Women in Asia Publication Series

MUKKUVAR WOMEN

ASIAN STUDIES ASSOCIATION OF AUSTRALIA
Women in Asia Publication Series

The Women in Asia Publication Series is a new publishing venture of the Asian Studies Association of Australia. It is intended to promote high quality scholarship about women in Asia, a subject of growing interest among students of Asia and of women's studies generally.

EDITORIAL COMMITTEE

C/- Politics Department
Monash University
Clayton, Victoria
AUSTRALIA

MUKKUVAR WOMEN

Gender, Hegemony and
Capitalist Transformation in
a South Indian Fishing Community

Kalpana Ram

London and New Jersey

To the memory of my great-grandfather, L.K. Anantha
Krishna Iyer, who pioneered Indian ethnography for the region
in which this book is set.

First published in 1991
Allen & Unwin Pty Ltd

Published in the rest of the world outside of Australia, New Zealand,
Southeast Asia and South Asia in 1991 by Zed Books Ltd, 57 Caledonian
Road, London N1 9BU and 165 First Avenue, Atlantic Highlands, New
Jersey 07716.

ISBN 1 85649 031 9

A catalogue record for this book is available from the British Library.
US CIP is available from the Library of Congress.

Set in 10/11pt Times by Graphicraft Typesetting Ltd., Hong Kong
Printed by Kim Hup Lee Printing, Singapore

Contents

Tables

Maps

Acknowledgements

The opportunity to acknowledge the many forms of assistance, guidance and nurturance I have received in pursuing this project comes as a welcome respite from the individualistic rigours of scholarship. First, I would like to thank my Mukkuvar 'family' in Kanyakumari: my intellectual companion, friend and sister, Stella; her mother 'Aataa' who nursed and fed me; and Stella's two lively children, Sheila and Babu, who accompanied me on many a relaxing evening walk along the beach at KaDalkarai Uuru. Secondly, I wish to thank the priests and nuns of Colachel and KaDalkarai Uuru, who provided a welcome point of intellectual exchange and discussion and willingly gave access to valuable parish records as well as village records relating to village associations and council meetings. The young Mukkuvar women, Lima Rose and Seraphim, I thank not only for their assistance in gathering survey material and translations, but for their daily companionship and continued friendship. Finally, I acknowledge gratefully the warmth, friendliness and patience of Mukkuvar villagers in providing me access to their unique way of life.

While in India, I also benefited from access to the facilities of the Centre for Development Studies in Trivandrum. Its library and Guest House, and the opportunity for discussions with staff and post-graduate students, made it an attractive port of call outside coastal Kanyakumari. The family home of Meena Ganesh, also in Trivandrum, provided a refuge in times of sickness and when the need for Brahman home-cooking and comforts became overwhelming.

Here in Australia, the task of writing the book has owed much to the staunch support and cooperation of several individuals. First and foremost, I thank Ian Bedford for providing a careful and painstaking reading of everything I write, for wielding a meticulous editorial pen and always being available to discuss ideas with. The fact that he simultaneously shares with me the joys and responsibilities of bringing up our daughter Kavita only makes his intellectual companionship all the sweeter to savour. I thank my supervisors Roger Keesing, Leslie Devereaux and Caroline Ifeka, who have provided generous support and commentary on successive drafts. The work was enriched by early discussions with Ranajit Guha, while Lenore Manderson commented on early drafts of Chapter 3. I thank my friends Margaret Jolly and Kathy Robinson for intellectually engaging with the broader issues addressed by the book. The work of transforming the thesis into a book has been aided and influenced by the detailed comments of two readers in particular—Michael Allen and Susan Bayly.

I thank Ria van de Zandt for the close attention and professional care with which she has typed the book, and for relieving me of a number of technical responsibilities along the way. Keith Mitchell has similarly taken on the technical responsibility for preparing maps and some of the figures. I also owe a debt to the Commonwealth Department of Education for the Postgraduate Research Award, and to The Australian National University which provided generous funding for the fieldwork.

Finally, I thank Roger Keesing and my sister Vandana Ram for adding to the quality of the book with their fine photographs.

A note on the transliteration of Tamil words, and Indian currency

The simplest alternative to the use of diacritical marks in transliterating Tamil words is that proposed by Harris (1982) on a model derived from Holmström (first published 1984). However, as a system of direct transliteration—which retains the non-distinction in Tamil between s, sh and ch, p and b, and so on—it proves too cumbersome to use when dealing with a regional dialect in which not all the words are formally Tamil words, and pronunciation is all-important. For this reason, a compromise system has been employed.

The symbols used in this book are as follows:

Vowels (exactly as in Harris):

a	(for short 'a')
aa	(for long 'a'); and similarly
i, ii	
u, uu	
e, ee ai i, oo au	

Consonants

k, g, s, sh, ch,	
T	(for retroflex 't')
t	(for dental 't')
D, N	(retroflex)
d, n, p, b, m, y, r, l, v,	
zh	(the loosely flapped retroflex 'r')
L	(retroflex 'l')

The above system has been used except where directly quoting from a text in which diacritical marks have been used. Personal names, geographical names and the names of castes are, however, spelt in their most common, modern anglicised forms.

Indian currency

The Indian rupee (Re) is divided into 100 naya paise. In 1983, the exchange rate was approximately Re9 = $1 (Australian), or Re15 = £1.

Introduction

To write of the Mukkuvars of Kanyakumari is to write of difference. In a predominantly Hindu agrarian society these are Catholic fishing people. The task of ethnographic writing is in this case bound up with the ultimately political challenge of shedding assumptions derived from the majority culture. In particular, any assumption on our part as ethnographers and scholars that all communities in South Asia live within the same moral and cultural universe of caste, the same shared hierarchy, fits ill with the lived experience of a semi-autonomous community such as the Mukkuvars.

To set out for the coast one boards a bus at Nagercoil, which has grown around the nucleus of an old weaving settlement. The bus journey from Nagercoil to Colachel, a port settlement, takes an hour along a highway that runs parallel to the coastline. On one side of the road there are paddy fields, dense groves of tapioca, jackfruit, tamarind, mango and banana—for Kanyakumari District is fertile, well endowed with rainfall and intensely cultivated. The groves enclose the homes of the main agricultural caste of the district, the Nadars, once humble toddy-tappers now transformed into a socially and economically powerful caste. From time to time, one flashes past ditches piled with rotting coconut husks to be beaten into coir rope.

For a time one can only sense the presence of the sea. But as one nears Colachel, the coastal villages at last come into view. The contrast is enormous. On the sandy soil there are no fruit trees— only some groves of coconut. Stripped of shade, or of the screening privacy of a compound, the houses of the fisherpeople swelter under a blazing sun, with the thatch roofs of the poor side by side with the plaster and cement houses of the well-to-do. The largest and most striking building in each village is the church, usually painted in shades of pastel cream, lime green and pink. Small covered alcoves house the shrines of the saints. Towards the end of the bus ride, there are few passengers left on the bus and it is easy to pick the Mukkuvars by their dialect and pronunciation of Tamil. The older women wearing rough cotton *cheelais* (saris) dyed a deep shade of indigo blue, their hair in a hastily tied knot, balance fish baskets or babies on their knees. Stepping off the bus at coastal villages such as Puduur, Muttam, Manavalakuruchi, one walks into the full dazzling glare of the sea and the beach under a hot sun. Out at sea, black objects bob and glisten—the *kaTTumarams* (catamarans) of the men, small boys floating near the beach on log rafts, the orange silhouettes of the occasional tamarind-dyed sails. On the beach are strewn nets and more craft—*kaTTumarams* and the *vaLLam* (dugout canoe). If it is *karamaDi* (beach-seining) season, one may see a row of fifteen to twenty men pulling at the rope that tows in the *karamaDi* net. In front of the church is the sandy open space that functions as village square. Here are held the *uuru kuuTam* (village meetings), scenes of excitable confrontations and high drama. Here too occur equally dramatic auctions during peak *netoli* (anchovy) season, when the haul is too large to be sold on the beach. But on most afternoons it is peaceful, with a few men sitting and mending their fishing nets or playing cards. The women are to be found only when one turns into the sandy lanes that run between the houses. There, outside their homes, women pound rice into meal or tend a small stall, sell a few miserable looking vegetables, and dry snacks to earn a bit of money. There are long queues of women at the water taps, waiting with plastic urns for a trickle of water. Others undertake the long walk, often over three kilometres, to bathe and fetch fresh water from springs in the paddy fields—for fresh water is an extremely scarce resource in these coastal villages.

This scene became extremely familiar to me as I took up residence in a coastal village with Stella, a widowed social worker, her two children and her old mother. Over a period of eighteen months, I became most familiar with the village where I lived, situated near Colachel, which I shall call 'KaDalkarai Uuru', or Seashore Place. Fishing villages differ from one another—they are highly dependent on the ecology of the particular stretch of coastline they happen to occupy. KaDalkarai Uuru was in fact one of the poorest villages in the district, since for technical reasons its fishermen can use only four types of gear as against the seven or eight utilised elsewhere. The continental shelf drops sharply away as one nears the cape. Villagers south of KaDalkarai Uuru have perfected a greater variety of deep-sea fishing techniques to compensate for the lack of off-shore fishing. I acquired a working familarity with other coastal villages as well, accompanying Stella on her health visits and later utilising networks of friends and acquaintances. In my general description of Mukkuvars as a coastal people, I draw on this broader framework of experience, as well as the more detailed information based on KaDalkarai Uuru.

However, it is the initial impression of the Mukkuvar country which captures in a visual image the essence of their relation to caste society. The Mukkuvars are located on the outer fringes of an ancient agrarian civilisation. Beyond them is the sea, on which their livelihood depends, offering them a ready if provisional escape from the low status that caste society affords them. Their geographical location is a metaphor not only for the social and economic marginality of the Mukkuvars but for the possibilities of an independent cultural identity which this marginality provides.

Fishing communities not only fall outside the framework of agricultural production—understood, in caste society, as civilisation tself—but, involved as they are in the acquisition and processing of a flesh food, they are bound to be treated, according to the perspective of the dominant culture, as a polluting caste. When the perspectives of the Mukkuvars themselves are taken into account ambiguities arise. To the Mukkuvars the sea is not only the physical terrain on which their work is performed: the work and the terrain also provide them with an alternative mode of self-representation, coherent in itself and owing nothing to the caste Hindu model. To the ideology of a caste hierarchy based on purity and pollution the Mukkuvars pose a counter-ideology of community based on a relationship of difference from and opposition to the model of agrarian society. Whereas the experience of untouchables working in the agrarian villages of Tamil Nadu serves to reinforce caste values (as shown by Moffat 1979), the work experience of fishing people promotes values of a different kind. The men—who put out to sea—are equipped with a masculine ideology of independence, individualism, bravery and resourcefulness. The experiences of the women, engaged in land-based activities, promote a value system which, while emphasising communal and social responsibility rather than individualism, still differs significantly from that of women in caste society.

I had come to this Mukkuvar community to explore the social forces at work in the lives of people in a community undergoing rapid historical transformation. My previous work (Ram 1981) had convinced me that the process of class formation, and the complex web of relations which links sections of the rural peasantry with the urban working classes and the casually employed sub-proletariat, could be best understood by examining the changing sexual division of labour. My original intention was to re-evaluate theories of class and economic development in the light of male-female relations. Through living with and writing about the Mukkuvars, however, my sense of the problem changed. My focus is no longer on class formation, or even on capitalist transformation as such, but on the variety of the forms of inequality and modalities through which power is exercised in this coastal community. While some of these forms are indeed the by-products of exposure to the world market, others are more deeply rooted. I have sought a way to incorporate in my account the part played by cultural and symbolic factors in shaping circumstances which are too often understood primarily in terms of the economy. One major thrust of the book will be to show how the Mukkuvars stand both inside and outside caste society. In so doing, I will challenge both Marxist economistic views of Indian society and global culturalist studies that see hierarchy and caste as a total paradigm of Indian society. In arguing for a more complex dialectical theory of culture, I use the marginality and ambiguity of the Mukkuvar fisherpeople as instruments with which to probe the foundation assumptions of anthropological Indology.

Indeed, there is something about the very region which invites such iconoclastic endeavours: Kanyakumari, situated at the crossroads of present-day Kerala and Tamil Nadu, stands heir to two rich and distinctive cultural complexes. The histories of both regions present a challenge to the colonial legacy of Indology: namely, the leaching of conflict out of representations of culture, and the creation of a static 'tradition' in which the category of caste is validated to the exclusion of all else, and made to operate as a frozen and impermeable entity.

In recent ethno-histories of these areas, the Brahmanic or Sanskritic paradigm of caste and of Hinduism, characterised by a cosmology of purity and pollution and a priestly ('Brahmanic') observance of ritual hierarchy, stands shorn of its claim to be the sole relevant framework of reference for south India. The Kerala coast has been home to Christian, Muslim and Jewish settlers from west Asia since the earliest centuries of the Christian era. These communities came in with the trade in pepper, spices and hardwoods which made the Malabar coast an integrated part of the Indian Ocean trading systems well before the first century AD (Bayly 1989). In Tamil Nadu, the Brahmanic order, far from being autonomous or all-encompassing, has been shown to be radically dependent on the political power of the kings, who gave the Brahmans land and wealth and sponsored the lavish construction of temples (Stein 1980). The kings, moreover, operated in terms of their own distinctive ideology of royal authority and honour (Dirks 1987). The nexus of kingly and priestly power is itself limited to the fertile riverine tracts of the Tamil country, and is in sharp contrast to the culture of the warrior and merchant castes, emphasising cosmologies and styles of worship that are quite different again (Mines 1984, Hiltebeitel 1988, Bayly 1989).

Groups such as the Mukkuvars, damned as 'impure' and 'untouchable' within a strictly Brahmanic interpretation of south Indian culture, nevertheless have available to them multiple points of reference: the multi-religious cosmopolitanism of the west coast, as well as the egalitarian, martial traditions of the warrior-merchant groups of Tamil Nadu.

As a study of social change and capitalist transformation, the book examines a series of interlinked phenomena: the new configurations of male and female labour-processes; the restructuring of women's access to and management of cash; the refashioning of marriage payments; and modifications in patterns of household formation. In addressing these areas, I acknowledge my debt to one of the key contributions of feminist theory since the 1970s, its insistent reappraisal of the connections between the private, domestic, familial world and the world of public, economic and political processes. The task of evaluating these interconnections historically has proved difficult for feminist theory, and this study may be viewed as a contribution to a continuing task, that of integrating the understanding of historical and cultural variability with the Western feminist project of the 1970s.

In my argument concerning the transformation of fishing communities, the cultural construction of gender occupies a central place. Capitalism, as it is generalised in the region, does not give rise to a singular, sexually undifferentiated pattern of class transformation. We find instead a strikingly differentiated response to the possibilities of wage labour which, where a woman is concerned, revolve around factors which make little sense within a purely economic definition: *where* the employment is located, the age of the woman, her marital status—factors which do not similarly apply in the case of men's wage work, and only begin to make sense if we locate them within a cultural framework which constructs male and female sexualities, male and female bodies, in entirely different ways.

The argument of this book is therefore an exercise in searching for a *language* that will satisfactorily allow us to explore the interconnections between areas kept disparate and unrelated in social theory: the labour process on the one hand, and sexuality/gender on the other. The problem is not dissimilar to the one Jameson explores in *The Political Unconscious*, where he discusses the concept of mediation:

> Mediation is the classical dialectical term for the establishment of relationships between, say, the formal analysis of a work of art and its social ground, or between the internal dynamics of the political state and its economic base ... If a modern characterisation of mediation is wanted, we will say that this operation is understood as a process of transcoding: as the invention of a set of terms, the strategic choice of a particular culture or language, such that the same terminology can be used to analyse and articulate two quite distinct types of objects or 'texts', or two very different structural levels of reality (Jameson:39–40).

Jameson's concern with mediation and transcoding stems from an attempt to combat the overwhelming tendency of the Marxist tradition to collapse the different 'levels' of social reality into what he would term the one hidden and fundamental 'master narrative', in terms of which everything else must be interpreted. It is in the course of discussing Althusser's critique of two unsatisfactory notions of causality employed in Marxism, namely, mechanical causality (the billiard ball model) and expressive causality, which requires all historical events or texts to be rewritten in terms of an 'allegorical master-narrative', that Jameson insists on the need for mediation, as against the search for identities.

In this book, one of the key sites on which this transcoding operation takes place is the human body itself. The body mediates between the economic disciplines of the labour processes and the sexual disciplines of gender identity. I explore the way women's bodies in the Catholic fishing communities are invested with a sexuality which is double-edged, in that it is dangerous to others as well as to the women themselves.

The part played by power relations in the constitution of femininity emerges with particular force in the realm of popular religion: but this is not a unitary field. Rather, religion is riven by multiple fault lines of contested power, not only between men and women, but between the Mukkuvars and the Catholic Church, and the Mukkuvars and caste Hindu society. The discourse of popular Catholicism contains and limits women, but it also constructs them as powerful, particularly in the domestic domain. I have located the sources of female autonomy and solidarity not only within the framework of this discourse, but also in the sexual division of labour and the specific version of domesticity found in a *fishing* community, where it well exceeds our conventional understanding of this term.

Recent anthropology has been characterised by a self-conscious project on the part of a variety of practitioners to challenge and revise the conventions of ethnographic writing (see contributions by Pratt, Crapanzano and Rosaldo in the collection of essays edited by Clifford and Marcus 1986). This book is not a part of such a project. However, for a number of reasons, it was not possible for me, as a fieldworker, to figure among the Mukkuvars in the role of an objective observer. The content of the book was itself partly shaped through my continual awareness of the deep ambiguities of my own experience as a fieldworker. As a woman of Tamil origin, a Brahman, whose family over three generations migrated to Burma, to Maharashtra and North India, and finally to Australia, my relations with Tamil villagers were in no sense a return to origins. Metaphors of identity and identification ('a woman studying women', 'a Tamil studying Tamils'), are as inappropriate to my experience as is the language of objectivity and neutrality. Instead, I experienced my cultural and sexual identity as shifting and makeshift, varying with my strategies of survival, which emphasised my status, now as 'foreigner', now as 'native'. The category of 'native' itself explodes into fragments under such circumstances: was I a native of the north (where I was brought up), or of the south (whose language I spoke, after a fashion)? Was I 'Brahman', as my speech indicated, and if so, what did my 'native' status mean in a society internally divided along profoundly hierarchical lines?

Certain of these tensions would be shared by any exile returning to the home country. But my experience was additionally determined by my being a woman. The male exile of Indian origin returning 'home' may be hyper-critical and detached (as was the Trinidadian V.S. Naipaul), and may be criticised in turn—but he does not bear the tremendous burden of representing the continuity of cultural tradition. In developing direct relations with colonial authority, men have had to evolve a culture of compromise, in which modes of dress and work, and even of resistance, have been shaped by a dialogue with colonialism. Women on the other hand bear the moral and symbolic weight of representing 'tradition' as this came to be defined in the interaction between a male elite and the coloniser. Such historical encounters, now being explored by scholars (Mani 1987, Ratte 1985), shape the experience of women today. Women's apparent adaptations to a Western model are viewed with a prurient curiosity, mixed with connotations of moral betrayal but also with anticipations of the sexual availability projected onto Western women. Far from stepping securely into the role of the observer, I was very much the observed. My best hope was to be subjected to the more benign versions of surveillance, to outright wonderment and curiosity, rather than to the brutal forms of sexual aggression and hostility. I was fortunate in the rural areas where my fieldwork was based. My experiences were less happy in the crowded, seething urban streets of Trivandrum. These experiences had more importance than can be conveyed by a few anecdotes in an introduction. They shaped the nature of interpretation itself.

My strategies of coping with everyday life alerted me to the strategic function of Mukkuvar culture itself. As I struggled, ineffectually, to efface the more obvious signs of my difference from 'traditional' Indian women, I began to view Mukkuvar culture also as a framework (itself undergoing change) within which the fisherpeople defined their identity in a hostile caste society. Above all, I experienced the tensions of my deviant status in my body, as I made daily efforts to learn anew how to walk, dress, move and speak. The experience focused my attention on the body as a prime locus for power relations. This attentiveness (which I could not escape) has in turn moulded my interpretation of the sexually specific nature of class formation.

In conclusion, a few words should be said about methodology and the language of the community I worked in. Mukkuvars speak a dialect of Tamil which is specific to their region and caste. Their speech reflects a regional continuity with the Malayalam-speaking people of Kerala as much as their affiliation to their Tamil-speaking neighbours to the east. The dialect has been further enriched by the Mukkuvar contact with the Portuguese and their brand of Christianity. At the same time, there are peculiarities of the dialect which set Mukkuvars apart as a coastal fishing community. Although I was able to communicate in my Brahmanical Tamil from my first visit, the services and translations of my field assistants were often indispensable.

My daily routines in KaDalkarai Uuru were structured around the task of conducting a detailed house-to-house survey, in the course of which I gathered basic information on age, educational levels, size of familial and residential units, as well as on areas of particular interest such as household formation, residential patterns, credit generation, marriage payments and health care. The survey in fact evolved into a loose and flexible set of rubrics, a structure I used as a point of entry for conversations with Mukkuvar men and women. I was able to ensure a reasonable range of contact with villagers from different parts of the village. Inevitably, however, I spent far more time with the women than with the men. Such an arrangement was socially and culturally more acceptable to the villagers. The men were away at sea for a good part of the day, and sometimes away from the village for months. In any case many of my concerns revolved more around the women than the men. In the women's company I came to travel up and down the coastal belt, but also into the interior, on visits to Christian and Hindu healers, Ayurvedic physicians and Western-style clinics. Much of the information on healing and health has not been included in the book, although it provides the basis for my discussion of popular Christianity.

My contacts were not limited to villagers and healers. The network of the local intelligentsia associated with the Church—priests and nuns of varied political persuasions, social workers and school teachers—provided a ready source of critical commentary on Mukkuvar life. My dialogue with them sharpened my thinking, and made fieldwork much more of a shared intellectual experience than it would otherwise have been.

Questions of methodology cannot be posed purely in terms of the practice of fieldwork alone. The structure of the book has been shaped just as much by the search for adequate representation of relationships between different levels of social reality. The movement of the chapters reflects this concern. Chapter 1 delineates the status of Mukkuvars as outsiders: their cultural orientations as fisherpeople, as Catholics and as a polluting caste. The chapter also sets up the basis on which the Mukkuvars are able, to a limited extent, to contest their ascribed status, not so much by open conflict, but by sidestepping the need to acknowledge their polluted status and constructing an alternative self-definition.

Chapters 2, 3 and 4 examine popular religion as a field of value and action within which we can explore the contradictory construction of femininity, female sexuality and the female body.

Chapter 5 explores the transformations in the political economy of fishing, both at the level of the structural forces at work, and in terms of the lived experience of the men who make a yearly journey to the port cities outside the district. The chapter therefore examines the historical impact of State policies on development, with its increasing emphasis on profitability and foreign exchange at the expense of the direct producers. At the same time, it seeks to explore what these policies have meant for the fishermen of Kanyakumari, in terms of the new patterns of work and leisure and their relationship to women.

Chapters 6 and 7 examine two of the crucial bases for women's empowerment in the community: their control of cash, and the system of kinship and household formation. However, these areas too are subject to redefinition on the basis of the new sexual economy. The domestic environment is being refashioned, and Chapter 8, which discusses the new features of marriage payments, highlights this process.

The last chapter before the conclusion assesses the interdependence of versions of sexuality and women's relationship to the labour process. I argue that, far from involving women in wider social networks of production and exchange, capitalism has in effect narrowed the horizons of their working lives. The world of wage labour and petty trade has little to offer women who wish to retain a measure of cultural acceptability and, indeed, their sexual respectability.

Neither men nor women have been subjected to a process which can be understood as inevitable, or as pre-ordained according to some general theory of ineluctable change, whether for better or for worse. The men continue to work with 'artisanal' craft and gear, even while combining this work, which *appears* 'traditional', with seasonal labour on mechanised craft. Women experience new, radically impoverished forms of domesticity precisely in their capacity as 'wage workers'. Both female and male experiences cast serious doubt on the validity of the master-narrative of unidirectional change which—whether in its liberal 'developmentalist' or its Marxist 'mode of production' guise—has long dominated metropolitan perspectives on 'the Third World'.

1 The Mukkuvars of Kanyakumari: on the margins of caste society

'Fringe-dwelling': cultural hierarchies of space

I begin my exploration of the Mukkuvars with a consideration of the physical landscape. I have taken the landscape as the basic metaphor of their marginal and ambiguous status in caste society. The idea of physical landscapes as a poetic metaphor is an old one in Tamil literature. The Tamil land is hierarchically divided into zones or *tinais* which denote both a geographical and a cultural identity to the people who live in each tinai. The identification between the Mukkuvars and their *naital tinai* or coastal zone provides the starting point of my account of these fringe-dwellers.

The close interconnections between occupational and spatial identity in a fishing community are well brought out by the two distinct folk-etymologies people offer for their caste name, 'Mukkuvar'. The first is recorded by A.K. Iyer, who writes at the turn of the century (1909) about the Mukkuvars of the Malabar coast: 'The word "Mukkuvar" is connected with the Canarese "Moger"; both the words come from the same root, which means "to dive"' (1909:266).

Possibly this derivation points to the engagement with pearl diving, a skill more prominent on the east Coromandel coast than in Kanyakumari—but at the very least, such an etymology stresses occupational specialisation in sea-based activities.

The second derivation, told to me by a Mukkuvar villager, stresses a geographical identity. Here the derivation is from the Tamil *mukku*, which means 'the tip' or 'the corner'. In this version, Mukkuvar denotes the people who occupy the very tip or edge of the land mass. In one sense, this geographical feeling of being at land's end is shared by the people of the district as a whole. Kanyakumari District is the smallest district of the state of Tamil Nadu, with an area of 654

1

square miles (approximately 1670 square kilometres). It is surrounded on three sides by ocean: the Arabian sea on the south-west,
the Bay of Bengal on the south-east and the Indian Ocean on the
south (see Map 1). The auspiciousness of this location, at the con-
fluence of three waters, is symbolically underlined by the substantial
temple of the virgin goddess, Kanyakumari, which gives the district
its name. The temple brings pilgrims and tourists from all parts of
India, and confirms the inhabitants' sense of occupying a territory of
unique significance.

In the case of the fishing castes, this sense of extreme location is
reinforced by occupational and demographic factors. Mukkuvar villages form a band of settlement on the western coastline extending
from the Cape as far north as the Malabar coast of Kerala. At both
ends of this band, the numbers of Mukkuvars thin out or are diluted
by a mixture of other fishing castes. From Muttom south to Cape
Comorin, a distance of about 19 kilometres, Mukkuvar settlements
are interspersed with the settlements of the Parava fishing caste. The
Parava in turn gain in numerical and social dominance as one rounds
the tip of the sub-continent and continues northwards along the east
coast (see Map 1).

This continuity of caste settlement is not merely a geographical
phenomenon. Marriage exchanges occur on a strictly endogamous
basis up and down the coastline. Work-related migratory trips take
the men on a seasonal basis from Kanyakumari to Kerala. Religious
pilgrimages to Christian shrines in other coastal communities and
continuities of linguistic usage keep alive a sense of solidarity and
oneness between the Mukkuvar settlements and, to a lesser extent,
between Mukkuvars and other fishing castes. Such social networks
cut across political divisions between Kerala and Tamil Nadu, and
mark out a unified cultural zone that corresponds more accurately to
the pre-1956 political unit that went by the name of the kingdom of
Travancore. In 1956, four administrative units known as *taluks*
(Agasteeswaram, Thovala, Kalkulam and Vilavancode) were excised
from the kingdom of Travancore and incorporated into Tamil Nadu
on the basis of the linguistic dominance of Tamil (see Maps 2 & 3).[1]
To Mukkuvars the realignments have brought with them a greater
absorption into the party politics of Tamil Nadu, as well as the
gradual 'Tamilisation' of the Mukkuvar dialect as Tamil becomes
the language of schooling and political mobilisation. However, the
social, economic and religious ties with Mukkuvars living across
the state border continue to keep alive a different unit of political
identification.

Within this band, stretching from Malabar to the Cape, the Mukkuvars live in one of the most densely populated areas in the world.
In the 67 kilometres of coastline within Kanyakumari District there
are at least forty villages. The district itself has one of the highest
population densities in India—726 per square kilometre. In coastal

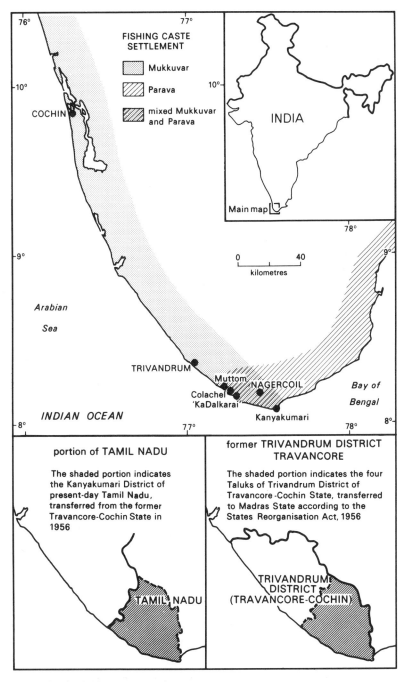

Map 1 (*top*): fishing caste settlement
Map 2 (*left*): former Trivandrum District, Travancore, pre-1956
Map 3 (*right*): the creation of Kanyakumari District, and its absorption into Tamil Nadu, 1956

villages the density is as high as 1000 per square kilometre (Sister Sophie 1980). The closely packed dwellings of the community and the poverty of much of the housing give the coastal strip an appearance more like a slum than a series of rural villages. One settlement begins almost where the other leaves off. If strong sentiments of solidarity link one village to the other, tremendous population pressures, taken with the precariousness of the economy, lead to the volatility, excitability and propensity for violence for which the Mukkuvars are well-known.[2]

To Mukkuvars, their close identification with the ocean—as people whose *thozil* or traditional occupation is *kaDal thozil* or 'work on the sea'—is inextricably bound up with their perception of themselves as fringe-dwellers. Not only does the caste's name get interpreted in terms of this perception, but the names given to fishing villages (such as KooDimonai, 'tip of the end') reflect it as well. Mukkuvars often refer to themselves as *KaDalkarai makkaL*, 'the people of the sea-shore'. Other castes may be referred to by their specific names. The Nadars, for example, whatever they may think of it, are still called ShaaNaar, and their place of settlement referred to as ChaaNaakuDi.[3] But the agricultural castes all merge into a bloc for the Mukkuvars who see a vast gulf separating them from the people of the *ul naaDu*, 'the interior'.

Communities may be referred to by direction alone. For Mukkuvars, *terkkai* (south) is north, towards the sea, and *vaDakkai* (north) is south, inland. The directions make sense only if one assumes the perspective of a people facing out to sea, taking the sea as their point of orientation. Such close identification between a people and a geographical location on the land is not confined to Mukkuvars alone. In Tamil country, one's *uuru*, usually translated as 'native place', is the first thing about a stranger one wants to know. One's *uuru* is also the first prefix attached to one's personal name, followed only secondarily by a patronym.[4] In Tamil literary traditions this identification takes on added dimensions of meaning. Every schoolchild attending a school where Tamil is the medium of instruction is made aware of the *ain tinai* or five zones (or landscapes) that characterise Tamil country.

The full elaboration of the *tinai* theme is to be found in the bardic and written literary traditions which crystallised in a corpus of poetry known as the Cankam literature. While the precise dating of this literature is still a matter of debate, it covers roughly the period between the first and sixth centuries AD.[5] The *ain tinai* form the allegorical basis of a highly elaborated poetic structure in which each landscape is attributed a set of stylised characteristics. Each *tinai* not only has its own flora and fauna, but its own poetic mood and its own *devan* or deity (Clothey 1978:24). Cankam poetry is divided by subject matter between two categories: *puram* (outside) and *akam* (interior). *Akam* deals with inner emotions, longings and love;

puram with external affairs of war, politics and trade. Each *tinai* has
its own dominant motifs of *akam* and *puram*, although the bulk of
Cankam poetry concentrates on *akam*.

An ancient literary tradition whose precise relation to the social
order of its own day is a matter of some controversy may seem
unlikely to directly affect the Mukkuvars of today. However, there
are certain aspects of the literature which reflect and codify cultural
attitudes that remain pervasive in Tamil society. In particular, the
organisation of physical landscapes and their associated cultures into
a hierarchical schema identifies the fisherpeople as the barbarians of
the coast, only just within the reach of civilisation. This attitude is
still found among the agricultural peoples of the district. The coastal
people refer to the agricultural hinterland as the *ul naaDu* or interior
landscape—also the title of a book of translations of Cankam poetry
by A.K. Ramanujan (1967). This coincidence is suggestive, since in
the poetic world *akam* and *puram* are not simply distinguished. *Akam*
is ranked above *puram*. In the religious *bhakti* cults of Tamil Nadu,
the outer is inessential, secondary and ultimately not as real or
important as the inner (Egnor 1978). The privileging of the interior
over the outer in religious and cultural attitudes metaphorically
captures the inferior outsider status of coastal people. At the apex of
the five *tinais* is the *marutam* or cultivated land, the 'centre of which
is generally the society and which represents a relatively advanced
civilisation' (Clothey 1978:24). At the bottom of the hierarchy is
the *palai*, or wilderness, 'desolate land generally symbolising the
area beyond the reach of civilisation' (Clothey 1978:24). *Naital*, or
the sea-shore tract, is placed only just above this absolute wilderness.
As the site of fishing and commerce it is within the reach of civilisation, but is ranked below the other two tracts—*mullai* or the forested
pastoral land, and *kurinci* or hill tract.

All the five *tinais* are represented in Kanyakumari District.
Although small, the district has a varied geography: the north-east is
an extension of the Western Ghats, forming a hilly tract (*kurinci*).
Forests (*mullai*) occupy more than thirty per cent of the geographical
area (Selvarathnam 1985:1961). The west and south-west are
bounded by the flat lowland of the *naital* or sea-coast. In a district
endowed with an average annual rainfall of 1470 mm, and a warm
sunny climate, the barren wasteland of the *palai* is less in evidence,
but the landscape does begin to resemble an arid plain as one moves
east into adjacent Tirunelveli District. However, *marutam* or cultivated land is the dominant *tinai*, not only culturally but in a geographical sense. Selvarathnam, an economist, describes the region as
one of the most intensely cultivated regions of Tamil Nadu, with very
little uncultivable or fallow land (1985). The bulk of the irrigated land
is under rice cultivation. Upland, non-irrigated areas are used for
drier crops such as tapioca and spices, while on the lowlands the

district has extensive fruit orchards, besides cashew, coconut and rubber plantations which account for forty per cent of the net cultivated area. Paddy and tapioca are now being rapidly displaced by the other cashcrops, but the historically dominant *tinai* in southern Travancore has been the rice-growing *marutam*, regarded by the codifiers of Tamil culture as the home of civilisation itself. From the perspective of the people of the *naital* (*naital makkaL*), the people of the *marutam* (*marutam makkaL*) are the key category against which they define themselves as 'Other'. These two *tinai* are fundamental to my account of the Mukkuvars. A detailed characterisation of them is to be found in Zvelebil's account of the Cankam literature (1973:98, 101).

Superimposed hierarchies

We have been referring to a hierarchy as old as the first century AD. In Iyer's account of the fishing castes of Malabar, written in 1909, a more familiar hierarchy is encountered. Mukkuvars are made to stand at a distance from the Brahmans, Kshatriyas and high caste Sudras. They may 'adore the deities in the Brahmanic temples by standing at a distance from the outer wall' (1909:274).

What is most striking in Iyer's account is the way the restrictions of caste and pollution coalesce perfectly with the geographical separation of the fishing castes, providing a structure for a segregation already in place. Tied to an occupation which places them on the outer perimeter of the land mass, the *naital makkaL* found themselves virtually prisoners of their own *tinai*, according to the rules of caste society. Iyer describes this for both the Mukkuvars and another fishing caste, the Katalarayans: 'They [the Katalarayans] were in former times considered an inferior race, and, as such, precluded from travelling along the public roads, and consequently obliged to keep to the sea-coast'(Iyer 1909:260).

In the case of the Mukkuvars, 'Being obliged to keep to the coast, and unable to bear the social disabilities, many became Christians and converts to Islam (Puislam or puthia Islams, or new Islams), and were thus elevated in the social scale' (ibid.:275).

Certainly, the burdens of low status in caste society would seem a powerful incentive to such forms of escape. However, the geographical containment of the Mukkuvars is not wholly to their disadvantage. Their degraded status in caste society is counterpointed by a strong sense of independence. Not only do the fisherpeople have their own unique *tinai*, but their occupation does not involve them in personalised relations of dependency and servitude to the higher castes in agricultural society. As a group, they are ranked by caste society as barbaric and impure, in a way similar to agricultural untouchable castes. But the agricultural untouchable castes are usually landless agricultural labourers, enmeshed within the same relations of production as the dominant castes. The Mukkuvars are able to sidestep this entire set of economic and cultural relations: the relations of production that define fishing are simply not to be equated with the relations of production in the *marutam tinai*. It is to this source of autonomy and identity—*kaDal thozil* or the work of the sea—that I next turn.

Fishing versus agriculture in the anthropology of 'the peasantry'

A debate that has intermittently recurred in anthropology concerns the place of fishing communities within what is defined as constituting the peasantry, or peasant society. It is intermittent because, with few exceptions, only those who have conducted fieldwork among fisher-people feel impelled to raise the problem (for example Firth 1966, Alexander 1982); the bulk of anthropological and political theorising on the question of the peasantry is conducted with agriculture as its sole framework of reference (for example, Wolf 1966, Shanin 1971, Barrington Moore 1967).

Those few ethnographies of maritime society concerned with questions of a comparative nature have tended to emphasise two peculiarities of fishing. Firstly, the ecological terrain and labour process of fishing, and the mode of surplus extraction within this labour process, are in sharp contrast to those of agriculture, in ways we shall examine in a moment. The second peculiarity, only superficially at variance with the first, is the ultimate dependency of the fishing community on the existence of a rural market, and on relations of exchange with the agricultural sector. Fishing economies cannot, by definition, be totally autonomous. Their specialisation in one economic product renders them particularly dependent on trade relations with the wider society. These peculiarities are established in two key ethnographies, among the few to attempt a thorough account of the various facets of economic life in two Asian fishing communities: Firth's classic *Malay Fishermen* (1966) and Alexander's *Sri Lankan Fishermen* (1982). Both books argue that despite occupying a niche defined by a distinctive technological sub-culture (Firth 1966:9), fishermen are nevertheless, in several important respects, 'the quintessential peasants' (Alexander 1982:255).

For Firth, the general criteria for characterising an economic activity as peasant production are applicable to both fishing and agriculture. These include the use of simple tools of trade; small units of production; the absence of a clear separation between owners of capital and the labourer; and a system of distribution governed by custom and long-term social relations rather than by purely economic criteria such as wages (Firth 1966:6–7). Firth's line of argument closely follows Marx's original distinction between pre-capitalist and

capitalist economies: the former does not allow a separation between
the economic level and other levels of society, nor does it accord a
primacy to the economy as the determinant level. Instead, kinship
and culture are integral components of the division of labour and the
relations of production. The economy is a 'moral economy', to use
the term employed by E.P. Thompson (1966:203) and more recently
by Scott (1976), and this is true of both fishing *and* agriculture in
pre-capitalist or peasant society. While Alexander lists different
criteria in his definition of 'peasant', for him too these apply to the
fishing community as much as to agriculture. Both sectors are
dependent on external markets, employ highly developed risk-sharing
procedures, include multiplex patron-client ties, and have a factional
mode of political competition (Alexander 1982:255).

These similarities do not erase the sharp contrasts between fishing
and agriculture. Firth lists these contrasts: agriculture is seasonal,
with long gaps of time without any direct income. Fishing, on the
other hand, makes possible daily increments in yield. The mode of
planning and saving adopted in each case is therefore vastly different,
with fishing weighted towards short-term planning, given the greater
uncertainty of an irregular daily income. The catch in fishing is
perishable and needs more labour and equipment for preservation
than do seasonal agricultural crops. While the entire family is involved in agriculture, the work of ocean fishing is restricted to men,
with women and children performing secondary tasks on shore. As an
item of diet, fishing is incomplete; it needs to be supplemented with
rice, so that full-time fishing is more intimately associated with an
exchange economy than is agriculture. Investments in fishing boats
and gear are not as permanent as investment in land and agricultural
tools, being liable to sudden damage and loss (Firth 1966:2–3).

Many of these aspects of fishing will be returned to in the pages
that follow. Firth's final comment on the sexual division of labour,
made here as one point among many, is my major concern. However,
at this stage let us pursue the rival characteristics of fishing and
agriculture in terms of the specificities of the social structure in India.

Resisting the totalising categories of 'caste' and 'class': the specificity of *Kadal Thozil*

The Indian agrarian peasantry has been characterised in sharply contrasting ways. British and European observers constructed an entity
known as the 'village community', a closed economy in which all
essential goods and services were to be found close at hand. The
supposed community was bound together by relations the colonialists
referred to as the *jajmani* system. Dumont (1980:97–99) gives us a
summary of the main features of this system: the form of the division
of labour is established through the use of hereditary personal rela-

tionships, each family having at its disposal a range of specialists. Payments and counter-payments are regulated by custom. The *jajman* (he who employs) and *praja* (the one employed) are bound together in a hierarchical solidarity. The main servants of the village enjoy an allotment of land from a communal fund set apart by the patron.

This romanticised picture of a closed, self-sufficient and mutually reciprocal community has been much criticised. Berreman (1962), Gough (1973), Mencher (1974), Beidelman (1959) and others have pointed to the pronounced element of economic exploitation that runs through the system. Others, such as Dumont, have insisted that the importation of certain European concepts specific to capitalist society, such as 'the individual' and 'the economy', be critically reappraised (1980:104*ff.*). Besides acknowledging the kind of fusion of culture, morality and economy typical of pre-capitalist society, Dumont has emphasised the specific features of Hindu religious ideology as the system of values that gives ultimate meaning to both economic and political power in caste society.

Whether we focus on economic relations of class exploitation, or on the moral and religious ideology that gives coherence and meaning to those relations, the question I wish to ask still remains the same: to what extent do these relations, whether of exploitation, power or hierarchy, shape the lives of people in fishing communities of southern India? To what extent does the distinctive technological sub-culture noted by Firth for fishing communities give scope for a different kind of moral economy, one in which labour is given meaning through different moral ideologies?

My purpose here is to highlight the place of fishing within the dominant agrarian order in India. All definitions of 'the peasantry', whether in agriculture or fishing, are now essentially theoretical reconstructions of a superseded past. The transformation of Indian agriculture by capitalist relations of production and a period of colonial domination is the subject of a vast literature in itself. The history of capitalism in fishing is comparatively less explored,[6] and it will be an important part of this book to establish what it has meant for the men and women of Kanyakumari District. It should be noted that Firth himself, writing in 1966, finds it impossible to maintain his earlier characterisation of Malay fishermen as 'peasants':

> Malay fishermen in Kelantan have to a considerable extent adopted mechanisation of their fishing fleet and side by side with this has come a change in the capital structure of the local fishing industry which has affected also the relation of the ordinary fisherman to the control of the enterprise in which he is engaged . . . It is no longer so appropriate to label the economy a peasant one now as it was in 1940 (1966:7).

Recognition of the complexity of the new mode of production must therefore shape discussion of the peculiarities of fishing in contrast to agriculture in Kanyakumari District. Yet what is striking is that although capitalism is now operative in both agriculture and fishing, it has not softened the contrasts between the two, or created as a labour force for both sectors an interchangeable or undifferentiated proletariat. Younger men in the Mukkuvar community, now facing increased pressures of competition from mechanised fishing and an increase in population, are searching for additional means of livelihood. But for now, at least, they do not even consider seeking employment in the agricultural sector, even if there were scope for further employment in an already overstrained labour market. A Mukkuvar, according to villagers, will only change his fishing occupation for an alternative that carries with it prestige and dignity, as well as additional income. One may enter the agricultural sector as a land owner or petty capitalist—as indeed some of the wealthier fishermen have managed to do (see Chapter 5)—with some pride. However, to work as an agricultural *labourer* is a definite fall in status. Similar considerations affect people's evaluation of work on mechanised fishing craft. The older values of artisanal or peasant fishing continue to remain alive and operative—albeit now in a new, oppositional context. These values are not simply free-floating cultural constructions. They are grounded in the continued persistence of artisanal fishing itself, which provides a necessary buffer against the fluctuating fortunes of an imported technology. I examine these difficulties in a later chapter. They have led to the formation of a peculiar proletariat with a foot in each of two camps.

Discussion of the place of fishing in the rural social structure of south India can be divided into two aspects—the relations of ownership, authority and distribution internal to fishing as a sector; and the relations of trade and exchange that articulate fishing with the wider economy. I will discuss each in turn.

Relations of economic differentiation within fishing communities in Kanyakumari District

How do relations of ownership over the means of production structure the fishing communities in Kanyakumari District? Are there inequalities of ownership? If so, how do these inequalities compare with those found in agrarian caste society?[7]

Technology

The means of production currently utilised in fishing are themselves associated with two quite different technologies. One of these may be called artisanal: the other was introduced in the post-colonial period. Each is further distinguished by quite different patterns of ownership and work, and they must therefore be examined separately.

The types of craft associated with artisanal technology commonly used in the district are the *kaTTumaram* (catamaran) and the *vaLLam* (plank canoe). The *kaTTumaram* (or *maram* 'tree' as it is more commonly called) consists of three to five logs of wood from the *chilla maram* (*Albyzzia stipulata*) tied together with coir ropes. The rope is tied around a cross piece of wood in the shape of stumped bull horns, which is placed at the ends of the logs. The logs are spaced to allow drainage and to reduce the effect of wave impact in heavy surf. Bamboo is lashed together for the gaff which holds the sails. Paddles too are made from bamboo poles 10 centimetres in diameter, which are peeled, cut to 2–2.5 m, and split in two.

KaTTumarams come in two sizes, each employed with a different type of fishing gear.[8] A small *kaTTumaram*, 3–4 metres long, is associated with hook and line fishing or *tuuNDil veelai*, as well as the small-meshed gill-nets such as the anchovy net (*kacha valai*), the sardine net (*chaalaa valai*), and the prawn net (*raal valai*). Larger *kaTTumarams* are 5–7 metres long and are used in pairs, together with boat seines called *taTTumaDi*. These nets are bell-shaped and have long wings of rope attached to either side. The two craft tow the hauling ropes at an equidistant angle; when a shoal is spotted the crews row towards it so as to sandwich the shoal between the craft.

The other type of craft, the *vaLLam*, is a kind of plank canoe or boat between 7 and 15 metres in length, 1 to 2 metres wide and between 0.7 to 1.5 metres deep. It is made by seaming together several planks of jungle jack with coir ropes. The inside is then coated with pitch to make it watertight. In Kanyakumari the *vaLLam* is used principally to operate shore-seine nets, known as the *karamaDi*. One end of the rope is left on shore while the *vaLLam* is rowed out by 3 or 4 men. As it moves out, the crews pay out the rope and wings of the *karamaDi* until the bag-like part of the net is reached. The bag's mouth is fitted with weights at the bottom and floats at the top to keep it open. Once the bag is dropped, the crew moves shoreward and delivers the wings and ropes of the other side of the net to the shore crew. The shore crew, numbering 15 to 20, pull in the two ends of the rope in synchrony. The crew on the craft meanwhile return to a position behind the seine and move shoreward with it to control the hauling according to water movement. Just before the bag reaches the shore, some of the crew jump into the water to close the mouth. The most commonly caught species include anchovy, tunny, carangid, pomfret, sardine and mackerel.

The technology introduced into the fishing economy of south India since the 1950s is appropriate for three types of fishing: gill-netting, shrimp trawling and purse seining. Three types of craft correspond. Gill-netters are about 8 or 9 metres long, use crews of four and employ wall-like nets in which the gills of fish get entangled. They cost, in 1982, between Re60 000 and 90 000. The longer shrimp trawlers, costing around Re160 000, comprise the majority of the mechanised boats operative in Kerala and Tamil Nadu.

Fishing with these is primarily for prawns, but the by-catch is also retained. The third type of mechanised vessel, the most recently introduced, is the purse-seiner, about 14 metres in length, employing up to 30 people and costing, in 1982, between Re700 000 and Re800 000. The purse-seiner operates on an encircling basis. A wall of webbing is released around a shoal of fish, and then pulled tight in the form of a purse. The catch sought in this form of fishing are oil sardines, whitebait and mackerel. Ninety-seven per cent of the mechanised boats used in south India fall into the category of small boats, about 9 to 10 metres long, originally designed for gill-net fishing, and later modified to accommodate stern trawling as the profitability of shrimps became apparent in the sixties.

Ownership

The new forms of work and ownership operative in the mechanised sector are discussed in Chapter 5, as is the role of the State in disseminating new technology. Fishermen in Kanyakumari District have become integrated into the new technological and social order of mechanised fishing principally not as *owners* of the mechanised craft/gear—although that was the ostensible purpose of the government's policies—but as workers. The ownership of the new means of production is concentrated in the large port towns of Kerala and eastern Tamil Nadu—and it is to these centres that Kanyakumari fishermen journey every year as a kind of seasonal proletariat. For the rest of the year, they continue to work in their own villages with their traditional craft and gear.

If we restrict discussion to what happens within the Mukkuvar villages, the data gathered at KaDalkarai Uuru indicate that ownership of the *vaLLam* and the *kaTTumaram* (and the types of fishing gear appropriate to these craft) is still a remarkably fluid and open-ended affair. Inequalities certainly exist between households, but do not lead to the perpetuation of rigid categories akin to classes. Owners and producers are not opposed to one another in structurally antagonistic relationships. Nor are they regularly distinguishable in caste terms to the degree found with agricultural landownership relations.

Table 1.1 shows the distribution of the means of production among fishing families in KaDalkarai Uuru. The data were gathered as part of an exhaustive house-to-house survey and census I conducted in KaDalkarai Uuru. The population of the village is 2776 and the number of residential units (generally kin-based households) is 288; however, the relevant unit of analysis for my purposes is not the residential household but the nuclear family, which operates among the Mukkuvars as the unit of ownership and income generation. There are 337 such nuclear families in the village. Of these, only 286

Table 1.1   Distribution of the means of production among fishing families in KaDalkarai Uuru

Economic category	Number of families (N = 286)	Percentage
1 'Masters' (owners of equipment worth Re10 000–20 000)	37	13.0
2 Self-employed (owning just enough equipment for subsistence)	59	20.6
3 'Coolies' or workers	103	36.0
4 Part-owner, part-'coolie'	87	30.4
Total	286	100.0

families (i.e., 85 per cent) derive all or a substantial portion of their income from fishing. The other 51 families (15 per cent) do not fish. They are the merchants, shop-keepers, barbers, church functionaries and salaried employees.

The wealthiest fishing families—those whose ownership or investment in the means of production is between Re10 and Re20 000—consist of 13 per cent of families in the village. Within this category fall the owners of *taTTumaDi* and *karamaDi* nets. The *taTTumaDi*, requiring two *kaTTumarams* for its operation, demanded an investment of Re1000 in 1983. The *karamaDi*, requiring a *vaLLam*, would represent an investment of anything between Re6000 and Re20 000, depending on the size of the *vaLLam* and the length and material of the net.

At the other extreme of the ownership ladder are families owning no equipment whatsoever, who work as 'coolies' on equipment belonging to other families. These are not wage labourers, but are paid on a share basis. Thirty-six per cent of families in KaDalkarai Uuru fall within this category of coolies.

Other families move seasonally in and out of the coolie category. These are families that own a small amount of equipment, but not enough to provide their families with subsistence throughout the year. Part-owner, and necessarily part-coolie, this category comprises 30.4 per cent of the families in the fieldwork village. Their existence serves to blur the distinction between owners and producers.

Finally, 20.6 per cent of families in this village are 'owners' of equipment, but in the most minimal sense: they own no more than a small *kaTTumaram* along with small-meshed gill-nets, perhaps supplementing their income with hook and line fishing. With this, they provide their families with little more than subsistence living, but on the other hand, they do not have to work as coolies for other families.

The fluidity of socio-economic categories in fishing villages

The data in Table 1.1 provide only the barest outline of the economy. They indicate an unequal distribution of the means of production, although the level of inequality compares favourably with similar estimates for agricultural villages (see the comparative estimate provided by Norr 1972). Such data in themselves are misleading. To them must be added the features that give the fishing economy its volatile character. Inequality in KaDalkarai Uuru is more fluid than Table 1.1 can suggest.

We should consider first the relative importance of economic investment in fishing equipment, an aspect noted by Firth (1966). Given the working conditions in the open surf, the risk of loss or damage to equipment is quite high and depreciation is rapid. This factor in itself produces a significant amount of downward mobility. Owners who lose their equipment become coolies. Families affected by the lack of income during the off season between September and December may plummet in economic assets by selling or pledging what equipment they have. However, upward mobility is also comparatively easy. The difference between coolie and owner status is not vast in monetary terms.

With a capital of Re750, a coolie can combine coolie work with hook and line fishing, while Re2000 to 5000 will enable the purchase of gill-nets. Even such amounts may be unobtainable in an uncertain and fluctuating economy, but the situation of a coolie is far more promising than that of an agricultural labourer aspiring to buy land and implements and set himself up as a cultivator. Besides considerations of mobility, relations of kinship and household formation specific to the Mukkuvar caste, place further limits on the degree to which economic accumulation occurs in any given household. The details of household formation are given in a later chapter (Chapter 7), but it may be noted here that processes of economic accumulation are strongly qualified by the tendency towards fissure and separation built into the Mukkuvar household. In a fishing economy, the accumulation of wealth and savings—which could be invested in the means of production—depends largely on the pooling of labour and income between able-bodied men. The number of cooperative males in a household is as much a determinant of a household's economic status, and of its political influence in the community, as is the level of ownership attained by that household.

There are therefore strong economic incentives for relations of unity and cooperation within kin-based households. This is reflected in the prosperity of the few households in KaDalkarai Uuru who have managed to keep together. In the village there are 33 families owning enough equipment to draw an income between Re800 and Re2700 in a good month. Leaving aside the difficulty of calculating incomes in fishing households, this sum may be contrasted with an average income of around Re300 a month reported by most families. Fourteen of these 33 families are organised as extended families, with at least two earning males pooling their incomes. When the household takes the form of a father and his unmarried sons working together, then the level of accumulation may be high enough to permit the purchase of mechanised equipment if these sons are prepared to work as seasonal fishermen in neighbouring regions during the local off season. Such a unified clan is celebrated in Mukkuvar culture as a *kaaka kuTumpam*, a term referring to the proverbial clan solidarity of crows in the bird kingdom.

However, there are in general more powerful cultural pulls in the opposite direction, towards fissure and the separation of extended households into their nuclear components. Chapter 7 will later on detail the great store set on the independence of these components. Joint families are thought to find it impossible to live together, owing to conflicting interests and resentments over the distribution of scarce resources. Sons therefore break away from parents soon after marriage. Even if they do not physically move out of the parents' home, incomes and expenditures will be budgeted separately. Large-scale equipment is not necessarily divided up in parallel fashion, but it is common for such possessions as small-meshed gill-nets and the small *kaTTumaram* to be sold, and a share of the cash value given over to a married son, who then works on his own. This is why the residentially-defined household cannot be used as the relevant economic unit of stratification.

This pattern of fissure in household formation has led to an extreme fragility in economic stratification. Fishing households may wax and wane in economic strength within the life cycle of the parental generation. But there are compensations: the tendency of households to fragment leads to the formation of interdependent economic units, which operate on a far wider basis than kin-based groupings. It is rare for one household to provide the entire crew needed for any form of fishing other than simple hook and line fishing. Crews may form around a core of closely related kin, such as fathers and unmarried sons, but will typically include a number of labourers not related by kinship. As Table 1.1 shows, 55 per cent of families (30 per cent coolie and 25 per cent part-coolie) provide labour for equipment owned by other families.

Economic interdependence is still compatible with a hierarchical organisation of the labour process. Indeed the coexistence of interdependence and hierarchy is at the heart of most characterisations of the agrarian community in India. So far, a number of the forms of hierarchy familiar from accounts of agrarian economies have been suggested as inapplicable for the Mukkuvars. Accumulation is limited by requirements of investment in artisanal fishing, and by the cultural logic of household formation. Moreover, the existence of a significant minority who move from being owners to coolies over the period of a year, sometimes from one day to the next, lends a fluidity to the relations between the two economic groups—as does the comparative ease with which a 'coolie' can set himself up as a hook and line fisherman if resources allow.

Division of labour

Two further factors modify potentially hierarchical relations between owners and non-owners: work relations on fishing expeditions and the share system of distribution. Where the first is concerned, I can only rely on the accounts provided in other ethnographies of owner/non-owner relations in craft working seas off the southern Tamil Nadu coast, since as a woman I was unable to accompany the men on their fishing expeditions. According to Norr (1972), the organisation of work teams in fishing expeditions is based on production require-ments of efficiency rather than on the requirements of hierarchical status. The exigencies of working the *kaTTumaram* in heavy surf where production time is measured in minutes rather than over days and weeks encourage swift and more cooperative decision-making. Tasks are relatively undifferentiated and the owners of the equipment are not present in a purely directive capacity. Owners organise the expedition, determine the type of equipment to use, organise the supply of equipment, and provide the raw material for its repair. However, the decisions required to put these materials into opera-tion, how long to fish, and where to fish, are made by the crew as a whole. The skill and experience of an owner may be recognised, and his judgement deferred to, but no privilege is attached to this. Seas-onal and daily fluctuations affect the catch far more than gradations of skill and management.

Distribution of catch

The share system of distributing the proceeds of the catch reflects and reinforces the comparative lack of differentiation between owners and workers. It is customary for the owner to be given a share equivalent to that given to a coolie. An owner could certainly earn twice the amount made by a labourer, but only by earning an extra share as a working crew member. In times of scarcity, moreover, the owner is virtually expected to forego his share, while continuing to bear all operational expenses. It should be remembered too that out of the return for his capital the owner is required to provide for repairs and upkeep.

Table 1.2 summarises the share system for different methods of fishing currently operative in KaDalkarai Uuru—as reported by villagers.

The relative homogeneity and the absence of sharp stratification between families engaged in fishing should not obscure the fact

Table 1.2   Share system for the methods of fishing operative in KaDalkarai Uuru

Type of fishing	Number of workers	Share
Small-meshed gill-nets (anchovy, sardines, prawns)	2	Division into three parts, with $\frac{1}{3}$ for ownership. $\frac{1}{3}$ for coolies
Hook and line work	1–2	Division into two, with owner given half for ownership and the rest divided into half each for labour
TaTTumadi (boat seine)	7–8	Division into nine parts, with owner receiving an extra $\frac{1}{9}$th
KaramaDi (shore-seine)	10	Net owner receives $\frac{1}{10}$th of a share, and the crew divide up the rest

Note: In all of these share allocations, about three per cent of the catch proceeds are reserved for young boys who help in loading equipment onto the boat and in hauling in shore-seine nets. Boys still serving an apprenticeship generally receive half the adult share, referred to as 'tea money'. In the *karamaDi* and *taTTumadi* operations, a further three per cent is allocated to the hereditary service subcastes in the village, principally the barber, and those in the service of the church such as the *melingi* or bell-ringer who calls people to attend mass at church.

that this is the homogeneity of poverty. A term commonly used of KaDalkarai Uuru is *paavangaL uDiya uuru*, a place of the wretched. A sixty-five year old woman singled out this village as particularly wretched: 'Our village is the worst of all, envy ridden. Here the types of fishing are less, and the catch is less. In Kadiapatnam [a village eight km away], there is now a good season. In this village, there may be at the most ten people who are better off—most are pretty ordinary, many are *paavam* [to be pitied].'

The Kanyakumari coastline is not alone in its poverty. In his study of a Sri Lankan fishing community, Alexander remarks that redistribution of income within the village would do little to alleviate its problems, and only bring the average household income up to the level of the poorest third of Sri Lanka's population (1982:53). A survey of Kerala fishing households undertaken in 1979 by the Department of Fisheries found that only three per cent had incomes above Re3000 per annum, while 50 per cent had incomes below Re1000 per annum. A third live in *kachaa* or semi-permanent housing. Only ten per cent have electricity, fewer have toilet facilities. Only a third have drinking water facilities within the ward in which they live. Such poverty is no longer purely a matter of traditional scarcities affecting fishing economies. It is the result of more general

18   *Mukkuvar Women*

processes which have integrated the fishing communities into a world
economic order, and disturbed their ecological environment (see
Chapter 5).

Traders and middlemen in Kadalkarai Uuru: a separate social class?

Is the shared poverty restricted to fishing families? In KaDalkarai
Uuru there are also households of fish traders, as well as households
where members draw the bulk of their income from newer wage-
earning occupations (see Table 1.3).

Let us first take the case of traders and middlemen with regard to
the question of poverty in relation to fishing households. Traders
have been described in some studies of fishing economies as particularly exploitative (Kurien 1985, Platteau 1982). The perishable nature
of fish as a commodity, particularly in the absence of facilities for
freezing and preserving it, dictates that fishermen must sell their
catch rapidly, and on any terms. Merchants, on the other hand, aim
at ensuring as large a share of the market as possible, and manipulate
relations of credit in order to ensure a steady supply. They therefore
advance loans to owners of equipment on the understanding that a
predetermined proportion of the sale proceeds accrues to them. The
merchants thus not only ensure their supply, but they are also able to
manipulate sales prices even during an official auction. The advantage to the fishermen is that there is no insistence on repayment of
the principal. The merchant has a vested interest in the continuation
of the relationship. Interest may be waived on days when the landings
are small or nil, since the interest is a stipulated percentage of the
catch. In KaDalkarai Uuru, loans from middlemen who dealt with
the purchase of *kaDavaa* (perch) are actually interest-free. However,
men wishing to change their allegiance to a particular merchant are
obliged by their previous merchant partner to pay a fine as well as to
return the principal.

The advent of mechanised fishing may not have turned fishermen
into owners, but it has produced an interest on the part of seafood
companies in the catch brought in even by artisanal fishermen. An
elaborate chain of middlemen has come into existence, linking the
companies with the fishermen. Some of the traders resident in
KaDalkarai Uuru now act as agents for the company at village level,
advancing loans in return for the privilege of choosing first from the
small seasonal catches of prawns. There are three agents working for
seafood companies currently resident in KaDalkarai Uuru (see Table
1.3). In the sample of 200 families on which I collected detailed
information on indebtedness and sources of credit, five families
nominated these agents as sources. One family listed a *kaDavaa*
middleman resident in the neighbouring township of Colachel as
operating in a similar fashion. The amounts advanced by these agents

Table 1.3   Occupational range and incomes in non-fishing households in KaDalkarai Uuru in 1983

Range of occupations in each household	Income for each occupation (rupees per month)	
1 Primary school teacher (F)	500	
Mechanic in Indian Rare Earths Company	500	
Total		1000
2 Dry-fish merchant	200	
Teacher (F)	500	
Social worker (F)	100	
Tailor (F)	200	
Total		1000
3 Teacher (F)	550	
Company job	400	
Tailor (F)	75	
Total		1025
4 Auctioneer	200–500 (2% of catch)	
Fish vendor (F)	75	
Total		275–575
5 Cycle-loader (trader using bicycle)	100–200	
6 Toddy shop assistant	600	
7 Middleman for prawn trade	400	
Supplementary sources of income:		
— rent from landownership	150	
— interest from money-lending	150	
Total		700
8 Primary school teacher (F)	500	
Teacher in polytechnic	1000	
Total		1500
9 Auctioneer	100–200	
Tailor (F)	200	
Social worker (F)	250	
Total		550–650
10 Home of *kannaku pillai* or church catechist, an office now abolished; the family now owns a shop selling spices, soda, fruit, etc.		
Shop	200	
Son: agent for prawn company	200	
Agent's supplementary sources of income:		
— cycle rental	100	
— radio rental	100	
— landownership	150	

Table 1.3   (cont.)

Range of occupations in each household	Income for each occupation (rupees per month)	
Another son is in the United Arab Emirates:		
— remittance	200	
Total		750
11 Agent for prawn company	400	
Supplementary income:		
— rent for land	150	
— interest for loans	150	
Total		700

ranged between Re350–500. Because these loans are given to fishing families in the form of advances, they are not perceived as debts. This makes it difficult to calculate the extent of such credit relations within the village.

Do these traders and middlemen constitute a separate social class and if so, are they better off than other Mukkuvars in the community? For KaDalkarai Uuru at least, the answers to both questions must be made separately. The traders, auctioneers and middlemen living within the village are poor and insignificant. Only the wives of fishermen who work as vendors would earn less than they do. Their status is generally low. The scale of their operations is small. Few can keep their families alive on the commissions and profits generated by their activities, so they have to supplement their commission with other small-scale activities: money-lending, running a small shop, renting out radio and sound equipment or bicycles. Some of the families also own paddy land as an additional source of income. Given all these supplementary sources of income, their overall economic status is not as precarious and fluctuating as that of fishing households. However, the trading families are socially indistinguishable from the fishing population—most trader households contain members who work as fishermen.

A similar observation may be made of households whose members draw income from waged occupations. Many of these teachers, clerks and social workers are women. Younger women are currently most active in seeking work outside the fishing economy itself (see Chapter 9). Their salaries are more regular and dependable than income from fishing and therefore highly valued. But here again, one finds that these women are the wives and daughters of fishermen. They do not belong to a separate salaried or wage-earning category of workers.

Only thirty families in KaDalkarai Uuru derive any part of their income from occupations other than fishing. Of these families, eighteen contain one or more members who are fishermen. Table 1.3 details information, gathered in a comprehensive village census, on the twelve families in the village which do not include anyone engaged in fishing. The table details the occupational mixture and the incomes within the non-fishing families. Their income is certainly more stable and even higher than that of fishing households. Despite this degree of differentiation the village is singularly homogeneous in terms of social class. There is no category of villagers who live entirely by renting out their equipment to coolie fishermen. Even the group of merchants, middlemen and salaried employees are a part of the class of direct producers in the fishing economy.

Trade-based relations with agrarian society: fisherpeople and the 'right-hand/left-hand' caste division

How does a relatively non-stratified economically homogeneous community without any significant internal caste divisions survive within caste society? How can so sharp a dichotomy between the fishing communities and the dominant agrarian society continue to exist, when fishing communities are dependent on the outside world for virtually every item they need in daily life? With the exception of fish, and a few other locally raised items such as poultry and pigs, these villages rely on agricultural markets for the supply of all items of immediate consumption and for the raw materials with which to construct the tools of production. The wood for the *kaTTumaram*, cotton for the fishing nets, even the tamarind dye for the sails must be bought. These relations of trade inextricably involve the fishing community with the wider economy.

Fishing communities therefore are involved in two distinct areas of economic activity: the work of fishing itself, and the trading occupations which sustain contact with the caste society of the interior. This distinction is reflected in the sexual division of labour in fishing society. Fishing itself is exclusively a male domain, although women are important in ancillary tasks such as weaving nets, salting and drying fish. In activities which require sustained contact with the outside world, however, women come into their own. Older women form a small but significant minority of fish traders. In this role they make regular trips to major agricultural markets within a vicinity of 15–20 kilometres. The purchase of rice, vegetables, firewood and other items of daily consumption falls for the most part on women. Market exchanges are conducted by women. Occasionally—although this is by no means typical—women working as fish vendors may strike up relations of direct barter with women from agricultural Nadar households, exchanging fish for rice and firewood. Trips into the interior for medical reasons are again women's business, for they are responsible for the household's health and welfare. For all the control exercised over their behaviour and freedom of movement, Mukkuvar women travel extensively throughout the district, both into the interior and up and down the coastal belt, consolidating the numerous credit-related transactions (see Chapter 6). In the course of their travels they are left in no doubt of the view held of them in the wider society. Distaste for aggressive and haggling 'fishwives' is there reinforced by caste values. Coming back from the markets after a day in the hot sun, fisherwomen who stop at a tea-house are served at the door, and must drink their tea separately, either standing outside or seated in the corner. If they use public transport to carry their baskets of fish to the market, they may be ordered off the bus at the whim of the conductor.

The question of Mukkuvar relations to caste society cannot therefore be discussed in identical terms for men and women. Among Mukkuvars, it is women who bear the brunt of their polluted status in caste society. Male work, oriented towards the sea rather than to the rest of society, enables men to escape similar pressures more readily. In Chapters 3 and 4 I explore the general capacity of Mukkuvar culture to selectively appropriate and recontextualise themes taken from the dominant religious culture. Despite others' devaluation of their occupation, Mukkuvars have in general retained a good opinion of themselves. The sources of their independence are located not only in the moral economy of fishing, but in the female-dominated sphere of exchange.

Trade relations involve not only a movement of women out into the hinterland, they also bring a range of hawkers, traders and specialists of various kinds to the fishing villages. First, there are different categories of merchants and fish traders who come to make direct purchases on the sea front. If we discount the Mukkuvar men and women resident within the community, the fish traders fall into two categories: the 'cycle-traders' and the larger merchants. The cycle-traders are men who live in the interior and who carry fish to the markets on bicycles. They may be members of the two local fishing castes, the Paravas and Mukkuvars, who have resettled in the interior, or they may be drawn from the Nadar or Muslim communities. The merchants who operate on a larger scale buy only in peak seasons, and then in bulk. Such merchants service more distant markets, and the produce is dried and transported in bullock carts or trucks. Their number includes the agents for seafood companies, who are part of a chain that ultimately supplies a national and even international market.

Other kinds of traders come into the fishing villages from the immediately contiguous hinterland to supply a service. They may set up small shops in Mukkuvar villages selling cigarettes, tea, soft drinks and small grocery items, or they may visit the village on a regular basis. Hawkers come through selling saris and clothing. Others are called in for specialised purposes: carpenters for house construction; jewellers; *vaidiyars* or medical specialists. These last-named are of different kinds and may travel from other districts of Tamil Nadu: the *korati* or gypsies selling feathers, charms and trinkets; the *raapaaDis* or night-singers, credited with occult powers; *mantravaaDis* or exorcists; *naaTu vaidiyars* or herbalists.

The distinctiveness of this trade-based relationship to caste society can be usefully situated within a wider social and historical context. Tamil society has long distinguished between castes related to other castes on the basis of trade and mercantile dealings and castes related to others on the basis of agricultural dependence and interdependence and ownership of land. The traditional form of this distinction is that between 'left-hand' and 'right-hand' castes. According to Mines:

> In medieval times (eleventh to thirteenth centuries) this economic dualism was manifested at the village level as a social dichotomy between the interdependent agricultural castes. This was symbolically represented in Tamil culture as a bifurcation of society into right-hand (*valangkai*) and left-hand (*iDangkai*) sections. The main agriculturalist castes and their interdependent service castes were members of the right-hand section; the artisans, itinerant merchants, and lesser agriculturalists were members of the left-hand section (1984:14).

The distinction has been given central analytical significance in some ethnographies (principally Beck 1972) but it must be used with caution. Scholars such as Stein (1980), working within a more rigorously historical framework, regard the distinction as having little contemporary currency (1980:175). Mines, in his study of an artisan-weaver caste, makes use of the distinction despite acknowledging that 'it is only a fading memory ... However something of the dichotomy persists in inter-caste relationships, beliefs and models for behaviour, local residential and temple organisation, caste administration and the contrasting customs of the castes' (1984:14).

We may proceed, as Mines does, on the understanding that whether or not the distinction is alive today among Tamils, it has played a shaping role in the past. The left-hand/right-hand dichotomy testifies to the relative autonomy (in some respects) of the historical traditions of Tamil Nadu. There was, in the past, a left-hand bloc of castes over whom Brahmans and the martial or kingly groups among agriculturalists failed to establish a continuing ascendancy. The model may no longer obtain, but it is suggestive in at least one respect: it points to the possibility of a generalised historical basis for the cultural heterogeneity manifested in some areas of South Indian society. In the case of the fishing caste—geographically distinct as it is—differences from the norms and practices of Hindu society may not, of course, stand in need of such an explanation. But it might also be argued that certain characteristics of the Mukkuvars, their relative cultural autonomy (Chapters 3 and 4), and aspects of their kinship system and processes of household formation, are manifestations of a more general pattern (see Chapter 7).

Fishing castes were never historically designated as belonging to either bloc. Theirs is a much more ambiguous status. But at least one scholar (David 1977) has been struck by the affinity between fishing castes and the mercantile and artisanal castes of the left-hand division. The distinction he draws is between 'bound' and 'unbound' castes: the latter, such as fishing, mercantile and artisanal castes, are said to enjoy a 'free-willing' relationship (in Tamil, *ishTamaana toDarpu*) with other castes, as compared with the 'bound' mode of ranking (*kaTTupaaDu toDarpu*) which is observed in the rest of society, principally among the agricultural castes considered as a bloc. The distinction drawn by David is equivalent to a distinction between caste blocs adhering to two models of exchange: that of market exchange, and that of the system called *jajmani* by Europeans. On the former model (which echoes certain of Weber's criteria for economic rationality), trade relations are unrestricted, whether by location or by social criteria, such as those of purity and pollution. Transactions are governed by supply and demand. The relation of buyer and seller is unicontextual, unlike the uneven and hierarchically governed exchange of caste society.

David is contrasting one ideal type with another. Trade transactions between fisherpeople and caste society do not conform to the model of rational economic behaviour he sketches. I have referred already to the various means of price-fixing followed by middlemen through the mechanism of loans, which tie the fisherman's catch and allow prices to be kept artificially low. At the same time, it is true also that fishermen do not feel hopelessly tied to any one source of credit. Transferring from one middleman to another may involve payment of a 'fine', but it can be done. Relations of credit are not reinforced by numerous non-monetary relations which tie the client in a network of dependencies, as is the case for agricultural society. Furthermore, fishing villages have evolved their own alternative sources of small-scale credit which reduce the power of the merchants in this respect (see Chapter 6). Other types of market imperfections could be mentioned, such as the small degree of direct barter between agricultural and fishing households. Even here, however, fisherwomen feel free to bargain for their goods, based on relative scarcity of the goods; there is no question of following traditionally established criteria of exchange out of loyalty to the agricultural household.

David's model, which he himself presents merely as description of two contrasting tendencies in Tamil society, is in fact a fertile model, useful in explaining many features of the fisherpeople. The world of the market, based on ethics of fairness and mutual benefit, as well as shrewd business behaviour, has left its mark on the values espoused by the trading women in the Mukkuvar community. These women cannot be compared to the wealthy and powerful merchant castes of the Left-bloc (Mines 1984)—they are still only the humblest and least powerful group of fish traders. Nevertheless, the fact that it is as traders or else as purchasers of services that women come into contact with caste society is all-important in explaining the difference between Mukkuvar women and women in agricultural untouchable castes, who may be called upon to provide everything from agricultural labour to domestic and sexual services for upper-caste men. David's description of *ishTamaana toDarpu* or free-willing relationships is even more apt when it comes to describing the masculine version of Mukkuvar identity which revolves around the work of fishing.

Masculinity and the caste identity of Mukkuvar fishermen

The self-definitions that collectively make up Mukkuvar caste identity are neither fixed nor defined exclusively by the work of fishing. The term 'identity' is being used in this book to incorporate several components, all of which converge to produce a sense of difference between Mukkuvars and the rest of society. These components include geographical, economic, religious and cultural elements.

In artisanal fishing, an ethos of individualism, freedom from unnecessary supervision, merges with a markedly male ideology of strength, virility, valour and competitiveness. Any work that entails loss of autonomy—even wage work as labourers in a city environment—is regarded by Mukkuvar men with contempt. Mukkuvar men do not readily consider taking up agricultural labour in times of seasonal unemployment.

About eight households in KaDalkarai Uuru have men away in the Middle East—working for the most part as construction workers or, at best, in small mechanical and electrical stores. The men go there in the hope of something much better, however, and their real status in the overseas labour market is usually shrouded in secrecy, sometimes even from their own families. For all the glamour of the clothes, cassette tape decks and gigantic portable radios that these men bring back to the village with them, there has been nothing resembling the enormous wave of immigration to the Middle East from neighbouring Kerala. For most Mukkuvar men, the only culturally acceptable alternatives to local fishing are working as labourers on mechanised fishing boats, or travelling with one's own artisanal equipment to other parts of the west coast. Work in the mechanised sector still presents a sharp contrast to artisanal fishing, in ways that are discussed in Chapter 5, but it is a form of work incorporating the men's skills and independent decision-making, qualities highly prized by the men.

The most prestigious form of artisanal fishing has been the most rudimentary one technologically—hook and line fishing. What is valued here is the high degree of skill and knowledge called for on the part of the individual fisherman. Such work is often referred to not as *tuuNDil veelai* or hook and line work, but as *maram thozil*, a hereditary occupation or calling in the European sense. The man engaged in such work has the much-envied opportunity of drawing in unusually large-sized single fish—the occasion of many tales and a certain individualistic pride. One man described it to me as the *thozil* where one can be the Raja of the *kaTTumaram*, alone and in full command. In purely economic terms, the hook and line fishing has been evaluated by marine economists as being efficient and economical. The gross earnings per man-hour-at-sea stand up well in comparison to other craft–gear combinations (Kurien and Willmann 1982). The prestige and glamour of a *tuuNDil* fisherman is reflected in his status as a highly desirable bridegroom, commanding high dowries (see Chapter 8). This type of fishing has suffered most through competition with mechanised fishing, and its gradual decline is mourned by men and women in the community.

Pride in individual initiative comes through in other areas as well. The oral history of the community is replete with stories of men learning and adapting to new technological influences. One man claimed, rightly or wrongly, that the technique of using the sail had been unknown around the Colachel area when he moved in after marriage some fifty years ago, and that he had successfully introduced it. Others point to the gradual replacement of cotton by nylon in net-weaving, and the range of adaptations to which the introduction of nylon twine has led.

Nylon nets, according to the men, have made possible hauls on a larger scale, and this in turn has necessitated the building of larger sized *kaTTumaram*. Fishermen have been curious enough to learn even from exploitative foreign influences. The ships that call into the natural harbour at Colachel take away mineral-laden sands mined next to the homes of the fisherpeople. According to John, a fisherman:

> Some fifteen to twenty years ago we learnt some techniques from the Japanese. Only the *kaTTumaram* fishermen learned all of them. Others could only master them in part. The Japanese themselves gave only the suggestions—but *kaTTumaram* fishermen are innovative. From the basic *tuuNDil*, they went on to *aayiram tuuNDilgaL* [a thousand hooks], tied in a row to blue thread, and thus tripled their catch.
>
> The men also discovered that Nylex cloth shines in the water and acts as bait for small fish.
>
> We have made a special line for the bigger fish, to prevent damaging their mouths.

Apart from a general pride in their occupation, self-respect and pride also take a regionally specific form. Mukkuvars regard themselves as the best fishermen on the west coast, and will boast with disarming openness about the way they are specially sought after by the owners of mechanised craft as far away as eastern Tamil Nadu, northern Kerala and even Orissa. Kerala, the region with which they are most familiar, is looked down on by Mukkuvars. Kerala fishermen, it is said, cannot manage the prestigious *tuuNDil* fishing, or perform deeds requiring bravery and skill with the same ease as Mukkuvar men. One man recounted an incident where the nets his crew had laid out were caught in the propeller of a mechanised fishing boat. The incident led to a violent clash between the two crews. Someone had to dive underwater and free the net. I quote from John's account: 'All the crew were local Kerala men. They did not know how to dive underwater and disentangle the net. So I did. It was very cold in the water and I cut my hand. They turned the boat back to shore to take me to hospital.'

Comradely relations with other crew members are shot through with competitiveness, and anxiety to prove one's strength, bravery and virility, whether out at sea or on land, in drinking, gambling and fighting. The fisherman James notes: 'There is a *chilla maram* [tree] near our house. Ignoring advice to leave it alone, I went and cut a limb off. I was unaffected by the milky poison, showing further my immunity against poison. Two snake bites have left me immune. It is believed that if you make yourself strong with liquor, even poisonous snakes will leave you unharmed.'

The cultural elaboration of healing arts is paralleled by an elaboration of arts of combat; among the fishermen, these are often expressed in fighting. Fishing villages have a reputation for violence among inlanders and especially among those officials who are forced to come into contact with fisherpeople—the parish priests, police and social workers. Fishing villages are nicknamed, often by their own inhabitants, in ways that reflect traditions of violence: KooDimonai has been renamed Sevantha MaNal or 'reddened sands', KoTTilpaaDu is known as KolaipaaDu, 'the place of killing'.

The propensity to violence seems rooted in men's work. Any violation of the principle of cooperation between one crew member and another, between one craft and another, or between one village and another is met with sabotage, scuttling or burning of equipment, or with physical brawls in which injury and death are possible. Violent episodes are common in the conflict between artisanal fishermen and the crews of mechanised boats.

The ideology of violence and daring blends easily with a martial *kshatriya* ethos, not so much characteristic of other untouchable castes as of mercantile-cum-warrior castes of the Left-bloc (Mines 1984). Indeed, the Mukkuvars, who have little by way of recorded history, boast of their strength in the service of indigenous rulers. 'The Battle of Colachel' (1741) is described in an official history of trade on the Malabar coast in the following terms:

A battle was fought on 10 August 1741, near the insignificant roadstead of Colachel tucked away in the far south of Malabar, between the armies of Martanda Varma [king of Travancore], and the Netherlands East India Company. The armies were not large and it was not much of a battle. But the Dutch lost it and the consequences gradually changed much that was traditional in Malabar (Das Gupta 1967:33).

In the oral history of the Mukkuvars, this incident has been transformed into a heroic occasion. Tales of physical bravery supplement the traditional pride of the fisherman in trickery and cunning. One version is offered by an educated Mukkuvar with great pride in community history:

> Though nothing as sophisticated as the navies of the Cholas and Pandya kings, the navy of the Travancore King did depend partly on the coastal people. In the famous battle with the Dutch, it was the coastal people who were lined up along the beach embankments with oars and poles aimed to look like guns. The Dutch drew anchor and half of them took fright and left. The other half came on land and their leader was taken prisoner to later become a martial advisor to the king. One of the cannon marks can still be seen on the *annam* rock [a rock shaped like a swan] near our village's beach. Till recently, a Dutch anchor rusted near the rocks and would tear the *karamaDi* as it was drawn.

In another version, the services rendered by the Mukkuvars to the king gives them official title to the part of the country they inhabit: 'At the time of the Dutch arrival, there was no one to drive them off. The fishermen offered their services to the Raja. They stood together at the beach, armed with oars. The Dutch, from a distance, believed them to have guns bigger than the ones they possessed, and took fright. The king, in gratitude, offered the fishermen a reward, and they asked for the *Mukku* [tip].'

It is perhaps not altogether surprising that the Mukkuvars of Kanyakumari have as their caste counterpart in Sri Lanka a group of Mukkuvars who espouse an ideology of chiefly conquest and have in fact historically assumed the role of chiefs and powerful landlords (McGilvray 1983). The socially powerful Mukkuvars of Sri Lanka are similar only in name to the Mukkuvars of Kanyakumari—but both groups have evolved a martial, combative ideology.

This ideology is all the more striking in the case of the Mukkuvar fishing caste of Kanyakumari, since they have neither land ownership nor military strength with which to underwrite their perception of themselves as *virakaarar* or brave men (David 1977). The work of fishing goes some way towards providing the basis for such a self-definition.

2 The Roman Catholic Church: petty Raja of the Mukkuvars

'Identity' as a relationally defined horizon of aspirations

An emphasis on structural differences between Mukkuvars and the rest of Tamil society can give a misleading impression of something immutable and pre-defined. In fact, all of these structural elements provide only the latent possibilities for identity, identity which is mobilised in the context of particular historical settings and the power relations between Mukkuvars and the outside world. Identity (including caste identity) does not precede the circumstances of the field in which it is produced. To caste Hindus, the Mukkuvars are polluted untouchables. The various positive statements of self-description that Mukkuvars offer the ethnographer must be read within the context of the politics of cultural power. For a polluted caste to represent itself as brave, innovative and adaptable to change, capable of cunning in response to challenge on sea or land, is a statement of resistance.

Which aspect of their marginality is used as a means of caste self-definition depends on the context. Against the threat of a police raid, the entire village may cooperate and see itself as a community in opposition to an alien state encountered principally as a punitive law-enforcing agency. Mukkuvars have increasingly begun to emphasise that they define themselves as Catholics as well as fisherpeople. This is again a response to political realignments, this time to mobilisations in the district by Hindu revivalist organisations. The communal clashes of 1982 between Christians and Hindus in Kanyakumari District figure prominently in accounts given by villagers of their recent perception of themselves as a community. Their descriptions vividly convey the way in which the various structural elements actually come alive in such a situation of hostility and conflict. During the period of religious conflict, the geographical continuity of coastal villages allowed the entire terrain of the *naital tinai* to function as an

29

enlarged collectivity. Instead of seeing themselves in terms of the crowded collection of conflicting households and individuals as residents of each village usually do, they saw themselves collectively, even across village lines: the unit of solidarity became the coastline itself. News was communicated by torch flares, and men travelled along the beaches without ever having to set foot in 'enemy territory'. At the same time, the vulnerability in the geographical and economic specialisation of the fishing castes became equally apparent. The agricultural castes were in a position to blockade the coastal villages, cutting off their access to essential commodities.

In this situation, the Mukkuvars fought as Catholics, under the leadership of the Roman Catholic Church—but unlike other Catholic castes in the district, they also mobilised along economic and geographic lines uniquely available to them as a fishing caste.

The church

To be untouchable, to be able to worship Hindu gods only from the outer wall and to be confined to the sea-shore to protect caste Hindus from one's polluting qualities would seem reason enough to seek to escape Hinduism. In addition, we have seen that fisherpeople are quasi-independent of upper caste power and patronage, with all relations with wider society mediated by trade. When an opportunity presented itself for the Mukkuvars to resolve the anomalies of their position in caste society, they took it.

The occasion arose with the arrival of the Portuguese Jesuits, first on the Malabar coast, and later on the Coromandel coast of eastern Tamil Nadu, in 1535. From the very start of Portuguese Catholic activity in south India, the question of conversion and proselytisation was bound up with issues of caste, power, status, economic interests and colonisation. To the Portuguese, religion and trade were activities so closely related as to seem all but indistinguishable in the enterprise of colonisation. As Roche puts it:

> The alliance of Portugal with the Papacy in Europe resulted in what church historians have called the 'padroado' jurisdiction. The jurisdiction which gave Portuguese kings direct administrative responsibility over ecclesiastical affairs had important repercussions in the colonies.
> Portuguese officialdom was characterised not only by captains and factors but also by the padres. Both captains and clerics acted as partners in christianisation and colonisation as servants of the king. Indigenous groups found that the clerics were powerful negotiators in winning the protection and support of the Portuguese officials (Roche 1984:41–42).

The earliest Portuguese presence was in Calicut, where from 1498 onward their trading and proselytising was carried out under the protective shadow of the forts. Their confinement to trading posts along the coastal belt remained a problem throughout the first century of missionary effort. The key successes of the period were the conversions of the fishing castes on the eastern and western coastline of south India. These conversions presented to the Roman Catholic Church a paradox with which it was to become only too familiar: conversion in India, while the result of efforts addressed, ideally, to the individual consciousness, was effective above all as a mass phenomenon. The conversions were an aspect of caste politics, of the jockeying of groups for a better position within the social order. If for the Portuguese Christianity was to a considerable extent an instrument of economic and political interests, precisely the same was true for those who converted.

Yet the process cannot be entirely reduced to considerations of material interest. Fishing communities which turned to Christianity in the first wave of conversions in the sixteenth century used religion not simply to climb a status ladder, but to consolidate and further emphasise a sense of separation and difference from the rest of caste society.

Of the Paravas, living on the east coast, Roche writes: 'The Parathars were people whose identity and social organisation was characterised by religion, exclusive settlements, kinship, closed marriage networks, constricted norms of social intercourse and an autonomous caste polity ... The pivotal element upholding the entire edifice of Parava social organisation, however, was the specialised corporate economy of the jati (1984:39–40).' The Mukkuvars shared all these characteristics. For both castes, Christianity has become a way of marking and further underlining their *jaati*, or communal identity.

There is, however, one crucial difference between the conversion experiences of these two fishing castes. The Paravas had a far more diversified occupational structure, one which included not only ocean fishing but a virtual monopoly over an extremely lucrative pearl fishing industry. Their economic strength contrasts with the precarious hand-to-mouth existence of the Mukkuvars. The social hierarchy, with caste notables at the apex, was much more highly elaborated among the Paravas who are, moreover, far better known: the interest of the *jaati* elite who acted as conscious and literate leaders has ensured the survival of a relatively rich body of historical evidence. There are now two detailed social histories of the Parava community, by Roche (1984) and Bayly (1981). The Mukkuvars, who were and still are a poor, illiterate community, have been the subject of little historical documentation. Their history remains wrapped in silence.

We know little of the Mukkuvar conversion, except that it followed that of the Parava conversion by ten years, and that it was a response to the missionary efforts of Francis Xavier, probably between 1544 and 1549. Xavier and subsequent missionaries worked also among lower status agricultural castes such as the Illuvans and the Pulayas

(Forrester 1979). To this day, however, the term 'Latin Catholics' means only one thing in the Travancore region: the fishing castes, principally the Mukkuvars.

On the reasons for their conversion we can only speculate. I have suggested that Christianity presented the Mukkuvars with a means of resolving the contradictions of an anomalous position in caste society, and of affirming an already powerful collective identity as the KaDalkarai *makkaL*, or the people of the sea-shore tract. In contrast to the case of the Paravas, there seem for them to have been no immediate economic and political benefits from conversion. However, recent historians of peasant movements have begun to accord fuller weight to non-economic motives even amongst the poorest strata. In his history of Christianity and its relationship with caste society, Forrester writes: 'What must never be neglected is that a conversion movement is like a kind of group identity crisis, in which the group passes through a negative rejection of their lowly place in Hindu society to a positive affirmation of a new social and religious identity (1980:71).'

Among the Mukkuvars, conversion was the result of a (probably explosive) combination of factors: the humiliations of untouchability being sharpened by the aspiration to autonomy and economic independence. This interpretation finds support in the literature on mass conversions to Christianity in the nineteenth century. Thus Forrester (1980) and Oddie (1977) argue that conversion movements begin among the more economically independent, and only later spread to the weaker sections of society.

The Roman Catholic Church

Whatever the Mukkuvars hoped to gain from conversion, the Catholic Church has not made it its business to alter their place within the overall social structure. The 'accommodationist' attitude of the Catholic Church towards caste society had been the subject of commentary. Forrester writes:

> Roman Catholic missions in India date from the coming of the Portuguese, and virtually from the beginning appear to have regarded the caste system as the given and religiously neutral structure of Indian society within which evangelisation, understood as the conversion of individuals without detaching them from their social context and also the conversion of whole caste groups, might proceed. Christianity, in other words, was seen as neither threatening nor undermining the caste system, but rather working within it and accommodating western social standards to the norms of caste (1979:14).

Little attempt was made to integrate fishing castes into a single church with the other higher caste Christian converts. Indeed, there was little effort made to integrate even the fishing castes themselves into one common church. According to Roche (1984:70): 'Jesuit directives clearly upheld Parava requests for separate churches and settlements from contiguous Christian fishing communities like the Mukkuvar and Careas'.

At the end of the first century of missionary effort, the Jesuits perceived with some dismay that their efforts had yielded success only among the coastal castes. It was a spectacular success, but not one which gave subsequent generations of missionaries cause for much pride. Christianity, it was felt, had remained trapped among a fringe population. The religion of the Parangis, as the Portuguese were known, had become synonymous with foreigners and polluting castes. Far from viewing this association as the basis for a critique of the caste system, the Jesuits set out to storm what they perceived as the citadel: the upper castes of the agrarian world. Robert de Nobili was one of the key architects of this later strategy, and Cronin (1959) captures in his biography of the priest the sense of frustration among Jesuits at the social unimportance of their converts: 'Too long, he decided, had conversions been made in the islands and along the beaches, protected, if necessary, by Portuguese guns. The time had come for the cross to outstrip the flag. The walls of India—what were they but fear of the unknown? The time had come for someone to penetrate the interior and convert those living in the heart of Southern India (1966:34).'

Under Nobili, the storming of the citadel came to mean a total accommodation to the rules of the caste order, observing every nicety required by pollution ideology. In a sense, the Jesuit was converted to Brahmanism before he succeeded in making any converts to Catholicism. His acceptance of the low status of the coastal castes has left its mark on subsequent relations between the Church and the Mukkuvars. Even today, parish priests view their term in coastal villages as something of an ordeal to be endured. Under the Roman Catholic Church, the Mukkuvars remained separate from other castes. They did not benefit from the concerted activity of educational, economic and social reform that was the hallmark of the nineteenth century Protestant missionary groups. That nineteenth century wave of conversion has left, as part of its legacy, a number of Protestant agricultural castes in Kanyakumari District, including the dominant Nadar caste. The gulf between the Mukkuvars and their relatively better educated, upwardly mobile Protestant neighbours is no less profound than the gulf between the Mukkuvars and Hindu agriculturists.

The education that was made available by the Jesuits, even at centres of educational activity such as Tuticorin in the east coast, was largely confined to catechetical schools or *veeda paLLikuuDam*, and seminaries. This level of education did not permit the fishing castes to enter the new dominant class of priests. If the powerful Paravas never became padres, there was even less opportunity for their poor cousins the Mukkuvars. Roche speculates that this may have been due to the early apprenticeship demanded of boys in a fishing economy. But the barriers ran deeper than this: until well into the twentieth century Roman bishops in Kerala were foreigners, and there were virtually no priests ordained from low caste backgrounds (Forrester 1980:111). Although the first Parava priest was ordained in 1894, the missionaries ordained high-ranking Paravas rather than non-elite fishermen (S. Bayly, personal communication, 1990).

The social gulf between priests and the community, and the lack of education within the Mukkuvar caste, has created problems for the Church. Since the period of conversion in the sixteenth century the Church has emerged as a powerful overlord, viewing the coastal belt as its own private territory, in both the economic and political sense. In the course of four hundred years, the Church has constituted itself as a quasi-State, operating within the boundaries of the official State of the day. It has levied its own taxes, adjudicated disputes between one village and another, or between individuals, and generally mediated the relations of people within its own territory with the outside world. Dumont has contrasted the fusion of secular and ritual power in the Christian church with their separation under Hinduism. In the European church, as he puts it, 'the supremacy of the spiritual' is 'expressed politically' (1980:72). In south India, among a fringe people, the Church's politicisation of religion has developed to even greater proportions. Villagers ironically refer to their parish priests as *kuTTi raja*, 'petty prince'.

The cornerstone of this self-appointed role has been the Church's arrogation of the right to levy taxes on the fisherpeople. In an arrangement which was operative until recently, a portion of the meagre surplus has been skimmed off in a tax known as the *kutukai*, a traditional term for a tax previously levied by the king of Travancore (Ramachandran 1981). In coastal Kanyakumari, the tax seems to have varied between 25–35 per cent of a good day's catch, payable once a week. The village of Muttom is on record as paying around 25 per cent (Selik 1980), while KaDalkarai Uuru has traditionally paid 35 per cent. Elsewhere along the coast the system is varied— in a fishing village in south Travandrum (Kerala), five per cent is extracted from every fisherman's daily catch (Vattamattam 1978). All over the Kerala and Kanyakumari coastline the right to collect this tax is in turn auctioned out to those men in the village who have the capital to bid and secure the place. In 1978 the auctioned price was 100000 rupees (Vattamattam 1978). In KaDalkarai Uuru, where the system ended fifteen years ago, the Church was paid off in three annual instalments. The person who secured the right to collect taxes also secured the right to appropriate a portion of the tax as his own commission. Access to such large amounts of capital would usually not have been available to an average fishing household. It was therefore the middlemen who became tax collectors. In KaDalkarai

Uuru, the same fish merchant held the right to collect dues for fifteen years.

The domination of the Church has a further dimension: it owns nearly all the land in and around these villages. In KaDalkarai Uuru, for example, it owns the two hectares of land on which the dwellings of the community are erected. While households do not pay rent to the Church, the owners of shops, and any other services located within the village (such as the health clinic or the post office), are obliged to do so. In recent years, mining companies such as the government-owned Indian Rare Earths Company have purchased village land from the Church. They now own 21 acres of land in the Uuru, and regular operations to extract sand containing rare minerals are now under way.

Finally, the Church lays claims to the produce of all coconut trees that grow in the village, and to the associated products, such as coir. The Church also derives an income from the monopoly it holds over the performance of life-cycle rituals—christening, marriage, funerals, first communions, etc. In KaDalkarai Uuru, the minimum charge for a marriage service is Re100; for a burial, a minimum of Re75. Some villagers bring in a more senior ranking priest from outside the village, paying for his travel and expenses.

The privileges of the priests may be meagre ones, but in a poor and fragile economy such as that of the Mukkuvars they stand out. These privileges include decent housing, regular meals, a cook, but above all, access to funds from taxes and landownership, supplemented by money coming in from outside agencies such as Church organisations, government departments and aid agencies. Villagers are suspicious; they gossip about such matters. The greater the rewards, real and supposed, the more they expose the Church to rumour, at worst to crisis. The Church is confronted by a subdued but chronic problem of legitimation among the villagers.

The Church's legitimisation of its power: the problem of hegemony

I have described the Church as a quasi-State, operating within the boundaries of the official State, with special powers of jurisdiction over the coastal population. As with every State, the Church has means of coercion in establishing and maintaining its domination—but over the past four hundred years has tried to exercise its authority through another mode of rule, involving the consent and participation of the subject population. This undertaking has been conceived by Gramsci as the establishment of hegemony. Hegemony depends, in the words of Adamson (1980:171), on ensuring control over 'the consensual basis of ... [the] political system', as contrasted with coercion sanctioned by violence. The Western bourgeois States,

36   *Mukkuvar Women*

which for Gramsci best exemplified hegemonic rule, relied on voluntary associations such as parties, unions and cultural institutions to reconcile the masses to the domination of one class over another. The task of the Church in establishing hegemony has been simplified enormously by its claim to be the sole earthly mediator between divinity and humanity. In a society such as India, where the dominant form of consciousness is religious, this claim represents an immensely powerful basis on which to build legitimacy and social power. At the same time, the traditional power granted to religious leaders within Hinduism cannot be readily claimed by the Church. The Catholic priests, unlike Brahmans, are part of a network which is at once more well-organised and centralised than Hinduism allows, and also more impersonal. The Catholic Church is simultaneously a religion and a bureaucracy in the Weberian sense of the term. It appoints priests to different parishes without any regard to their caste or social background, nor can priests develop long-range and intimate ties with the people of any particular village. Brahman elites base a considerable part of their hegemony on the basis of hereditary office and their participation in the community life of a village over a period of generations. Their power as a caste group is further strengthened by the continuity of association between particular individuals of that caste and the community as a whole. Parish priests cannot rely on this further source of legitimacy.

The problem is further compounded by the foreign origins of the Church in India, and by the relative failure of the Church to recruit members of the converted castes into the priesthood (Forrester 1980). Such priests as are recruited from the Tamil population come overwhelmingly from the agricultural castes.[1]

When appointed to a parish in a fishing community, the Tamil priest is scarcely more at home than a foreigner would be. He will not stay long enough to develop ties within the community. The priest is likely to regard the Mukkuvars as uncouth, quarrelling and ignorant—and in turn the villagers feel free to scrutinise and criticise the priests. Some priests are given irreverent nicknames (such as 'Chemmeen' or Red Fish), even by the young girls of the village. They are often young and vulnerable. Their behaviour is watched closely, and any association with young women is a subject of continuous gossip and censure. Those priests who have no awareness of the peculiarly Mukkuvar appropriation of the Catholic Church as part of their own communal identity view their many responsibilities in a coastal parish as an oppressive burden.

Furthermore, the Church as an institution—one in which secular and religious authority are united—does not provide a secure basis for the exercise of moral legitimacy in a society dominated by Hinduism. In Hinduism, Mukkuvar villages have the basis of a powerful critique of the Church's association with economic power. The Hindu ideal of the supreme spiritual authority is that of the renouncer, who has given up all attachment to all interests pursued within civil society (Dumont 1980). This ideal retains force among the Mukkuvars. Men of knowledge within the community, known as *aasaans*, are respected for taking a vow never to accept money for their religio-medical skills. The Church's handling of money, whether through taxes or from outside sources, is the target of increasing criticism and dissatisfaction. In the next chapter, I discuss the theme of *poraamai* or envy in its proper context. This powerful form of resentment, when directed at the church, gains further fuel from the moral stance which holds that a religious power should be seen to be above all worldly concerns.

The responses of the Church to these serious problems—which are inherent in its structure—take two forms. One has been the development, with Church encouragement, of an indigenous and popular Catholicism, with a base in voluntary religious organisations and in mass cults surrounding the Virgin Mary and the saints. The second response has been to invoke the example of the Church as the special representative of the Mukkuvar community, as a neutral arbiter above all individual interests, acting in a paternal spirit to ensure the majority's welfare.

The nature of popular Catholicism is examined in the next chapter. There the perspective will be that of the villagers, but here it should be stressed that the initiatives in establishing such a mass base were taken by the Church itself. Although Mukkuvars have only recently been recruited into the priesthood, they could aspire to becoming ecclesiastical functionaries (*karyasthanis*) of the Church within their own village. In 1542, Xavier introduced a number of offices: the *kanakapillais* (catechists), *modoms* (overseers of ecclesiastical duties), the *ubadesiars* (sacristans), and the *vaatiyaars* (teachers in the *veeda paLLikudams* or religious schools) (Roche 1984:67). While working under the direction of the individual parish priests, these functionaries have developed their own stake in the continued power and presence of the Church. In turn, the functionaries and the priests have worked closely in cooperation with the traditional headmen or elders of the villages. These elders have less prestige than those of the *jaati talaivar* of the east coast Parava community, nor are the structures within which they operate as centralised. But they have been important sources of support for the church. Some villagers view this situation as a political trade-off between the Church and the *pradhani* or headmen: the Church provides the headmen with economic funds, the latter provides the political support necessary for the Church's rule. Benedict, the school teacher, observed that:

> The village hierarchy could be described thus: the emperors are the rich boat owners; the kings are the educated teachers, the president is the priest; the strong men are the *uuchaalis*. An *uuchaali* is a man who knows how to talk, and make self-aggrandising noises regardless of the justice or

injustice of the situation. His family can usually command manpower, and they should have proved themselves in conflicts. They have the strength to make the priest seek their support rather than the other way around. In fact, the priest, though an authority, is also an honorary figure like the president, who must align himself with important men in the village. The *uuchaalis* are still today the movers behind the scene—as all over India, democracy is just a veneer. '*Uuchaalism*' is not as violent as '*goondaism*' in the north of India. There may not be any murderous bashings. But opposition to an *uuchaali* can make one's life very difficult—one may find oneself barred from buying fish or carrying on a normal life. Also, many of the main fights in the village are in fact those between gangs of *uuchaalis* and their supporters. You know the saying, '*kallum kallum modinal taan neruppu varum*' (only when one stone clashes with another is there fire). The priest may bribe *uuchaalis* with drink, flattery and loans of money— once that is done, they will implement his decisions in the village. '*Kovil poonai kadavul ku anjaadu*' (the temple cat is not afraid of god—the priest is the least godly of all in his conduct). Boat owners also have their own backing—the strong men for the emperors. The educated and the teachers settle disputes in the village, but play favorites so that their decisions are followed by a feast, like the monkey that 'settled' the dispute between cats and ate well out of it. The educated, with better sense and morals, simply stay out of village politics. As in the story of the monkey and the bird. The monkey was taking shelter under a tree, shivering in the rain. The bird looked down, snug in its nest and advised it to similarly build a nest for future need. In a rage, the monkey climbed the tree and pulled the nest to pieces. Never tell wisdom to fools—they will drag you down.

Stella, the social worker, was equally cynical about this collusion:

It was a corrupt system. Government aid such as raw material for nets, would be taken off by the *pradhani* and his strong-men, many of them uneducated and deriving their authority only from appeals to traditional and familial strength in the village. Many poor fishermen were quite unaware of this corruption. They may occasionally be called in by one of the leaders, their health and well-being enquired after, and be given a little money to repair their huts. They would go away extremely pleased and grateful for the benevolence of their leader, little suspecting that they had only been given a tiny fraction of what was their due.

There was also the collusion between the traditional leaders and the priests. The priest secured their allegiance by giving them a cut of the money obtained through taxes or through ownership of coconut groves. Little of this tax money found its way to the people; most of it would be used for the upkeep of the church—repairs and endless extensions with occasional token welfare gestures like repairing some thatched roofs and improving civil amenities. The gulf in the lifestyle of the priest and the people was vast, but accepted by the latter. If anyone challenged this set-up, the *uuchaalis* would go around and abuse the individual.

In addition to collaborating with the *pradhanis* and fostering a group of ecclesiastical functionaries, the Church set up a number of voluntary associations in charge of organising lessons in catechism or of rituals such as First Communion, the festivals of the Saints and other Christian feast days. These religious organisations draw in village participation, and are particularly important to women. Several of the organisations in KaDalkarai Uuru are exclusively women's associations—the *Marai Kalvi Asaariyaigal Manram*, which conducts catechism classes; the *Christian VaaLva Sangam*, an attempt to revitalise village religious life; the Little Way Association, in charge of village religious functions.

The participation of villagers has been sought by the Church ever since the time of Pare Henriquez, St Francis Xavier's immediate successor among the Paravas. Henriquez was dissatisfied with Xavier's mechanical insistence on rote memorisation of Catholic doctrine and the destruction of Hindu idols. He lived in coastal settlements on the Parava coast, encouraging the literary study of Tamil among parishioners. It was Henriquez who established the Confraternities of Charity, the earliest predecessors of the Church voluntary associations found in coastal villages today.

Most significant of these means of ensuring popular participation was the introduction by the Jesuits of cults devoted to the Virgin Mary and the Saints. In 1582, the Jesuits imported among the Paravas a statue of Our Lady of the Snows from Manila, and established in Tuticorin a cult of the Virgin which became a focal point of caste identity (see Roche 1984 and Bayly 1981 for details). The Virgin and the Saints have become guardians of village welfare among the Mukkuvars as well. Priests have encouraged villagers to adopt a saint as a village patron, and to celebrate that saint's festival with special community pride. Erected outside each church is a special shrine dedicated to the village's patron saint. The official Sunday sermons are held in the church, but in addition, priests deliver informal sermons at the shrines of the saints. Evening prayers are held before the shrines on the beach sand, the villagers kneeling with flickering candles in the open air.

A second way in which the Church has sought to establish a hegemonic position among fishing communities has been its promulgation of a paternalistic ideology in which the Church is depicted as community representative and leader. In terms of this ideology, the Church's ownership of land and collection of taxes are portrayed as exercised on behalf of the community itself. The taxes are represented as a common fund belonging to the entire *uuru*. Needy villagers are encouraged to apply to the Church for loans. Alternatively, the Church may purchase land on behalf of the villagers, for example to rehouse the homeless in the wake of monsoonal flooding. All Church-owned land is referred to by villagers as *uuru nilam* or land belonging to the *uuru* as a whole.

In this fashion the Church is able to turn to its advantage what in other contexts may seem a drawback: the social distance that separates it from the villagers. The Church is perceived as above sectional conflicts, uninterested in factionalism. Land belonging to the Church

is communal in one important sense—it is a bulwark against ownership by any one wealthy individual. Where private individuals have
recently bought land and rented it out to other villagers—a result of
recent changes in the political economy of fishing—the enrichment of
these individuals has been much resented in the village, particularly
by those living on the rented property. But money spent on refur-
bishing the Church, on firecrackers, sound equipment or lavish
entertainment on *tiruvinaL* or festival occasions, is not necessarily
seen as misappropriation of village funds by the Church. Often such
expenditure is a source of village pride.

However, it is in the Church's exercise of prestige and authority in
dispute settlement that its resemblance to a mini-State is most striking. The gulf between seafaring and agricultural society in this respect
reinforces the role of the Church. Mukkuvars are reluctant to take
their disputes outside the community. Modern agencies of law enforcement, such as the police, find Mukkuvars elusive and resistant to
their authority. The visit of a police vehicle is a sure sign for men to
take off to sea, and for women to adopt elaborate games of trickery
and to feign ignorance. The priest is one of the few people whom the
Mukkuvars will trust to help solve their conflicts. In his dual capacity
as insider (special representative of the community) and educated outsider, the priest both settles disputes and mediates with the outside
world. In settling the disputes the priest may consult the *pradhanis*,
or call an *uuru kuuTam* or village meeting in which only men can
participate. I give below a list taken from village records at the
neighbouring village of KooDimonai of the kinds of conflicts brought
before the priest:

(i)   The priest is requested to arrange peace talks between two families in
the village, a dispute which has brought in related kin from other villages;
(ii)   A woman fish vendor complains: her husband is away on seasonal
migration, and she is being harassed by the family of her daughter's lover
for not keeping closer watch on her daughter's movements. The other
family is threatening to dishonour her other three daughters, and she seeks
protection;
(iii)   The owner of a home wants compensation for being turned out of his
home by a man returning home from seasonal migration. The latter
refused to recognise the sale of the home, organised by his family in his
absence;
(iv)   A woman demands the return of her money from a family to which
she loaned Re20 000 in order to purchase a mechanised boat. The
borrower family has left the village with her money:
(v)   A request is made for an additional water-pipe to be located in the
village, and for the priest to approach the municipality on behalf of the
villagers;
(vi)   Mechanised boats in KooDimonai are said to be causing disturbances
to *kaTTumarams* operating in another village, Enayam Putenturai;
(vii)   The primary school requests another teacher;
(viii)   Two *kaTTumarams* have been found missing by men from the

neighbouring village, and they suspect they have been stolen from KooDimonai. They request the priest to find them and return the equipment;
(ix) A request is made from a neighbouring village for joint action over securing proper water facilities from local government.

It is clear from the variety of requests flowing towards the priest that the authority he exercises is a mixture of different elements. Not only is he the moral and spiritual mentor, but he exercises the secular authority to allocate village funds, to mediate disputes between families, factions and classes, and to negotiate with the official State in order to secure better facilities for his constituency. The coercive dimensions of this authority should not be overlooked. These have historically taken the form of moral as well as physical sanctions. Moral sanctions may take the form of denying baptism to illegitimate children, denying the right to burial in the common village grounds and enforcing rituals of submission and public humiliation such as requiring a couple guilty of adultery to parade around a village with a cross in their hands. Behind these lies the sanction of physical reprisals: this is the significance of the *uuchaalis* or strong-men referred to earlier.

Hegemony is never an accomplished fact that can be taken for granted—it is a relationship in which the consent of the dominated must be continually re-established and affirmed or negotiated by both sides. In the next chapter I examine the way in which the popular Catholicism of the villagers continually threatens to run outside the confines defined by the Church.

Moreover, the wider social framework within which Church and villagers seek mutual accommodation is itself subject to change. The Church nowadays has to relate to a much more centralised form of State authority, which places greater restrictions on its own jurisdiction over the coastal people. At the same time, with the emergence of political parties, unions and cooperatives, villagers are themselves offered alternative sources of patronage and allegiance. The village of KaDalkarai Uuru does not stand alone. Under the structure of local government it has been amalgamated into the Panchayat of Colachel. Politicians and political parties offer an alternative route to admissions into schools and jobs, protection from the police and help in legal cases. Although the Mukkuvars have had little caste representation in either the State Parliament or Legislative Assembly, some sections of the caste are actively campaigning to have themselves reclassified as a 'Backward Caste', an official designation which provides for special protective legislative status and material concessions. There is also some feeling that the coastal belt should be granted the status of a separate political constituency.

With the emergence of a new source of conflict between artisanal and mechanised technology, political associations have sprung up to represent artisanal fishermen. The associations, while maintaining a certain distrustful distance from all official political parties, now offer villagers another mode of organising themselves and of establishing links with fishing communities all over Tamil Nadu, and increasingly, federating with similar associations all over India. In KaDalkarai Uuru, organisations such as *Meenavar Urumai Paadakaapu Sangam* (Society for the Protection of Fishermen's Rights) are voluntary political associations of this kind. Government-run cooperatives offer a further source of access to material goods such as funds to purchase nets and mechanised fishing gear. Finally, the various arms of the State, its law enforcement agencies and its welfare services (catering for health, sanitation, roads electricity, education), continually threaten to supplant the monopoly of the Church over these functions.

What is remarkable is not so much the existence of external limits on the Church's power, but the extent to which the Church has managed to utilise even some of these potential rival agencies to consolidate its own influence. Neither police nor government officials are keen to deal directly with the Mukkuvars. Their villages are seldom visited by anyone from the Fisheries Department or the Health or Education Departments. An outbreak of typhoid or cholera (a very common occurrence) may bring a team of government health workers to innoculate villagers. Otherwise, the government prefers to deal with the parish priests. Villagers, for their part, rely on the education, social class and experience of the priest to plead their cause with the Block Development Officer, the municipality authorities, the police and the bank managers. Rural development programmes, whether government-based or funded by Church agencies, are obliged to work through the local power structure with the priest at its apex.

Nevertheless, certain irreversible realignments have occurred in the power relation between Church and villagers. The tax traditionally paid by villagers, the *kutukai*, has been discontinued in many coastal villages. In KaDalkarai Uuru it ended fifteen years ago, in other villages about seven years ago. Villagers talk of an erosion in the respect for the priesthood and of a growing resentment of the contract system. The resentment has become acute with awareness of the gradual deterioration in economic conditions, particularly the decreasing size of the fishing catch. The following remark of a woman fish vendor is typical of this sentiment: 'We used to get so much *kudipu meen* [big jawed jumper] and *vaalai* [mackerel] that we had to employ all kinds of kin and relatives to dry and salt the fish, which we sent to Ceylon. Today we survive only through the little bit of prawn that is available. A man in this district tried to secure his bid on the *kutukai*, but had to drop it because he was running at a loss.'

According to several villagers, matters came to a head in a year of great *varme* or scarcity. One villager described it in this way:

We had the practice of borrowing money from the church in one lump sum and then dividing it equally among the needy households in the village. It would be borrowed in the lean months and returned in peak season. However, in this particular year, the catch which had been deteriorating steadily, was worse than ever before. When it was time to return the money loaned from the church, the men began to grumble, and argue that the church should take its due out of its *kutukai* tax.

For fifteen years after this the Church did not insist on the tax. The *kutukai* was re-introduced in the name of raising funds for the purchase of land on which to construct new housing, and involved payment of a daily tax of five per cent. However, it was so bitterly resented by the villagers that after several households simply refused to pay it, the attempt collapsed in a year. While variants of this tax continue to exist in some coastal villages, the system no longer rests on secure foundations.

Finally, forces of reform and social criticism are active within the Church itself. Catholic social service organisations, mobilising around issues of women's employment and the establishment of community services, have become an important force for social change in the district as a whole. In Kerala, parish priests have led fishermen in their agitations against the disruption caused by unregulated trawling. In Kanyakumari District, where the impact of mechanised fishing has been indirect (resulting mainly in the creation of a migrant labour force), the priests have concentrated more on the establishment of 'Basic Communities', following a model for encouraging community-based self-government and religious growth which originated in the Latin American slums. Participation in these schemes has offered villagers a means of political education and has led to the emergence of a group of articulate critics and reformers within the Mukkuvar community. Teachers and social workers such as Bernard and Stella are part of this emerging group of activists and intellectuals. To the extent that campaigns for employment, health facilities and community amenities are encouraged by groups within the Catholic Church, we may be witnessing the evolution of new forms of legitimation, which will ensure the continued leadership of the Church despite realignments in the relations of power between Church and villagers.

Conclusion

In the last two chapters I have argued that the Mukkuvars, on the borders of caste society, have a distinctive subculture of their own. To explain this subculture I have sought to identify three components. The Mukkuvars are geographically separate from caste Hindus. Because of their occupation, their system of values is relatively non-hierarchical. They are Catholics. In varying ways they have used all three of these characteristics to reject, or elude, the low ranking assigned to the community according to the rules of caste. From the Mukkuvar perspective, caste or *jaati* is viewed as the form of their communal identity. The hierarchical elements of the system as a whole are minimised. For the Mukkuvars, caste stands for their difference from Hindu society, not their subordination to it. Their ancient rivalry with other social groups (principally these days with the Nadars) is represented by the Mukkuvars not in terms of status within a hierarchy, but in terms of a contest between their own, coherent social entity and another.

It has been argued, most powerfully by Dumont (1980:201*ff.*) that alternative identities do not last long in caste society without striking some compromise with the principle of hierarchy. He refers particularly to the identities supplied by minority religions such as Islam and Christianity. But his argument is too general; it must be qualified by closer reference to the particularities of local configurations of power.[2] In the coastal villages, the Jesuits, as has been seen, were quite willing to compromise with the principle of hierarchy, and fit into the caste structure, but the people they converted had in their fishing economy a powerful basis for keeping themselves aloof from caste society. Among the Mukkuvars, Catholicism has found its place within a structure of difference rather than of hierarchy.

The next two chapters explore this difference as it is articulated in terms of a specific version of religion and femininity.

Pulling in the *karamaDi* (beach-seine net)

Dyeing the sail in tamarind liquid outside the village church

The village church, KaDalkarai Uuru

The beach as men's space

Mending torn nets on
the beach

Mary the healer, praying to St Michael to be possessed by his divine grace

Picture card of Velankanni Maataa, sold outside the shrine at Raja Uuru

The village patron, St Anthony, in his shrine on the beach at KaDalkarai

Mary healing in trance state

The embodiment of a
different style of healing:
Gomati, Hindu healer, living
across the road from the
coastal villagers

Women's spaces, women's (unpaid) work: fetching water

Bathing children

Grinding spices for the evening meal

Weaving the nets. An older woman helps the girls for a while

Pounding rice into flour

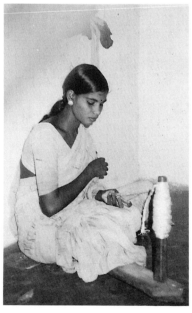

Making thread for fishing nets

A trader in rice and spices operates her shop from her porch

Seraphim, my research assistant, taking in tailoring work

Author with women and children
of KaDalkarai Uuru

A *kuTTai kaari*

A group of fish traders share a joke

3   Popular religion and femininity (1): the disciplining of the female body in popular Catholicism

One of the contributions of the social sciences, particularly anthropology, psychology and sociology, has been to show how the human body is used to support power struggles, as a place where the dominant group inscribes its systems of domination, its taboos and punishments. But if this is true for the human body in general, it is all the more true for the female body, which seems to be the prime material for the symbolism of power and writing on hierarchy, domination and exploitation. The female body as a field of writing, initiation and discourse on power, domination and exploitation seems a constant aspect of human societies, whatever the degree of development of their means of production

> *Woman in the Muslim Unconscious*
> Fatna A. Sabbah (1984:17)

This chapter bridges two themes of the book. I have characterised the distinctive features of the Mukkuvar community as a whole. I now shift to the theme which dominates the rest of the book: the lives of Mukkuvar women and the structures and forces that shape them. As with all moments of transition, there is a particular need at this point to clarify the nature of the linkages and the points of mediation between the two themes I have outlined.

It will be clear even at this early stage that in raising the question of women in a community such as the Mukkuvars, we will have to situate themes of gender in a very specific social context. I have char-acterised the Mukkuvars as a ritually impure low-ranking caste in the Hindu hierarchy, who have nevertheless avoided the total economic and social subservience of untouchable agricultural castes. Further, if we conceive of property purely in terms of individual rights to possession and use of material goods, then we are dealing with a community where property has only limited importance. The means of production in this definition are distributed remarkably evenly, in comparison to those in agricultural communities, and inequality, where it exists, is volatile. All of these features, which place the Mukkuvar in a rather unique relationship to the wider system of social stratification in India, must necessarily shape the nature of the relations between the sexes, and the situation of women.

Yet in the course of conceptualising the relation between gender and wider systems of power, we are haunted by a kind of crude nineteenth-century materialism. Ideologies of femininity, particularly in their more severe and restrictive aspects such as seclusion and segregation, are all too frequently conceived as the peculiar burden of women in the propertied upper strata of society. This is sometimes noted as a curious paradox: women's freedom from surveillance is supposedly in inverse proportion to their economic power as members of a class or caste. Jeffrey's book on seclusion among the Pirzada women of the Nizammuddin Sufi shrine in Delhi states the general argument as it has been framed for India:

> The Indian situation, then presents a paradox. It is mainly—but not exclusively—women from the poorest sectors who work outside their homes, and have greatest equality with their menfolk at home. By contrast, the cloistered women who do not work are women whose menfolk wield the greatest influence in the world outside the home, and who, as several writers have commented, experience marked inequalities between spouses in these richer families, often signalled by women when they cover their heads, lower their eyes, or employ polite and circumlocutory forms of address (1979:32).

The nineteenth-century tradition I refer to received its most influential and densely argued version in Engels' thesis attributing women's subordination to the development of private property. The control of female sexuality became imperative in this context, and was ensured through the institutionalisation of monogamous marriage (1884).[1] The argument continues to resurface with remarkable persistence in contemporary social theory. Recently, both Goody (1976) and, in a slightly different form, Boserup (1970) have maintained that it is economic surplus, the establishment of a privileged non-productive class, which leads to seclusion, concealment, chaperonage, segregation and arranged marriages. Even theorists who, dealing with caste-based societies, are reluctant totally to reduce the problem to economic terms, see the concern with female purity merely as a by-product of maintaining the caste privileges of the community as a whole (Yalman 1963).

Materialism of this kind has left us with a troubling legacy in our depiction of the lives of women in the poor non-propertied classes. Cultural control of female sexuality and, in a sense, the problem of culture itself, become the province of the upper classes. For those who own few means of production, and in addition have little economic stake in the niceties of caste purity, the problem must be 'economic'. But does this economy operate in a naked fashion, bereft of cultural signification, simply because one is dealing with the dispossessed?

A community such as the Mukkuvars, with minimal internal economic stratification, ranked low in both caste and class terms, should provide the ideal setting for relative equality between the sexes and freedom from the cultural disciplining of female sexuality—according to the axioms of the materialist thesis. Yet the most striking feature of the sexual division of labour in Mukkuvar society is one which is so deeply entrenched that it may even be passed over by the outside observer—women are *barred* from utilising the resources of the ocean, except through their relationships with men. They may not pursue the most lucrative occupation open to a sea-faring community, which is also the activity central to the community's self-definition: the activity of fishing itself.

However, to understand the constitution of the fundamental dispossession of women, we need to distance ourselves sharply from the notion that such dispossession is to be located in a separate sphere called 'the economic', where property and the means of production are thing-like entities which one either possesses or is barred from. Such a conceptualisation may mislead us, in the Mukkuvar case, into postulating an egalitarian society, when on closer examination that egalitarianism turns out to be confined to men only.

The issues are partly clarified by extending our concept of property to include non-material means of production. As early as 1929 Lowie coined the term 'incorporeal property' to describe certain privileges which constitute wealth in certain societies. These privileges may include the proprietorship of certain skills, knowledge of rituals, songs and legends. Among the Mukkuvars, the incorporeal property comprises the transmission of specialised skills in the operation of fishing gear, knowledge of fishing grounds, the breeding habits of the fish, navigation skills, astronomy, and so on. These skills are essential in working and utilising the natural resources of the ocean.

The acquisition of these skills is in turn regulated by another key component of incorporeal property: the rights to space. It is only recently that the operation of 'sea tenure' has been recognised at all: fishermen were thought to operate in a purely individualistic way in utilising the sea as a 'common property resource' (see Alexander 1984 for a critique). These rules of sea tenure are defined on the basis of social membership, the *uuru* or village one belongs to, ethical rules governing the laying of nets and the division of catch—but most importantly, the element usually forgotten in the study of sea tenure—on the basis of one's sex.

From the vantage point of the women, sea-tenure itself is a narrow component of the wider social distribution of space: norms governing the sexual distribution of space on land in fact pre-empt the question of who has rights to the sea at all. These norms prohibit women from gaining access to the sea, and even to the spaces most intimately associated with the work of fishing: the sea-front and the beach. Since the skills of fishing are largely acquired in the course of the labour performed in these spaces, the sexual distribution of space must be seen as crucial in the unequal distribution of those resources which Bourdieu (1977) describes as 'cultural capital'.

In describing the rights to space and to the skills acquired through those rights as cultural capital, we are not merely extending the scope of the materialist concepts of property and capital. We are doing more: we are inserting the notion of culture into the very construction of capital. We are concerned here in particular with those aspects of culture which involve the construction of sexual difference and sexual inequality. The sexual distribution of space is itself an aspect of a wider cultural project by which male and female bodies are governed by radically different rules, prescriptions and minute observances, as among the Kabyle of North Africa whom we encounter in Bordieu's ethnography:

> Bodily *hexis* is political mythology realized, *em-bodied*, turned into a
> permanent disposition, a durable manner of standing, speaking, and
> thereby of *feeling* and *thinking*. The oppositions which mythico-ritual logic
> makes between the male and the female and which organize the whole
> system of values reappear, for example, in the gestures and movements of
> the body, in the form of the opposition between the straight and the bent,
> or between assurance and restraint . . . In short, the specifically feminine
> virtue, *lahia*, modesty, restraint, reserve, orient the whole female body
> downwards, towards the ground, the inside, the house, whereas male
> excellence, *nif*, is asserted in movement upwards, outwards, towards other
> men (Bourdieu, 1977:93–94).

It will be among the chief concerns of this and the next chapter to describe the rules and practices of physical containment and discipline which help to create the sexually appropriate, gendered body among Mukkuvar women. These rules bear some resemblance to the *purdah* complex of the north, discussed by anthropologists such as Sharma (1978, 1980), Jacobson (1982) and Jeffrey (1979). Mukkuvar women are excluded from certain spaces, notably the sea and the beach. The onus is on them to maintain a physical separation from men if they venture into this masculine space. The enforcement of this restriction is nuanced according to the age and marital status of the women. Young girls are prohibited from a very early age from swimming and playing in the surf, and from becoming familiar with the sea the way boys do. Boys on the other hand are actively encouraged to perform small tasks for the men as soon as they are physically able to do so—helping in pulling in beach-seine nets, stacking equipment, in return for which they may get to earn small sums of money.

Two per cent of the catch is put aside to pay such young helpers. By the age of eleven, boys are actively recruited to go out to sea, although they only earn their full share of the catch when they are much older. Girls lose more and more of their access to the sea and sea-front as they grow into puberty. Young unmarried girls are regarded as having no legitimate business on the beach. However, women over the age of forty, usually married, enjoy greater freedoms in this respect. On the few occasions when a female presence on the beach is prominent—in peak fishing seasons, for example, when female labour is needed to sort and dry the fish—it is the older married women of the household who come out to engage in these tasks.

The exclusion of women from certain spaces designated as masculine, and the gradual expansion of female access to those spaces along with seniority and marriage, is familiar to us from descriptions of the purdah complex in the north. Unlike the north, however, the veiling behaviour is largely metaphoric: no actual veil or purdah is used. Nor is there veiling behaviour of any kind in front of affines or the people of one's husband's village. This difference may be traced back to radical differences between the kinship systems of the south and the north (see Chapter 7).

A similar modification occurs in the sense in which Mukkuvar women may be said to be consigned to 'the domestic sphere', and to the further assumption by which the space of the domestic is equated to the interior of the house. Here again, the association between women and the domestic takes a symbolic rather than a literal form. Female identity and subjectivity is firmly anchored in the tasks of social reproduction performed as the wives, mothers and daughters of men. However, these tasks are defined unusually broadly in the fishing community, and permit the actual space of 'the domestic' to spill over from the confines of the house, into the alleys of the village, and much further, into numerous journeys and pilgrimages that take women up and down the coastal belt and into the agrarian hinterland. However, when engaged in activities which cannot be readily identified as domestic—activities undertaken for pleasure, relaxation, or even economic activities such as trade—women lose the privilege of safe and legitimate conduct in spaces which revert to their primary status as male spaces.

It is only in the space inside and around the house, together with areas associated with domestic labour—the wells and taps, certain parts of the river—that female presence is unproblematic and not in need of legitimation. Relaxation, for women, must be found sitting on the front porch of the house, or in sandy lanes just outside the house. Although men have a parallel close association with the sea and the beach where all the gear and boats are stored, with many men preferring to spend even their nights sleeping on the beach in the cool of the open air, men do not need to justify their presence outside this space. For relaxation and adventure, they have access to other public spaces such as the village square (usually in front of the parish church), the toddy shop, the shady groves of coconut palm lining the beach and, if they are in the mood, the cinema houses and tea-shops in the larger township of Colachel. Potentially, the public venues of the world are open to them.

Although women's spaces are not subject to the same radical closure as northern purdah, the association between women and the domestic continues to structure women's access to space. There are some forms of work performed by Mukkuvar women, such as fish trading, which are not domestic, and which take women onto the beach as well as into markets outside the coastal belt. These women occupy sites dominated not only by Mukkuvar men but men from other castes and religions. For precisely these reasons, however, such activities are heavily hedged about with restrictions—and only a minority of older women engage in them. Further, even the older women do not quite escape the taint of disreputability, both in the eyes of the outside world and within the Mukkuvar community itself. In fish trading, as in other female activities, the sexualisation of the female body makes attributes such as age and marital status highly significant in the degree of closure and strictness with which female space is defined. For young unmarried girls, association with the domestic sphere is no mere metaphor, but may become very real indeed, particularly after puberty.

Women's exclusion from fishing, and the restrictions placed on their access to trade could, of course, be discussed as so many 'economic facts'. To do so would limit us to accepting social processes as reified structures. Access to the means of production is as much a cultural construct as an economic resource. Deeply imbued notions of female modesty, chastity and invisibility outside the domestic cannot be relegated to a merely reproductive status, as legitimising an economic dependency accomplished 'elsewhere'. Mukkuvars themselves, while taking the sexual division of labour for granted, if questioned on the matter do not argue that the division of labour is either biologically ordained or a purely natural order of things. Their responses are framed in terms of the violation of cultural values entailed in permitting women to engage in work in male-dominated spaces without suitable safeguards.

It is not merely that the violation of such cultural norms would be dangerous for women. Women themselves are seen as dangerous—to men. The degree and nature of the danger depend on the age and social position of the woman concerned, but women as a category share the stigma of being designated dangerous, particularly to the male pursuit of hazardous activities such as fishing. Fishing itself is a highly ritualised form of productive activity. In contrast to the land, which has been at least partially domesticated through agriculture, the sea has not been tamed or socialised. Technology and skills cannot guarantee human safety, let alone some degree of predictability and periodicity in the relationship between labour and productivity. Purely materialistic explanations of the labour process therefore stand little chance of plausibility to the fisherpeople themselves. Attempts at controlling the environment focus therefore on ritual, rather than technology. All tools of trade, their fishing craft and gear, particularly prior to their first use at sea, must receive religious consecration. The Mukkuvars utilise their parish priests for these purposes. The priests pray over the craft, and offer the insurance of divine blessings for the future luck and safety of the craft. Individuals in fishing villages who claim some knowledge of Hindu *mantra-vaadam*, described by a practitioner as the juggling of sounds or *aksharam* said to have begun with the origin of the world itself, are able to exchange their knowledge for a share in the fishing catch. By utilising their *mantram* to attract fish into nets (and also deflect fish out of the nets of rivals) these men collect five per cent of the total catch from the crew they have helped. Significantly, the type of fishing where magic is used most frequently is the *karamaDi* or beach-seine, precisely where human skills and expertise are least related to productivity.

In this supernaturally informed understanding of work, women are seen as a particularly potent threat to the successful fruition of men's work activities. A woman crossing a man's path as he is setting out to sea is said to make the sea rough. Women must therefore stay out of sight when men are setting out with boats. Young girls, who were among my closest companions, would never take the shortest route between coastal villages, which lay along the beach-front itself, if they knew the men were likely to be launching their craft. Wrongful conduct on the part of women may be held responsible for the failure of economic ventures at sea, and may be regarded as putting at risk the safety and welfare of the men themselves—a belief which has peculiar and terrible force in an occupation with daily risk and uncertainty. The popular novel by Kerala writer Thakazhi Sivasankara Pillai (1962), *Chemmeen*, emphasises that in fishing society the man is entrusted to a girl rather than the other way around. It is women, by their prayers and chastity, who bring the men safe home from the sea.

The construction of femininity in Mukkuvar society is a peculiarly contradictory affair: on the one hand, the view of female sexuality and the female body is one which excludes women from key areas of production, and even structures their entry into other areas of economic activity, such as trade and marketing. On the other hand, the exclusion of women from key areas of production is qualified by a second movement which uses exclusion and confinement as the basis for a kind of female power over men. The conduct of women holds powers of life and death over men in Pillai's novel. The view is one which has much wider resonance than the fishing communities, and according to recent ethnographic writing, is at the core of a Tamil view of femininity (Wadley 1977, 1980; Baker-Reynolds 1978; Egnor 1978). Among the Mukkuvars, the powers of women are not simply mysterious psychic attributes projected onto women by male anxiety—the view of women as powerful is well grounded in the considerable responsibilities that women exercise. Within the space allocated as female, the domestic domain, women are seen as supreme and as the basis for social continuity from one generation to the next, between one household and the next. Coastal villagers arrange marriages for their daughters which are designed to keep them close at hand, as reliable supports, while sons are seen as wayward (see Chapter 7). The daily uncertainties of male-based fishing operations are compensated by the elaborate monetary redistribution of resources organised by women who are in charge of the daily reproduction of labour power and familial social relations (see Chapter 6).

It is this twin movement, of exclusion and reconstitution of the female presence, which provides the structure to my presentation of women in Mukkuvar society. In paying equal attention to both aspects it is possible to avoid representing ideology as a set of purely repressive external constraints. Rather, we need to see how culture also produces a positive identity and a subjectivity which has a stake in the current system, even among those most severely penalised by adherence to its norms.

I begin this investigation by giving theoretical priority to understanding the cultural logic which shapes gender ideology. What are the elements which are utilised in the Mukkuvar construction of femininity and how are they assembled in this marginalised community? What are the specific constraints and disciplines imposed on women in the name of this construct of femininity? The exploration takes me into an account of the religious culture, which has at its centre a particular view of the feminine. This version of religion, while in many ways specific to the community, and to the Catholic peasantry in the district, also bears certain relationships to the religion of the Tamil low caste Hindu, to Tamil religion as a whole, and finally, to themes which are common to south Asian religion. The logic of this movement into ever-widening cultural circles is given by the very nature of the subject: femininity and sexuality are so much at the heart of relationships of power that they can no more be contained by boundaries of caste, religion and region than can relationships of domination and subordination. The structure of this chapter reflects this zig-zagging movement in and out of Mukkuvar society.

The interconnections between Mukkuvars and wider society are today sharpened by the advent of new forms of mass cultural consumption such as films. With their potent construction of gender and their great popularity among the Mukkuvar youth, their importance in popular culture as a cross-caste, cross-class phenomenon cannot be underestimated and a fuller account of the subject I have chosen would necessarily include an investigation of film. I have concentrated instead on that more archaic form of popular culture, religion itself. At the same time, my interest is not in reinstating the theme of a homogeneous 'South Asian culture' in a new form—rather it is in placing the recognition of difference at the centre of ethnographic reconstruction. In this respect, Chapter 3 carries over many of the themes of Chapters 1 and 2, tracing further the religious and cultural counterpart to the economic and social distance between fisherpeople and agricultural Tamil Nadu.

The preoccupations of popular Catholicism: the centrality of the body and the feminine principle

At the heart of Mukkuvar religion is a concern with the immediate local environment and the various axes of everyday life: work, illness, misfortune, human love, desire and envy. Instead of treating these concerns as mundane or this-worldly, villagers invest them with divinity. Their idea of divinity evades neat classification into Western-derived categories or binary oppositions such as nature and culture. Rather, divinity stands somewhere between these two poles, and derives much of its conceptual power from an ability to shift in emphasis from one pole to the other, never to be quite pinned down. Thus, for all its supernatural force, divinity is experienced by villagers in a direct fashion in the course of their daily lives, while moving around the local environment of the village or the sea. While fishing, for example, the Mukkuvar experience the sea as an ambivalent power—benevolent and sustaining in some of its moods, but unpredictably wrathful, dangerous and terrible in its toll on human life and on the frail technology fashioned by the fisherpeople. Similarly, the environment of the village is at once both a territorial unit and a religious category which forms the basis of the most intense points of spiritual fervour in cults of the Virgin and the Catholic saints, who function as village guardians and patrons.

Paradigmatic of this focus on the local environment is the human body itself, which is the most direct means by which Mukkuvars experience the reality of divine force. The body epitomises the shifting nature of meanings in popular religion between the material and the supernatural. The body is on the one hand subject to the physiological rhythms of birth, sexual maturation, illness and death. On the other hand it is also the site for divine and supernatural intervention. Supernatural interventions are made possible by the continual changes and fluctuations within the body. These changes are conceived of partly as a matter of imbalance in the various humors which are said to compose the body, and partly as imbalances created by the psychic existential pitfalls of being human. The paramount emotion underlying Mukkuvar analysis of psychic and social imbalance is the sentiment of *poraamai* or envy. It refers to the infinite capacity of human beings to want what cannot be had, a capacity which turns rancid with frustration. It is therefore a subset of the broader category of desire, in this case desire full of resentment over the good fortune of another. It is *poraamai* which underlies attempts by villagers to employ sorcery on one another, thus providing the entry point for supernatural agencies to attack. In a community where even daily food is an uncertainty, *poraamai* need not focus on anything extraordinary: even the ability of a neighbouring family to feed itself may be sufficient. An old woman was described as one who was so envious that she would 'resent the smoke from a neighbour's hearth'. Cooking itself is a surreptitious activity—evidence of seeming plenty sparks off *poraamai*, quarrels and dissension even between kin living under one roof. Women are careful to make no sound when cooking rice. Similarly, if one lets it be seen that one is making *puTTu* (a steamed dish of rice flour and coconut) or any *panihaaram* (item of cooked food), things will start to go wrong with the food itself: the steam will not erupt, the flour will 'drink' a lot of oil. Fear of arousing envy feeds into the distribution of resources and living arrangements, the management of food and income within households (see details in Chapter 7).

Relations of envy, always active, have come into greater prominence in this time of great social upheaval: new forms of capital accumulation, new deployments of human labour power, social movements for reorganising the power of the Catholic Church are all transforming the fishing villages. Such changes are experienced as introducing disequilibrium, exciting deep-lying resentments. The principal divisions in the community are therefore, in this account, not ones of caste or religion, but rather by-products of people's own nature. Mukkuvars see themselves as a wretched people. A common self-description is as 'a place of suffering' ('*Idu paavankal udiya uuru*'). The suffering is that of sinners—*paavam* in Tamil refers simultaneously to the objects of pity, and to sin itself.

Disequilibrium, the absence of harmony, may thus be socially generated, but finds its symbolic locus in the excesses of a desiring psyche. The framework of *poraamai* fundamentally alters the significance of the various elements of popular religion which dwell on the purely physiological aspects of the body. Critical details of this dimension of popular thought derive from the indigenous medical model of the south Indian branch of the Ayurvedic tradition, known as Siddha Vaidya. In this tradition, the body is composed of three humors or elements (*naaDigal*): *vaadam* (air), *pitam* (heat, phlegm)

and *srerpaaNam* (bile, water).[2] The relationship between Siddha
Vaidya and popular practice is complex and not at all the transformation of a highly elaborated naturalistic discourse into a crude and
simplified version, using only certain basic categories.[3] The rendition
of 'popularisation' to mean simplification is extremely easy to fall
into, given the deeply elitist history of the term itself, where the
culture of the 'masses' has been viewed as the debasement of elite
culture to its lowest common denominator (see reflections by
Raymond Williams on this question, 1976:285–323). Rather, the
process apparent in Mukkuvar appropriation of Siddha Vaidya's
model of the body is one in which those concepts which are richest in
symbolic meaning and relevant to the villager's apprehension of the
environment are taken up, and transformed by re-absorption into the
Mukkuvars' own interpretation. Bodily balance, in the Mukkuvar
view, becomes not merely a matter of maintaining physical health,
but a way of maintaining harmony between humanity and divinity—
if only in the negative sense of minimising harmful supernatural
interventions in human affairs. The notion of attraction between certain subversive elements in the body and the subversive or harmful
elements in the supernatural hierarchy is a particularly striking
feature of the way the theory of humoral balance is linked with a
religious theory of the body. Within the body, the hot or heat-
producing humors are the most troublesome and dangerous elements.
Heat in turn is associated with energy, with sexuality, envy and, in a
more general sense, with desire itself. Thus popular definitions of
heat escape not only the confines of humoral theory, but a purely
physiological rendition of the body.[4] A predominance of the hot
desiring elements attracts the lower beings in the supernatural
hierarchy, since there is a direct affinity and even identity between
the two.

It is this desire and heat which can not only attract the troublesome
elements in the supernatural, but can also transform human beings
into these supernatural beings. Unnatural and untimely deaths of
individuals leave their spirits dissatisfied and in limbo, unable to rest.
As *peey* (spirits) and *aavi* (ghosts) they linger close to humanity,
always looking for a crack or lesion in the social fabric of the community or in the physical body, waiting to reoccupy a living being. To
Mukkuvars, the presence of the supernatural can be known directly
through such possession—but it has to be gauged through the use of
interpretive devices. Analysts and interpreters skilled in the art
of reading the signs of possession and illness come in the form of
Christian faith healers (the *kaNaku shollaravaa*, or those who make
divine calculations), and Hindu *mantravaaDis*, as well as more
experienced members of the Mukkuvar community. These analysts
use as their text the symptoms of the body in much the same way that
the psychoanalytic method gauges the presence of the unconscious

in terms of its effects—the slips and utterances of language, the hysterical twitches and above all, the *aaTam* or dance of the *peey-* or demon-infested body.

The task of these analysts is aided by a striking literalism in the form taken by bodily manifestation of the supernatural. Bodies of living human beings occupied by spirits of the dissatisfied dead will exhibit the precise bodily characteristics of the violent death which overtook the spirit's previous occupant. Thus a person possessed by the spirit of a hanged man will have his/her possession fit with his/her tongue hanging out. If the possession occurs with the person clutching his/her own neck, the onlookers may assume the spirit's previous owner died of strangulation. A Mukkuvar spirit possessing the body of an inlander is instantly identifiable by the insatiable craving for fish exhibited by the possessed.

The same literalism comes up again in the use of symbolic offerings to placate and mediate between humanity and the supernatural. Afflictions of the body may be lifted by symbolically surrendering to the divinity that organ or limb most affected by disease. A small silver replica of the arm or leg or organ is offered to the deity, along with other offerings collectively known as *paDukkai*. The common practice of shaving one's hair at the shrine of the deity is an extension of the same bodily symbolism. The head occupies a key place in the merging of medical and religious discourses. The head stores the heat generated by desire, as well as the spiritual power generated by the meditative and bodily practice of *yoga*, which establishes control over that desire. Pride and egoistic arrogance are described as *'talaikku eriuDuthu'*, literally, 'it has mounted to his head'. Sacrifice of hair is therefore a statement of submission before divine will, an attempt to curb and control the erratic and desirous body. It forms a part of a continuum of forms of bodily self-mortification in Tamil popular religion.

The use of talismans and icons follows a similar principle, which grounds religious meaning on the materiality of the body. Mukkuvar villagers will wear a *tahaDu* or metal cylinder, with a special *mantra* (in this case a Christian prayer) inscribed on it. It is worn tied around the waist and derives its full efficacy not merely from the prayer, but from actually being worn on the body to ward off evil spirits.[5] Sorcery, the manipulation of those evil spirits, also works along similar principles: using mud on which the proposed victim has urinated, hair or thread from their clothes. Proper disposal of bodily effluents such as menstrual blood, the blood of afterbirth and the placenta of the newly born infant, become vitally important in minimising the chances of sorcery attacks.

The illnesses of the body therefore constitute not only problems which Mukkuvars take to their divinities, but also the site and locus of divine intervention. The simple literalism of bodily symbolism is less straightforward than it might seem, because of ambiguities surrounding the conceptualisation of the body and its relationship to the supernatural. Illness and possession are both a curse and a blessing. They may indicate the presence of malign demonic powers, or they may be a mark of divine grace. The distinction between illness and possession is itself blurred—certain illnesses such as smallpox are seen as forms of possession. Serious bouts of illness are an affliction, but also key opportunities to experience the power of the divine in the form of surrender and faith. Illness is therefore a pathway to prove faith and receive grace, as well as being one of the symptoms of love. This love may be of an earthly erotic nature, or it may be religious fervour—in both cases the symptoms are similar. The blurring of religious and erotic forms of love found in Mukkuvar devotional faith is also the subject of a rich religious literary tradition in south India, where we find explicit elaboration of these themes. In the tradition of Viraha Bhakti (Hardy 1983:138*ff.*), separation from the divine is modelled on the experience of earthly lovers. Further, the whims of divinity are in essence as unknowable and changeable as the moods of one's lover—the deity may be benign and gracious one moment, and wrathful and vengeful the next. What makes the semiotics of bodily possession a source of endless speculation among the Mukkuvars is that both these moods of divinity make themselves known through very similar bodily symptoms of illness and possession.

The cult of the Virgin and the Saints

The ambiguities inherent in popular representations of the suffering and possessed body, shapes the nature of religious worship. Mukkuvars take up the key female figure offered to them by the Christian divine hierarchy, the Virgin Mary, and elevate her to a position of primacy. Along with the saints, who enjoy cults of their own, the Virgin Mary governs most of the concerns of their religion: affliction, uncertainty related to the problems of daily material fluctuations in the food available to each household, mass epidemics. In the key area of men's safety at sea, the cult of Mary reigns supreme.

Mother Mary is not only rescued from her position of derivative importance as the Mother of Christ, but the Christian emphasis on the anomalous juxtaposition of virginity and motherhood is resolved by dropping all reference to her virginity. To Mukkuvars she is Maataa or the Mother, but she may be worshipped in many forms defined by her multiple powers, in her varied territorial bases in particular shrines. The most powerful of these forms is the Velankanni Maataa, named after the shrine of Velankanni in Tanjore District. Here her special powers are in combating disease and healing illness. She also cures in her form as Arogya Maataa, or Our Lady of Health, and is especially noted for curing cholera, which has replaced smallpox as the most dreadful of epidemic diseases, and is known as *kolle*

58   *Mukkuvar Women*

noyvu or killer-disease. The Census of India in its detailed account of
the Fairs and Festivals of Madras (vol.9, part VII B 1961) is moved to
describe the Tanjore shrine of Velankanni as the 'Lourdes of India'
on account of the many miraculous cures offered by the Maataa who
resides there. The annual festival (29 August–8 September) is a high
point for Christians all over south India, and Mukkuvars make a
special effort to journey to the shrine as thanksgiving if the Maataa
responds to their prayers. Mukkuvars also worship Maataa in various
advocations: as Lourdes Maataa, Fatima Maataa, Thesnevees
Maataa, Poondi Maataa and Kaannike Maataa.

The saints are an essential part of this idiosyncratic interpretation
of the Church's message. St Michael (Mikheel), exorciser of evil
spirits, St George, slayer of demons, St Anthony (Anthoniar) and St
Sebastian are all guardian deities of the coastal villages. Villagers
have added to the list certain saints altogether unknown to the
Church—KaDalkarai villagers regard themselves as protected not
only by St Anthony, housed in the official shrine, but Alexiar (St
Alex) who has been equipped with a complete hagiography. As
patron saints of the villages, the powers of these figures suggest a
world that is localised, both territorially and in terms of immediacy to
the world of human affliction. Worshipped in annual village festivals,
the saints and the Maataa are the focus of much monetary and
emotional investment.

The powers of the saints and of Maataa gain their full efficacy
only through contact with or possession of the bodies of villagers.
A woman reports: 'Some of us pray to St Anthony and consult a
specialist such as the one at Kadiapatnam [another fishing village],
who prays over a *tahaDu* and then inscribes a prayer in it. We call
this an Anthoniar*eeDu*, and tie it to our waist for protection against
evil spirits.'

The Maataa and the saints take on many of the ironies and com-
plexities of popular depictions of divinity—they both cure possession
and cure through possession. Selected human beings become the
medium for the Maataa and the saints, and these people are able to
cure and divine, while possessed by sacred power. Further, most
healers report that their powers were given to them after a period of
trial in which illness as well as other forms of misfortune figured
prominently. Other ironies also come in: the Maataa not only cures
diseases, and may be sought through the experience of disease, but
she may also be implicated in the causation of disease. Two accounts
offered by older Mukkuvar women, recounting their experience of
epidemics, suggest this complex association between the Maataa and
disease, which is more than just a relation of healing. The first
concerns a smallpox epidemic, the second, cholera:

Small-pox ('vyssori', or 'ammai noyvu')   Amma [Mother—that is, the
goddess] decides on a number of victims. She brings a *naaru petti* [woven

box made of coir] visible only to the victims. From this she takes or gives the pox. The leaders of the ghosts of the deceased come back to take the victims 10–15 days after the start of the disease. The fifth, seventh, ninth, eleventh, and thirteenth days are all critical—if the fever has not gone down in less than thirteen days, the person will die. A net is laid on the streets—invisible to all. If one sights the ghosts, it is crucial not to take fright.

Cholera ('kolle noyvu' or killer disease) I have seen a huge number of people dying: five more dead by the time we buried five. In cholera epidemics, their ghosts would teem, 14 000 of them, some sitting on a palanquin, like the 'strong men from PaanDee', with four bearers on either side. These ghosts come back to spread the disease further. Dressed grandly, they proceed through the village—anyone taking fright on sighting them will die. Unknown to the people, Arogya Maataa is seated inside the palanquin, to guard us. Only her shadow can be seen. The barking of the dogs warned us of the coming of the cholera *kuuTam* [crowd]. We set out water in an urn to slake their thirst and their heat. They dislike noise and light: that is why we now burn electric lights and have the radio on all night when we have a cholera epidemic.

Femininity and popular Catholicism

I have outlined a particular conception of divine and spiritual powers among the Mukkuvars: it is one which is rooted in daily life, and in the material, tangible aspects of the local environment, in the labour process, and in the corporeal body. At the same time there is a deep-seated ambiguity in the relation between humanity and divinity—the divinity is a maverick one, capable of curing, nourishing and sustaining human beings as well as destroying humanity in a wanton manner.

This view of religious power is intimately tied to a particular view of femininity and the female principle. At one level the relation between divinity and femininity could be read as one of homology, a 'structural relation of parallelism' (Jameson 1981:43). Femininity, like divinity, is powerfully ambivalent. Women have the power to generate and sustain human life; in this capacity, Mukkuvar culture celebrates their fertility in puberty rituals, and in its evaluation of the positive advantages of having daughters. At the same time, women have the powers of destruction and danger to the social order, particularly to men. Allowed unrestricted freedom of movement, thought and speech, if their bodies and sexuality are untrammelled by restrictions of clothing, marriage and ritual control, then women's powers have the same unpredictable capacity to bring destruction to human life as the deities have.

In Hinduism, this power has a name—*sakti*. However, it remains only implicit in Mukkuvar conceptualisation of femininity. As with divinity, so also the female force or *sakti* cannot be categorised as either purely biological and natural or as social and cultural.

Although women are thought to be born with an inherent force, the force is operative only within culture, and women exercise it through female roles that are culturally defined. As women act as financial managers, child carers, cooks, health carers and religious organisers their powers mature and grow. At the same time, *sakti* retains the stamp of its origins in the physical materiality of women's bodies, and shows the more menacing side of its Janus-face at times when the specificity of women's bodies is most apparent: at menstruation and at childbirth. I have tried in my presentation to preserve rather than merge these two distinct levels of meaning: they provide the tension that marks the space of femininity in the culture as something at once at the core of the social institutions (community, family), and as something always threatening to overflow and disintegrate the patriarchal order. I will examine the implications of this view further, in detailing the rituals of control in Mukkuvar culture which are aimed at the daily containment of women's bodies. The characteristic and contradictory mark of femininity—conservative and yet threatening—finds its local formulation in these rituals.

But the relation between the divine and the feminine is more intimate than allowed by a formal relation of homology. Femininity also enters as a crucial principle in the very shaping of popular religion. This is clear in the elevation of the Maataa to the primary position of worship in the Mukkuvar pantheon. The sea, conceived of as divinity, is either directly referred to as KaDal Amma—the sea as maternal female—or else is seen as the special province of the Christian female deity, the Maataa. For men, the people directly exposed to the dangers of the sea, the relationship to the Maataa is an intense and private affair between the individual and the god, unmediated by institutions such as the Church, the parish priest and land-based social networks. It is exemplified in the short, intense prayer directed to the Maataa in the hour of crisis out at sea, as the following accounts suggest:

John: I pray to the Arogya Maataa. On the way to Ramewswaram, our engine overheated and there were no other boats in sight. We were at least three miles off-shore, and started swimming. Hungry, giddy and hurt, we fought against the wind and prayed to the Maataa and found ourselves ashore. My church is in my heart, at sea—not in the *kovil* [temple].

The second account is taken from the recounting of a disaster which has left a deep impression on villagers. A cyclone hit five boats on their way to fish in Orissa, and sixteen men perished in the storm. One of the survivors recounts his trial and the faith which sustained them:

There were eleven of us on this boat, for eleven days with no food or water. We drank rain water, and once we managed to kill a stork. We prayed to the Maataa, who brought us ashore in a jungle infested with demons. There we saw the ghosts of the men who died with us. To this day, I wake up shivering if the sound of the surf is high and I cannot go fishing if the sea is rough. We returned later to the Velankanni Maataa and shaved our hair [as an offering].

For women, the expression of religious faith is intertwined with their social responsibilities. Faith is demonstrated through regular church attendance, by organising the social details of church festivals—arranging decorations, cooking special foods, conducting catechism classes, organising children for their First Communion, and so on. Female responsibility for the health and welfare of their families dominates women's religious preoccupations and involves them in a series of pilgrimages to healers of different kinds, and to the various shrines of Maataa and the saints which dominate the Christians' sacred geography.

Through these pilgrimages, which take the Mukkuvars all over Tamil Nadu, their religious culture is integrated into the wider Christian and Hindu religious communities of south India. Such forms of interaction will necessarily have to be considered to explain the remarkable way in which the figure of the Virgin has been transformed in popular Catholicism. Summarising the descriptions offered so far of her various attributes: she is worshipped as a central figure of importance in her own right, not as mother or wife to a male divinity; her divinity is visualised within the confines of earthly concerns; and in particular, her power is experienced through the mode of bodily possession.

It would be more than easy to explain this transformation as a case of simple syncretism, of incorporation from Hinduism, or even as a direct continuity from a pre-Christian past. The latter argument could be supported by ethnographic evidence indicating that goddess worship has historically been an important feature of religion among Hindu fishing communities in south India.[6]

However, Mukkuvar relations with Hinduism are not straightforward at all: they are considerably complicated in ways that take us back to the economic and social paradoxes of their position in caste society. The Mukkuvar people's implicit consciousness of their minority status profoundly affects their interaction with the dominant culture. The Virgin takes on many of the attributes of goddess worship in Tamil Nadu, but she also diverges in ways that are crucial.

The splitting of the feminine, and the hegemony of the Catholic Church

Mukkuvar Catholicism is predicated not only on the worship of the female principle in the form of the Virgin, but on a Manichean opposition of good and evil supernatural beings. The female principle predominates on both sides of this divide. On the side of good is a divine social hierarchy headed by the figure of Mary, Maataa and her helpers the saints. On the side of evil or affliction are the Hindu goddess Issakai (locally pronounced 'Eseki'), and her demon (*pishaashu*) companions, SuDalai MaaDan (locally pronounced 'Cholla MaaDan'), the demon of the cemetery or burning grounds, and Vannara MaaDan. Below the Hindu goddess and her demons are several lesser beings, also essentially afflictive in character: the *aavi* (ghosts) of the dead and *peey* (spirits). Maataa Mary and the saints are necessary to regulate, exorcise, countermand and protect humanity against the forces of evil which bring sickness, affliction and daily tribulation. The forces of affliction, personified as Hindu supernatural beings, express in concentrated form the traditional Tamil etiology of misfortune, quite distinct from the Sanskritic doctrine of karma. Baker-Reynolds notes the contrast succinctly:

> Suffering, disease, poverty and misfortune are viewed in ancient Tamil
> Nadu, and we may add today as well, as disruptive events caused, not by
> karma, but by *ananku*, capricious, destructive, unpredictable power at
> loose in the world, waiting to wreak havoc on the lives of the unwary.
> Suffering results not from an ineluctable law of cause and effect, deeds
> bearing fruit, but from an irascible, erratic, uncontrolled power.
> Happiness, fortune and well-being result, not from good deeds, but
> from control over *ananku* (1978:70).

What is distinctive about the Mukkuvars' conceptualisation of the matter, however, is that the capricious and destructive qualities of *ananku* are not generalised to all supernatural beings—rather, they are specifically confined to Hindu divinity. The Christian divinities are quite unproblematically benign and benevolent in their disposition. Thus, securing happiness and good fortune is not here merely a matter of control of *ananku*, but the Christian control of *ananku*, personified as the supremacy of Maataa and the saints over Hindu divinity.

The benign Christian deities and the malign Hindu deities are diametrically opposed in their respective attitudes towards human beings. The opposition is not of the binary kind suggested by the anthropologist Mandelbaum between what he calls humanity's 'transcendental' concerns and its 'pragmatic' concerns (Mandelbaum 1966:19). Mary and the saints are not occupied with anything more lofty than that which concerns the Hindu afflictive deities. Both sides are involved in the daily human affairs which are at the centre of this religion—and their battle is waged through the medium of the human body.

The battle beween good and evil, once it is conceptualised as a battle between a Christian and a Hindu goddess, immediately renders the relationship of Mukkuvars to Hinduism an antagonistic one. Issakai (Eseki) as worshipped by local Hindu castes in Kanyakumari District is a village goddess with a complex range of meanings. Later I examine the full range of meanings in a discussion of the place of

the village goddess in south Indian peasant religion. What is important to note at this point is that in opposing the Virgin to Issakai,
the Mukkuvars split the unity of the opposing qualities of femininity
embodied in the village goddess of Hinduism. The Virgin Mary,
although partaking of some of the characteristics of the village goddess in her complex relationship to disease and possession, remains
for the most part serene, smiling, eternally placid and the embodiment of a purely benevolent idea of the maternal feminine. Popular
iconography in major shrines such as Raja Uuru which draw
hundreds of Christians every week depict her in robes of blue, head
covered and perfectly compatible with the Church's version of
femininity unsullied by anger or desire. The parish priests feel quite
comfortable taking advantage of the Virgin as Maataa, and her popularity, to hammer home their message of godly love. Several sermons
I heard utilised the image of the Virgin rather than Jesus—
her motherly love for her earthly children was the image used to
concretise the idea of divine mercy. There were also explicit
appeals to the mothers in the audience as people intuitively equipped
to understand the nature of godly love.

The 'cleaning up' of the official image of the feminine by the
Church has only succeeded in driving the disorderly and unruly
elements of femininity underground, to be projected onto a Hindu
goddess. In this process of repression and projection, the Hindu
Issakai is also reduced to a simple meaning. She has none of the
beneficent healing qualities that Hindu worshippers attribute to her—
instead, she is evil incarnate, the pagan devil that the Church has
done its best to suppress. Church attitudes to sexuality, particularly in
women, are as punitive in these fishing villages as in the homelands of
Catholicism. Sexuality is tolerated only within the confines of
Church-approved marriages. Illegitimate children are refused baptism
and burial in the common graveyard, which reinforces beliefs
regarding the production of ghosts through incomplete deaths.
Certain archaic practices were till recently quite common in coastal
villages: a couple found guilty of sex outside marriage were punished
by having to parade the village while holding a cross (*koDi piDikar-
adu*), and paid the church a fine. Divorce is prohibited by the
Church, and this injunction is closely adhered to; although informal
separations and re-alliances are certainly frequent (see p.176), there
is no formal divorce. Abortions are prohibited, and therefore performed illegitimately, resulting in the deaths of at least two women in
recent years in the village of KaDalkarai. Individual parish priests
who have come in contact with reformist ideology are now willing to
modify some of the harsher aspects of previous practice, but the
accompanying values remain internalised by the villagers, not least of
all by the women. Mukkuvar women fight one another with a stock of
semi-ritualised insults and abuses, delivered with the entire body bent
forward and the finger used to jab home each insult. The basis for

one set of insults is the accusation of infidelity to one's husband: '*Ni eesha panDari*' ('You are everybody's wife'), '*Ni eesha moLe*' ('You are everybody's woman'). This is swiftly followed by the taunt of losing one's husband's favour, with the material consequence of losing access to daily food: '*Onakku shoru tandana? Onakku meenu tandana?*' ('Did he feed you rice today? Did he feed you fish today?'). Worst of all, there is the taunt of having rendered oneself a barren woman by agreeing to medical sterilisation: '*Ne poi kuthindu vandi ya*' ('Did you go and stick needles into yourself?').

Yet all of the efforts of the Church to suppress certain aspects of feminine sexuality have resulted only in a form of split consciousness within popular religion. This is apparent in the conflicting interpretations of sickness and possession that rage against one another in the discourse of villagers:

> Because we are sick and in hardship, or to seek good fortune, we have to believe in Kali, and Murugan.
>
> The priest sees this as a sin and advises us not to go to these *mantravaaDis*.
>
> According to our faith, *pishaashu* (demons) are something each person is tempted by—but we have a *sammanasu* (conscience) as well. The priest tells us simply to pray to God to strengthen us and give us good fortune...
>
> The *pishaashu* schemes to drag us into hell-fire. It does not reside inside us, but exists outside as *aavi* (spirit).
>
> Then there is the *pishaashu* of people who have died unnaturally ... But I say, it is not anyone's spirit which comes back—since once dead, no one can return—but rather the same *pishaashu* which roams free and invisible, and masquerades as dead people.
>
> (Claramma, a woman of 45, pers. comm.)

To a certain extent, these tensions are specific to the Mukkuvars—an extension of their structural constitution by the Catholic Church and the polarities of fishing versus agriculture, as a distinctive minority bloc opposed to the dominant presence of the Hindu peasantry. Anthropology testifies to the frequency with which spirits are projected onto the alien: either as an exotic property of the conquered native [Taussig 1980a, 1980b), or as the property of the outsider, coming always from the other village or the opposing tribe (Lewis 1971). Evidently, spirits become actors in the drama of human politics.

In the case of the Mukkuvars, the threat of the dominant culture swamping their own sub-culture is so intense that it cannot be safely kept at a distance. The local village environment, the very territorial base of the Christian patron saints, is itself infested with invading Hindu spirits. Certain areas of the Mukkuvar village serve as the traditional loci for Hindu spirits. The village of KaDalkarai is said to have originally included up to a hundred Hindu families as recently as fifty years ago. Today, one solitary house is occupied by a Hindu Harijan family who have lived there for four generations. According to the seventy-year-old man who works sporadically for the fishing community by fetching down coconuts from the trees, the original Hindu community was employed in dyeing cloth, and gradually moved out in search of employment. In a sense, whether this Hindu presence in the Mukkuvar village was fact or myth is beside the point—the psychic traces of their previous presence continue to erupt in the form of the spirits they have left behind. The geographical locus for their spirits is a site where an old Hindu temple, one of three, is said to have existed. It has now been built over by a residential dwelling. A young bride who came to live in this home about fifteen years ago, from her native village in Kerala, experienced periodic possession by the Hindu spirits and temple deities for a period of ten years after marriage. Now dormant, the attacks earned her the generic term of *peey kaari* or devil-woman. Her visions, which began nineteen days after marriage, she describes as being of the *devate* or deities of the Hindu temple: male and female, dressed grandly with conch (suggestive of Visnu) and flowers, with seven accompanying tokens of divinity. Her possession is preceded by a long line of other supernatural occurrences on the old temple site: urns of water placed on the ground were swallowed up, while other women have experienced possession on entering the house.

For educated men who have had exposure to the world outside the *kutti raajyam* (little kingdom) of the Church, the Hindu presence is a part of the Mukkuvars' own cultural heritage, and a valuable means of recording a history that the Church has tried to erase. One of these educated men, Mariya Nayakam, was a mine of information on the village's past history, which was bound up with a pre-Christian past. The old Hindu temple, according to him, was dedicated to the goddess Kumari Amman (Virgin Goddess), and was one of a series of three temples, two of which have since been engulfed by the sea. For most villagers, however, such identification with pre-Christian traditions emerges only in states of disease and possession. In ordinary states of consciousness, Hinduism may be experienced as distinctly unpleasurable. One villager told me she could not bear it when taking a trip on one of the buses that takes loads of pilgrims around the Tamil countryside, and the bus stopped at a Hindu temple—the smells coming out of there made her feel ill.

The very terms of its constitution signals the contradictory nature of popular religion among Mukkuvars. In elevating the Virgin, in experiencing her divinity in forms more appropriate to Hindu worship, and finally, in continually opening themselves to the invasion of Hindu demons and spirits, Mukkuvars have shaped a religion which escapes the definitions and controls of the Church, and makes Mukkuvars a part of the Tamil Hindu peasantry. However, in defining all the invading Hindu spirits as evil, and in particular, defining all the angry and wrathful aspects of femininity as evil, the Mukkuvars have allowed the Church to establish its ultimate hegemony. In a sense, then, the discursive representations of femininity are at the heart of this tension between the hegemonic and counter-hegemonic aspects of popular Catholicism. In this tension also lie some of the seeds of unity and disunity within the popular consciousness of the peasantry. Insofar as the Church's definitions of good and evil are hegemonic in popular consciousness, the potential for communal mobilisation under the Church's leadership is always latent, and not merely a function of external political manipulation.[7]

So far I have referred to the relationship of Mukkuvars to Hinduism, and to the goddess tradition in particular, as though Hinduism were a unitary or unified culture. This is indeed what one would assume from recent ethnographic writing on Tamil women (Wadley 1977, 1980; Baker Reynolds 1978; Egnor 1978) which inadequately interrogates the self-presentation of the dominant castes. As a result, religion and culture are presented as a unity, with one coherent and commonly accepted version (or even two divergent but complementary models) of divinity and femininity. From the point of view of the Mukkuvars, this is bound to be grossly inadequate, since their version of religion displays a marked tendency to incorporate selectively, subvert and play with the codes of the dominant culture. When Mukkuvars invert the Hindu worship of Issakai to make her the feared and despised embodiment of all evil, they are not inverting Hindu culture as a whole—rather, they are inverting a particular strand of Hinduism. The goddess tradition of Tamil Nadu boasts many more versions of a female deity than Issakai—versions which are culturally far more valorised, such as the great mother goddess Meenakshi worshipped in the temple of Madurai, or even the district's very own virgin goddess, Kanyakumari, worshipped at the tip of the sub-continent. These goddesses are Sanskritic goddesses, if by that we mean all that is purest and hierarchically most elevated in Hindu culture (Coburn 1984:10*ff*.). Yet it is the little-known 'Eseki' (Issakai) who haunts the Mukkuvars, not the great Sanskritic goddesses. Who is Issakai and what does she stand for in Hinduism? What vision of femininity is it which both fascinates and repels the Mukkuvars? On the other hand, what does Mukkuvar indifference to the Sanskritic goddess signify?

We can answer these questions only by stepping back a little from Mukkuvar culture to examine the cultural tensions which internally divide the dominant Hindu religion itself.

The goddess in Sanskritic and non-Sanskritic traditions: the case of Tamil Hinduism

All over India the cult of the feminine as divine is marked by a cultural struggle between a conception of female energy, *sakti*, as the primary activating principle in the universe—and on the other hand, a rendition of the female principle as supportive, benign and subordinated to the male principle. The struggle may be roughly correlated with the historic tension between Brahmanic or Sanskritic and non-Brahmanic traditions. Robinson (1985) characterises the two traditions in the following way:

> Brahmanic Hinduism is a Sanskrit-based priestly tradition emphasising formal ritual. Although as a religious tradition brahmanic worship has received patronage from all castes, brahmanic worship has been maintained in the custody of *purohits* (ritual officiants) belonging to the highest ranked caste, the brahmans. Non-Brahmanic Hinduism, expressed through regional languages, is a composite of diverse devotional practices emphasising modes of worship which either de-emphasize or obviate the priestly role. This general categorisation bears critical significance with regard to the religious role of Hindu women in that historically, brahmanic Hinduism has tended to objectify and exclude women, whereas non-brahmanic Hindu traditions have tended to provide for full recognition and active participation by women (p.182).

As a consort, the goddess is not a partner to a male god but, as O'Flaherty has pointed out, she is a 'mere appendage, far inferior in power and status to her spouse' (1980). As consort to the male gods Visnu and Siva, as the wifely and submissive Parvati and Lakshmi, she is robbed not only of primacy, but her capacity to inflict anger and destruction on mankind. Fittingly, this is accomplished, as in the earthly family, through the binding mechanism of marriage. By contrast, in her role as Sakti the goddess' feminine roles of wife and mother are not only secondary but inessential to her powers. To quote Robinson again, 'As Kali, the Devi governs time and unleashes destruction; as Maya she afflicts and heals, provides and withholds, rewards and punishes' (1985:182). In this sense, the term 'Mother Goddess' is a misleading title for her.

The struggle between the two conceptions of the goddess is less than an opposition between a truly female-centred, woman-defined religion and a patriarchal one. Both versions are ultimately phallo-centric, both stress the necessity for male control over the dangerous aspects of the feminine. It is simply that in Sanskritic Hinduism the danger is quenched, and the control is a *fait accompli*. Sakti cults, although emphasising the feminine principle as an integral part of religious consciousness, do not necessarily emphasise the centrality of women to actual religious practice. Indeed, possession by the goddess, insofar as it is seen as a kind of erotic bonding, may be deemed more appropriate for followers of the male sex (Beck 1981). Cult rituals dedicated to Sakti worship frequently focus entirely on male devotees. Kakar (1981) has argued that the ambivalent figure of the all-consuming mother goddess embodies unconscious male fears based in the infant's early relation to its mother, particularly in India where the male child is the object of the mother's undivided attention and deflected eroticism. Nor is there any necessary correlation between a religious discourse which assigns symbolic primacy to a female figure, and the actual social status enjoyed by women in that very historical period.[8]

With these important caveats in mind, it is still important to distinguish between different manifestations of phallocentric religion—not merely as moments of a forgotten history, but as a site of continuing conflict, in which non-Sanskritic themes continue to provide the resources for subordinated groups to seize upon at moments of resistance to cultural hegemony.

In Tamil Nadu, the twentieth century non-Brahman movement has been attempting to purify Tamil culture of all Brahman elements, which are seen for these purposes as external accretions brought in by Aryan invaders. The impulse of cultural revolt has here been encapsulated by the logic of regional nationalism, a process which has lent itself to elite domination by non-Brahman groups. Scholarship on Tamil religion is also largely overshadowed by the politics of non-Brahmanism, with scholars, even of Western origin, being drawn into the debate or at least having to define their positions in relation to it. Hart (1974, 1975) and Zvelebil (1973) argue for being able to extract a complete vision of non-Aryan culture and society from the sophisticated and socially descriptive literature of the Cankam period, while others such as Hardy (1983) argue that while the literature depicts a distinctively southern complex, it is one where Tamil, Sanskrit-Brahman, Buddhist, Jain and many other influences are intertwined in a complex whole.

For my purposes, it is not necessary to argue that Brahman hegemony is either fictitious or easily disentangled from the culture as a whole. The non-Brahman tradition in the south is undoubtedly a dominated tradition, entailing the formal recognition of the supremacy of Brahmanic texts and rituals and, within the divine hierarchy, the ascendancy of the Sanskritic version of the goddess. However, the non-Brahmanic traditions have survived, and have succeeded in impressing their own hallmarks upon the religion as a whole. It is sufficient for me to take the minimalist position granted by Hardy:

> [We may postulate] a very archaic and universally Indian form of popular religion of non Aryan origin. But while in the North this folk religion never stood a chance of asserting itself, of reaching any autonomy or sophistication, because of centuries of Upanisadic ideology, the situation in the South was different. Not only could a high culture evolve here independently of the North, a cult in which common 'folk' elements were intrinsically amalgamated with typical Tamil features like Murugan [an early Tamil god], but the pressures from Upanisadic ideology were of a much more restricted duration and impact. (Jainism and Buddhism dominated the southern scene for not more than 3–4 centuries.) (1983:141).

Sanskritic gods such as Visnu and Siva have been worshipped in the south in modes pre-established by early Tamil religion. The hallmark of this worship is ecstatic–mystic cults, often involving possession, a markedly sensual use of incense and flowers in worship, and an emphasis on direct unmediated relationship with the divine. The *bhakti* cults in Tamil Nadu begin early. Krishna devotionalism reaches its peak in the seventh century onwards with the Alwar poets (Hardy 1983). The worship of Siva associated with the Nayanar poets, covers a period of six hundred years, beginning in 550 AD and going up to the twelfth century (Zvelebel 1973:186). Hardy's study of Vaisnavite devotionalism (1983) lists three key features as coming from the earlier form of religion implicit in the Cankam literature: (a) the absence of a clear awareness of transcendence, which allows for the visualisation of the divine within the confines of earthly reality; (b) the sensual character of worship; (c) the ecstasy of emotions in which the divine is felt to be present, which links (a) and (b); and (d) lastly the exclusively female cults of Sankam literature resurfacing in the later *bhakti* worship, in which the psychology of religious awareness is female (p.140).

According to Egnor (1978), the femaleness of religious consciousness in *bhakti* involves the glorification of the qualities traditionally ascribed to femininity, as being the most appropriate attitude to adopt in the worship of divinity. Thus, love and erotic relations with the divine are preferred to the intellectual discipline of yoga and *tapascharya* (rigorous meditation). The internal, soft, yielding core of human consciousness is not only superior to the external, rigid and masculine in consciousness but the former must melt this outer rigidity through the power of love. Woman, according to Egnor's informants who are devotees of Siva, is the source of feeling and the teacher of the soul in matters of love and grace. In this view, woman is original, and man derivative. The confinement of women in the interior of the home is glorified as an indication of women's superior wisdom in rejecting the world of the inessential exterior.

There are striking continuities between the early conceptions of divinity and the present-day worship which have been kept alive in the *bhakti* tradition. The continuities are particularly traceable in representations of the feminine. The concept of *ananku* is especially significant in this respect, being in many ways a very early forerunner of the concept of *sakti*. Hart (1975:42–43) describes the religion of the early Tamils as 'an animistic one in which divine forces were conceived of as immanent within actual objects and as potentially harmful. These divine forces, called *ananku*, were for the most part not personified as gods.' Baker-Reynolds (1978), also drawing on an earlier article by Hart, gives us the following etymology of the concept:

> *Ananku* is a term that applies both to the possessor of power and to the power itself, and as a verb, to the action of that power or possessor of power. As a verb, *ananku* refers to a host of distressful actions—to strike, vex, afflict, kill, fear, and to suffer, be afflicted, vexed etc. As a noun,

ananku means pain, fear, disease and those who possess *ananku* and hence are known by the term *ananku* by metonymy, are malevolent deity and woman. *Ananku*, thus, is essentially a malevolent, dangerous power, and those who possess it are, therefore, malevolent, vexing and dangerous persons or deities (p.69).

Again we come across the linking of divine power and women. Hart in fact goes so far as to argue that the early Tamil view of *ananku* as something which clings to a woman, in particular, may be seen as 'the origin of many pan-Indian customs which have to do with women': in particular, the practices of imposing chastity, self-restraint, seclusion at times of acute danger such as childbirth, menstruation and widowhood. That is, the dangers of *ananku* are particularly crystallised at times when women's bodies are perceived (in this phallocentric rendition) as 'out of control', either due to biological phenomena such as menstruation and childbirth, or at times when social (male) control is weakened, such as after the death of a woman's busband. Baker-Reynolds confirms this: it is the breasts, loins and outflows of women which are particularly credited with possessing *ananku*. Hart's interpretations of the pre-Aryan roots of pollution, female seclusion, and even untouchability, are controversial matters. What is not controversial, however, is the centrality of a notion of divine power as something which is known through the alien possession of one's body: either in the form of disease, or in the form of emotional possession, as love/ecstasy and ecstatic dance. The possession may be inflicted on the sufferer by divine whim, but may also be summoned to take hold of the body through ecstatic dance (Hardy 1983:133). The early Tamil usage of the term *katavul*, which in medieval times came to denote a transcendental God, has been argued by Hardy to have had a primary meaning closer to our terms 'supernatural' and 'divine', and to be understandable only in conjunction with the allied concept of *ananku* (1983:131–2).

The seeds for simultaneously deifying and restricting women are therefore already present in the very earliest records we have of religious worship in Tamil Nadu. We are now in a better position to evaluate the characteristically south Indian nuances of goddess worship. *Ananku* is both a precursor of the later *sakti* cults, and a basis for giving this pan-Indian religious tradition its localised meaning. Even the worship of the Sanskritised goddess acquires a specific meaning in a culture where women's *sakti* is said to lie behind everything, and where accounts of creation often take the female as the first principle (Beck 1974:7). The most submissive of Sanskritic rituals may acquire different connotations in such a context. Baker-Reynolds (1978) documents the female rituals focusing around the renewal of the *tali*, the ornament most symbolic of women's status as wives in Tamil Nadu. Tali rituals, undertaken by Brahman and non-Brahman women alike to attain and safeguard the status of *sumangali* (an auspicious married woman) are directed at the Sanskritic, prestigious and married form of the goddess, celebrated as Meenakshi of Madurai, or Kamakshi of Kanchipuram (to name only two of the most prominent forms of the goddess). Yet the form of the *tali* ritual is not merely one of supplication, as one might expect in a ritual designed to renew and reaffirm the status of wife as the only legitimate status for women. It also takes the form of challenge, even a defiant challenge which Baker-Reynolds interprets as taking the following form: 'If I have been the faithful and chaste wife which I know myself to have been, I defy the goddess on the basis of my acquired powers, to deprive me of my status of *sumangali*.'[9]

The basis on which women are able to challenge the gods themselves regarding the term of life granted to their husbands rests on a view of women as both naturally and culturally placed to acquire immense spiritual powers. Partly, as we have seen in the archaic concept of *ananku*, the power is immanent in women, something their bodies are afflicted/blessed with. However, and here we must again note a definitive break with the Western associations between women and nature, women are also granted the capacity to increase those immanent powers through the terrible self-restraint imposed on them by cultural codes. The rigorous *dharma* of a chaste wife is not merely an externally imposed obligation of obedience to patriarchal will—it is also the means of accumulating powers comparable to the tapascharya of a male yogi. Indeed, in a very popular Tamil myth cited by Baker-Reynolds, the power of a disciplined wife emerges as superior to male yogic power in a direct confrontation between the two. The Tamil epic *Cilappadikaram*, described by Beck as 'one of the most famous and beloved epics of south India', centrally features the wrath of a chaste and abandoned wife, not on behalf of herself, but on behalf of her husband who is wrongfully accused of theft and put to death by the King of Madurai. The city is burnt to the ground by the wrath of the heroine Kannagi, when she rips off her left breast, as we now know a prime location of divine power, and flings it to the ground.

However, it is in the worship of the village goddess in contemporary Tamil Nadu that the early conception of femininity and divinity survives in its least altered form. Brubaker, in his study of village goddesses (1978, 1979), contrasts their prominence and centrality in the south to the religion of the north. In the north, he argues, the village deity is male. In the south, the deity is not only female, but worship of the goddess is highly elaborated, and expressive of common fundamental patterns. Given the minor role of female deities in Vedic literature, indigenous local goddesses have contributed to the 'feminisation of divinity in Hinduism'.

Although Brubaker does not associate the two, it is possible to make a number of connections between early Tamil religion and the village goddess. As in the concept of *ananku*, the village goddess captures the simultaneously destructive and redemptive capacities of the divine. Brubaker describes the goddess as the 'ambivalent mistress', both ravaging and renewing village life through the calamities of famine, flood, fire and disease. In the same way as with the religion of the Cankam period, the concept of divinity embodied in the goddess is not primarily a transcendental one: it is encountered primarily in the local environment, that of the village, and it is encountered most intensely through the most localised of all environments: the human body itself.

In her role as the symbolic centre of the village, the goddess demarcates the divine and the demonic—but in her paradigmatic form she fuses the two. This paradigmatic form is her possession of the human form, through disease and mystical, emotional identification. Brubaker describes the linkage between the goddess and disease as 'complex and multivalent':

> Not only does the presence of the goddess normally keep the disease demons at bay, and her power ensure their eventual expulsion on those occasions when their assaults have succeeded, but she is often said, on the contrary, to inflict the epidemic herself as a punishment of her people. In addition, the disease may be experienced as her immediate manifestation, quite apart from any intent to punish: suddenly and mysteriously emerging from her usual quiescent state, she possesses some of her people, and their symptoms are evidence of her awesome aliveness. Yet again, there are various symbolic expressions of the goddess herself as a victim of the disease. Epidemic disease, then, is something the goddess suffers, something she is, something she inflicts, and something she combats. In other words, the relationship between the goddess and this paradigmatic threat to her people takes every possible form (Brubaker 1979:130).

The characteristic experience of divine *ananku* as possession, which is inflicted, but which can be summoned to take hold of the human body by ecstatic dance (Hardy 1983:133), also survives in the typical form of worship for the village goddess. Earlier, worship was held at times of crisis; now it has been regularised into an annual village festival, partly due to the greater degree of human control over certain forms of epidemic disease such as smallpox which is the 'special' disease of the goddess. If *bhakti* represents the infiltration of ecstatic modes of worship into the Sanskritic realm, the festivals of the village goddess exemplify the primacy of the non-Sanskritic traditions of worship. Here the use of blood sacrifice, liquor, ecstatic possession and dancing, various forms of bodily chastisement and self-inflicted tortures (of which the mildest form would be lifting pots of water, *kavati*, for the goddess' bath, and the cruelest would include self-mutilation of the mouth and parts of the body, hook swinging, and fire-walking), come into their own.

Since the very worship of the goddess in this form is an inversion of the Sanskritic religious hierarchy, it is fitting that her worship is the occasion for social inversion. In the rituals themselves, it is the castes ranging from the middle to the very lowest of the social order which attain prominence: the barbers and washermen who are of middling 'purity', and the untouchable groupings such as the Paraiyan and Cakkiliyans in Tamil Nadu, and the Madigas and Malas in Telugu-speaking Andhra Pradesh (Brubaker 1979, Beck 1981). The very lowest of the low, untouchable women, also come into the centre of the religious stage at the festivals of the goddess. Elmore records the figure of the Matangi, an unmarried woman in the Madiga community, who, in a state of exulting possession subjected the upper castes to foul abuse and insult (Elmore 1925:29).

We have now located the specific religious terrain on which to identify the relation between Mukkuvar popular Catholicism and Hinduism. The former occupies, within Catholicism, the structural position of the tradition of the village goddess in Tamil popular Hinduism. In attributing a high proportion of disease and affliction to the hostile presence of the goddess Eseki (*Issakai*) and her demons Cholla MaaDan and VaNNaara MaaDan, Mukkuvars forge an antagonistic but nevertheless intimate relationship with *non*-Sanskritic Hinduism. The particular form taken by the invading goddess betrays her highly localised origins in the geography and caste structure of the region.

For Eseki is to be found only in the area corresponding to the old kingdom of Travancore. She is a wrathful and Kali-like form of the goddess most central to the low-caste cults of the region—the Bhagavathi Amman (sometimes referred to as Mariamman) of ManDaikkaDu. The annual festival of Bhagavathi Amman, held at the temple of ManDaikkaDu, differs significantly from the worship of the main Sanskritic goddess of the area, the Kanyakumari or virgin goddess. Where Kanyakumari's temple at the Cape attracts pilgrims, including high-caste pilgrims from all over India, Bhagavathi Amman attracts low-caste pilgrims confined to the regional geography of the old Travancore (which includes areas now part of Kerala). The annual festival of Bhagavathi Amman, unlike the steady trickle of pilgrims to the goddess of the Cape, is a focus of intense religious fervour.

The Mukkuvars from the cluster of villages around KaDalkarai Uuru are far more familiar with Bhagavathi Amman than with Kanyakumari. First, there is the geographical proximity of Bhagavathi Amman, whose temple is situated only five kilometres from KaDalkarai Uuru. Second, and more importantly, the annual festival at ManDaikkaDu, with its low-caste worshippers, is far more accessible to the fisherpeople than the worship of the goddess at the Cape. Mukkuvars act as temporary hosts to the pilgrims who come to ManDaikkaDu, offering them food and shelter. The Mukkuvars offer access through their own villages to the pilgrims bathing in the sea. By contrast, the worship of the Sanskritic goddess at the Cape has, particularly in recent times, not only excluded the fisherpeople, but has disrupted their residential and working areas.[10]

The controversies and tensions surrounding the figure of the goddess seem endless. The Mukkuvars are familiar with the worship of the non-Sanskritic goddess, Bhagavathi Amman, but incorporate her as the evil figure Eseki with her demon companions. But Hinduism itself is not clear-cut in its interpretation of these figures. The Hindu priest at ManDaikkaDu disassociates himself from the part Issakai and MaaDan play in Hindu low-caste cults.[11] Far from viewing them as fully fledged deities in their own right, he explains them as creations of Siva, created to slay Rudra (O'Flaherty 1975:118–122). On the priest's view, the low castes are elevating minions of Siva into deities challenging the paramount figures of the Hindu pantheon. That his suspicions may be justified is confirmed by the data in the Village Survey Monographs of the 1961 Census (Kanyakumari District vol.ix, Madras) which reveal that Nadars worship Mariamman, the Paraiyars worship Sudalai ('Cholla') Mada Swami and Kadamalai Amman, the Maravars worship various versions of the Amman (Vadakkuvasalli Amman, Muthara Amman).

The idea that popular religion is a field of struggle, not simply of cultural reintegration, is a particularly controversial one in the context of Indian anthropology. Treatments of the subject are still largely within the framework of structural functionalism. The worship of the village goddess is accepted by many scholars at face value as the common joint worship of the one power by all, irrespective of caste. Indeed, the very primacy of the untouchable castes in her worship at festivals is seen as proof of the integrative capacity of the cult and its reaffirmation of the interdependence between the highest and the lowest (Brubaker 1979, Beck 1981). Gluckmann's model of 'ritual rebellion' (1963), despite the many anthropological challenges it has subsequently received (Babcock 1978 gives an overview), continues to vitiate an otherwise brilliant interpretation of a Mariamman festival offered by Beck (1981).

In the case of a religious minority such as the Mukkuvars, popular religion is even more of a battleground than it is for low-caste Hindus. Their anomalous status in caste society has been outlined in the previous chapter. The fisherpeople are a degraded, low caste community in the eyes of Hindu upper castes, yet they are not dependent for their economic livelihood on the culturally hegemonic upper castes. Relations with Hinduism are therefore bound to be marked by a profound ambivalence, even hostility. What is of particular interest is the way that all of these struggles over cultural meaning and autonomy coalesce around contesting discursive representations of femininity. Implicit in Mukkuvar relations to the Sanskritic and the non-Sanskritic goddess are different conceptions of religion as well as of gender.[12] It is through these ambiguities and potentially open-ended play of meanings that the culture retains its symbolic polyphony and politically double-edged possibilities. Women are able to manipulate these meanings in conscious and unconscious ways, just as the Mukkuvars, also a minority, are able as a community to establish varied relations with different strands of Tamil culture. The next chapter examines the theme of cultural contestation in more detail.

4 Popular religion and femininity (2): the signification of the female body as a culturally contested zone

Brahmans liken the menstruous woman to four types of untouchables, each corresponding to a day of menstruation with a concomitant rise in the social hierarchy:
first day—Paracci, fisherwoman;
second day—Cakkili, shoe-maker;
third day—Canatti, toddy tapper;
fourth day—Vannati, washer woman.

To keep the tali strong
Baker-Reynolds (1978:101–102)

Consider for a moment this striking portrayal of the equivalence of the untouchable and the polluted menstruous woman, and the further equivalence of the fisherwoman with the menstruous woman in her most polluted phase. The humiliating force of this equivalence powerfully evokes the dilemmas of a low-caste community which wishes to contest its devaluation by the dominant culture. Chapter 1 noted that certain aspects of Mukkuvar life, principally their '*kaDal thozil*' or 'work of the sea', places the community in a uniquely favourable position to reject the lowly status offered to them by a caste order based on a hierarchy of purity. What are the implications of this generalised resistance for the way femininity is perceived and signified within the community?

The two conditions, untouchability and femininity, are closely intertwined. The analogy between woman and untouchable is no mere linguistic device. Insofar as Hinduism can be characterised as Sanskritic, that is, as based on formalised ritual adherence to the values of purity and pollution, the religion has had severely disabling

76

social effects for both groups. Krygier (1982:78–79) has noted some of the implications of this relationship of homology between woman and untouchable. She points out that the Brahmanic Upanayana rite of initiation for boys is restricted to the twice-born castes; there is no initiation rite for girls. Only twice-born castes can study the sacred Vedas; women similarly are not allowed to read the Vedas or to worship any deity with Vedic mantras.

We are led therefore to a significant problem bound to arise where members of a low caste attempt to contest the definition of their caste as impure. Notions of impurity and of femininity are closely bound up in Brahmanical discourse. In what ways is the intimate and devastating force of this connection registered in Mukkuvar representations of femininity and the female body? We pose this question while recognising that the female body is more than a passive register of the process by which the caste bids for self-respect. It is the occasion and the site for such communal contestation. There is only a partial truth in the notion of the Mukkuvars as an unbound caste, enjoying a structural autonomy from mainstream agrarian social relations. This interpretation can be maintained only as long as we allow men's work to stand for the entire Mukkuvar social order.

Women's work on the other hand requires of them a continuous task of mediation between the community and the outside world. Older women, who form a small but significant minority of fish traders, work alongside men from other castes and communities in markets and auctions. Even as cooks and childcarers, and in their efforts to raise credit, consult doctors and healers and sustain alliances of marriage and friendship, women's activities carry them not only outside the domestic dwelling but away from the coastal belt into the interior of the district. In other words, responsibility for the daily reproduction of Mukkuvar society and culture falls on the women. Women also control the management and expenditure of cash, and run what is virtually a parallel economy operating on credit which enables the community to survive the fluctuations and the instability of the male-dominated official economy.

The centrality given to women by the sexual division of labour is further accentuated by the kinship system, which will be the subject of detailed examination in Chapter 8 and therefore requires only brief reference here. The Mukkuvars share with the rest of Tamil Nadu a Dravidian system of kinship. The idealised form is that of cross-cousin marriage, of a man to his mother's brother's daughter or father's sister's daughter (who are classed together) and their classificatory equivalents. Where marriage joins closely related cross-cousins, the woman is in a comparatively strong position. Not only does she already have familiar relations with her affines, but she is able to continue to have intimate bonds with her own natal family, lessening the rupture in her life occasioned by marriage. Among the Mukkuvars this system of kinship is accompanied by a distinct bias in favour of marrying daughters to men within the same village, or else in closely contiguous villages, which further consolidates the continuity in women's lives.

The range of women's economic and social activities poses an indirect challenge to male patriarchal precedence. This factor itself threatens to undermine not only male dominance but the entire community's effort to conserve self-respect and a degree of cultural autonomy. Women are far more exposed than men to evaluation from outsiders, an evaluation structured not only by notions of pollution (which direct attention to their membership of a fishing caste) but by upper caste models of femininity. Outsiders are accustomed to a far more confined and restrictive version of femininity than they find among Mukkuvar women.

Insofar as female behaviour is continually over-interpreted and made the bearer of multiple levels of signification, the very notion of an autonomous Mukkuvar identity founders. The threat of hostile outsider evaluation of female potency as signifying lack of sexual restraint and dishonour to the community has radical implications for the disciplining of the female body within the community. Indeed, the very placing of ethnographic boundaries around 'the community' becomes problematic. For this reason Mukkuvar constructions of femininity cannot simply be regarded as if they were self-contained cultural artefacts, to be patiently reconstructed by anthropological exegesis. Nor can one speak of a straightforward encounter between a low caste of homogeneous outlook and a monolithic Hindu cultural system. Mukkuvar perception itself distinguishes between separate and often mutually contradictory strands of Hinduism. While the Hindu codes emphasising purity and pollution (those I have labelled Sanskritic) may be rejected or at least disregarded, the Mukkuvars have been so strongly affected by elements of popular Hinduism that the worship of the Virgin significantly replicates elements in the cult of the Tamil village goddess, raising the feminine to a new status of paramountcy. Yet, as we have already begun to glimpse in the previous chapter, the Mukkuvar relationship to popular Hinduism is problematic. It cannot be assimilated into a simple category of Hindu-Christian 'syncretism', a term which effectively obscures power relations and the element of conflict in cultural processes, suggesting simple amalgamation instead.

A neutral term such as syncretism does not do justice to the form of repression which occurs in the interiorisation of Hinduism. The cult of the Tamil goddess is incorporated into popular Christianity only at a price: the goddess is split in two. The Church's traditional antipathy towards indigenous religion and its institutional dominance over coastal villages ensures that instead of the 'ambivalent mistress' (Brubaker 1978), with her fluid alternation between nurturing and demonic aspects, there remain two reified entities, implacably hostile to one another: the good Virgin and the bad Eseki. Far from allowing a comfortable interchange between religious communities, popular Christianity posits Hinduism as an evil and invasive force, responsible for sickness, misfortune and suffering.

The first half of this chapter examines the shift in the signification of the female body within the Mukkuvar community, from a construction of the female body as polluted to an attribution of power, danger and sexuality instead. Although the account focuses on ritual and daily activity in the community, consideration of the semantic and cultural field involved in the signification of women's bodies entails a continual crossing over the boundaries of the coastal zone.

The second half of the chapter moves from an account which contents itself with elaborating an implicitly masculine representation of the female body, to an account which involves women as active participants in the elaboration and construction of cultural meaning. Through the mode of spirit possession, in the opposed but dialectically related roles of healer and patient, women play with, mock, utilise and occasionally invert codes of cultural signification which cross-hatch the female body. In doing so, they fashion a modality of resistance and contestation uniquely their own.

The suppression of the motif of 'pollution' in the Mukkuvar community

If we examine each of the contexts where ritual impurity normally occurs in Hindu society—birth, death and menstruation, as well as more minor pollutions such as saliva, urine and faeces—we find that pollution ideology has left only minor traces in Mukkuvar society.

The closest the coastal villages come to having a sub-caste responsible for polluting activities are the members of the barber households. Barbers are distinguished in Mukkuvar villages by membership of the Parava fishing caste. Villages with Parava populations try further to distinguish themselves from their lowly barbers by calling them Chuna Paravas, referring to the practice of extracting lime from the burning of sea shells.

Barbers have ritual functions associated with death: it is their job to carry news of death to all relevant kin of the deceased, and it is also their job to dig graves and cover the bodies. Their ritual functions are not restricted to polluting occasions, however. The barber also has an important role in that most auspicious of all occasions, marriage. One day before the wedding, the Mukkuvars have a ritual called the *Muhachavara Chadanku*, in which the face of the bridegroom is ceremonially shaved by the barber. In return, the barber is given ritual payment of a *dhoti* from the groom, and money from other relatives of the groom. Despite this, the fundamentally lower status of the barbers is undeniable. In this relation of fishermen and barber we find something of the patron-client relationships of caste society: the fishermen act as patrons, setting aside two per cent of a good catch as payment for the caste's services. For the rest, barbers have to rely on the generosity of guests at weddings, and of the kin notified by them of death. The fundamental dependency on the goodwill of the rest of the villagers is felt keenly by the barbers, who describe their job as lowly, leaving them at the mercy of all, irrespective of status.

However, the sub-caste of barbers does not concentrate within itself other polluting tasks, as happens in Hindu society. Thus barbers' wives do not necessarily act as midwives or washerwomen. Instead, midwives are simply ordinary Mukkuvar women who perform midwifery in addition to their other chores and tasks. While this skill may be passed on from mother to daughter, a woman who shows special aptitude and the all-important capacity, called *arudal*, to give the woman in labour courage and comfort may 'become' a midwife simply by virtue of the community's recognition and reliance on her services. I received no indication that such women are regarded as having performed a task in any way polluting or requiring purification. As we shall see, birth is considered a time of considerable danger to mother and infant, but this does not entail a view of the mother's body as polluting. Observances such as the ritual head bath may certainly carry overtones of purification, but this does not accord with the systematic omission of purificatory acts in the ritual complex.

Death, for example, is ritualised by the officiating of the priest, and congregational singing. The body itself is cleaned, dusted with white powder and sprinkled with rose water, to be then dressed in new clothes. This is as far as purificatory ceremonies go. The family does not observe 'death pollution' after the funeral. The death is commemorated with special prayers after intervals of eight and thirty days, but there is no evidence that mourners keep to a special regime during this thirty-day period. Subsequently, death anniversaries are marked only by a prayer.

Menstruation rites show up this selectivity in the absorption of Hindu values even more clearly. The first menstruation, which is marked in Tamil society as an auspicious and celebratory occasion, is an important part of the Mukkuvar female life-cycle. Even here, some of the purificatory rituals, such as calling on a priest to cleanse the house, are omitted. The Christian priest is not at all involved in puberty ceremonies nor, on the whole, in birth ceremonies, where he involves himself only at a considerably later stage, when the child is taken to church for baptism.

In Tamil Hindu society not simply menarche but every menstruation is marked by ritual—and unlike the menarche ceremony, subsequent menstruations are accompanied not by celebration but by seclusion, which carries strong overtones of fear of pollution, since it is accompanied by a ban on public worship and domestic cooking. The practice of menstrual seclusion is conspicuously absent among the Mukkuvars. Women cook, go out to work, attend church services during menstruation—although women who become direct vessels of divine grace, mediums, do draw the line at healing in the name of divinity while menstruating. They rarely get the *muzhi* or divine gaze at such times, and often report the cessation of all menstruation and sexual activity after becoming mediums. Even here, however, there are in Mukkuvar practice marked differences from the kinds of purificatory measures taken by their Hindu equivalents. Mediums curing in the name of the Hindu deities will never appear for a trance session without a purificatory bath, sacred ash (*veebudi*) and *kumkum* on the forehead and a fresh sari. Christian mediums by contrast, appear dirty and unwashed, hair uncombed, wearing old nylon saris.

In a state-wide survey of practices surrounding menstruation, Ferro Luzzi (1974) found a noticeable absence of pollution observation in southern Tamil Nadu. On the reader's closer investigation of the survey results, this finding turns out to be related to the distribution of certain Christian fishing castes: 'It is in fact, mostly due to the Christian fisherwomen, the Mukkuvan and Paravan of Terunelveli and Kanyakumari District, as well as to a number of Nadar and Maravar women, who for economic reasons, have to work' (1974:128).

Menstruation is described by Hindu Tamils in negative terms, emphasising the *tiiTu* or pollution inherent in the phenomenon. They call it *duuram* (distance), *viiTukku duuram* (distance from the house), or *viiTukku veLLeelai* (outside the house). Mukkuvar women, by contrast, call it *maatha viLLakkam* or the monthly cleansing, or else *kare varum*, the coming of blood/colour.

Traces of a purity consciousness there are bound to be—Mukkuvar society does not exist in isolation. Outsiders' views of fishing people impinge on the community, and in particular on women who have to deal with other castes in the course of their work as traders. Similarly, young Mukkuvar children going to school are in a position to observe and imbibe the purity consciousness of their school friends. On the whole, however, anyone importing these norms into the community is given short shrift. A young girl who refused to accept food eaten by another in deference to saliva pollution was gossiped about and criticised for 'putting on airs' and raising herself above the community. My own presence as a Brahman in their midst occasioned only curiosity, often of the mildest variety. Only the priests and the more educated villagers knew enough of Brahmanical prestige to regard my vegetarianism as a challenge. For them it became a matter of pride to convert me to eating fish. For the rest, Brahmans were a distant and alien caste, whose norms of vegetarianism and purity were only a dimly heard of curiosity. It was my power as an educated outsider who might have influential connections which occasioned much more interest and jockeying for attention and favours.

The absence of the pollution hierarchy cannot be related in any simple way to economic imperatives such as the 'need for women to go out and work' (Ferro Luzzi 1974:128). Rather, I suggest it may be linked in a more complex way to the men's exemption from direct servitude to upper castes, which gives a firm basis for the community's ability to distance itself from a metaphysic damaging to the struggle for a more dignified and positive communal identity.

Mukkuvar women as the forbidden Eseki: the signification of the female body in Mukkuvar culture

American ethnographers of Tamil culture (Beck 1974, Baker-Reynolds 1978) are fond of quoting a Tamil proverb to highlight the dual vision of femininity in Tamil Nadu: '*Aavatum peNaale, alivatum peNaale*—Through woman there is being, and through woman there is obliteration also.'

Mukkuvar rituals and beliefs attest to the direct continuities between the fishing community and the rest of the Tamil population. Female sexuality is attributed both an auspicious modality and a dangerous one. That there is both celebration and control of female sexuality to be found in these rituals is only superficially a paradox. Women are not the only group to be simultaneously accredited with magical, superhuman powers on the one hand, and on the other treated as dangerous, wild, and in need of control from the dominant group. Recent work by Taussig on the European view of the South American Indian amply bears out this ambivalence in the discourse of the powerful (1987).

At the same time, the view of Tamil femininity elaborated in American ethnography (Beck 1974, Baker-Reynolds 1978, Wadley 1980 and Egnor 1978) becomes rendered as some kind of timeless cultural essence: 'the Tamil view' or 'the Mukkuvar view' of women. It is necessary to view such cultural representations as fully grounded in the structure of kinship and the division of labour. Furthermore, such structures are subject to historical modification, as the rest of the book is concerned to demonstrate. These structural modifications will in turn alter and modify the kinds of discursive representations under examination here, although not in an immediately direct or mechanical fashion.

I begin my examination of ritual and belief with those aspects of Mukkuvar culture which seem to vindicate and even celebrate the maturation of female sexuality and, in a broader sense, women's physical and spiritual energy or *sakti*.

Female energy as auspicious, divine power

Feminine *sakti*, at the core of Mukkuvar conceptions of the divine, defies the thesis that patriarchy assigns women a simple meaning, or even a simple identification with sexuality, biology or nature (Ortner 1974, Ardener 1975a, 1975b)—an unsatisfactory and misleading philosophical position which has left its stamp on the feminist-inspired American ethnography on Tamil women (Wadley 1980, Baker-Reynolds 1978, Egnor 1978). Female *sakti*, a category simultaneously referring to the cultural and the biological, is manifest in a girl before the first appearance of sexuality, which is believed to occur only at puberty. Young virginal daughters have an auspicious quality which is not simply an anticipation of their later sexual potential. Beck (1974) cites the benefits that the mere presence of such girls brings to their father and brothers, benefits which are jealously guarded and only reluctantly given up to the husbands the girls will later marry.[1] Among the Mukkuvars brothers in particular play a key role in warding off potential husbands and suitors for the girl. Certainly this configuration is a classic patriarchal mode of guarding women's chastity. Yet the brother-sister bond among Mukkuvars goes well beyond the role of male guardianship which elsewhere (e.g. in the north of India) must strictly end with the marriage of the woman. A woman as sister and daughter continues to provide, for her natal family, loyalty and, if possible, financial assistance even after her marriage. Cases of married brothers and sisters living together with their respective families are certainly not unknown (see Chapter 8).

Yet the virgin daughter has neither the full sexuality nor the culturally controlled *sakti* of the sexually mature woman. Such controls, only achieved by the mechanism of marriage, consummation and motherhood, are of course beneficial primarily to men, and signal underlying male fears. But there are some curious twists in the form taken by cultural signification: for submission and chastity are also the pathway to spiritual power in this society. Thus the woman who is chaste wife and loving mother is also seen as practising a form of spiritual austerity in which she is able to cultivate her own inherent *sakti*. In Tamil Hinduism, the consort goddess, sexually mature and chaste, has greater spiritual power and prestige than the virgin goddesses such as Kanyakumari. Among Mukkuvars, and in Tamil culture generally, such a view permits women to claim special access to divine powers belonging to the highest levels of the religious hierarchy. I examine women's utilisation of such ambiguities in the next section.

The Mukkuvar, in their view of the unmarried girl, first as child, then as pubescent virgin, reflect all these different shades of meaning found in the wider culture. The birth of a daughter is valued not as economic necessity but as the coming into the world of a person to be treasured and loved: '*aashaikku pen*', 'for love, one has a girl'. She is a source of emotional comfort and security in the parents' old age: all characteristics one normally associates in the Indian context with parental valorisation of sons. The sharp contrasts in views are in turn based on the material structures of kinship and the division of labour outlined briefly earlier.

The appearance of fertility in the young girl brings together a number of related concerns and beliefs. First and foremost, it is welcomed by a public ritual statement of the girl's maturation, her enhanced status and her potential availability in marriage. McGilvray (1982) reports that the onset of menstruation is seen by Tamils in Sri Lanka as both result and proof of the fact that the female body has an excess of waste blood. Blood is the locus of bodily energy; Mukkuvar villagers are deeply fearful of Western medical surgery due to the loss of blood incurred in the process: '*Rattam ooTam kammi aividum*', 'the flow of blood will decrease'. In producing this excess blood, menstruating girls indicate their increase in energy and bodily heat and the appearance of sexuality and fertility. (In losing the excess blood, according to McGilvray's informants, they allow the possibility of male dominance.) This is a phenomenon which is to be celebrated and at the same time carefully ushered in with cultural codification and restraints. The twin concerns are reflected in the Mukkuvar menarche ceremony.

Puu punida niiraTu: *the menarche ceremony*

The terms used to describe the menarche ceremony are themselves celebratory. The dominant motif is that of flowering, the terms *puu punida niiraTu* and *pushpavadi* both playing on the metaphor of blossoming. As with the flower-like fragrance the woman is said to emit immediately after her wedding, in the period following sexual initiation and experience—a fragrance immensely attractive to demons—maturation in a woman is a pleasurable and important event. The other term commonly used for this ceremony, *chaDangu*, is a term used only to describe highly auspicious ceremonies such as marriage.

The very existence of menarche rituals has been highlighted as a conspicuous contrast to attitudes towards female puberty in northern India by Wadley (1980), who has worked predominantly in the north. She argues that until recently, anthropological interpretation has focused on the relationship between the control of female sexuality and caste purity (e.g. Yalman 1963), but has neglected to recognise the other side of the picture—which emerges only when we consider that 'in the north, puberty is not only not celebrated, but is hidden' (1980:163). Equally significantly, such puberty rituals disappear, even in the south, in direct proportion to the dominance of an ideology which emphasises female sexuality as a purely negative and embarrassing phenomenon. McGilvray has noted this historical process occurring among the Muslim population in Sri Lanka as a result of an increasing pan-Islamic consciousness (1982).

The Mukkuvar ceremony itself, as described to me, can be retold briefly as follows:

> The girl is secluded for seven days. During this period she is not allowed to work or go out. On the first day of menstruation, the girl is fed special

foods by specified kinswomen. Generally, these women are senior women, but they are usually related in ways signifying a special interest in the girl's marriageability and fertility. These are the wives of the mother's brothers, whose sons are potential grooms for the girl. Also involved are the girl's brothers' wives, reflecting a concern further away in time, but also related to the kinship system: the future daughters of the pubescent girl will provide the brides for the sons borne by the girl's brothers' wives.

The foods that the girl is fed are also significant. She is given raw eggs, sesame oil, as well as a dish of rice flour steamed with coconut milk and grated coconut called *puTTu*.

Those who have the financial means to entertain others will invite others to call formally on the girl on the third, fourth or seventh day. These include not only kin, but acquaintances and friends in the village.

On the seventh day, the same women who fed the girl special foods on the first day now give her a ritual bath, which must importantly include the bathing of the head. The girl is dressed in jewellery and in an expensive sari for the first time. The clothes may be presented by wealthier kin.

So far I have concentrated on those aspects of the ceremony which emphasise the festive celebration of female sexuality, an attitude which springs from the distinctive features of the kinship system. A fuller examination of the ceremony refers us to the other paramount concern of the culture: the containment of the female body, which is replayed over and over in metaphors and social practices of cooling, binding and secluding the female body.

Metaphors of power and domination over the female body

Cooling

I have spoken already of the Mukkuvar preoccupation with regulating the body's heat and its humoral balance. The theme is found in Tamil medical culture and is continually reinforced among Mukkuvar villagers by the diagnoses and prescriptions of Siddha Vaidya doctors. However, the everyday dietary and bathing practices of the Mukkuvars, as well as their rituals, indicate a relatively autonomous existence of this concern with bodily balance in popular culture.[2] This autonomy is clearest, as I also indicated earlier, where the humoral theory of the body found in Siddha Vaidya merges with religious explanations of illness and misfortune. The fusion is expressed in a particularly dramatic fashion in beliefs concerning the female body. The female body is more prone than the male body to act in a disorderly way, subvert the harmony of human affairs and invite unwanted supernatural attention. The other vulnerable beings are infants, but their condition is so intimately linked with dependence on the maternal body that one may be excused for subsuming them under this discussion of the female body. The physiological rhythms of the female body, its periodic flux, are the occasion for and the site of supernatural intervention. The physiology itself creates transitions—puberty, with its dramatic flow of blood which subsequently recurs every month, pregnancy and childbirth—which are times of great ambiguity and change. They constitute the cracks and weak points in the relation between humanity and the malign powers.[3]

Overheating of the female body occurs whenever there is a concentrated accumulation of blood. This occurs periodically at menstruation and again during pregnancy. At both times great concern is shown over the kinds of food the woman is allowed to eat, in accordance with the heating and cooling properties allocated to foods, liquids and spices (see Note 3, Ch.3). The woman must above all avoid heating foods. The pubescent girl is given sesame oil and coconut milk, both cooling foods. *PuTTu*, the steamed dish, avoids the eruptive qualities of foods cooked in oil. In pregnancy, complaints such as the swelling of feet during the later stages are treated with coconut milk and garlic heated together and had as a drink—a balance of heating and cooling elements, perhaps reflecting the same tension between enhancing fertility and reducing body heat. During labour a woman is offered hot liquids such as hot coffee or hot water to speed up the delivery by adding to body heat. Immediately after birth, by contrast, the midwife may give the mother a cooling mixture of ginger, pepper and oil from the leaf of the margosa tree (*veepa ellai*).

The addition of details concerning these Mukkuvar home remedies betrays a more complex set of linkages. The use of margosa tree-oil in birth and in the treatment of the pubertal girl in other regions (McGilvray 1982) is particularly significant. *Veepa ellai* or the leaf of the margosa tree is associated not only with combating heat and heat-induced diseases (Beck 1969) but with the Goddess. It is the Goddess who brings *shuuTu vyaadigal* or heat-diseases, most paradigmatically the disease of smallpox, which Mukkuvars call *ammai noyvu*, or the disease of the Mother. Both the oil and the leaf of the margosa tree help to reduce the heat of the Goddess who has possessed the victim of the disease. The use of the same oil in cooling the woman during menstruation and after birth is strongly suggestive of close association with an angry, hot Goddess.

The association is strengthened when we consider daily practices surrounding bathing. The daily bath is extremely important. It is normally taken in cold running water, and liberal amounts must be available to cool the body satisfactorily. My own use of one bucket of water (all I could carry back to the privacy of my own room), was considered miserably inadequate, as was my practice of neglecting to douse my head daily with large quantities of cold water. Only in states where the body has lost large quantities of blood and energy is hot water used. In the twelve days that the post-partum mother is kept secluded, her emissions are said to be draining her of heat and energy, and she therefore bathes in extremely hot water. (This is balanced by massaging her with cooling turmeric.) The ritual bath taken by the pubescent girl at the end of the menarche ritual is in keeping with these general principles. Here too, she bathes in cold water, and it must specifically involve wetting and cooling the head and hair.

The emphasis on the head deserves closer attention, for it reveals certain features common to both sexes, but some specific to the female. In ordinary bathing, not only is the head wetted and doused with water, but the scalp must previously be liberally massaged with oils such as groundnut oil or coconut oil. The concentration of cooling devices on the head harks back to statements made earlier regarding the primacy of the head in the bodily symbolism of devotional religion. Bodily energy in both men and women is portrayed in yogic theory as accumulating in the head. In men, it is the source and reservoir of semen. In women, however, the accumulation of heat in the head sparks off associations of the angry Goddess.

The Tamil association between smallpox and the Goddess intensifies around the head of the patient. Beck has elaborated a little on this theme (1981). The sores of the smallpox are viewed metaphorically as eyes, and are thought to be the eruptions of excessive internal heat. Blindness is often the result of smallpox, and this is linked to ideas about the loss of vision because of unreasoning lust and self-pride. Finally, the appearance of 'extra' eyes or pox sores on the face or head in the course of the disease are the definitive sign of the presence of the Goddess.

The Mukkuvar goddess, the Virgin, is unable to condense within her symbolism all the multivalent relations to the disease contained in the Hindu goddess. In the statements of the older villagers, there is still the ambiguity whereby the Maataa both brings and cures the diseases of smallpox and even cholera (see quotes on pp.58–59), but for the most part the Maataa's association with disease is a purely benign and curative one. The Church's teachings have not been able to intervene as powerfully in shaping Mukkuvar notions of the earthly female, however. The human woman is still perceived as a source of danger, disorder and power. This becomes clearer still when we turn to the recurring metaphor of binding the female body.

Binding

Kenneth David (in Wadley 1980) has analysed binding as a recurring theme in the life-cycle rituals of Tamil women. The key emphasis is on covering and binding the parts of the female body that are focal points of *sakti* and sexuality: the breasts and loins, but also the head and more specifically the hair on one's head. The degree of binding varies in direct proportion to the maturation of the woman.

I begin with an account of hair. Hair may be worn cropped short by very young girls. After five or six years, it must be oiled and plaited, allowed to hang down the back as a braid. After the puberty ceremony, and particularly after marriage, the adult woman wears her hair in a tightly coiled cone-shaped knot at the back of the head. Henceforth a woman can leave her hair unbound only when allowing it to dry after a bath. Unbound female hair outside the context of bathing signifies disorder and extreme emotion: the grief of widow-hood, anger, sexual passion or demonic possession. Tamil and pan-Indian epics such as the Mahabharata bear out the power of this motif. The Tamil epic *Silappadikaram* stresses the potential for destruction in the wrath of the chaste wife, by describing her loosened hair:

> This is the widowed heroine Kannaki confronting the king of Madurai with the injustice of his execution of her husband, before she goes on to actually burn down the city with her anger:
> Her lily eyes streamed with water;
> in her hand, a single anklet (proving her innocence)
> her form untenanted by life.
> What evil have I done that I saw her,
> her black hair spread like a forest?
> The king of Maturai beheld her
> and terrified he died.
>
> (*Cilappatikaram*, 20, venpa 2, transl. Hart 1975:105)

Similarly, the Mahabharata evokes the long period of exile endured by the heroic Pandavas as one of social inversion. The key signifier of this social inversion is the vow of the queen Draupadi to leave her hair dishevelled until it has been braided by one of her five husbands with hands steeped in the blood of her sexual aggressors (Hiltebeitel 1981).

The binding of hair and garments are closely interlinked in mean-ing and intention. If we continue with the example of Draupadi for a moment, the dishevelling of Draupadi's hair by the sexual aggressors is combined with the pulling of her garments—both are symbolic of an assault on her sexual chastity. The two motifs are closely fused in some narratives of the Mahabharata (e.g. the *Kesambharakarsana* or the pulling of hair and garments; see Hiltebeitel 1981:183).

Among the Mukkuvar, as with Tamils in general, the puberty ceremony marks the transition from the free and unencumbered form of dress belonging to early childhood and girlhood to the binding garment of womanhood, the *chelai* (Tamil) or sari. Each phase of dress is increasingly more restrictive of female movement. Very young girls may be seen wearing Western style dresses. From the age of five onwards they wear a long skirt coming down to their ankles and a top (*paavaaDai chokkai*). Between twelve and puberty, they may wear *paavaaDai-meelaakku*, which adds to the long skirt and top a light cloth draped to cover the girl's breasts. Finally, the *chelai* or sari, eight or nine yards of cloth, is wound completely around the female body. Particular emphasis is placed on training girls to be aware at all times that the top of the sari covers their breasts—even while engaged in physically demanding tasks. Remember that *ananku* was thought to be specially located in women's sexual parts. An early Tamil poem covers both the stress on binding hair and covering the sexual parts as the key points of transition to womanhood:

> Your breasts are maturing
> your sharp teeth shine.
> Your hair is in a top-knot.
> You wear a cool leaf-dress.
> From now on
> do not go here and there with your wandering girlfriends.
> Our ancient town has old places with attacking gods (ananku).
> We are entrusted with protecting you.
> Do not go where you went before.
> You are no longer a little girl, O wise child,
> but have become a woman.
> Do not go outside.
>
> (*Akam* 7, quoted in Baker-Reynolds 1978:71)

Allowing a girl to linger on in the dress of childhood after sexual maturation—as occurred in the somewhat more cosmopolitan family with which I lived—is heavily associated by villagers with lack of modesty and chastity. The girl is open to hostile mockery and abuse.

The symbolism of binding reaches its most explicit statement of male control in the wedding ceremony. Mukkuvars have retained in their Catholic ceremony the ritual of central importance in the Tamil marriage ritual: the tying of the *tali* around the woman's neck by her husband. In an extensive analysis of *tali* symbolism, Baker-Reynolds describes the tying of the *tali* as the definitive act whereby 'a man binds, ties and harnesses [the woman] to him, and to his family with a symbol of the lineage he represents. He defines the parameters of her activities; he attempts to control her; he lays claim to her powers of fertility. He also indicates his responsibilities' (1978:230).

Seclusion

Seclusion merges the symbolic motifs of containment with the deployment of power. I have earlier raised the question of inter-relations between the gender-coding of space and women's separation from the means of production. The gender-coding of space, which less politely comes down to restrictions on the female use of space, now emerges as part and parcel of the more general concern with containing women through the regulation and regimentation of their bodies.

Seclusion at its most severe, restriction to the four walls of the home, occurs only at very specific moments in the Mukkuvar woman's life: the first menstruation (but not subsequent menstruations) and then again for twelve days after childbirth. I have indicated already the considerable significance of this divergence from the Hindu practice of secluding women at every monthly period. It implies that the seclusions which do occur among the Mukkuvar are concerned with the danger of female power rather than with pollution. At menarche and childbirth women are a threat to people around them, but they are simultaneously people in danger due to the attraction their heat and blood hold for supernatural forces. Just as the divine female in Hindu religion actually suffers the diseases she inflicts and cures in others, so also the Mukkuvar female is open to suffering the dangers of demonic possession and spirit attack that she could bring on others in the community. The seclusion of women at these times is accompanied by the attempt to guard and protect them with pieces of iron to stave off demons and spirits. The area where the secluded woman bathes after childbirth is specially constructed to collect her outflows of blood. A pit is constructed in the corner of the hut and covered over with planks of wood. The woman bathes standing on these planks, and at the end of the twelve days the pit is sealed up with several articles having been placed in it: a piece of iron or a knife, a bit of salt and a bit of chili. I have already mentioned the odour of sexual activity, *puu maNam* (the smell of flowers), said to be particularly strong and attractive to demons in the period immediately after marriage. The husband, by contrast, does not suffer from any similar association with demons on account of his sexual activity.

The associations between the normal functioning of female reproduction and demonology are numerous. Ghosts witnessed during labour or pregnancy make the labour more protracted and painful. A house in which there has been more than one difficult childbirth will be suspected of harbouring spirits and not be used for that purpose again. The motif of binding occurs again at birth, the woman's stomach being bound afterwards with cloth. This is said to help the uterus contract, and to help the organs return to their normal place, but is also linked with the distancing of evil spirits.[4]

Men are also vulnerable to attack from demons in particular physical locations: the graveyard, where ghosts lurk and where *mantravaadis* come to steal the parts of the body they need for sorcery, the parts of the village associated with repeated death such as a point along the beachfront where two young boys were swept away, demarcations between villages, the paddy fields if traversed late at night, and so on. But, men are not counselled to stay indoors for this reason; rather they are armed with counsel on what to do if confronted with a ghost or demon, such as never showing fear. Women must seek safety in domestic seclusion. Even a trip outside the house at night to urinate may bring on demon attack.

Given the demonological interpretation of the ordinary female reproductive cycle, it is not surprising that problems of infertility, over-bleeding, spontaneous abortions, irregularity or delayed menstruation are all likely to be interpreted in the idiom of the supernatural. Again, early modern Europe provides striking similarities, with its associations between womb disorders and the supernatural. The association has persisted right down to the psychoanalytic view of hysteria as a peculiarly feminine disorder.[5] I give below just one example of such an interpretation by Mukkuvar villagers:

Virgin [a woman's name] is childless due to suffering spontaneous abortions. She has consulted numerous *naaTu vaidiyarkal* (dispensers of indigenous medicine), and is currently under treatment for the relief of menstrual pain which her doctor diagnoses as the key to her other gynaecological troubles. However, she says her body cannot assimilate the herbal medicines and dietary restrictions recommended by Siddha Vaidya doctors.

She has also been on numerous pilgrimages—to Velankanni two years in a row; Periya and Chinna Eduthuvai for two years; Uvari (pronounced Ovadi in local dialect) in Tiruneveli District, the shrine of St Anthony, Raja Uuru of St Michael; and Balaramapuram (pronounced Valrapuram) en route to Trivandrum in Kerala. Her most significant pilgrimage was to Balaramapuram. She went there with a stomach bloated from the inability to pass urine, and began to experience relief en route. At Balaramapuram a medium divined that someone had placed a sorcery offering in their house. A messenger was sent to ask the old parents of Virgin's husband to purify the house, to keep it free of fish and cooking smells. On the appointed day, three assistants of the medium, one man and two women, came to dig out the ensorcelled material. In one corner of the house, they found a bundle containing coconut, *kumkum* (vermilion powder worn on a woman's forehead), incense, *vetalai* (betel nut leaf). These are all considered items of worship in Hinduism. The medium's assistants replaced this material with a spear, symbol of St Sebastian who died a martyr's death by spearing.

Two months later, her husband found another magical bundle, as he slept near the front porch. The next morning his attempt to go fishing was unsuccessful. They called the parish priest to pray over it and burn the material with ground nut oil.

Virgin took the remains of these magical materials back to Balaramapuram and asked the saints why no punishment was being meted out to the evil doers who had repeated their attempts at sorcery. She left it in God's hands and came home.

Virgin believes her enemies have since been punished. She believes that her enemies are her husband's relatives who would like her to die childless. Prior to marriage, her husband lived with his father's sister and their family. His *atai* (aunt) wished him to marry her own daughter, instead of which he married Virgin. Virgin and her husband tried living with his aunt and her family for a while immediately after marriage—but she found that her husband's income was kept out of her hands, and she was hardly allowed access to money. Even her dowry jewellery was taken from her—and this precipitated separation. However, the aunt and her family continue to plot Virgin's downfall, especially since friction began to develop between Virgin and her husband. If Virgin were to die childless, her husband would not continue to live with her old parents. Virgin feels the only reason she is being kept alive by God is to protect her parents from being totally deserted in their old age.

Social conflict, as expressed in the idiom of sorcery, is conceived by Mukkuvars in terms of the human body as the point of entry for supernatural intervention. In this conception, the female body, already invested with complex associations of divinity and malignity, is well equipped to be assigned a very special susceptibility to attacks of sorcery and spirit possession. However, the body is a meeting ground for multiple relations of power, not merely those of men over women. If female sexuality and fertility are valuable but coveted and troublesome resources, so also are the resources of the male body, most important of which is its labour power. Social conflict over the control of these resources comes up most acutely at the time of settling marriage alliances. Marriage is the social mechanism whereby female fertility and male labour power are redirected from one family to another. Given that sorcery is the dominant idiom of conflict, it is not surprising that sorcery figures regularly in accounts of marriage alliances and love affairs:

(1) A young woman of 19 tells me of her love affair with a boy who has since married another. She comes from a family of many children and few assets. His family owned a mechanised boat and expected to marry a family which could supply capital for buying complementary equipment such as nets. Their love affair was therefore opposed. The boy suggested an elopement, which the girl refused. Soon after, the girl's parents formally proposed marriage to the boy's family, which they refused. The girl believed that the boy's parents called in a *mantravaadi* to use a love charm on the boy, for he willingly agreed to marry a girl of their choice soon after.

(2) Vijaya comes from a village in the interior of the district; her parents are fish traders. Her family was poor since her father died while young. She has experienced spirit possession at different times in her life since the age of eighteen. The first time was before marriage. The spirit which haunts her has declared itself to be the ghost of a married woman who lived near Vijaya's childhood home, and who killed herself with poison as a result of her husband's repeated suspicions regarding her sexual fidelity. The circumstances of Vijaya's marriage have been surrounded with tension. She met James, her husband, while visiting her elder sister who has married into KaDalkarai Uuru. *Pazhakam* or acquaintance occurred between James and Vijaya. The idea of marriage was opposed by James' mother owing to the poverty of Vijaya's family. She also feared that James would set up a separate establishment after marriage, and deprive them of his labour power and income. James stood firm, fought with his family, and went and brought Vijaya to stay at his elder sister's home. The conflict was smoothed over by mediators, respected men in the village, who persuaded James' mother to accept a token dowry. However, James' mother's fears have come true. Vijaya experienced possession attacks five days after her

marriage, and the spirit demanded that James and Vijaya move out of his family home. They now live with Vijaya's elder sister and her family, and James no longer works with his father.

The above accounts—only excerpts from what are far more involved case studies—are sufficient to show the regular conflict that can occur between parental regulation of marriage and their children's desires. The former is aimed at the social control of the children's labour and sexuality, while the latter continually threatens to stray outside these boundaries. The conflict has become particularly acute in the context of changing relations of production, as marriage, with the chance it affords to extract dowry payments, has become one of the few avenues for capital accumulation (see Chapters 5 and 8). But it is the girls who bear the brunt of the surveillance and containment, dictated both by parental marital strategies and by the cultural construction of their bodies.

The Virgin against Eseki: religious consciousness among Christian women of Kanyakumari District

This section examines the themes of this chapter from a different vantage point—that of the women themselves, who have so far been discussed as the passive objects, rather than the agents, of cultural rules and practices. Just as Mukkuvars select and reinterpret the elements of the dominant culture, so the women are able to a certain extent to manipulate and even exploit to their advantage the qualities patriarchy ascribes to them. This manoeuvrability is made possible by the fact that the dominant culture is itself full of internal contradictions, ironies and ambiguities, which create a potential space for the contestation of cultural meaning. In the Christian fishing villages the rituals of binding, cooling and seclusion implicitly attribute to women a dangerous power not officially recognised by Church doctrine. Women physically take on the attributes of this illicit identity through the medium of illness and possession. The figure of the demonised Hindu goddess affects men and women alike; but in entering the bodies of women it enables them to challenge the daily discipline of living within the confines of respectable femininity.

My examination necessarily takes us, once again, outside the confines of the fishing community. Just as Mukkuvars incorporate and reassemble themes from Hinduism, so also their modes of worship and pilgrimage and their attempts to cure themselves of illness and demonic possession integrate them into a wider religious community of Christians, peasants of the district and even all over Tamil Nadu. The modes of resistance employed by Mukkuvar women in possession and illness are not unique to them as members of a fishing community. Rather, they are specific to them as members of a Christian peasant community, which includes members of many different denominations (among them, Church of South India, Pentecostal Church and Protestant groups).

My pursuit of the theme of female illness, possession and religious consciousness took me repeatedly out of the fishing villages, accompanying Mukkuvar women on their journeys to the agrarian hinterland. The women visited healers, Christian women who began their cures in the name of the Virgin and the saints, and further directed them to a network of shrines dotted all over the Tamil Nadu countryside. The importance of the healers to these women cannot be underestimated. It was the healers who functioned as intermediaries between Mukkuvar Christians and the wider Christian world of rural Tamil Nadu. The settings for this interaction between Christians (and indeed, some Hindus as well) were the shrines. Confirmed in their faith and directed by the healers, scores of women at a time pitted the demons possessing them against the powers of the Christian divinities.

The battle of the Virgin against Eseki, the two female figures who symbolise the battle between good and evil in popular Christianity, is strikingly transposed to an earthly plane by the battle of the healer against the demonically possessed. Their contest produces and disperses among the peasant population images and meanings which confirm the bodily experience of religion. Where the healer and the demonically possessed are, in addition, women, we are in a position to explore the additional inflections of meaning that women bring to this popular religion.

I examine the details of this contest—between the discourse of the divine and the discourse of the demonic—in two parts.

The discourse of the divine: the healers

Nowhere are the rival tendencies within popular Christianity—in its moments of complicity as well as of resistance to the dominant culture—made clearer than in the figure of the healer. Healers constitute themselves as key intermediaries in the dialogue between good and evil, between the Virgin and Eseki. Insofar as they are successful in this role, they unwittingly usurp one of the key bases of the official Church's legitimacy. The Church, already uneasy about the very existence of an unorthodox dialogue between the Virgin and Eseki, is even more nervous about the existence of mediators and intermediaries who are produced and legitimised in ways that are outside the Church's control.

Yet this is not to say that the healers ostensibly oppose their values to Christian ones—indeed, healers would like to claim the legitimacy of the Church's approval, and see themselves as co-partners in a common fight against Hindu demons and false gods. Ths discourse of the divine as elaborated by the healers is imbued with a latent and sometimes overt hostility towards indigenous Hindu religious figures. My consideration of the healers in Kanyakumari District bears some affinity with recent work on peasant healers. Folk healers have been analysed elsewhere as crystallising and activating peasant consciousness, as organic peasant intellectuals in the Gramscian sense (Connor 1982). Taussig has in turn analysed dispensers of magical medicine in South America as mediating and articulating 'the differences that both divide and constitute the wholeness of society' (class, race, town/country, etc.) (1980a, 1987). The description of healers as mediating and articulating oppositions seems to have particular relevance to their function with respect to the Mukkuvars—linking fishing and agricultural populations, mediating Christian and Hindu religions. The function of mediation is not to be understood as one of erasing the differences, or even of rendering the relations non-antagonistic. In the case of the Christian healers, the antagonism latent in a minority consciousness is kept alive. Hindu gods and goddesses are repeatedly berated, and held responsible for a great variety of misfortunes and sicknesses affecting the Christians. At the same time, in giving a bodily reality to the power of the Virgin and the saints, the healers unconsciously replicate the very Hindu popular consciousness they are ostensibly opposing. The iconography and visual detail of Christian images of the saints (male and female) and the Maataa come alive as they possess the body of the healer, appearing to her in dreams and visions, and are each given a specific mode of curing.

Mary is a woman in her forties who cures in a trance state while variously possessed by St Michael, St Anthony and the Maataa. The Maataa speaks in a more singing, rhythmic chanting voice, the saints with more staccato bursts. The saints have a more dialogic interchange with their patients—Mary will then talk to her clients with eyes open, and the interaction takes on a question and answer form. When the Maataa speaks, Mary has her eyes closed and is more withdrawn from her surroundings. The style of Tamil adopted is more formal than Mary's ordinary conversation.

These details vary from healer to healer. Mariam conducts all her healing with her back to her clients, kneeling facing the shrine which contains images of the Christian deities. However, her voice varies like Mary's, depending on which divinity speaks, and it becomes particularly fierce when she receives visitations on Wednesdays from Verghese (or St George), the one who binds the fleeing demon.

Not only the voice but the body of the healer must be altered to permit divinity to leave and enter. Mary has a kind of yawn at the beginning and end of her trance sessions, since the mouth is where the spirit enters and leaves. Her speech is punctuated by a kind of choking sound, between a cough and a clearing of the throat. Other healers, particularly when curing in a place where the divinity's presence is very strong, such as St Michael's shrine at Raja Uuru, become convulsed and shaken while possessed, hoarse of voice and drenched with sweat while healing.

The specific visual imagery of iconography becomes supremely important in the way healers bring divinity to life. St Michael is usually depicted with one sandalled foot on a speared slain demon, the other foot on the ground. When St Michael speaks through Mary, she places her foot, the *chaapaati kaalu* or the sandalled foot, on the back of a patient diagnosed of demonic possession. In Mary's visions, the Maataa appears in robes of blue, surrounded by rays of light as she descends from the sky.

In the curing sessions, the antagonism of Christian versus Hindu merges with the vigorously assertive mode in which faith healers seek to attract and keep clients. In Hinduism, curing sessions of a parallel nature are opportunities for the healer to demand greater human faith and following for the deity which has possessed him/her (Moffatt 1979, Moreno 1985). A similar atmosphere of aggressive interrogation and demands made of clients prevails among the Christian healers as well, but in their hands, such a form of social transaction becomes, in addition, a chance to demonstrate the inadequacy and evils of the dominant religion. Their opening remarks usually seek to establish the all-encompassing knowledge of the divinity possessing the healer:

Healer: *MahaLe* (Daughter)/*Mahane*(Son)
[as Maataa or saint]   Do not be afraid.
                        Rid yourself of all mistrust.
                        I know your sorrows and misfortunes.
                        I know the tears you have shed,
                        the misfortunes you have borne.

Healers usually build up a degree of extended contact with clients, since the saint or Maataa commands a number of return visits. At each sitting, the divinity commands the client to state publicly whether or not she is feeling a distinct improvement. Any success is stressed:

Healer: You came here with no faith in me.
[as St Michael]   Your husband was missing for three months,
                        and you had no money or word from him.
                        I told you not to be afraid.
                        He has now returned, has he not?

Client: Yes, he has.
[a Hindu Nadar]

Healer: Yet you had no faith.
                        You have visited my shrine at Raja Uuru.
                        Now you wish to know when you can safely
                        bring your pregnant daughter home from her
                        in-laws. Trust me in this also.

Curers usually demand a consistent and overt show of faith from the clients—by a specified number of visits to the most important local shrine of the saint or the Maataa, by donations of money. Although the subject of economic contributions—their extent and degree of compulsion—is a matter of debate between healers as well as in the peasant population generally, some healers will, in trance state, rebuke clients for not bringing enough donations as evidence of their inadequate faith. Much is made of occasions (such as the one described above), when the client is Hindu. In the interchange reported below, the client is a Hindu man worried about his failing eyesight, accompanied by his daughter:

Healer: [as St Michael]	[After opening remarks] Do not worship false gods any more. Where has it got you? [Throws holy water on his face] Are you not feeling better already?
Client [slowly]:	Yes.
Healer:	[waits for this to sink into the audience] You are in the early stages of *muulai kaachal* [brain fever]. See an English *marundu vaidiyar* [allopathic doctor]. You are being plagued by the ghost of a man who lived on street x. He was your companion on walks. [Rubs the man's back with wax from candles burning in front of the domestic shrine.] This will guard you against the *aavi* [ghost]. I wonder why none of my devotees brings me fresh candles (*molaguthiri*). You must come back to me for six visits. But do not wait to seek English *marundu* [medicine] for your complaint.

Healers who convert from Hinduism to Christianity as part of their divine ordination also report a similar Manichaean struggle between Christian and Hindu deities. Mariam, now a healer, was born into a Hindu family and was sent to a convent to work as a tailor. She continued to visit churches after her marriage, much to her mother-in-law's disapproval. She neglected the worship and upkeep of the household shrine, and became seriously ill. She refused hospitalisation and remained impervious to Hindu exorcism, asking only to be taken to St Michael's shrine at Raja Uuru. When finally taken there she lay rigid and without food for three days, at the end of which the saint came and told her: 'I have brought you, destined to die, back to life. But I will not let you live in the place inhabited by Satan. Destroy the Hindu shrine in your household and I will come and live there instead.'

The command could not be obeyed without conflict with the family, who were finally forced by Mariam's repeated serious illness and continuous visions to agree to her seeking baptism.

The efforts of the Christian healers to assert the supremacy of Christian deities over Hindu ones is contested from within the Christian population itself. In the discourse of the possessed, the visual characteristics of the Christian images and the linguistic and bodily signs of the healers in turn become material for mockery.

The discourse of the demonic

The demonic discourse is the 'Other' of the Christian divine, inverting the latter, mocking it and threatening it. At the same time it is a dialectical Other in which the distance between the two discourses is not as vast as it may first seem, and seeming opposition can even become identity. Both discourses share the same characteristic way of expressing a form of consciousness through condensed bodily metaphors.

In shrines such as Raja Uuru, where I did most of my observation of public rituals of possession and healing, the possessed pour out their anger and mockery at Christian divinities. Here, any physical or visual characteristic of the Christian divinity becomes the target for mockery and abuse, often quite clever in its transformation of the established interpretation. Thus the sandalled foot of St Michael, his *chaapathi kaal*, becomes his *nonDi kaal*, his lame foot: with one foot raised off the ground, leaning on his spear, he is mocked as a disabled, feeble old man. He is called *kuruDu kaNa*, the blind one, a *moTTai* or bald one. Similarly, the Virgin Mother's serene composure is transformed by the demonic discourse into a kind of complacency. Women go running up to her pedestalled existence inside her shrine, and shake their fist at her, demand to know who she thinks she is, seated smugly and snugly behind the steel bars that now cover her shrine. They ask what she is afraid of that she has to cower behind steel bars. Adolescent girls come repeatedly rushing over, and slap their hands on the wall immediately under the bars, and occasionally rattle the bars themselves. I was told that previously the shrine had been covered only with a glass casing, but this was repeatedly broken by the possessed.

I will concentrate here on the interpretation of female possession as paradigmatic of the discourse of the demonic. It is in women that the discourse of bodily possession—both demonic and divine—finds its fullest expression. This is true even at an empirical level: a very high proportion of both faith healers and the demonically possessed that I came across in Kanyakumari District were women. However, I am here referring primarily to the semiotics of bodily possession, not to its incidence. The female body is paradigmatic in the sense that it is able to convey the full range of the meanings codified through possession. This is particularly striking in the inversions which are the dominant trope of demonic possession. Hayden White (1978) elaborates on the meaning of trope in contemporary literary criticism:

> Tropes generate figures of speech or thought by their variation from what is 'normally' expected, and by the associations they establish between concepts normally felt not to be related or to be related in ways different from that suggested in the trope used … it is always not only a deviation *from* one possible, proper meaning, but also a deviation *towards* another meaning, conception, or ideal of what is right and proper *and true* 'in reality'. Thus considered, troping is both a movement *from* one notion of the ways things are related *to* another notion, and a connection between things so that they can be expressed in a language that takes account of the possibility of their being expressed otherwise (p.2).

In the sense discussed above, the entire discourse of the demonic can be seen as one gigantic trope, expressed not through texts but through 'the usually neglected phonic, graphic, corporeal supports' of texts and social practices (Gross 1986:128), a combination of bodily movement, words, gestures. The aim of this bodily discourse is also specific to the feminine: possessed women continually play with, invert and mock the cultural construction of femininity, directing their play at the locally produced metaphors of binding, cooling and seclusion with which the female body is disciplined. The cult of the village goddess, even when entering Christian women in an illicit manner, continues to keep alive the range of potentialities in much the same way as the image of the unruly woman on top kept open a way of symbolising social alternatives in early modern Europe (Davis 1978).

At Raaja Uuru, one can witness the visible transformation of women from respectable femininity to disorderly demon-goddess. The focal point of this transformation is the dance of the demon, *peey aaTam*. The women are brought by their families and by healers to dance. At first, resisting this expectation, the possessed women sit very still, head covered, sari demurely wrapped around. Only their eyes, fiercely brooding in an inward stare, betray that they are not the same as other ordinary worshippers gathered there. The dance or *peey aaTam* has many different levels of meaning. At one level it signifies the power of Christian divinity over the demonic—by dancing, the demon has had to make its presence overt instead of existing only through its effects, the symptoms. The powerful presence of the saints and the Virgin at the shrines torments the demon in the women—and the dance is therefore at one level an expression of torment. The *aaTam* acknowledges this dimension by bodily symbols of torment and chastisement. Women may dance with their arms pinned together at the wrist, held at the back of the body as if bound by the invisible ropes tied there by the saint. Women may roll over and over on the ground, with their ankles similarly pinned together.

To all onlookers, this is the divine work of St Michael punishing the demon.

At the same time, *peey aaTam* is utilised by the women as a moment of physical liberation, a breaking loose from the daily restraints imposed on the female body. The utilisation of dance in ecstatic possession has a long history in Tamil religion. Descriptions of this phenomenon go as far back as the poetry of the Cankam period. In the *akam* poems from this period, dance is the mode by which the healer is able to enter into a trance:

> ... man could for particular purposes call upon a special medium, the velan, 'he who (holds) the spear'; he was a kind of soothsayer or shaman, who by getting possessed by Murukan could divine the cause of various diseases, when he had entered into a trance induced by a frenzied dance and had consulted the *kalanku* oracle. In akam poems, a particular genre developed in which the velan is called to cure the sickness of a girl which in reality only her lover can cure. For example: 'My friend! When my mother, on account of my "illness", arranges for the velan to come, will that velan be able to find out about my affair with the lord of the fragrant country, when he is in the frenzy of possession?' (Hardy 1983:138–139).

His dance is called *veriyaTu*, the dance of wild frenzy. But the dance had a religious significance far wider than the figure of the healer, particularly for women. Thus from this Cankam literature we hear of 'the large market place where festivals never cease, which is crowded with girls (dancing) the *veriyaTu* of Cevvel' (Hardy 1983:139).

Under the Church's regime, dance is no longer a legitimate mode of religious experience. Indeed, there is no longer any form of dance available to men or women in the fishing community. Through the now familiar mechanism of displacement, *aaTam* re-emerges as the prime signifier of the forbidden, in the possession of Christian patients by the Hindu demonic. It still retains its old place as the crucial medium available to the healer in the cure of illness/possession, but it is no longer the healer who dances. Rather it is the worshipper of the Hindu deity, redefined as the sick patient. Sickness and possession are, however, highly ambiguous phenomena—they both reflect social expectations of the patient (that they will dance, that this dance is an expression of torment, acknowledging the power of social/ religious norms), and constitute a transgression and rupture of those norms.

In the course of the *peey aaTam*, Christian women systematically invert every one of the symbolic yet corporeal modes of containment examined so far.

Hair, usually bound, is released from its knot to hang loosely. As the women roll in the sand in front of the shrine and leap in the air, the hair acquires a wild and unkempt appearance. As the women sway with head hanging forward, the hair is used to sweep the sand. Covering the face, the hair hangs limp, then is thrown back and forth as the head thrashes around. The mere sight of Kannagi's unbound hair was sufficient to cause the terrified king of Madurai to die (see earlier reference to epic, on p.88). These women are deliberately using hair as a symbolic weapon, drawing on the rich chain of associations of unbound female hair to produce a state of awe and terror among spectators.

The sari loses its normal modest draping quality. It is now hitched up and tucked into the *paavaaDai*, or underskirt, while the *talappu* which usually covers the breasts is tucked into the side of the sari. For women now turn into acrobats: running up towards the saint ensconced in his shrine, they break into wild somersaults, and swing with their arms wound around the pillars of the *mandapam* or covering of the shrine, occasionally shinning up the pillars. Men claim that a possessed woman, infused with the strength of a tiger, can fight a man.

The adolescent girls, who form a kind of sub-group among the possessed, give the vivid impression of enjoyment, as against older women who may look troubled and angry. These young girls perform not as individuals, but as a collective. They move with a bobbing, jaunty step, hand on hip, taking delight in their freedom of movement and speech. In the course of their wanderings they may descend on faith healers, taunting and defying them. The possession of the girls merges with a kind of play, delighting in verbal games with healers, swinging around pillars, and somersaulting. Recent commentary on female hysteria and possession has attempted to make just such a suggestive connection between the theatre of the body in possession, and in other contexts such as those of circus acrobats and the play of children (Clement 1986). Clement brings them together in her commentary on the 'rite of the swing' among women said to have been bitten by the tarantula spider:

A rhythmic motion, which reproduces the rocking of infancy, pacifies. A motion reproducing the way Arachne was suspended by Athena in the threads of her web. Spider, hanged doll, the pleasure of a swing. The women swing, swing from it, don't give a hang for it, make fun of it: the Greek ritual of sacred swings is the same childish game as that of little girls' swinging (1986:21).

To the outsider at Raja Uuru, the inappropriate feeling of being present at a festival or carnival rather than among the sick and suffering is enhanced by the loud laughter and the clapping of hands from the possessed women. Young girls in Mukkuvar villages who are being schooled in the norms of femininity are told sternly by elder women when they laugh too loudly and openly: '*Pallai kaaTaade*', or 'do not show your teeth'. Open and unabashed laughter in a woman is as unpleasant as an animal baring its fangs, the snarling of a beast that shows its teeth. The possessed women blur the distinction between animal and human by inverting the signs of femininity.

Finally, there is the strong element of mockery and taunting which predominates in the speech of the possessed women. I have mentioned this feature earlier, but it deserves to be underlined since it is a striking component of the pleasure principle, the libidinous semiotic in Kristeva's sense, which surfaces here.[6] At the same time, since it emerges in the form of speech, and is not confined to bodily symptoms, the repressed is here allowed to make some impact on the conscious, to have some efficacy through the symbolic order of language. The licentious speech of the oppressed classes has always been a notable feature of their enjoyment in the *charivari* of the carnival (Davis Gordon 1978, Darnton 1984, Guha 1983). Mockery and strong language are certainly not alien to the daily speech of Mukkuvar women—but there is a difference between everyday abuse and the mockery of possessed women. I have already described the form taken by daily forms of mockery—often directed principally at other women, and reinforcing the patriarchal norms for female conduct. Among the possessed, it is directed outward, at divinity itself. The women taunt the capacity of the Christian divinities even to begin to understand and correctly identify the nature of the demonic, let alone attempt to control it. An eighteen year old shouts out: '*Ei, kuruDu kaNa* (blind one)—not even the *mantravaadis* could drive me out. Why should you think of yourself any more highly?' The speech is punctuated by loud derisory snorting sounds which identify the demonic.

The young girls hive off, run as a collective pack, hunt their prey: divinity itself. Confrontation with the divine reaches its keenest delight when the divine can answer back in human form, through the faith healers. Where the healer is also a woman, we have the ultimate spectacle: woman against woman, one representing the patriarchal Virgin/Christian Maataa, the other representing the Hindu goddess turned demon. In the excerpt quoted below, the young girls are taking full advantage of the ambiguity in the popular interpretation of Catholicism: Virgin and goddess/demon are supposed to be antithetical. Yet both possess the human body and only a very practiced and knowing reading of the bodily text can distinguish one from the other. All healers who cure as Virgin or saint depend on the maverick element of social acceptance for credibility. Most healers in fact begin their careers under a cloud of suspicion that it is the demon disguised as saint which speaks through them. It is this fine line separating community acceptance from rejection which the girls continually try to erode when mocking the healers:

Girls: *Ei paaTi* (old woman)—can you tell everyone what kind of a demon I am?

Healer: I know how tormented you are already. I will send you even greater torment until you leave.

Girls: Do you expect us to believe that you are Mikheel
                          (St Michael)? If everyone could turn into a Michael,
                          what is the point of coming into a shrine? People
                          may as well stay at home! In fact, it is not Michael
                          at all—only Cholla (Sudalai) MaaDan pretending to
                          be Michael, the old *nonDi kaal* (cripple). See—we
                          have disrupted your *muzhi* (trance state), and you
                          cannot fool these people any more.

In my account of the gender-specific production of bodily symbols I
have tried to avoid the dual tendencies of psychoanalytic and sociological reductionism that vitiate the literature on possession. My
own account of female possession gives central place to the women's
experience of cultural/bodily discipline. Recent feminist criticism of
psychoanalysis for the way it has obliterated the question of sexual
difference is apposite here (Clement 1986, Irigaray 1985). Anthropology has utilised a version of psychoanalysis which is not only
alarmingly crude (matted locks equal 'sublated penis emerging from
the head' (Obeyesekere 1981:34)), but which fails to interrogate the
phallocentrism of psychoanalysis with its 'predesignated masculine
categories, for example uncastrated woman = masculinity complex;
normal femininity = castration' (Gross 1986:135). Under the mas-
querade of a 'human' subjectivity, of a generalised human body in
which 'matted locks' have the same meaning for male and female
ascetics ('sublated penis', of course), Obeyesekere is able to obliterate the entire question of sexual difference despite the fact that
nearly all his material is based on the experience of female possession. A masculinist interpretation is meant to stand for the whole
of human experience. Even where the orthodox psychoanalytic
paradigm allows the question of sexual difference to be raised, as in
Kakar's two books on Indian culture (1981) and healing (1982), far
greater time and sympathy is spent on male fears, anxieties and
repressions than on female ones. Once again, the reductionism of
orthodox psychoanalysis presents an obstacle—in Kakar's hands, the
possession of women in India may have its fascinating local colour,
but ultimately they are all expressing a simple repressed sexual wish
framed by the familiar predesignated masculine categories referred to
above. The complex interplay of the different relations of power that
feed into the possession of the Christian women in Kanyakumari are
here emptied of their content.

     I am arguing that as long as the strategies of power inscribed on the
body are predicated on the sex of the human subject, bodily forms of
representation and inversion must also be read in a gendered way. At
the same time, this reading must give attention to the specific mode
in which possessed women speak—not in conscious sociological
commentary but with unconscious references back to the bodily basis

of femininity and divinity in popular culture. The sociological analysis of possession ignores this unconscious dimension, even while it has enabled anthropologists (Lewis 1971, Brown *et al*. 1981, Freed and Freed 1964) to note, with varying degrees of sophistication, the links between femininity and possession. In this genre, social powerlessness, sometimes accentuated by social transformation (Constantinides 1978, Curley 1973) is responsible for the production of possession in women and other disadvantaged groups. But is there no difference between women and other disadvantaged groups? In this account it is difficult to see any. Freed and Freed write: 'Opler mentions eight women who suspected ghosts and sought the aid of a shaman because of menstrual pain, death of children, barrenness, miscarriage and other ailments' (1964:170). Social tension may underlie possession, but why does it find its specific expression in the illnesses of female gynaecology? Once again, the specific content of the popular discourse on divinity and femininity in countries such as India disappears from sight.

Instead the sociological idiom focuses attention on the function of possession—is it reproducing the social order by providing a safety valve for the tensions in the system, or is it changing that order? Ultimately, this is an important question, but I have not introduced it in the foregoing analysis due to its tendency to deflect attention from a careful examination of the discourse itself. I would, however, like to close this section by pointing out that the possession of women as illness is like the malady of the twentieth century hysteric, rather than the ritual rebellion of the annual festival which has preoccupied anthropologists since Gluckmann: it cannot be planned for and put away at the end of a specified period to allow a return to normality. As such, it disrupts and ruptures the orderly reproduction of daily life and of the domestic domain, which depends crucially on the labour and cooperation of women. Illness and possession may mean the difference between a family being able to survive economically or not in communities such as the Mukkuvars, where labour power is almost the sole means of production. Illness and possession may end in cure, but they also have a disturbing tendency to recur when all seems settled: the threat of women turning into angry goddesses and demons is ever-present.

Further, possession by its very nature renders itself open to multiple interpretations within Tamil culture. It may be illness, evidence of a malign, harmful demonic presence—or it may be the exaltation of the highest form of religious experience open to humanity. Illness itself may signify disease or erotic love. To make the matter even more complex, the difference between these various phenomena can only be established through possession, in the body of the healer. Women have historically taken advantage of these open-ended possibilities—passing off the illness of forbidden erotic love as ordinary illness (Hardy 1983:138–139), or else resisting parental control of their sexuality in the name of a higher, divine bridegroom. Christian women, denied a place in the formal positions of authority within the Church, disadvantaged by poverty, illiteracy and gender, continually play on these culturally given possibilities as well, to permit them direct access to divinity. Since it is never unequivocally clear that it is the demon and not a god speaking through them, peasant women suspected of demonic possession may still strive to convince all that they are the vessels of divine grace and power. In this way, they can constitute themselves as healers, and establish a position which transcends the confines of family, kin-group, village and even caste, to cater to the peasant community.

Their establishment as healers is always open to challenge and reinterpretation—as the taunts of the demonically possessed at Raja Uuru indicate. What is not held against them, as it would be in elite religion, is their low status as poor peasant women. Indeed, their poverty and low status are emphasised in the self-representation of these healers. In detailed case histories I collected of four faith healers, the suffering caused by poverty and gender is further underlined by a period of prolonged suffering as illness, death and loss of family fortune threaten the household of the woman who has embarked on the path to divine grace. In retrospect, this period is interpreted as the trial one must undergo in order to achieve this state (cf. Obeyesekere's exegesis of the 'dark night of the soul' experienced by Sinhalese women healers). Egnor (1980) also describes the deliberate adoption of dirty, 'low caste' habits among the Hindu Tamil healers she met. Far from being a handicap, low status and the experience of being the lowest of low—a woman from the despised castes—can be turned into a positive advantage in popular religion.

Ultimately, the non-reproductive status of popular religion, and women's use of popular religion, can be pursued as a thesis only by examining the fear and contempt it inspires in the discourse of the elite. I close my examination of popular Catholicism among the Mukkuvars with a brief look at the attitudes of the Church.

The Church and popular Christianity

Priest A (two years the parish priest at KaDalkarai Uuru):

> Yes, I believe there can be possession by the devil. The *kaNaku* (faith) healers I totally oppose, since it is the devils speaking with the voice of angels. First, God would never lie—yet many of the healers' predictions are wrong. Second, judge a tree by its fruits. Yet there was a murder attempt in KaDalkarai Uuru following the 'revelation' by a healer that his neighbour had stolen his watch. God would not cause this kind of conflict. Third, look at the gap between the lives of the healers and the divine powers they claim. They are dirty, ignorant and have no purity of heart.

Genuine *peey aaTam* is recognisable by its insatiable frenzy, its fear of anything to do with the church. If cured, such cases exhibit extraordinary devotion to the church and become powerful lay preachers themselves. The majority of cases are simply psychological disorder caused by accumulated tension—disappointment in love, domestic strife, etc. A great deal of imitation is involved in such cases. I saw a young boy in KaDalkarai Uuru begin imitating the assistants to a *mantravaadi* who came to remove a *tahaDu* from his household. Such cases can respond to individual attention. I have conducted prayer groups for such people, aimed not at any devils, but at giving them peace of mind. I have also forbidden the performance of *peey aaTam* at the shrines of the saints in the parishes I work in, and such a stern stance has often curbed the outbreak of a whole wave of hysteric dancing and healing.

The *kaNaku* healers who have told you they have the sanction of the church for their activities are mistaken. They ask us priests to come and pray at their house—and we cannot refuse such a request. This they then interpret as giving our blessing to their enterprise.

Priest B (parish priest transferred from Madurai to the coastal village of KooDimonai):

We believe in evil, but not in the personalised possession of individuals by evil. There may be a few genuine cases of devil possession. For such an eventuality one or two priests in a Diocese may have learnt special prayers. But it is not needed in anything like the numbers that it occurs in the villagers' diagnoses. If people come to us with what they say is possession, we say an ordinary prayer. It seems to help them. But most are social problems. Evil itself is a social problem.

School teacher at Colachel:

Most possession cases are due to mental tension, as you can see from the high incidence among women. The tensions come from the husband's drinking, children's behaviour, overcrowding, fighting, envy, competition, everyone watching one another.

Males pass on family responsibilities to women and do not suffer as much.

There are also the true cases of possession—to be detected by the extraordinary qualities of the possessed. They recognise the names of strangers, speak foreign languages, know of events occurring in distant parts of the world. Possession by 'Hindu' spirits is simply because the more fearsome Hindu idols look demon-like to our fisherpeople. So they say it is Kali who is in them.

But there are also cases of pure fright:

ArunDavan kannuku
IrunDatillam Peey
(To the eyes of a fearful man
Everything around seems a demon.)

The shock of an uncanny encounter can affect the mind badly and encourage us to snatch at ready-made explanations.

In the responses of the priests to the phenomenon of Mukkuvar religiosity one can detect at least two lines of thought, both mutually in tension, but which unite in opposition to popular religion. The first is the official stance of the Church, which as an institution concerned with the spiritual welfare of humanity is bound to recognise the power and reality of evil, incarnated as the Devil. In the orthodox religious idiom, then, the 'reality' and distinct possibility of possession by evil is acknowledged—indeed it is the task of the Church to oppose and conquer the presence of evil and sin. Priests are therefore obliged to admit the possibility of Satanic possession, and must respond to villagers' requests for spiritual help in driving out such evil. Priests are thus unable to maintain a complete aloofness and distance from popular religion—they are implicated by reciting prayers at the request of individuals or in prayer groups, and by blessing objects of iconic status such as rosary beads over the bodies of sick or possessed villagers.

However, recognising the 'reality' of divine possession, in villagers who speak and heal as the saints and the Maataa, is quite another matter. Such villagers threaten the twin bases of the church's claim to power: its 'monopoly over mediation between man and God', to use Stirrat's phrase (1981); and its capacity to heal and cleanse humanity of sin and affliction.

Weber's notion of 'institutionalised charisma', where charisma lies not at the level of the person but at the level of the institution is elaborated by Turner (1984) with reference to traditions of sainthood in Islam and Christianity. He argues that the length of the process of canonisation ensured that 'all saints are orthodox and dead' (p.68) and cites research that the 'official' saints of the Church have been predominantly recruited from dominant, privileged classes.

The capacity of Mukkuvars and other Catholic sections of the Kanyakumari peasantry to make fluid transitions from demonic to divine possession, without any intervention or mediation from the Church, is a potent threat to this official control over the religious commodity of charisma. It must be noted immediately that the threat is not necessarily intended by the healers themselves. *KaNaku* healers would in fact be extremely gratified by the approval and ratification of the Church, and hanker for such legitimacy. Healers often tell stories of a visit from the local priest, and of their success in allaying doubts in the priest's mind about their own authenticity:

> Father James visited me when I first started getting the *muzhi*. He visited me three days in a row. He questioned me, asked why a regular church attender such as myself should behave in this fashion. I replied that if it was the devil speaking through me, I could not continue to attend church. He finally was satisfied, and gave me permission to continue, on the condition that I only use Christian prayers to heal people, and that I use my powers to convert people from non-Christian beliefs. (Mary, the healer)

While priests deny ever legitimising such activities (see priest A's statement), the popularity of a healer working from a base at her own domestic shrine may indeed spark off an attempt at cooption by the Church. Such an attempt was made at a healer's shrine in the inland village of TheruvakaDai, where the priest offered to lead a weekly prayer at the shrine. The arrangement was resisted by the healer since he would have had to accede to the shrine being closed for the rest of the week by the priest, thus cutting off the healer's access to divine power. Further, as priest A's statement acknowledges, priests are not above prohibiting transactions between healers, the possessed and the divinity by forbidding *peey aaTam* around the Church's premises. The statements of the priests therefore show none of the sanguine attitude towards healers and villagers suggested by the notion of a complementary division of labour between a 'transcendent' and a 'pragmatic' religious complex. Rather, the entire framework of priestly intervention is one of discrediting the distinctive features of popular Catholicism.

Compare for a moment such attitudes with those of the Brahman priest at ManDaikkaDu towards low-caste Hindu cults. There is a striking convergence of elite religious attitudes to be noted. The complaint of some of the more educated Mukkuvars that 'the coastal people are made to feel ashamed of their speech and ways by the priests who are trying to make Brahmans of our girls' acquires its full resonance only when placed in this context.

In this attempt to discredit popular Catholicism the traditional stance of the Church has been joined and aided by a somewhat unlikely argument of recent origin: that of sociological positivism and rationalism. Through the influence of liberation theology on the Church in south India, those such as priest B are now inclined to look upon villagers as 'the oppressed'. In this view, while a small minority of possessed are still in the clutches of the devil 'speaking in the voice of angels', the rest are simply sick, psychologically disturbed, and suffering from social problems. We are back in the realm of Western logocentrism that is evident in the sociological accounts of possession found in anthropology—once again, the denial and supercession of the place of the body in popular religion by a conscious, rational discourse.

Such a misplaced rationalism merges rather easily with an elitist attitude towards popular culture and religion. Liberation theology may be the particular conduit through which Western rationalism has influenced priestly attitudes, but it is conveyed equally effectively through schooling and the kind of education it inculcates. It represents a stance which unites priests even with educated Mukkuvars who would be inclined to be fiercely critical of priestly power and corruption on all other fronts. The language of the school teacher, a Mukkuvar staunchly opposed to the Church's power, is virtually indistinguishable from the priests'. In both cases, the Mukkuvar villagers emerge as impressionable, fearful—always inferior. In the new version of priestly religion, one may attack social problems, but religion is still individualistic. Each individual villager is supposed to be ruled by his or her *sammanasu* or conscience and utilise nothing but prayers to conquer and combat the evil in themselves. The fact that villagers allow evil and good to battle it out externally, as the Virgin and the Demon; that they experience this battle in a collective mode, as part of a group at the healers' shrines or at the shrines of the saints; that they experience this collectivity through the medium of their bodies and in an altered state of consciousness—all these features are still anathema to the new radicalism in the Church and among educated villagers. One may almost speak of a 'Protestant Catholicism' in the making, one perhaps even further from popular Catholicism than the traditional stance of the Roman Catholic Church.

Popular religion as cultural struggle

Mukkuvar popular religion has acquired some of its specific features from its involvement in a terrain which may be defined as a cultural battlefield. The ability to mark out an autonomous stance in a cultural terrain is directly related to the strength (economic, political) of the partners engaged in battle. As part of a broad grouping of castes, the artisan-merchant bloc, fisherpeople have enjoyed a cultural autonomy which must be related to (but cannot be wholly explained by) their freedom from economic subservience. One can easily imagine how much more heavily compromised would be the religious practices of economically dependent castes such as landless agricultural labourers. Moffatt's ethnography of just such a group (1979) testifies to their replication of Sanskritic hierarchies within their own religious cults—but his dismay at having to report this also testifies to an underlying misconceived quest for an autonomous subjectivity among the subjugated.

At the same time Moffat—and indeed most functionalist interpreters of religion—underestimate the tensions which underlie hegemony, and which require that hegemony to be constantly re-affirmed and reconstructed. Growing evidence indicates that castes penalised by Sanskritic beliefs will modify them to allow themselves a measure of dignity and some capacity to shape their own lives. Moffatt's own ethnography shows how different are the explanations offered by Brahmans and untouchables on the origins of caste and untouchability. The former stress karma, the notion of untouchables having earned their low status by an accumulation of impurities. The latter typically stress upper caste trickery and their own naivety in allowing themselves to lose status. Kolenda (1964) presents similar evidence

on the sweepers' view of karma theory. Even such minor modifications and inflections are important for groups whose situation is
defined by their extreme dependency.

Cultural processes, whether of myth or ritual, may reflect the
standpoint of the hegemonic elite by synthesising and defusing latent
antagonisms, which is why functionalist interpretations (such as
Beck's otherwise excellent account, published in 1981, of the goddess
festival in village Tamil Nadu) retain a surface plausibility and force.
However, what such interpretations fail to do is to interrogate these
as process, or bear witness to the interplay of power. Guha (1985)
attempts such a deconstruction in his account of the myths surrounding the lunar eclipse and the use that untouchable ex-tribal groupings
have made of these myths.

A possible pitfall here is simply to equate non-Sanskritic elements
with an inherent class bias in favour of the dominated. Neither
Sanskritic nor non-Sanskritic ideology is inherently 'elite' or 'subaltern'. Rather, the two constitute distinctive moments of religious
history which now coexist and constitute cultural resources or raw
material for different classes or caste blocs to define and utilise. It
would, however, be fair to say that given the overwhelming utilisation
of Sanskritic ideology to uphold caste and patriarchal supremacy,
groups seeking to subvert this supremacy have found richer materials
to hand in the non-Sanskritic tradition which has proved particularly
forceful in the context of colonialism and post-colonial transformations. The contrast drawn within the non-Brahman movement of the
south, between Brahmanism and a Dravidian culture uncorrupted by
Brahman importations, parallels the contrast drawn by the urban
untouchable ideologies of the Lucknow Charmars studied by Khare
(1984), between an Indic tradition (Buddhist, Jain and ascetic
religious traditions) and the Hindu tradition. Parallel political appro-
priations of the goddess tradition have occurred in the nationalist
movement (Ratte 1985) and more recently, in the urban feminist
movement in the 1970s. Such utilisations represent comparatively
articulate, conscious challenges to cultural and political hegemony.
In the case of the popular Catholicism found in Kanyakumari and
among castes such as the Mukkuvars, the antagonisms between elite
and subaltern interpretations are no more than implicit.

In viewing popular religion as a site of cultural struggle I am
signalling a break from the characterisation of world religions as
composed of two complementary complexes (Mandelbaum 1966). In
such formulations, the place of the body in peasant religiosity is
recognised and at the same time mis-recognised. In Mandelbaum's
characterisation, popular religion serves as an example of a pragmatic
complex which complements a transcendental complex. The first
problem here lies with the effacement of the relation between social
class, power and religious culture. Each complex may have different
concerns and be serviced by different personnel (shamans and

priests), but both are adhered to by all sections of Indian society and in the same manner. Here the problem of power and struggle disappears entirely in a cosy relationship of mutual affirmation and homogeneity in the different sections of the social structure.

The second problem is one which would remain even if we reintroduced questions of class and power into this schema. This has to do with the characterisation of popular religion as pragmatic. It comes up again in Bryan Turner's recent article (1984). In discussing the relation between scholarly and mass Islam, he places the matter squarely in class terms: 'Rather than treating Islam as a "decline" from or "corruption" of pure Islam, popular religion may be regarded as a form of "practiced Islam" and the relationship between scholarly religion and its popular manifestations as an interaction between social groups interpreting their practices by reference to common formulae' (pp.55–56).

However, when it comes to characterising the 'mundane interests and needs' of the rural peasantry, we find in Turner a strikingly behaviourist interpretation: these are about the 'acquisition of remedies and cures'. First pragmatic, and now mundane! Certainly, popular religion sets up its own practices, exemplified in the pilgrimages to shrines and healers. The healers give the religious paradigm its efficacy, the point at which it is demonstrated to have a real transformative power over the material world. But to reduce the discourse to the pragmatic cure-seeking behaviour of the peasantry is to rob it of its own specific assemblage of meanings.

Yet another way of minimising popular religion is not only to interpret it as concerned with cure-seeking behaviour, but to see illness as a 'liminal' period during which all religious and social taboos are suspended. The readiness of popular believers to cross religious boundaries is here again reduced to a kind of pragmatism. The desperation of people during illness is enough to drive them to try anything: a Christian faith healer, a Hindu *mantravaadi*, Western allopathic medicine. Such eclectic strategies are, of course, striking features of villagers' approach to illness. However, the reason they are able to move with such ease from one to the other relates back to the problematic, one which not only relates peasants divided by official religious barriers, but one which integrates the peasant view of illness with the peasant view of the place of the body in religion, as a part of everyday life.

In order to dispute this behaviourism I have examined the distinctive and systematic interrelation of concepts in popular Catholicism. This is a consciousness necessarily eclectic, deriving strands from diverse sources. However, the principle of selectivity in the way they are incorporated emphasises some elements, gives different inflections to others while yet other, fundamentally incompatible, elements are suppressed altogether.[7] With regard to Hinduism, the Sanskritic construction of divinity and femininity along the grid of purity and

pollution is virtually suppressed. Popular Hindu images of a multivalent conceptualisation of femininity have more resonance—but cannot
be incorporated untransformed due to tensions between Christian
fishing castes and Hindu agricultural ones. The tensions allow the
Church to reaffirm and establish its hegemony over the coastal
people. We thus have the splitting of the multivalent goddess and
the projection of her anger onto the Hindu population.

In my analysis, therefore, the actual content of the popular religious consciousness is vital to analysing the kinds of relationships
(of antagonism, transformation, suppression) that this consciousness
forges with the rest of the peasantry and with elite culture. In his
'Deconstruction of the popular', Stuart Hall argues that it is the
tension between the culture of the elite and the culture of the
periphery which determines what is popular from one historical
period to the next (1981). For him, the content of each category
(elite/popular cultural activity) is irrelevant to the definition of the
popular in any given period: it is forces and relations which sustain
the difference. Hall's approach, a useful corrective to a trivially
descriptive social history, seems unduly structuralist in the end.
Anthropological traditions, thanks to the care given by the ethnographer to content and detail, have always had some inbuilt corrective
to the construction of content-less structuralist boxes—but have been
notably deficient in paying attention to the central way in which
power is implicated in the production of knowledge. Representations
of Indian culture as a unified and shared set of meanings, which
forego the investigation of hegemony as an ongoing process, which is
always under some form of contestation, are striking illustrations of
this critical failure. Practices which have contributed to this failure
are now under challenge within anthropology as a result of a more
generalised critique of conventional modes of representation in
Western social theory. An introduction by Clifford to a set of essays
on the practice of ethnographic writing (Clifford and Marcus 1986),
states: 'If culture is not an object to be described, neither is it a
unified corpus of symbols and meanings that can be definitively
interpreted. Culture is contested, temporal and emergent' (p.19).

5 The new political economy of gender: capitalism and the creation of a seasonal male proletariat

If local relations of power have played their part in shaping the nature of popular culture among the Mukkuvars, supra-local relations of power have also to be taken into account, for the community has been exposed to new forces for change originating in the outside world. There have been changes in the alignment of classes in the post-colonial State, leading to the formulation of new economic policies stressing modernisation and development. These policies in turn have encouraged the emergence of new forms of investment in the production process of fishing. Artisanal fishing has been assigned its place in a world capitalist system. Work, marriage and living patterns, even the most intimate facets of life in the Mukkuvar community, are now liable to transformation by this overwhelming new force in their lives. We need to take a step back, as it were, to examine the forms of determination occasioned by the articulation of Mukkuvar men and women into a global mode of production.

Every year, around September–October, the start of the local 'lean' season in fishing, a flurry of activity sweeps the coastal villages of Kanyakumari, carrying with it a rhythm quite different from that of ordinary male departures to and from the ocean. This time, the men are preparing for a much longer absence from the village, designed to allow them to seek alternative employment during the seasonal slump in local fishing. Instead of the usual 5–8 hours, the absence will last a minimum of two months, and for many as long as seven months. Some are destined to work on mechanised fishing vessels in various parts of the southern coast, while others set off with their *kaTTumaram* and artisanal fishing gear to work in Kerala.[1] In the village of KaDalkarai, a little more than half the households (52 per cent) contribute at least one male member to this annual outflux.[2]

A population movement of such major proportions is in itself of considerable sociological importance. But when it is, in addition, sharply differentiated along sexual lines, it becomes quite central to my examination of the relationship between gender and capitalism.

I begin by looking at the introduction of new systems of payment in the mechanised fishing sector, entailing altered relations between owners and workers. I then go on to trace some of the implications of the prolonged physical separation of male workers from the home, a new factor brought to bear on the relations between men and women. The world of the village or *uuru*—when viewed from the perspective of newly proletarianised younger men—is increasingly a world of women and of leisure.

For the men working on mechanised boats, there are two principal destinations: Rameswaram, in the eastern district of Tamil Nadu known as Ramanathapuram; and centres of mechanised fishing in Kerala such as Cochin and Ernakulam. There are also a few other ports of call of lesser importance to Kanyakumari men—Keezkarai, also situated in Ramanathapuram District, and Tuticorin, located in the Tirunelveli District of Tamil Nadu. There are also men who have in the recent past travelled much further afield, to states such as Karnataka and even Orissa. Table 5.1 sets out the data for the village of KaDalkarai, indicating the rough proportions of households involved in each of these different destinations.

Work in the mechanised fishing sector

The different centres of mechanised fishing in Kerala and eastern Tamil Nadu offer contrasting conditions of employment to the men they attract every year from Kanyakumari District. In Kerala, for example, the men are paid on a share basis, whereas in Rameswaram they are paid fixed wages. The significance of these differences will be made clear shortly. No matter where they work, however, the men are subject to a fundamental alteration in the way that the product of labour is distributed between the owners of equipment and the labourers. The new share system of payment in Kerala is only superficially similar to the one used in KaDalkarai Uuru. From a situation where men working on a *KaTTumaram* could expect more than 60 per cent of the divisible earnings, in Kerala they can now expect to share between themselves only about 40 per cent of the takings, while the owners' share mounts to 60 per cent. As a percentage of gross earnings, the men's share amounts to much less than this—13 per cent in mechanised trawlers, and 26 per cent in gill-netters (Vijayan 1980). The share system operative in Orissa grants an even larger share to the owner—he gets 70 per cent of the divisible income, leaving 30 per cent for the crew to share.

Typically, a crew would consist of four or five workers: a master, a driver and two or three deckhands. The divisible earnings are calculated after various deductions have been made. The major portion of

Table 5.1   **Households involved in seasonal migration in KaDalkarai Uuru**

Destinations within Tamil Nadu	Number of households contributing at least one male member
Rameswaram	65
Keezkarai	9
Tiruchendoor	2
Madras	2
Pondicherry	1
Tuticorin	3
Destinations outside Tamil Nadu	
Kerala	57
Andhra Pradesh	2
Karnataka	1
Orissa	4
Mysore	1

Note: The above information would have to be modified for other coastal villages, which exhibit a different emphasis in destinations. The adjoining villages of Vaniakudi and Kurumbanai for example, send men to Karnataka in greater numbers than is the case for KaDalkarai Uuru.

these deductions is made up of fuel costs. Also included in the deductions is the *beta* (money for meals cooked on board), as well as the 'tea money' (which is usually a small amount such as Re5 per person per day). One villager in KaDalkarai Uuru calculated the proportions of the different deductions to be of the following order: If the total catch is worth Re1000, then Re200 goes on diesel, Re200 on food, plus Re5 per person for tea.

By the time all these deductions are made, workers often feel it is simply not worth their effort to work on mechanised craft: 'At least one gets something most days on the *maram [kaTTumaram]*, whereas in the boat, the costs of diesel and so on eat up most of the catch. One has to catch a lot to make any money' (a KaDalkarai villager, personal communication).

Nevertheless, Kanyakumari fishermen prefer working under a share system to the wage system. In Orissa, the fishermen from Kanyakumari, Kerala and other parts of Tamil Nadu have tended to avoid working for boat-owners who pay by the wage system of payment. It is left to the less skilled Telugu fishermen to supply the labour for these owners (Vijayan 1980). In Rameswaram, where the only operative system of payment is wage labour, the men have no choice.

It is easy to see why men express a resistance to working under such a system: in Rameswaram, a driver receives Re350 in monthly wages, but the coolies or other workers would receive as little as Re50 per month, plus a *beta* of Re2 daily. Food, worth Re2 per person, is provided daily, even when the men are not working. In this system, incentives are not built into the mode of payment itself but come in the form of a bonus. A percentage of the catch—usually around two per cent—is paid when the catch is above Re600.

Having said this, I have as yet described only the quantitative dimension of the changes in working relationships between the owner of the means of production and the labourers. More profound still are the qualitative changes. No longer is the owner simply another villager who happens to be luckier—often on a purely temporary basis—but who still works alongside the rest of the crew, accepting only one extra share as compensation for his upkeep of the equipment. In the new system, the owner may still work with the crew, but this is no longer necessarily the case, and he is entitled to claim a share, purely on ownership grounds, which is far in excess of that claimable by men contributing the labour.

The economic distance between owners and workers is accentuated by regional and linguistic barriers. Given the vast labour catchment areas drawn upon by mechanised fishing, labour recruitment is necessarily mediated by the intervention of labour brokers—a function usually fulfilled by the driver of a mechanised boat. Such labour contractors and brokers have a long and continuing history in the traditions of labour recruitment in colonial and post-colonial India.[3]

Little is known about the life in the migrant settlements set up by seasonal workers in the centres of mechanised fishing. It would be premature to speculate on the impact of labour recruitment on the nature of the emergent labour force among fishermen. Reliance on the driver to supply the crew certainly accentuates region-based and even village-based forms of recruitment, which in turn creates divisions not only between owners and labourers, but within the workforce itself.

A crucial dimension characterising the institution of the labour broker in other parts of Indian industry is, however, missing in the fishing community. While the driver may attempt to 'settle in' the other crew members from his community, there seem to be none of the various forms of labour control and paternalistic modes of hierarchy between the driver and crew members which are characteristic of the *jobber* in the textile industry or the *sardar* in the construction industry.[4] The function of labour control is so alien to the usual work situation of fishermen that a foreman class has had to be created afresh by the owners of mechanised boats. In Orissa, the boat-owners have created a category of supervisors to control and watch the migrant workers. The supervisors are drawn, not from the fishing community at all, but from among educated unemployed youth in Kerala (Vijayan 1980).

Within the immigrant labour force, Kanyakumari fishermen have emerged as a labour aristocracy—as skilled, highly prized and sought-after fishermen to operate the new mechanised boats. On the basis of this special status, men from Kanyakumari and Kerala have been able to bargain for themselves an entirely more favourable mode of

payment than have the men from Andhra Pradesh and Orissa. While
the former are paid on a share basis, the latter have had to settle
for a fixed daily *beta* of Re7.50 (Vijayan 1980). Distinctions of
skill within the workforce are thus compounded and further institutionalised by different regional backgrounds and different economic
circumstances.

The economic logic which drives men from artisanal fishing work to
mechanised fishing cannot be faulted in monetary terms. While the
return to labour is far reduced in the new system of payment, each
individual income may still be higher than in artisanal fishing, and
according to Kurien and Willman (1982:47), the average worker on a
trawler may earn twice that of a *kaTTumaram* fisherman.

What is masked by this impeccable economic logic, however, is an
entire social revolution. A fisherman's journal, sections of which I
reproduce under two headings below, marks the point of entry for my
exploration of male experiences of work and the domestic sphere.

THE WORLD OF WORK AND MEN

January 6th:

I left for Kerala and arrived in Trivandrum. I caught
the East Cannanore Express to Ernakulam. I left
my belongings with friends and went to the pictures.
There was no room anywhere to sleep—so I slept on
the harbour platform. Most men here sleep this way
anyway.

January 7th:

I went to the harbour and the boat was in. I drove it
and berthed it after the fish were sold. Laser, the
maamaa [maternal uncle] of the boat-owner came
fishing with us. We left at 3 pm in the evening, with
gill-net. At 5.30 pm we started laying out the nets,
and completed this at 6.30. We then exchanged
stories—about local fishing, exchanged information.
Only after that was there light talk. We slept
between 9 and 12 pm, but always in fear of a ship
running into us. One always has to be a watchman.
We began hauling the nets at 12, completed this at
3. At 3 am we headed back for the shore, arriving at
5 to eat old food and bathed.

January 9th:

Tellicheri, Kerala: We went fishing at 4 am. We laid
our prawn net. It was not yet dawn—about 5 am—
when we hauled in our nets, to find them torn by
another boat's propeller. This caused a fight and we
seized the other boat's net. We frightened the other
boat-owner and he ran off. In our joy over this, we
neglected our own nets—and found that it had got
caught up in the propeller of our boat. All the crew
were local Kerala men—they did not know how to
go under water and disentangle the net. So I did. It
was very cold in the water—and I cut my hand.

They turned the boat back to shore to take me to hospital.

January 10th:

I reported for work as usual, but the owner of the boat kept me ashore. There is no pleasure in that—all my friends are at work, and there is only the cinema to go to.

January 19th:

I am now working on a boat at Neendakara.[5] We have just hauled fish worth Re503. This is a place of *suham* [contentment]. There is time to sleep, one can get off the boat and rest. I have a woman friend who is like a sister to me. She is now the wife of the boat-owner, but is also from Puthenthurai.[6] I played with their child and slept, but worried about my wife's delivery and her sterilisation operation. I miss her attentions. An ant kept troubling my ear, and I thought of how she would have soothed me. I want to go to Muscat, but I want to take the family with me—get my wife to see the world. God—help my wife.

February 1st:

I am on the boat. We could not locate the reef. Up till 11.45 pm we were just running around. At 12 pm we located it. Big fish, around in twos and threes. This is a new experience for me. I also caught a big one. Perkman's hand hit my forehead and it swelled up. At 6 am we turned back to the shore. At 9.30 am we were ashore. We packed the fish in ice and were home at 12. Verghese's wife told me of a letter for me which she had opened and read. I grieved in my mind.

February 2nd:

My mind is still heavy. We went to sell the fish to the company. Jervasin's mother asked for the letter. Re1078 was the price we got for the fish. On coming back, a friend in Customs called me and told me he could sell his boat's diesel on the sly. I said I would reply later. I got the letter and read it. I have been deceived—my wife writes I have had a girl child. Worse, she writes of being grieved at not having me by her side. She told me of her sterilisation operation and the pain it had caused. The electricity had been cut during the operation, delaying it. There was not even enough money on hand to buy milk. I must ask someone's permission and go back to see her. I am decided on this. I found the sum for my return fare as follows—the food money, Re64, and my share of Re60. From Neendakara I left at 3 pm. I am going home to console my wife.

THE WORLD OF IDLENESS, KINSHIP AND WOMEN

January 1st:

Today is the new year. I pray for improvement in my life, and before I get off my straw mat, my wife awoke me with a sweet in my mouth. I put one half of it back in her mouth. My nephew wished me a new year. My *maami* [mother-in-law] seems upset with me. I played with my children. I went and bathed along with my children. There I wished Carmel Mary a long life. After eating I slept. At 4.30 I had lunch. I joked with *maami* and made her happy with me. We began speaking again. Only after that did I have *nimmadi* [peace of mind]. I am now going to bed.

January 2nd:

We could not go to Kerala because of disturbances there between *kaTTumaram* and boat-owners. *Akka's* [elder sister's] husband came from Rameswaram. I told him of the hot water she had spilled on herself while he was away. I also confessed I had not been able to visit her at the time. He went without saying a word and bought me a cup of tea.

January 3rd:

There is a *chilla maram* [poisonous tree] near our house. Ignoring advice to leave it alone, I went and cut a limb off it. I was unaffected by the milky poison —showing further my immunity against poison. Two snake bites have left me immune. It is believed that if you make yourself strong with liquor, even poisonous snakes will leave you unharmed.

[Away on mechanised fishing boats]

February 3rd:

Arrived safe back in the village. I bought Horlicks and Boost worth Re20 for my wife. Her mother was not at home when I arrived. She had gone to my *kolundi* [wife's younger sister] in Pallam. My wife has had her sterilisation operation. For three months she must not have *uDal uravu* [sexual relations]. But I had relations with her. She cried out that she had a pain in her belly. I consoled her. At 8 pm *maami* came home. Until then, I did everything for my wife. I went and bought her medicine so that she did not need to walk.

February 4th:

I was to go back to Kerala today, but didn't. I was told by *akka* [elder sister] that *maami* did not help my wife during delivery. I did not say anything to *maami*. I borrowed Re25 from *akka*. A man came from Pallam and said that Millus' sister-in-law's husband was seriously ill. I went there at once. My

maami has forced my *kolundi* to wed against her
wishes. But I could not bring myself to dislike the
mapillai [bridegroom]—he has already arrived, after
all. The real reason is that my *kolundi*, who I value
as my life, is one whose welfare I pray for. I
therefore prayed for Millus. God—give Millus a
good life.

February 6th:

Today is Kannike Maataa's *thiruvilla* [feast day].
This morning Rajni came to seek our blessings for
her *pudu nanmai* [First Communion]. We blessed
her and gave her Re5. We owe Mary Re337 for the
chit fund.[7] She came on aggressive and I put her off.
Even after taking the eighth *chit*, we are short of
Re1000. We have to give Re445.

Akka came and spoke of my going overseas. Not
having anyone to help her, my wife asked *akka* to
stay behind. Agnes accused me of having put a
mantra [sorcery] spell on her boat. That sorely
troubled my mind.

The experience of time and work intensity: *kaTTumaram* versus the trawler

The excerpts quoted above, dealing with the life of a migrant fisherman, are taken from the journal kept by a fisherman living in neighbouring Colachel. The man, whom I shall call John, was in some
ways atypical of other men who worked as immigrant fishermen.
Young and ambitious, he had committed himself to working right
through the year away from home, with casual jobs on mechanised
craft. However, he was employed not as an unskilled worker but as
the driver, implying some degree of mechanical skill. As the journal
reveals, he was further planning a trip to try his luck overseas, in
the Middle East. The very fact of his keeping a journal sets the
man apart from other fishermen in his degree of literacy and
self-reflexivity. Nevertheless, the record he has kept of daily life in
the village and at work in Kerala highlights themes shared by other
men in the village.

Although the journal represents only a brief period of John's life, it
covers two significantly distinct parts of an immigrant fisherman's life:
periods in the village, waiting to go back to work in Kerala (or
elsewhere), as well as working periods in mechanised fishing. While
there are other threads to be picked out of this unique text, we will
begin with this, one of the most salient dichotomies in the lives of
Kanyakumari fishermen today. Work, for a good part of the year, is
located in a space geographically and culturally distinguished from
the village, while the village itself becomes synonymous with idleness,
involvement in family affairs, and a structuring of days and nights

completely different to the intensive work schedules dictacted by mechanised fishing.

A good deal of social history dealing with the transition from pre-capitalist to industrial capitalism has been concerned precisely with tracing this process whereby new barriers are created between 'work' on the one hand and 'leisure' on the other. As long as labour contained within it elements of self-fulfilment, relaxation and sheer enjoyment, the frenetic pursuit of such pleasures outside the confines of work, as we know it today, remained unnecessary. It has been left to the anthropologists and historians to remind those living under advanced capitalism in the West that such divisions are neither necessary nor universal.

KaTTumaram *fishing*

The first thing that strikes one about *kaTTumaram* fishing is its discontinuity. Work is regulated both by the seasons and by the patterns of nature, which may vary from day to day. Rough surf may make setting out to fish impossible or dangerous; the wind may not be favourable; the current may be one that cannot be risked in case it prevents a timely return to the shore (Kurien and Willman 1982:46). The maximum number of days men would fish in a year would rarely exceed 105 out of 365. Furthermore, these working days are concentrated into 'peak seasons' for the more important species such as anchovy, sardines, mackerel and prawns.[8] During these seasons, the pace of work for the men, and for the women waiting at the shore, is frantic: as against the single but long-drawn out trip that men might take during other periods, the peak season witnesses several trips back and forth during a single day. Fishing during the slack season has built into it long periods of waiting. The women, who may not be particularly in evidence on the beach in the slack season, are drawn into heavy labour at peak times, and are continually on the beach to dry and guard their men's catch, and eventually to salt and sell it.

For the men, days spent not working—and this includes the Sunday of every week, as well as much longer stretches of time when the weather is inclement, or fish not available—are spent in more or less complete idleness. Some ancillary tasks related to fishing may be undertaken, such as sewing and finishing nets woven by women, mending them or dyeing the sails in tamarind-based dye. The men also make their own paddles from bamboo poles, but the making of boats and sails is left to specialists. Apart from these tasks, time on land is spent eating, sleeping, gambling, drinking and visiting nearby tea-shops and movie theatres. One might see these activities as periods of physical renewal—the necessary other side to the total exhaustion of intensive labour, often concentrated in periods of minutes when swift decisions have to be taken and nets hauled. To a certain extent the pattern is one dictated by the peculiarities of fishing: the entire production cycle, as far as the men are concerned, is compressed into a day. Unlike the long drawn out rhythms of agrarian seasons, production time is measured in minutes rather than days and weeks. The location of production—out at sea—itself dictates separation from the land-based world of leisure, recreation, the family and women.

My earlier discussion (in Chapter 1) of the persistence of a substantial degree of egalitarianism in the working relationships of crews in artisanal fishing, the absence of marked polarisation between the owners and workers, or between their families, and the remarkable degree of class and caste homogeneity in villages such as KaDalkarai Uuru, would all suggest that artisanal fishermen share with other pre-capitalist groups (such as self-employed artisans and small farmers) a substantial degree of control over their working lives. It remains to be seen how the advent of mechanised fishing has affected this characteristic quality of men's work.

A final word about work and leisure patterns in the village—the alternation of activity and complete idleness must be specifically seen as a feature of male work. To the extent that female work is ancillary to the sphere of male production—in activities such as weaving nets, drying and salting fish, and to a certain extent handling the sale of fish—women are also subject to the same rhythm of seasonality, tides, currents, winds and the movement of shoals of fish. However, women's work includes that other range of activities: food preparation, the care of the young, nursing the sick and tending to the men when they are home; their work dictates a very distinct mode of working. Geographical movement away from the land is not a precondition for commencing work.

Divisions between work and non-work are blurred by combining a great variety of tasks. A typical female task such as the weaving of nets is much more likely to be interrupted by the demands of childcare, housework, the arrival of one of the men, than are the male tasks associated with fishing. It is an index of how ingrained the sexual division of labour becomes that such punctuations of one's tasks are not regarded as interruptions at all, by either men or women, but rather as of the nature of women's work per se. At the same time, the extent to which women are able to mix their tasks, and combine them with a certain degree of social interaction—for example, groups of women may decide to sit down together to weave nets and sing songs or talk—is also a powerful index of the degree to which their labour process is not dictated by the external authority of a manager or supervisor, either in the shape of a boat-owner or his appointed agent.

But if women's work is less supervised than men's work, it is also more continuous.[9] It is therefore important to make it clear that when we talk of the transitions in men's work rhythms we have in no sense said anything as yet about what the women are experiencing.

Trawler fishing

What then of the new work discipline proposed by mechanised fishing? The alteration on the agenda is potentially a vast one. Mechanised trawlers can fish all the year round. Being mechanised and proceeding to sea from protected harbours, they are far less susceptible to rough weather and heavy surf. This means that they propose a work intensity and regularity which far exceeds even the few types of fishing—such as hook and line or the combination of drift-net and *kaTTumaram*—which could theoretically operate at any time of the year (see Kurien and Willman 1982:67–70).

While men may work harder in artisanal fishing than they do in mechanised fishing in any one given quarter, the pressure of work is far more relentless and the total work intensity much higher in mechanised work. Associated with the increase of intensity is the evolution of a greater degree of predictability and technological control over the production process. Where previous technology depended on waiting for the catch to come to the *kaTTumaram*, shrimp trawlers and purse-seiners operate on a more active principle— trawlers plough and sweep the sea bed, while purse-seiners encircle shoals of fish. These methods, which permit a more even and predictable curve of production through the year, also encourage the owners of the equipment to increase the intensity with which capital and labour are put to work. As a result, the absolute output increases and there is a more even distribution of catch (Kurien and Willman 1982).

If we refer back to John's journal at this stage (page 117), the discussion of transition in time and labour intensity sheds a new meaning on the way he meticulously records the time taken by each stage of the labour process: the departure from shore, the laying out of the nets, hauling them in, turning back, the arrival on shore. Each entry marks the completion of one stage of the process. On shore another cycle begins with the packing of the fish in ice—something John would not have seen often in Kanyakumari fishing—the sale of the fish to the company, the realisation of cash payment.

Apart from the intensity of the work routines—including long night shifts, in which one always has to be a watchman, even while snatching a few winks, for fear of a ship running into the trawler— something else comes across from the descriptions. This is the way in which work provides the dominant framework and meaning in the lives of migrant workers. For men taken out of their village and the social network provided by the community there, the work routines assume the importance they do in the journal because they hold within them almost the entire ensemble of social relations that life as a migrant fisherman has to offer them.

The situation is rendered all the more acute by the fact that the routines obtain only on a seasonal, temporary basis and there is seldom the opportunity to forge lasting relationships outside the workplace. Until John signs on for work and is out at sea, he has little contact with other people, little opportunity for an exchange of stories or catching up with local news—'light talk', as John calls it. These opportunities occur in the lulls between periods of intensive activity on the boat. The various dramas that are enacted as part of these intensive work periods—the discovery of a new breeding ground, of new types of fish, finding one's nets torn and the consequent challenge and fight with the other crew, being the one to dive underwater and rescue the net—all provide the daily dimension of adventure that fishermen thrive on.

Away from this work context, staying back on shore to rest his injury, John mopes around, at a loss to know what to do: 'There is no pleasure in that—all my friends are at work, and there is only the cinema for entertainment.' This loss of purpose affects any fisherman on land, particularly when kept there by sickness or injury. One of the most embittered men I came across was a young man in KaDalkarai Uuru who was physically immobile and no longer able to fish as a result of a gunshot wound incurred from police firings at the communal riots of 1982. In less extreme circumstances, village society normally has enough overlapping social networks to sustain periods of inactivity. The city instead offers enjoyment based on passive consumption, the pleasure of the spectacle. Some men, like John, are bored by such pleasures. For others they outstrip anything the village can provide. A man who had come back to the village in the middle of a work season due to lack of adequate catch in Kerala complained: 'You see me back here today, lying around here due to the lack of any fish out there. In Kerala, on an "off" day like this, I would have gone out for tea, seen the cinema, drunk *shaarayam* [country liquor], watched ships and foreigners. There is a lot of "jolly"[10] there.' Other pleasures include the purchase of manufactured commodities such as wrist watches and transistors, and fashionable clothes. In poorer regions such as Orissa such lavish habits have created resentments among the local, less skilled fishermen: 'The Kerala and Tamil Nadu migrant fishermen spend a good deal of their earnings in luxurious consumer goods when they earn much money during the good season. But this itself has led to many problems for them. The local people who still have traditional and feudal values do not like the "superfluous" life style of the migrant workers' (Vijayan 1980:33).

Similar discrepancies arise when the men come back to the villages of Kanyakumari, resulting in tensions between the households that send men out and those which do not, and between the fishing community and the agricultural castes who see the finery—young fishermen in their flared trousers and platform-heeled thongs, wrist watches and transistors have the reputation of being the 'flashiest' people in the district—but not the continuing poverty of the community.

Transition between different modes of work

Transition from agriculture to urban industrial capitalism can be a harsh and often shocking experience for peasants (see Berger 1975 for a phenomenological description of the experience). In the case of Kanyakumari fishermen, the harshness and abruptness of the transition is considerably softened by a number of factors. First, they are still employed as fishermen. Second, even mechanised fishing requires skill and initiative in the men. John's journal is full of episodes showing the continued role of skill, luck, chance and excitement. No time and motion study could be conducted on such varied activities— a sure indication that the rigid work norms of industrial capitalism cannot be fully instituted here.

The skill and initiative still required of the men hired in mechanised fishing also allows them, particularly the favoured men from Kanyakumari, to exercise some considerable degree of control over the production process and over the terms of the labour contract. If, on the one hand they have lost in terms of the distribution of the product, on the other they have retained some degree of flexibility as to how they work when they are out at sea. As well they exercise some influence over how long they work, the holidays and breaks they would like to take. The very fact that a labourer such as John is able to read of his wife's illness, announce his decision to ask for permission to go back and see her ('I am decided on this'), and arrive at home the next day is an indication of his power as a skilled worker who is respected by the boat-owner and his family, and can therefore absent himself and still come back to a job. The strain of migration is softened when it is to a place such as Kerala, which is close to Kanyakumari, and where the men are 'respected' by the boat-owners for whom they work. Due to this geographical and social proximity, trips back to the village are frequent, structured around social occasions requiring their presence: the birth of a child, illness at home, religious festivals such as Christmas and Easter.

Such control over the terms of the labour contract can in no way be taken for granted even by Kanyakumari fishermen. In Rameswaram, where the men have been unable to insist on modes of payment along a share basis, they are wage labourers in a much fuller sense of the term. Here they are further away from home, more vulnerable as migrant labourers. Even though they are linguistically more at home in the east coast of Tamil Nadu, a greater cultural gulf separates them from the local people than in Kerala, which was previously a part of the same state of Travancore as was Kanyakumari. Today the ties born of marriage exchanges still occasionally link the fishing villages of Kanyakumari with those of southern Kerala. John, for example, stays with the family of a woman originally from a Kanyakumari fishing village, now married to a boat-owner in Neendakara. Such ties do not connect the east and west coast of Tamil Nadu. Men talking about Rameswaram often emphasised the physical rigours of life there: 'The water there is salty and scarce, the air is no good and there is excessive heat. We came back disease-ridden.'

Their problems in Rameswaram contain another dimension relating to a greater compulsion from boat-owners to work as dictated. For example, boat workers are forced by the owners to poach in the more lucrative off-shore waters of Sri Lanka. This means that men have to work with the constant fear of being detected by Sri Lankan patrol boats, which is usually followed by harassment, or physical intimidation or, occasionally, arrest. The women worry about this added danger to which their men are exposed: 'The customs men beat up our men. Their work is harder there. When they tell us the stories of getting beaten up we feel anxious and unable to help them. They say they cannot even eat their *kanji* [rice gruel] in peace for fear of the patrol boats. We send them there for earning money and expose them to these dangers' (personal communication).[11]

Furthermore, cases of cheating the men out of money that was due to them are frequently reported for Rameswaram and Orissa: 'Things are getting worse in Rameswaram', one man said. 'There are fights, the owners get stingy about payments if the catch is not large.' For Orissa, Vijayan reports that 'Cheating and irregularity in payments seem to be a common occurrence and happened in three out of the five boat samples' (1980:28). Complaints about the food and living conditions in Rameswaram were also common. This is a woman whose three brothers work in Rameswaram:

They sleep out on the beach at night, and work from two in the morning until 8 or 10 in the morning. The afternoon lunch is given by the boat owners, but it is so bad that my brothers can't eat it. They prefer to spend Re10 a day on buying their own food. At night they are given *kanji* [gruel] by the owners. On Sundays, as soon as they get the chance, the men go out to eat hotel food and see the cinema.

A great many considerations govern men's preferences as to where they work, of which strictly economic considerations are only one aspect. Kerala is preferred over Rameswaram, not only because the men prefer a share system to wages. Of equal importance to them is the degree to which they can expect a 'fair deal', which includes respect for their skills, freedom from persecution while they go about their work, and fair dealings between boat-owner and coolies in terms of pay and food. For John, what defines a work place as 'a place of *suham* [contentment]' is that 'there is time to sleep, one can get off the boat and rest'. Where a man feels unable to replenish the labour expended in fishing, he may decide it is simply not worth going back.

For this is the ultimate weapon still in the hands of the men in Kanyakumari: they are only a quasi-proletariat, for the simple reason that they have not been totally divested of the means of production or, at least, of access to it. For the same reason, they are not totally at the mercy even of the harsher regime of the Rameswaram boat-owners. If conditions get too harsh, the men simply stay away in droves and revert back to their old patterns of either tightening their belts during the local off season or doing a bit of local fishing where they can. It is a readily available alternative, utilised in a number of contexts. Some men stop going on seasonal migration once they marry and have a family, finding the lengthy separations too physically uncomfortable as they grow older. Others try taking their families with them to live in Rameswaram; but many return, often after a period as long as four or five years, complaining of the brackish undrinkable water, malaria and excessive heat.

The point is, however, that as long as the men have an alternative way of earning their living to working on mechanised boats, any transition to new work rhythms of a more regular and stable, but also of a more externally imposed kind, is necessarily going to remain partial. Equally important in mediating between old and new patterns of men's work is the form taken by the sexual division of labour.

An important sub-text running through the journal concerns John's relations with women, both in his home village and in Kerala. The access men have on a regular basis to their own village and their kin is an important source of stability and continuity between old and new patterns of work and living. It is women, above all, who symbolise this continuity. When John writes of his work in Kerala: 'This is a place of *suham* [contentment]', he is referring not only to the greater opportunities Kerala offers for following a self-directed pattern of work, but to the women in the family of the boat-owner, with whom he lives. He immediately goes on to add: 'I have a woman friend who is like a sister to me, now the wife of the boat owner, who is from Puthenthurai.'

An essential component of men's preference for work in Kerala is the degree to which they feel at home with the local culture—in turn, central to the constitution of 'home', is their relationship to the local women. Patterns of inter-marriage between coastal fishing villages in Kanyakumari and Kerala mean that women move between the two regions and mediate the cultural differences that men might otherwise experience more sharply in the course of their work-migration. Apart from this, the Kanyakumari men feel comfortable and at ease with Kerala coastal women. Many men commented on the ease with which they could get along with the girls in Kerala, often to the detriment of the women they left behind in Kanyakumari. 'We have a lot of contact with the girls—they don't run away and hide like our Tamil girls,' said one hook-and-line fisherman. 'They serve us like they were our daughters ... The girls there work like tigers, not lazy like ours,' said an older man. The ease of relationships opens up possibilities for lasting associations between Kanyakumari men and

Kerala women, occasionally disrupting relationships with the women left behind. Cases of adultery are becoming common, and a case of bigamy was under examination by the newly instituted village council in the neighbouring village of KooDimonai.

However, the centrality of women to men's concept of home also means that the period away from Kanyakumari is usually most sharply symbolised in their minds by the absence of their own women. 'I miss her attentions,' John writes, while worrying about his wife's ability to cope with birth and subsequent sterilisation. 'An ant kept troubling my ear, and I thought of how she would have soothed me.' Likewise, his return to the village is experienced most vividly in the 'attentions' his wife pays him: waking him up on New Year's Day with a home-cooked sweet in his mouth, a gesture which conveys both intimacy and domesticity. He promptly gives her half to share, in a further romantic gesture. It should be mentioned that John's marriage was a 'love-marriage', and that he was currently supporting his younger brother's choice against the opposition of the two sets of parents concerned. Often the love-marriage means no more than that the girl and the boy formed a degree of intimacy in the very course of marriage negotiations. In these cases dowry is still paid, for reasons of prestige, but the dowry is a reduced amount.

Apart from a man's wife, his female relations as a group are key figures in conveying to him the news about events, grievances, domestic tensions, social obligations yet to be fulfilled, and insults to family honour. John's elder sister tells him that his wife's mother did not adequately care for his wife during delivery—and he broods over this. John's deep attachment to his wife's younger sister is another reason for his hostility towards his mother-in-law: she has been wed against her wishes in John's absence. Yet for her sake he prays for the groom's recovery from his recent illness. John's wife, his wife's mother and younger sister have become the key figures in his life: the only member of his own family who figures in this excerpt is another woman, his own elder sister. Although this is an excerpt from the journal kept by one man, the women-centredness of John's view of the village, as well as its matrifocal and uxorilocal bias, is a feature of the kinship system among the Mukkuvars, which is explored in a subsequent chapter.

I will come back towards the end of the chapter to a discussion of the particular view of femininity and romanticism which comes through the journal's various entries, and the light this sheds on a shift that is taking place from the more traditional male constructions of femininity examined in the previous chapter. But first, I move back from the activities of the Mukkuvar community to examine the wider set of social relations with which their own economy has become articulated over the last forty years. The examination involves bringing into our analysis some understanding of the policies of the emergent post-colonial State in India with regard to fisheries, and to the rural economy more generally. It is only in terms of this wider setting that the new patterns of work and gender relations can be properly understood.

The economic transformation of Indian fisheries

In discussing the influence of new forms of technology and patterns of migration, I must first of all make clear that I am not discussing the first exposure of some isolated rural community to technological innovation or even foreign influences. As Chapter 1 has already indicated, the people pride themselves on responding to new technological innovations and readily adapting foreign ideas to their own conditions. Coastal people are doubly exposed to wider economies—they have been open to the foreign influences of other maritime traders and to the agrarian economies of the hinterland. Historical records on such a marginal people are scarce, perhaps non-existent, but we can usefully utilise the methods Kosambi pioneered for India in an attempt to extract history from material artefacts and tools (1956). The *kaTTumaram*, for example, is conjecturably of Polynesian origin, while the *vaLLam* bears distinct traces of Arab influence (Kurien and Mathew 1982). Types of fishing techniques also bear the mark of overseas conquerers and maritime traders. Kurien and Mathew (1982) hold that the boat-seine technique is unmistakably of Spanish origin, while the shore-seine or *karamaDi* was introduced by the Portuguese. Possibly the only 'indigenous' techniques in Kerala and Kanyakumari are the use of hook and line and cast-nets.

The migratory movements of the fishermen themselves are reflected in the gradual regional shifts that occur in the use of different types of equipment. To take just the two regions that influence the technology used in Kanyakumari, Tamil Nadu and Kerala, it may be noted that the *kaTTumaram* is characteristic of the eastern coast of Tamil Nadu, where the seas are rougher. The craft typical of Kerala is the *vaanchi*, a type of dugout canoe predominant today in the northern Kozhikode and Cannanore regions of Kerala.

South of Trivandrum, however, the *kaTTumaram* begins to make its appearance, and by the time one reaches Cape Comorin is extremely prominent. At least one study has speculated that it was the fishermen of Tamil Nadu who brought the *kaTTumaram* to Kerala (Vattamattam 1978).

I have already noted in the first chapter that the exclusive concentration on the production of one item, fish, has rendered coastal settlements totally reliant on trade with the hinterland for access to nearly every item of consumption and the raw materials for constructing the tools of production. Therefore neither trade nor monetisation, nor even technological innovation, is at the heart of the recent dramatic changes that have swept over the fishing communities. This needs to be stressed because 'development' is often equated with a change from a simple subsistence-style economy to a market economy based on monetisation (Platteau 1982).

Ethnographic predilection for portraying villages as isolated and self-sufficient units is now increasingly seen to be inadequate, even for agrarian villages. Such a stereotype would have been undermined even sooner if our picture of peasant India had taken the coastal people into account. Planners and developers at the national policy-making level tend to concur with the biases of social theory in this respect, conceiving their task as the introduction of history and progress to timeless, changeless rural communities. The National Planning Committee of 1946 saw the fisherpeople as primitive and crude—referring primarily to their technology, but imperceptibly extending the evaluation to the people themselves: 'existing modes of fishing are largely of a primitive character, carried on by ignorant, unorganised and ill-equipped fishermen. Their techniques are rudimentary, their tackle elementary, and their capital equipment slight and inefficient' (Shah 1948, cited in Kurien 1985).

Sociological research on the impact of planning and development has interpreted social change primarily in terms of technology. There are now many studies of the areas of the Kerala coast which have received large inputs of funds and technological aid, both foreign and national government funding (see Platteau 1982, Gulati 1983, Kurien 1985). Whether the research comes down in favour of the nature of development in these areas, or is critical, is for the moment irrelevant. The point is that we are left to assume that the rest of the coastline, which represents the great majority of people who have not been direct recipients of aid projects, remains traditional, unchanging, perhaps 'primitive'. Districts such as Kanyakumari, where fishing is still predominantly non-mechanised, are rarely chosen for the study of social change.

Yet the use of non-mechanised technology is itself virtually no guide to the nature of the social relations of production within which the technology is embedded and utilised. Thus, while artisanal technology may be seemingly unchanged in its technical aspects, it is in fact now employed in producing for a world capitalist market. Fishing for the commodity at the heart of the new thrust towards foreign markets and foreign exchange—prawns and crustaceans—has been largely conducted, not by the modern, mechanised fishing boats, but by men working artisanal technology: 'Between 1961–69, of the 237 tonnes of prawns landed, as much as 70 per cent was caught by these artisanal fishermen' (Kurien 1985:A77).

Similarly deceptive is the contrast that is sometimes drawn between 'natural migration' dictated by the location of the fish and the evolution of craft and gear, and the more recent type of migration 'in search of jobs rather than fish' (Vijayan 1980, Mathew and Kurien

1982). Both types of migration not only coexist, but mutually interact. The account given by the men from KaDalkarai Uuru indicated a great deal of flexibility in moving from one type of work to the other: those who found life as a coolie on mechanised craft too difficult or unsatisfactory would revert to taking their *kaTTumaram* to various parts of Kerala and working as hook-and-line fishermen in the lean months. A more serious problem in regarding the latter kind of migration as natural is indicated by the case histories I collected of previous generations of fishermen in the village. There was no-one in the village of KaDalkarai who had picked up patterns of seasonal migration from his father or grandfather. The earliest instance of seasonal migration dated back thirty years, followed by another which began twenty-eight years back. The bulk of migration undertaken by those working with *kaTTumaram*, hook and line, falls within the period of the last ten years—which are also the years in which the migration to centres of mechanised fishing has become established.

In this village at least, both types of labour migration are a response to a new set of social relations. It is 'job-seeking' migration which is actually setting the pattern and outlining a new range of possibilities for those self-employed men working with non-mechanised equipment. Finally, the labour migration of men from Kanyakumari seeking work in Kerala, eastern Tamil Nadu, Karnataka and Orissa shows that regions which have not been directly affected by the technology of the labour process may nevertheless be integrally absorbed into a new social dynamic which creates inequalities both within communities and between one region and another.

Kanyakumari as an 'underdeveloped' zone

The new modernisation package introduces technological change, but not in a social or political vacuum. Inequality, the lack of producer control over the new technology, the rapidity with which the technology has been monopolised by large business firms rather than the fishing community itself, the utilisation of fishermen as labourers rather than owners of mechanised craft—features described over the next few pages—are all the symptoms of the capitalist nature of development. Once development is guided by the search for profits, the designation of some regions as backward labour catchment areas, and others as metropoles of commercial activity, is inevitable. Regions with proximity to State funding, either through geographical proximity, as in the case of Madras, or through the presence of powerful business lobbies, are more likely to be recipients of aid and investment. Alternatively, regions richly endowed with items of seafood judged lucrative on the export market, such as prawns and crustaceans, attract such investment through the logic of the market. The disparities are evident in figures on the district-wide distribution

of marine craft, and on other aspects of new technological facilities in
ice-making, cold storage and freezing (Marine Fisheries Information
Service, August 1981).

Kanyakumari emerges from these figures as having the highest
number of non-mechanised craft, and the lowest proportion of
takings from the mechanised sector, with only 0.09 per cent as
against the 60 per cent and 51 per cent for the districts of Madras
and Ramanathapuram respectively (Directorate of Fisheries, Tamil
Nadu, 1981). Unlike fishing centres in other states, such as Cochin in
Kerala, Kanyakumari has no developed harbour. Plans to develop a
harbour at Colachel have been mooted for some time, but funds
from the State government have not been forthcoming. Storage and
processing facilities are still run along traditional lines, with smaller
varieties of fish—anchovies, silverbellies and white sardines—sun-
dried directly on the beach without the addition of salt, while larger
varieties—shark, rock cod, rays, perch—are salted, rinsed and sun-
dried. A privately owned canning plant at Nagercoil, one of only two
such plants in the entire State, had to close down due to the high cost
of canning and the low demand for canned products. No facilities for
freezing are provided by the government (Directorate of Fisheries,
Tamil Nadu)—what little there is has been built on private initiative.
Efforts by the Colachel Fishermen's Cooperative Society to build an
ice plant foundered for lack of sufficient funds to pump fresh water
from outside Colachel, there being a scarcity of non-saline water in
most coastal villages. Along with this, efforts at marketing dry fish
collapsed due to scarcity of funds for transport costs.

The lack of investment is related to the lack of an effective industrial lobby in the district, but it is also the result of the overwhelming
emphasis, in the rationale of current government policy, on the
export of internationally lucrative species of seafood. Kanyakumari
District does not have the estuaries and the wide continental shelf
required for the breeding of prawns—the continental shelf in fact
drops sharply away as one nears the Cape. As a result, the small ten
metre trawlers used in India fail to find much scope for profitable
fishing close to the coastline. The little investment that has occurred
within the district is concentrated in the town of Colachel, where 130
mechanised craft alternate between working locally part of the year,
and in Kerala and Tiruchendoor for other parts of the year.

Trawler ownership was initially sponsored by cooperatives, which
were (and have remained) the local arm of government policy.
Although the credit they provide has had some purely 'welfare'
objectives, such as providing relief during the lean months in the
fishing seasonal cycle, cooperatives have been virtually synonymous
with the push towards mechanisation. The cooperative at Colachel,
functioning under the administrative control of the Director of
Fisheries, offers loans to fishermen for the purchase of mechanised

trawlers, but has suffered from a gradual phasing out of government subsidies.

Difficulty in meeting the cost of repayments has progressively driven the smaller producers within the community to bankruptcy, allowing a pattern of monopolisation to set in very quickly. Ownership of the 130 trawlers in Colachel, initially dispersed among sixty-five members of the cooperative, has today become concentrated, with seven households owning twenty per cent of all operating trawlers. If this group of richer fishermen were given the encouragement by the government they vehemently argue for, and if fluctuations in the international economy had not turned against them in the mid-seventies, they might become a local entrepreneurial class. That group of households has already moved away from risky investments in ocean fishing to more secure remuneration from investment in coconut and paddy land, as well as the ownership of local small-scale rural industry such as coir-making units. The secretary of the Boat Owners Association in Colachel expressed the deep sense of frustration among these local emergent capitalists at the neglect of the government:

> Colachel has a majority of *kaTTumaram* owners, which means that the AIDMK [the ruling party] sides with them in order to gain votes. The government has so far given only small donations and midday meals—it has no policies for the community as a whole. The government will not let us get on with the job of development, leave alone helping us with it. It hedges us about with restrictions. Yet, the *kaTTumaram* sentences boys to remain uneducated—they start at the age of seven, whereas they can study and later work on mechanised boats. The AIDMK has neglected this district. Only about twenty-five people would have bought boats with the government's help (interview, March 1983).

The sudden dropping away of the continental shelf in Kanyakumari District, combined with the high cost of fuel, forces small-scale entrepreneurs such as the Colachel owners of mechanised boats to operate in the same areas as the artisanal fishermen, thus competing for the same resources and adding to the economic pressures on those utilising non-mechanised technology.

Male outmigration as a consequence of scarce local employment

Development, if by this one means the introduction of new technology and its widespread utilisation, has not taken root in Kanyakumari fisheries, nor has it generated the promised benefits of local employment. The annual out-migration of the men makes more sense when we further consider the paucity of locally available alternative forms of employment. The only employment for men in KaDalkarai Uuru and Colachel other than fishing is the ferrying of goods to the ships that occasionally call in at the natural harbour of Colachel. The irony of this is that the men are, for the most part, ferrying out sackfuls of sand that has been mined from their own beaches, beaches on which their houses are erected. The ships, calling from Japan, UK, France, Yugoslavia, Taiwan and Korea, take on as cargo sand mined by the government-owned Indian Rare Earth Company. The sand contains oxides of uranium and rutile, and the mining is conducted along open-cut lines, affecting all beaches between Colachel and Manavala Kuruchi, a distance of some sixteen kilometres of heavily settled coastline. The erosion of the beachfront has already had an impact on the poorly constructed dwellings of the fisherpeople, which are now more vulnerable than ever to the hazards of the wind and rain during the monsoon season.

There is no compensatory employment available for fishermen in the mining company itself. The only work it has generated for them is loading sand and ferrying it to the ships in the larger *vaLLam* craft. The work is arduous and dangerous, with a high rate of accidents. Wages are extremely low, with the men being paid Re1.05 per bag of sand, which works out on average to Re10–15 per day per person. The work is disliked intensely by most, but poorer households have no choice but to send their men. Efforts at unionising the *vaLLam* workers have so far been thwarted by the contractors, who are drawn from the small set of wealthy boat-owning families. With this the range of options for local employment is virtually exhausted. Work in the agricultural sector of the district is impossible to find in an already overstrained labour market, where the class of agricultural labourers grew in far greater numbers than the class of owner-cultivators in the period 1961 to 1980 (Nair, Sivanandan and Ratnam 1984). In any case, fishermen are loath to exchange the prestige and self-directedness of fishing for the life of an agricultural labourer.

The relative underdevelopment of Kanyakumari fisheries is directly related to the development of other parts of the western and eastern coastline of south India. Both are by-products of the logic of profitability. Although the district has not been the target of technological revolution, the work performed by the men as seasonal immigrant labourers in other districts and states, and even the work they perform with artisanal technology, are all part of a supra-regional, and potentially a world-wide, set of market relations.

KaTTumaram *fishermen's opposition to mechanised fishing*

That the *kaTTumaram* fishermen journey yearly to work as seasonal labourers for mechanised trawlers does not signify a complete acceptance of new modes of fishing. An increasingly vocal and organised fishermen's lobby is placing considerable pressure on the State to exercise control over the operations of mechanised vessels. Organised action is a new and foreign experience for the men of the coastal villages. Far more to their taste is quick and direct action—sabotage, the scuttling or burning of a trawler in reprisal for a slashed net or the loss of daily catch, a physical brawl with the crew of mechanised boats (in which stab wounds and death are possibilities). John's journal indicates such methods have not been left behind. These modes of dealing out justice have, however, proven inadequate in resisting the systematic transgression of the moral economy of artisanal fishing by the activities of large-scale producers.

Due to the traditional neglect of the fishing community by organised political parties and unions, the unionism within the fishing community fiercely proclaims its independence and its non-political nature. In the Indian context, this can only mean autonomy from direct affiliation with any of the major political parties. The agenda of the new organisations is if anything more potent and wide-ranging than that of the by-now bureaucratised parties of the Right or Left. Their demands go all the way from arguing for the limitation of the fishing operations of mechanised boats, to an analysis of the social causes of poverty in the fishing community. The tactics adopted in recent years have been increasingly agitational: demonstrations, hunger strikes, picketing, road-blocks, and 'fill the jail' campaigns.

The organisations have repeatedly drawn attention to the impact of mechanised fishing on the ecology and livelihood of the thousands of small-scale producers using non-mechanised technology, who provide, in Tamil Nadu, an estimated seventy per cent of the total catch (FAO–SIDA Report 1983). Specific criticisms have been made of each of the three new techniques—gill-netting, shrimp trawling and purse-seining. Gill-netting is criticised for the wall-like deployment of the nets, which prevents the movement of fish from offshore to inshore waters, and for scaring away fish that would have otherwise found their way into the traditional inshore nets. Shrimp trawlers are opposed for their operation through June-August, which is the breeding season for most species of fish, and for causing damage to the eggs and young fish. The ploughing and sweeping of the sea-bed by the trawling nets is felt to lead to the depletion and ultimate destruction of marine resources. The purse-seiner is opposed because it competes with the small producers for their traditional catch: oil sardine, whitebait and mackerel.

Scientific opinion remains equivocal about the technical accuracy of these claims, but recent economic trends have been alarming enough to move the State government of Kerala to appoint a committee of government officers, scientists and trade union representatives to examine the dramatic downturn in the total catch of several important species of fish in the State. According to the report of this committee (1981), sea-fish production rose steadily until the mid-seventies, both in Kerala and at the national level. However, after 1976, while the national all-India figures continued to show an increase, in Kerala the figures fell from four hundred thousand to three hundred thousand tonnes between 1976 and 1980. Among the most severely affected species were oil sardines and mackerel, both targets of the purse-seining technique.

The agitation of the small-scale producers runs directly counter to the immediate inclination of both regional and national governments, which is to take advantage of the quick and easy profits from exporting frozen prawns to an international market. Any commitment on the part of the government to treating fisheries as a source of cheap protein for low-income rural and urban consumers—a commitment much in evidence through the fifties—has been long abandoned in favour of capital intensive technology, which effectively prices the product out of the reach of traditional consumers. Since the 1970s, the central government has been encouraging international capital with Indian subsidiary interests (companies such as Tata, Kelvinator, Union Carbide, Indian Tobacco Company, Parry, Brittania, etc.), offering them loans at low rates of interest to invest in export-oriented marine fishing. Trawlers acquired in this way are eligible for rebate on excise duty. During my period of fieldwork, a task force on marine products set up by the national government in 1982 was still intent on offering major concessions to large industrial concerns.[12]

Inevitably this policy has encouraged the growth of a class of purse-seine operators and merchants enjoying links with the international export market whose political muscle far outweighs the fishermen's lobby. In 1982, the purse-seine operators in Cochin went on strike, against legislative restrictions on trawler fishing, backed by the Mechanised Boat Owners Association, the Fish Merchants Association and the Ice Manufacturers Association (Kovakanandy 1984). Such pressure has ensured that concessions extracted from the government by the small producers (concessions such as the 1977 Ordinance designed to restrict the operation of trawlers to specific depth zones, areas and seasons) remain largely empty pieces of legislation, neither enforced nor policed.

The fisherpeople, only too aware of the destructive tendencies inherent in the unchecked operation of mechanised fishing, and offered at best only seasonal employment as labourers on the craft of the more wealthy and powerful, show little inclination to abandon their traditional modes of fishing. In the last decade, far from giving way gracefully to the technological harbingers of modernity and progress, the fisherpeople have showed a stubborn tendency to persist and even proliferate their artisanal craft and gear: 'Going by the aggregate counts of traditional fishing craft alone, the increase was of the order of around 10 per cent from 30594 in 1972 to 34112 in 1979. The number of artisanal fishermen increased from around 90000 to 106000' (Kurien 1985:A77).

The work experience of the men of Kanyakumari is not directly explainable, in the terms we have inherited from Marxism, as a transition to capitalism or an irresistible movement forward in history. Nor do the complications introduced into the model in the 1970s, such as notions of 'quasi' or 'partial' proletarianisation, adequately escape the underlying teleology of this narrative form. In a style not dissimilar to that experienced by other (urban) labouring classes in India (see Ram 1981), the Mukkuvars' exposure to global economic relations in the post-Independence era has only encouraged an exaggeration of 'old' forms of work, which now are given a fundamentally new significance. The division of labour between the sexes follows a similar logic of exaggeration and reinterpretation, as the female half of the potential labour force remains behind in the village during the annual exodus of men. I discuss this dimension in the next section.

Women and migration

The seasonal proletariat that journeys yearly to the ports of Kerala and eastern Tamil Nadu is almost exclusively male. All the changes have profound repercussions on women, but the men emerge as the primary actors. It is timely at this point to reflect more consciously on the implications of the process for women.

Women are able to mediate the new experiences for men by virtue of their cultural and economic association with the native *uuru*. They rarely accompany the men on their seasonal trips. 'Family migration', while not unheard of in the community, rarely lasts for long. Five families in KaDalkari Uuru had returned to the village after attempting to settle in the port town of Rameswaram. If we set aside for the moment the notable exception of some young educated girls in the Mukkuvar community who have migrated to neighbouring districts and states in pursuit of professional training and jobs, the norm for the bulk of the uneducated female population is to remain in the village while the men migrate. This pattern is closer to the sex-role implications of industrialisation in the north of India, where rural-urban migration is overwhelmingly male (Zachariah 1968, Gore 1970), than to the southern pattern, where the transition to industrialisation and urbanisation is more gradual, characterised by a far greater incidence of family migration (Murphy 1976, Menefee Singh 1984).

The similarity to the north Indian pattern is complicated by the peculiarities of fishing. Men's absence from the village during their trips to neighbouring districts and states is only an extension of the usual demands of fishing, which keep them substantially out of the land-based activities of the family and the village. Nevertheless, two tendencies in the Mukkuvar pattern of proletarianisation are still strikingly similar to the north: first, the inclination of the men to keep their stake in the local economy alive even while they try to earn money in the urban industrial economy; and secondly, the consolidation of this rural-urban nexus by the tendency of women to remain locked into the rural sector.

Any attempt to theorise the sexual polarisation in the Mukkuvar pattern of proletarianisation must begin by clearing away some of the unsatisfactory assumptions in the literature on migration in India. Most literature on the subject has in fact very little to say about the imbalance in the ratio of men to women in rural-urban migration. The underlying assumption is that women's movement, unlike men's, is not governed by economic motives but by kin and marital ties. In the jargon of migration studies, women's movement is purely 'associational' (governed by their relation to men); hence a study of immigrant labour in Bombay city by the Joshis (1976) justifies its concentration on male workers by describing any economic activity on the part of female immigrants as 'incidental to the fact that they are in the city' (1976:138).

There are at least two sorts of problems inherent in such an approach. The first is that by assuming women's economic marginality we are led to underestimate the various types of work that women do perform. Even if we take an extremely narrow view of production as the generation of income (a view this book is concerned to dismantle) in KaDalkarai Uuru, all women in the five families which had returned from Rameswaram had been earning income during the period of migration. So had their children. But the work they performed tended to be casual, irregular, small-scale, and often confined to the home. The women had taken in tailoring at home; the older women had worked as petty traders in the sale and purchase of fish. The children had sold shells and trinkets to tourists, and helped in loading and unloading the boats. Such work is easily overlooked, unless the researcher is already sensitive to the rather elusive and problematic nature of women's economic activity—and it is precisely such sensitivity which is sacrificed by assuming the incidental and marginal nature of such forms of work.

A more striking refutation of the thesis that women's migration is purely associational comes from the younger generation of Mukkuvar women. Girls in their late teens and early twenties are increasingly prepared and even encouraged to find better paid employment than is available in the local environment. There are very few jobs available to girls even in the context of the wider urban economy: at best they can hope to be trained and employed as teachers, social workers, clerical assistants and typists. Many attend local typing and book-keeping classes in neighbouring Colachel, but those hoping to teach will travel much further afield in order to obtain training and jobs (see Chapter 9 for details). The phenomenon of young girls travelling interstate to Karnataka to train in Catholic-run colleges, or to other parts of Tamil Nadu to work as teachers, is no longer unheard of.

The jobs and the training available to the girls are severely limited by restrictions designed to protect their modesty and respectability. They must accept the chaperonage of the church where the family and community can no longer function as safeguards. Nevertheless, they do migrate for work-related reasons, without immediate reliance on any man—in stark contrast to the associational model of female migration. The ability of these younger women to migrate, work and support their families at home—all of which are characteristics associated with sons in the wider culture—can be fully understood only in the context of the unusually wide responsibilities shouldered by women in Mukkuvar communities. A full discussion of the phenomenon of the young educated group of women appears in the final chapter.

Even this preliminary discussion alerts us to the social restrictions which are uniquely applied to women. Clearly, men and women do not have identical work experiences, nor do they bear the same relationship to economic processes. The fundamental problem with the dominant model of migration is not that it differentiates between male and female experience, but that it fails to treat sexual differentiation in social processes (whether they be urbanisation, industrialisation, or migration) as deeply problematic and in need of explanation.

A similar deep-seated indifference to questions of sexual differentiation within the emerging proletariat has been characteristic of scholarship shaped by a nationalist Left historiography. Here the focus has been on the capital/labour antagonism, and the unwillingness of colonial capital to bear the full costs of reproducing the labour power of the industrial working class. The continuing part-peasant character of the Indian industrial workforce, which has largely retained its rural roots, is explained by the failure of industrialisation to provide adequate housing or a family wage to workers (Thorner 1957, Mersch 1974, Omvedt 1978).

It would not be hard to extend such an economic analysis to the Mukkuvar case. Colonies of immigrant labourers in Orissa, Karnataka and eastern Tamil Nadu are notorious for lacking any proper facilities for housing, water or sanitation. Accounts of these colonies are few, but an FAO working paper on the living quarters of fishermen from Andhra Pradesh working in Orissa notes:

> The most severe social problems in fishing communities are found in the temporary and semi-temporary villages of the migrant Andhra fishermen ... The community consists of filthy unorganised congestions of overcrowded small thatched huts where the fishermen and their large families live. Basic communal facilities are non-existent. Their hygienic conditions leave everything to be desired (FAO 1977).

Mukkuvars who have lived under such conditions also speak of the lack of drinking water, the overcrowding and the malaria—but they translate it into their own cultural categories of bodily health. Living conditions such as the above are said to aggrevate greatly the imbalance of bodily humors. In particular, the central category of body heat or *shuuTu* comes into play. *ShuuTu* and *shuuTu vyaadigaL* (heat-induced diseases) are said by the Mukkuvars to proliferate in the immigrant colonies. The numbers who are defeated by such conditions certainly include the families who have attempted to settle in places such as Rameswaram, but they also include men who have gone there on their own but given up the life of the seasonal labourer, unable to withstand the *shuuTu*.

The question of living conditions itself is not to be appraised in an objective or purely economic manner. It has quite different meanings for men and for women. Employers who fail to provide adequate shelter and housing for their workers may be acting in terms of their interests as a class, but they deter women from moving outside their homes in the villages far more effectively than they deter men. According to Mukkuvar cultural norms, men require less housing than women. They may sleep on harbour platforms while waiting for accommodation, as John records in his journal, or they may sleep out in the open on beaches, as they do back in their native *uuru*. Women must be guarded not only against the elements, but perhaps even more urgently, against a loss of sexual modesty and respectability. If such measures cannot be guaranteed, the village seems a more secure environment in which to keep them.

The result of this interaction between the class interests of boatowners and Mukkuvar cultural norms regarding femininity is that Mukkuvar women cannot avail themselves of the few ancillary areas of female employment which have sprung up around the centres of mechanised fishing. This has been documented for the big centres of prawn fishing in southern Kerala by Gulati (1983), who describes the rise of small-scale but relatively successful female entrepreneurs in the prawn business recruited from the Latin Catholic fishing community. Among the Hindu fishing communities of this same area, the women have found seasonal wage employment in the processing of prawns, in small sheds where an all-female workforce peels and deveins the prawns.

Kanyakumari has not been favoured by the vagaries of the international market, for reasons discussed in the previous section. This means there is little generation of local employment for men or women, but where men have the relative freedom of travelling to sell their labour power elsewhere, women are denied even the minimal and ambiguous 'freedom' of the wage-labourer under capitalist relations of production. Proletarianisation is therefore a gender-specific category which has a specific historical trajectory for men and women even within the same caste, class and community.

Forced into a relatively passive relationship to industrialisation, the women in the coastal villages bear witness to a historically new and changing relationship between the sexes.

Migration and women's new relationship to cash

The separation, both geographical and social, between male and female worlds is not a new feature of Mukkuvar society. The male monopoly over the skills of fishing has traditionally ensured that men and women not only had to perform different tasks, but that they were located spatially in different spheres. The dispossession of women from the work of fishing has always had its compensations, however inadequate.

One curious feature of male/female relations in the Mukkuvar community until recently was that it represented in many ways an inversion of those situations, highlighted by feminist anthropology and history, in which women have been central to production, but failed to control the cash benefits flowing from their work (Sanday 1974, Molyneux 1981). Here women have been barred from the central productive role in the community—but they control the cash flow from that production. Women keep track of the accounts, of how much they are owed for each catch, for reasons which are explored more carefully in the next chapter. The next chapter also examines the women's larger role in the village's credit economy, in which they give and receive loans in an elaborate network of informal transactions which counterbalance the vicissitudes of the male-dominated formal economy of production. Men rarely challenge this female control over cash. They may quarrel over the precise amount that is given to them as personal 'pocket money', and they may even abuse women physically to get them to hand over more drink money. But the basic premise that women should control the income and budget for all household expenses is rarely challenged.

This female responsibility for economic decision-making and for ensuring the family's daily survival is reflected in the strikingly shrewd and business-like way in which women speak of the impact of their men's annual outmigration. Where male evaluations of the new work experience are nuanced by non-economic considerations of equity, fair play, work satisfaction, comradeship and emotional relationships in the new workplace, as well as the problems of danger and hardship they face while away, women by contrast emphasise the impact of the outmigration on their ability to survive economically as a household, and the quantity of cash that flows back in the form of remittances. The following quotes from village women highlight this preoccupation:

> We allow them [the men] to go there in case they get lucky—if they do, they may earn anything up to Re2000, of which they could send back up to a half. But that is rare.

> The life of fisherfolk is uncertain and hard anyway—here or there. But if they [the men] were here, there would be nothing in the lean season. At least from there we get something.

Yes, there is anxiety. But—there is also the expectation of something being
sent back.

Despite the higher expenses there I would say we still benefit—here we
could only meet daily expenses. But there not only is the catch greater, but
the men send it to us in one lump sum of Re500, which encourages us to
spend it on capital equipment, or in paying off a debt.

A subtle shift in terms of the traditional female control over cash is
now taking place. While men work locally, women are able to maintain the right to allocate the cash income according to their priorities.
But as men work much farther afield women have to accept whatever
the men choose to send home, and this is often only a fraction of the
amount earned. While recognising the greater costs of living in port
towns, the women felt that male inexperience at budgeting and taking
responsibility for their earnings substantially whittled away at the
income: 'They send back sometimes up to Re200 a month. The
expenses are greater there—but they spend "over". They do not know
how to look after themselves there and the cost of living is greater.'
There is always a slight mistrust of the account men give of their
expenses. While one woman marvelled at the discrepancies between
village and city prices, another was quick to add: 'Well, there is no
one there to check on what they say.' In many households, there was
no monthly remittance—only the occasional amount to bail out a
crisis at home, which the women have to struggle to bring to the
men's attention: 'My three sons all work in Rameswaram as coolies,
but they only send money when they hear of hardship at home. Even
then, they have no savings to send home—they borrow in order to
send us Re2–300.'
The experience of women in handling budgets has gone hand in
hand with an awareness of the many needs of the family, while men
have felt justified in spending their money on gambling, drink and
pictures. Such a scenario fits in well with studies of household
budgets in other rural communities (Sharma 1980). Women's
allowances are utilised in the upkeep of the household, and if they
earn their income is regarded as a household resource, whereas men
assume the right to spend their money on personal items or outside
commitments shared with other men rather than their families
(Standing and Bandopadhyay 1985). The shift in control over cash
from female to male hands therefore has profound implications for
the overall welfare of the household as a whole, as well as for the
status of the women themselves.
In the journal kept by John we have an indication of the new note
of romanticism in the younger men who spend a good deal of their
working lives away from the village. The case of John, who no longer
works locally at all, is but a more accentuated version of the experience of more than half the men in KaDalkarai Uuru for some part of
the year. In the vision of 'the women left behind' which emerges in

John's journal, there is virtually no recognition of the economic role played by women. The older men of the previous generation are much readier to concede that women are economic decision-makers, so far as the household is concerned, and that is as it should be. This acknowledgement was the foundation of their view of women as powerful and dangerous, elaborated in the previous chapter. The 'new woman' who inhabits the pages of John's journal resembles her predecessor in her confinement to the interior of home. That space was always defined as feminine. What is new is that there is now no hint of danger, or of power that needs to be controlled. She inhabits the house out of a sweetness and passivity of nature, rather than to ensure her powers are checked. John's wife is seen as a comforter, provider of tender and softening influences.

Previously, women's social networks, extending into the hinterland and up and down the coastal belt, have in some ways outstripped the men's horizons, limited as they are by their confinement to a relatively small tract of the sea coast. Now, however, the balance is shifting. Men are travelling to places far outside the district, and coming back with an aura of glamour and experience. For John to be able to say that he wants to show his wife the world bespeaks an entire revolution, both in the ideology of gender and in the reality of power relations between the sexes.

Conclusion

Social processes in a small locality such as KaDalkarai Uuru are inextricably linked to transformations in regional, national and international political economies. Kanyakumari, a region which is by no means a stranger to foreign maritime intrusions, and possessing a complex technological history of its own, is paradoxically emerging from its latest encounter with an international economy as a 'backward' zone, left only with a highly skilled labour force as an exportable resource. Faced with an economic logic which diverts capital and employment only to regions endowed with marine species profitable in the international market—a finite resource at best—the fishermen of Kanyakumari have responded with a number of survival strategies. They work as labourers on mechanised boats as a skilled and relatively privileged workforce, but combine such work with *kaTTumaram* fishing in local waters. In their capacity as small producers, they try to organise politically to check the power of the trawler owners.

However, even these survival strategies are not simple economic responses. They are shaped by constructions of gender and sexuality explored in previous chapters. Women's movement—unlike men's—is charged with sexual meanings and subject to surveillance. Men and women are therefore forging fundamentally different relationships to the world of cash, commodities and wage labour.

My data on credit, kinship, marriage payments and women's work needs to be read in the light of this fundamentally changing historical context. In what follows I am concerned not only with the analysis of gender relations, but with demonstrating the historical character and the economic/political basis for aspects of the community's existence.

6 The underground female economy: women's credit networks and the social reproduction of fishing households

A contradiction dominates the sexual division of labour in the Mukkuvar fishing community. Women are excluded from the central economic task of fishing and from access to the economic and cultural capital related to performing this task, yet the very monopoly exercised by men over these resources has certain results paradoxical to the smooth maintenance of male dominance. In performing the pivotal tasks of the fishing economy, men must necessarily absent themselves for long periods from the land-based society of the village, which is the locus for social reproduction. Further, the experience of proletarianisation is lengthening these periods of male absence. In contrast with agricultural society, where patriarchal cultural rules are buttressed by the actual physical presence of the menfolk, the sexual division of labour in fishing society leaves women in charge of all activities based in the household.

The close association, even identification, between women and the domestic economy of the household only superficially resembles the association between femininity and responsibility for familial welfare found in the dominant version of Tamil culture. In the dominant version, women are *of* the domestic sphere, are *contained* by the interior space of the house, without being able to lay claim to the ultimate decision-making responsibility pertaining to the domestic sphere (Baker-Reynolds 1978). Without necessarily setting out to transgress the dominant codes of Tamil culture, Mukkuvar women find themselves in a very different position. Indeed, their very efforts to fulfil the cultural requirement of ensuring familial stability, survival and welfare forces them to assume roles that take them well outside the traditionally female spheres of influence.

Men are unable and unwilling, by virtue of their exhausting pre-occupations out at sea, to follow through the financial transactions that flow on from the initial auction of the fish catch and which are

145

realised only after their sale at the markets. Women keep track of what is owed to their husbands and receive the money as well as making the decisions regarding the allocation of this scarce cash resource to various urgent familial needs.

Further, women find themselves in the position of having to mediate between the temporal rhythms of male and female activities in fishing society. The periodicity of fishing is governed by the seasons, tides and winds, as well as by sheer chance. The economic contribution of men is necessarily sporadic and uneven. When there is a spectacular catch, there is a flood of money, while lean fishing seasons mean dearth and hunger in the home. Women's social responsibilities, however, are a continuous daily process and have a distinctive rhythm of their own which is in direct tension with the vagaries of the fishing economy. This area concerns not only the family's biological survival—and this means finding money for food, clothing, housing repairs and medical expenses—but also the broader strategies of social reproduction involved in marriage, kinship and religious practices. These strategies may involve raising sums of money for dowry, marriage expenses and pilgrimages, payment for the education or training of children, or finding the money to send a son overseas in search of work. Such monetary demands are renewed, if not on a daily basis, then certainly with a regularity that fits uneasily with the uncertainties of the male-dominated sphere of fishing.

This chapter explores the economic strategies Mukkuvar women have evolved in their role as mediators between the contradictory rhythms of male and female spheres of activity. The strategies revolve around an elaborate network of credit which constitutes a submerged but virtually parallel economy. Indeed, it would be no exaggeration to say that the underground activity of the women confounds the conventional erection of conceptual walls between 'male economic production' and 'female social reproduction'. This female credit economy is complementary to the male economy of fishing, but is nowhere as visible or as openly accessible. Where the work of fishing is visually striking and apparent in the teams of men pulling in the *karamaDi* at the sea-front, or in the noise and bustle of an auction, women's credit transactions are conducted in relative privacy and obscurity, being based on networks of neighbourhood, residence and kinship which take time for the outside observer to penetrate. The credit economy is an informal one, in that there are few institutional manifestations of the transactions, let alone organised offices or office-bearers. Instead we find a multitude of small-scale transactions, with women acting as borrowers and lenders, involving a range of households known to them through associations of marriage, kinship, common work experiences and friendships, or else through the services of female intermediaries who also utilise similar social networks. The credit networks are a supreme example of local, community-based strategies. They are thickest where marriage and residential ties overlap, within the village itself, but they also reach out to all villages linked by marriage and kinship, which effectively brings in the entire coastal zone. That is, the generation of credit derives its social basis from precisely those social relations and activities which are the peculiar domain of women in Mukkuvar society. Gender, or more precisely, the female orientation of this parallel economy, is therefore inextricably woven into my account of the specific features of the credit economy.

The data on the credit network were gathered through the questions on debts, loans and sources of credit, the specific reasons why loans were taken, included in my village census which covered all households in the village of KaDalkarai Uuru. The percentages and figures presented in this chapter are based on a random sample of 100 households. Information on debts and loans was comparatively easy to collect: most women in the village were keen to stress their bad fortune to an outsider assumed to have influential contacts, in the hope that some form of material assistance might flow out of the information I collected. By contrast, information on assets and income was much harder to acquire, since it was feared that this would arouse the envy of other villagers and generate the possibility of sorcery attacks. There were a few instances where the female head of the household was hard to find at home, usually in cases where the woman was a small-scale fish trader, as well as a few cases where I was blandly assured that there were no debts whatsoever. In the former case, I found that the men of the house were totally unable to volunteer any information on debts, loans or weekly budgets, and had to rely instead on the women's close relatives—a mother or sister, sometimes even a neighbour, who seemed to have a reasonably good idea of the loans and debts incurred by the missing woman. The amount would often be discussed and modified by the small group of onlookers from immediately surrounding huts or dwellings which usually gathered around during the interviews. Even if the resulting information was not always completely accurate, this public knowledge about the financial dealings of each household was itself striking corroboration of the social relations underlying the informal economy. The chronic and structural roots of indebtedness are indicated by the fact that 97 per cent of the households included in the random sample did have debts to report. In the case of the remaining three per cent who reported no debts, I have accepted their statement at face value, but have taken the precaution of substituting them with three other households with debts to compensate for possible withholding of information.

The female orientation of the credit economy, and its operation

Perhaps the most striking feature of the credit network is its deprofessionalisation of the role of the money-lender. This is achieved in two ways.

Firstly, nearly every household in the fishing village has the opportunity both to lend and to borrow. The basis for turning money-
lender is not the existence of a permanent cash surplus greater than
other villagers, but rather a shared predicament common to all fishing
households. The irregularity of income creates not only seasonal
variations, but also temporary inequalities between households. All
households are aware that by lending money they not only secure a
little extra income based on the interest their loan will earn, but they
also secure the reciprocal right to borrow when they themselves are
in need of cash. Although participants in the transactions think only
of their own survival, the system operates as a whole to redistribute
income through the village remarkably effectively, ensuring the
survival of the community as a whole rather than of a few lucky
households.

Secondly, the typical pattern of raising credit is to disperse the role
of creditor among as many households as possible. This is done partly
as a deliberate strategy, to lessen potential build-up of tension between debtors and creditors and to increase one's flexibility in paying
off one's debts in smaller amounts. It is also, however, a reflection of
the poverty of the community as a whole—usually no one individual
has large sums of money at her disposal to lend to others. Loans are
therefore taken and given by ordinary fishing households, with the
women lending and borrowing money on an ad hoc basis.

A relatively minor exception to this rule is a small group of women
who rely on money-lending as one of their occupations. Most of these
are elderly widows who are too old to work as fish-traders. In KaDalkarai Uuru, four out of the six women who were described as regular
loan-givers were elderly widows manipulating the few assets at their
disposal to raise funds—selling or renting their dead husband's fishing
equipment, trading rice, obtaining rent from a little land they may
own, receiving a government pension for widows—and in turn, lending out some of these funds to generate a little extra income. Of the
other two women, one belonged to the household of a male fish-
trader, and therefore had access to more stable funds based on trade
and land ownership rather than fishing. The sixth woman belonged to
an ordinary fishing family, but needed to make enough income to
finance her son's training and lent money out as a means of doing so.
This small group of female money-lenders therefore constitutes the
less fortunate wives of fishermen, not a social category in their own
right. Some of the small-scale female rice traders offered credit, but
usually on a daily basis, that is, women who bought rice and spices
from them in the morning would be given till nightfall to pay for
them.

Far more typical is the situation where a household is approached
because of its greater resources than the borrowing household. The
borrowing woman would simply describe the transaction as 'from the
next person' (*'aDuta aaL kiTTerundu'*), or from people 'around
the place' who stood in no special relationship to her.

It would of course be difficult to approach an entirely unrelated household. Furthermore, households with surplus are reluctant to advertise them in case their creditors turn up at the door. Such fears are compounded by the chronic fear of envy. These problems are overcome by the use of women who act as intermediaries and go-betweens, a function which allows credit networks to operate as overlapping social networks instead of being discrete, discontinuous social circles. Here again, a small number of women may be approached to act as intermediaries because of their reputation for access to a wide circle of acquaintances and contacts. These women do not charge any extra fee for their services, instead taking a 'cut' from the money they raise. This cut is eventually repaid, so it is not a form of payment. What the intermediaries derive from the arrangement is access to credit for themselves, yet another mechanism by which the available cash flow gets distributed among needy households.

Women who are earmarked as intermediaries are no more representative of the credit system than the women who act as full-time money-lenders. A much wider category of women act as intermediaries on a casual basis. A typical example would be the woman asking her married daughter to act as intermediary with her husband's relatives or her friends. If the daughter has moved outside KaDalkarai Uuru village after marriage, then the credit network is that much enlarged. Alternatively, a woman married into KaDalkarai Uuru may go back to her natal kin in her own village for a loan. Go-betweens such as these facilitate the extension of the money market beyond the village.

The items used by the women as collateral in this credit system point to its specifically local and female orientation. Fishing nets and gear appear as items of surety, and are utilised flexibly, without depriving the owner of their use during the productive seasons. Even more popular, however, are items of female wealth: jewellery, gold, brass cooking vessels, and these days, government-issued rice ration cards.

Women themselves, if questioned on the matter, will point out that jewellery enjoys a number of advantages that make it useful to employ as collateral: it has a ready resale value on the market, and is not susceptible to depreciation in market value over time. Further, from the point of view of the debtor, jewellery can be reclaimed piecemeal over time, as and when small amounts of cash come to hand: a necklace may be reclaimed at one point, the earrings at another time.

The key advantage of jewellery from the point of view of a female-run credit network is that it is one item of wealth which passes, as dowry, into female control at the time of marriage. Ostensibly meant for personal use, jewellery and gold have in fact operated as the surety in a kind of collective female survival fund.

Women's preference for jewellery as collateral is once again confirmed when one compares rates of interest charged at six-monthly intervals on types of surety. Where fishing equipment and cooking vessels are charged five per cent, jewellery is charged only three per cent. Even the mode of reckoning interest carries the stamp of an essentially cooperative enterprise. Women may grant each other 'grace periods' in which loans are free of interest—sometimes as long as one-third of the period of borrowing. The interest-free period may be contracted as an incentive to speedier return. As one women put it to me: 'If you return a loan within three months, you pay interest on two of these months, but if you return it in five, the interest is on four months.' These arrangements may be further modified according to the degree of familiarity between the households, or alternatively, the familiarity with the intermediary. There are cases where the interest is waived altogether. The use of jewellery as collateral represents one of the few positive features of an otherwise unequal system of inheritance between men and women. (In Chapter 8, we see how this feature of the dowry system is currently being eroded by the demand for huge sums of cash.)

The ability of women to forge strong social bonds with each other is one of the crucial bases of the credit network, since loans are generated on the basis of ties of kinship, neighbourhood, work association and friendship between women. The pattern of loan taking closely mirrors the pattern of marriage, kinship and household formation. These patterns are discussed in more detail in the next chapter, so it is sufficient to say here that both loans and kinship networks are tightly clustered within the village. Of the 258 loans noted and detailed in the survey, 173 were taken from within KaDalkarai Uuru, while 85 loans were taken from outside. This follows the same contours as marriage patterns, where roughly half the women in the village can expect to stay on in their own village after marriage. The high proportion of intra-village marriages allows for a continuity of association between generations of women, with marriage and neighbourhood ties overlapping one another instead of the disruption that marriage usually entails for women in cases where village exogamy and virilocality are the prevailing social norms. Successive generations of women are found living quite close to one another in the village, making for strong ties built over lifetimes.

Similarly, where credit flows between villages, it tends to follow the channels already carved out by marriage exchange. Given the strict observance of rules of caste endogamy, this means that not only marriage exchange but credit exchange between fishing and agricultural villages is extremely rare. If ties of kinship and marriage facilitate the exchange of credit between coastal communities, these same ties also create the obligation for such financial assistance to be rendered. Indeed, marriage exchanges may depend on the financial exchanges between women. Married daughters are expected to help raise the dowry for their younger unmarried sisters—by using their own jewellery, or by drawing upon the jewellery of their female associates if necessary. The dowry of a previous generation of married women helps finance the marriages of the present generation of unmarried girls.

Kinship ties that can be called upon to raise loans may be wide-ranging. One may seek the assistance of an elder sister's daughter, who in turn may have lived in a different village; a niece's husband's family, and so on. The ties can be expanded one circle further if one has strong friendships with other women, who can then be prevailed on to utilise *their* kinship ties, as well as their jewellery, to raise loans with. Thus, in one case, it was a friend who utilised her own contacts and kin to raise three separate loans from the neighbouring village to finance her god-daughter's dowry.

A typical transaction could therefore involve many female ties, as the following study of social ties involved in raising money for a dowry indicates:

The amount to be raised for a daughter's dowry is: Re10 000. The mother (X) therefore turns to the following sources:
1 Re3000 from her married daughter, who was married only two years ago and therefore still has much of her jewellery intact. She is now living with her mother, in a case of uxorilocal residence, which makes it easier for her mother to have access to her dowry. The daughter contributes cash as well as access to some of her jewellery with which to seek loans elsewhere.
2 Re2000 from the mother's sister, married into Periavillai, another coastal village in Kanyakumari District. The money is raised by X's sister approaching a friend of hers with the jewellery given by X's married daughter. The loan generated here has to be re-paid at the rate of three per cent every six months.
3 X's son, living in KaDalkarai Uuru, gives Re2500.
4 X's husband's sister's daughter, lives in the coastal village of Manakudi, 25 km away. She contributes Re1500.
5 A friend in KaDalkarai Uuru gives access to using her jewellery as surety. This is in turn placed with another household, also in KaDalkarai Uuru, to generate a loan of Re500.
6 A friend in the neighbouring township of Colachel gives Re100.
7 An intermediary is approached, who in turn approaches a friend of hers, using jewellery as surety. Re400 is raised in this way.

The above account represents an actual case, and a number of variations are possible in each of its features. Nets may be used instead of jewellery; there may be a greater proportion of individuals with no kin ties involved in giving loans. Loans for dowries tend to involve kin links more than other types of loans: a dowry is more of a family concern, and one where a great amount of money has to be generated in a hurry. Daily needs, on the other hand, involving smaller sums of money, draw on neighbourhood ties to a greater extent.

The importance of social continuity in providing the basis for women's ability to generate finances is strikingly illustrated by the few cases where marriage has disrupted these associations. In one case, the woman who has married into KaDalkarai Uuru is not from a coastal village, but from an interior village called Kulithurai. In this household, loans are arranged and organised by her husband. She explains this in terms of simply not having the trust of villagers in KaDalkarai Uuru, or the local contacts for the kinds of transactions involved.

In addition to the marriage and neighbourhood ties emphasised so far, women also utilise work-based associations. Much of women's work is performed within the framework of familial obligations, often in the very niches and alleyways between the dwellings. Nets are woven, and rice, grain and spices are pounded by women gathered in clusters in makeshift work groups set up in between residences. Waiting for water at wells and taps, as well as bathing in the rivers and canals, become all-female communal activities due to the cultural, gender-based definitions of space and work. In more public and paid forms of female work such as petty trading, particularly fish trading, women's work can involve complex social cooperative arrangements with other women. Women can come together in a flexible team called a *kuuTam*, with four or five women sharing the tasks of buying at the beach, drying fish and travelling to rural markets to sell the catch (for details see Chapter 9). The mateship developed in this context extends itself to various forms of practical assistance that traders may offer one another. In one case, I came across a trader sheltering a widowed workmate in her own home, since the latter was otherwise virtually homeless. Such assistance also spills over into the area of offering one another loans, or acting as intermediaries for one another.

Fish-traders also develop contacts outside the coastal belt itself. Occasionally, this may take the form of non-monetised barter with agricultural households, particularly the main agricultural castes living at close quarters, the Nadars. Raising loans from the Nadars is sometimes preferred by village women, since they feel it has the advantage of leading to fewer daily conflicts with other villagers. Another woman had developed contacts with the Hindus of Colachel through tailoring work. She rented a room to a Hindu family and earned Re100–150 per month on this basis. Friendships across caste also spring up in other contexts, such as shared religious pilgrimages to healers and Christian shrines, or in the small medical nursing homes that women may use in childbirth or illness.

Relationships or friendships which are established in these various ways may be consolidated by the institution of being a godmother to a friend's child. Friendships are taken seriously, and are given a name: *kumbadri* (from the Portuguese compadre), is used more commonly to describe female friends than the Sanskritised term *snehidi*. Close friendships may be translated into fictive kin relationships through the practice of asking a friend to be a godmother (*toTTamma* or *talai toTTamma*). Godmothers are required to attend the child's christening, its First Communion (*podu nanmai*), its menarche ceremony if a girl, and marriage. At each of these occasions there is a gift of money and clothes. A *toTTamma* may therefore be turned to when the god-child's marriage is being arranged, in order to loan money, or to act as intermediary with her own kin and friends. Occasionally, the obligation to help may be reciprocated by the god-child as well.

The informal system of loan-giving and taking among women co-exists with other more formal systems of savings which are also run by women. Chief among these is the chit fund. The system has been described by Hill in the following manner:

> This system involves all the members of a group, formed expressly for the purpose, in making regular cash contributions perhaps weekly or monthly, into a common pool, one member taking the whole kitty on each occasion until each has had her turn. Unless the members who have already received their share can be relied upon to continue to contribute, the group will fail, so it is essential that they should know each other well and should respect the convenor (1982:17).

In KaDalkarai Uuru, the convener is also paid a commission, which is about five per cent of the amount collected every month. Although the system is strictly speaking a savings scheme and not a credit system, it is part of the range of economic strategies employed by women in the fishing community.

Comparison of female credit networks with other forms of rural credit

If we compare female credit networks with other systems of credit available to the fishing community, several features immediately stand out. First, credit available to men in the workaday economy, from merchants and middlemen as well as from those who work as agents for sea-food merchants, is for long-term economic purposes, thus perpetuating the reproduction of relations of power and dependency between creditors and debtors. In these relations, profit is not realised wholly, or even principally, through the interest charged on the loan—although high interest rates are a crucial part of the way the relationship of indebtedness is reproduced, often across generations. Rather, the profit involved is long-term, where the money-lender gains access either directly to the labour of the producer, or more indirectly to the products of that labour. The continuity of the rights to this access takes priority over all other considerations from the point of view of the money-lender, often even at the expense of short-term monetary gain.

Thus, some middlemen and boat-owners who lend money to their crew members are willing to waive all interest or *vaTTi*, and apply little pressure for the return of the loan. Instead, the penalty is applied on the severance of the debt-relationship, when a 'fine' must be paid. The fine is all the more severe if the relationship is discontinued during peak fishing seasons, when the labour of the producer is particularly valuable. The characteristic flavour of rural credit has been noted by some (such as Friedmann 1979) to lie in this far-reaching relationship between interest and labour extraction:

> Interest rates are often so high that repayment is impossible, extending the debt relation indefinitely. At the same time, these interest rates are nominal, since money is often not involved either in the loan, or even more frequently, in the repayment. The pre-capitalist debt relationship is exploitative, and the mechanism of appropriation of surplus labour is interest (cited Harris 1982:189).

One of the means by which such exploitation is secured in fishing economies is price-fixing. By advancing credit to producers and pre-booking a portion of the catch, the merchant is able to fix the price well in advance, and usually at a rate lower than the producer would otherwise be able to obtain at market rates. In coastal villages in Kerala, it is common practice for boat-owners to advance loans to their crew as a means of ensuring sufficient labour power.

By contrast, the women's credit economy does not lead to the concentration of economic power in the hands of creditors, the obligations of the debtors being distributed over a very wide range of people, all owed relatively small amounts. Further, all the creditors are themselves producers—there is no social or class distinction between creditors and debtors. This underlines the way all these credit transactions have been deprofessionalised. Although certain individuals excel in raising credit and others are known to be good sources of credit, these individuals are not entirely representative of the way the system works. Finally, women's credit networks manipulate social relations to generate credit—whereas, to put the contrast in its most striking form, mercantile credit manipulates credit and interest rates in order to generate the kind of social relations most conducive to further profit for the merchant.

The hidden aspect of the operation of credit from merchants and middlemen is reflected in the mystified form in which it appears to villagers. If one may use a formulation derived from Marx's analysis of the wage form in capitalist society, the very form in which this kind of credit is made available renders it opaque to producers. My questions on the extent of debt and the sources of credit initially brought no mention of middlemen, agents or merchants—instead, I heard only of neighbours, kinswomen and acquaintances. Persistent questioning revealed that villagers view credit from middlemen and merchants as advances (and the English word would sometimes be used) rather than as debts, or *kaDan*. Since the form taken by repayment of advances was often, indeed typically, non-monetary, involving surrendering a portion of the catch, villagers did not view it as repaying a loan, but rather as their having received a sum of payment earlier rather than later. Most villagers urged me not to include these sums when calculating the extent of their indebtedness.

The form taken by the credit relationship between women, on the other hand, is relatively transparent as a relationship of debt. The interest rate results in some profit for the creditor, but at the same time, the structure of the interest rate, with an initial interest-free period built into it, emphasises the creditor's stake in the speedy return of the loan, rather than in the perpetuation of economic and social dependency.

In any case, the interest rates charged by women within Mukkuvar villages compare favourably to the interest rates charged in agricultural villages. Harris (1982:188*ff.*) summarises the available ethnographic evidence for India in his study of a village in the North Arcot District of Tamil Nadu. He records a range of interest which begins at 14 per cent of all produce, going up till 25–30 per cent in North Arcot District. In the particular village where he worked, the rates amounted to one-sixth by volume, which he records as unusually low compared to the 18–24 per cent per annum on major loans elsewhere in village India, and as even more of a contrast with the notorious rates recorded for the Purnea District of Bihar, where two units must be repaid for every one borrowed (Biggs and Burns, cited Harris 1982). These interest rates are all calculated on an annual basis. But even when we double the six-monthly interest rates charged in coastal Kanyakumari to render them comparable, the rates still compare favourably: 6 per cent per annum for jewellery collateral; and 10 per cent per annum on all other forms of collateral.

In offering this contrast, I do not mean to suggest that credit relations between individual women are necessarily free of conflict. The two cases given below amply illustrate the physical violence and even social upheaval which may result from the antagonism of debtors and creditors. Nevertheless the partners in such relations are evenly matched, and inability to pay results in the rupture of social bonds rather than in the perpetuation of debt bondage across generations.

Case studies of conflict generated by credit relations between women

Case A

Family A and Family B were quite friendly. One of the women in Family A ran a chit fund, and her husband, being related to Family B, had extended them small loans out of her earnings. A fight developed when the former tried to reclaim some of the loans, and was denied reimbursement. There was verbal abuse and some fighting. That night, the men from family B came over and hit the woman who was responsible for giving them the loans. The conflict escalated when the men from Family A returned to find the woman lying in a heap. In the ensuing fight, one of the young men from Family B was killed. A case was filed with the police, and one of the young men in Family A served a commuted sentence of seven years. Family A was also driven out of the village by the other family, and they fled to Colachel, leaving all their possessions to be claimed by the other family. Family B in fact gained a substantial amount monetarily. Not only were their loans cancelled, but they claimed money from the insurance company on the basis of a loss in their working capacity. They also claimed a government grant designed to encourage widow remarriage, by marrying their second son to the widow of the dead elder son. It has been hard to verify some of the extent of these financial gains since most accounts from other villagers are unsympathetic, but the decline of the other group, family A, seems indisputable.

Case B

This quarrel involves four households: A, B, C, D. The relationships between the households illustrate some of the overlapping ties of work and kinship in the village. Household C buys the prawn catch from household B, while the eldest son of household A works for household B. The wife of household A has also borrowed money from a fourth household, D. A diagram of these relations would look like this:

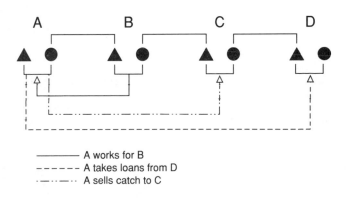

――――――― A works for B
― ― ― ― ― A takes loans from D
·―··―·· A sells catch to C

The woman from household D asked the woman from household A, whom we shall call X, to repay her loan. X asked her to wait, since her son had long been expecting payment from household C for a catch of prawns, after which she would be able to repay the loan. This was overheard by the daughter of household C, who was infuriated by the way her family affairs had been revealed in a way that did not reflect well on them. The girl, X's husband's niece, stole up behind her and dealt her a severe blow on the head with a piece of wood. As a result, X developed fits (*janni*), and was taken to various hospitals for treatment, and is currently receiving treatment from an *asan*, or practitioner of Siddha Vaidya. Her younger brother advised her to file a police complaint, which she has done.

While the above cases illustrate the considerable conflict and violence which may occur at the individual level, we are still justified in characterising the system as a whole as possessing a cooperative flavour lacking in other forms of rural credit.

The final contrast between the two forms of credit lies in their gender-specificity. The credit offered by merchants, middlemen or boat-owners typically is based on the relations of production and the activities of production, which have been monopolised by men. Thus agents and middlemen anxious to have a steady and assured source of catch at non-competitive prices will approach the fishermen with promises of an advance on future sales. Similarly, the owner of fishing boats and equipment will be approached by the male crew who work for him. As against this, we have already seen how the small-scale loans generated by women base themselves in female-dominated spheres of social relations.

I end this section by extending the comparison of women's credit with the more formal institutions of rural credit, namely banks and cooperatives. Only very few loans are taken by Mukkuvar villagers from these formal institutions. Of the total number of 258 loans which I recorded in the 100 households, only 5.43 per cent were borrowed from banks, the local cooperative and the local credit society. The reasons for this lack of popularity are not hard to locate. First, government-based institutions are not prepared to accept the particular range of assets available in fishing villages. Banks will not accept fishing gear and nets as collateral, and neither banks nor the local cooperative will accept items such as brass cooking vessels. True, banks would accept jewellery as surety, but they offer less money in exchange for a given quantity of gold than women are prepared to offer each other. Thus banks offer anything between Re800–1200 per ten grams (approximately) of gold (locally, one *pavan*), whereas village women readily offer Re1200 for the same amount.

Secondly, banks and cooperatives define the purposes for which credit may legitimately be given according to extremely narrow criteria, where only production-related goals are deemed acceptable and production is defined as short-term investment in purchasing or improving the means of production. This immediately renders unacceptable the vast majority of purposes for which women seek loans. While I was unable to obtain details on the purpose of every one of the loans taken by the households included in the sample, only 21 per cent of the loans for which details were made available may be described as related to production, and this figure is based on a much broader definition of production than that used by banks and cooperatives. For example, I have included loans which were taken to invest in a son or daughter's education and training, or to send a son overseas in search of work. For the remaining 79 per cent of the loans, taken for needs such as daily requirements for food, medical bills, house repairs and social obligations such as dowry and pilgrimage, formal sources of credit are unavailable.

In areas such as neighbouring Kerala, where the impact of rural credit schemes and bank loans is more considerable than in Tamil Nadu, the fishing communities have tended to bypass the restrictions imposed by these formal sources of credit. Here, credit-worthy households which have the assets to satisfy banks and credit societies borrow from the banks and re-lend the money at higher rates of interest as consumption loans to the rest of the community (Naik, social worker in Trivandrum, personal communication).

In defining production to separate it artificially from the encompassing complex of social relations, and in doing so rendering the former a legitimate, credit-worthy goal, banks and government cooperatives have perhaps unwittingly discounted many of women's activities in the fishing community. Although there is now some awareness among community-based aid organisations and church groups in Kanyakumari District that there is a need for credit in some areas of women's work such as fish trading and net-weaving, the main trend ignores the vast bulk of work that occurs in simply keeping the household alive in between the peaks of the fishing cycle. Nor have government-based institutions been fully cognisant that financial dealings in fishing societies such as Kanyakumari's are largely 'women's business'. Loans designed to make new technological innovations in fishing available to the community continue to be offered to men, although women are more often involved in raising loans for the purchase of nets, gear and *kaTTumaram*. In raising money for such purposes, women pawn their jewellery and call on the same sorts of ties they utilise for consumption loans. The division between production and consumption is therefore somewhat artificial, from the point of view of the women who make the financial decisions in both spheres and who are increasingly being called upon to provide cash from their dowries for new patterns of male work (see Chapter 8).

Politically motivated groups with goals that are explicitly female-centred have begun to deal with the problem of supplying credit to women in the poorer labouring classes in necessarily novel and radical ways. The best publicised and possibly the most successful of these ventures is the Self Employed Women's Association (SEWA) in Ahmedabad, Gujarat, which has utilised its original basis in the trade union movement to enrol vast groups of women hitherto untouched by the union movement (Jain 1980). The enrolment of such groups is an enormous improvement on the economic reductionism practiced by banks, cooperatives and credit societies, where all social problems are reduced to the level of financial transactions. As Thorner pointed out in the 1950s, it is precisely in their greater sensitivity to local economics as well as personal relationships that the traditional money-lenders have emerged victorious from the challenge of government efforts to uproot 'the evils of usury' (1964:27 *en passim*).

What is less often noted is the fact that rural populations have not been entirely lacking in initiative in setting up their own small-scale and cooperative modes of credit circulation, whose flexibility and roots in local networks could well be examined more carefully even by the more socially progressive brands of middle-class interventionism represented by SEWA. Systems such as those described for KaDalkarai Uuru have their broad counterparts in agricultural villages, as Harris' brief description of *cillaRai* (small change) loans in one village would suggest (1982). He describes these as 'small loans which are usually taken for consumption purposes for short periods', and although there are six villagers (four men and two women) particularly known as money-lenders, the pattern of the credit market is known locally as 'rolling' or 'lending and borrowing'—that is, a villager may simultaneously be owing money and be owed money (1982:189). Harris concludes by stating that 'Those farmers who do have funds try to keep their money circulating, and it appears that the money market may not be subject to oligopolistic control' (1982:190). Hill also argues in favour of localised systems of credit where creditors and debtors are in day-to-day communication within the village, 'a situation which does not necessarily imply the existence of any patron/client relationship' (1982:216).

It is even rarer to come across any explicit reflection on the value of such localised credit systems in suggesting more effective ways of reaching women currently disadvantaged by the terms and definitions employed by formal institutions of credit. It is here that the system evolved by the women of coastal Kanyakumari seems particularly rich. It is timely to ask ourselves the question: what are the links between the social, small-scale and local nature of Kanyakumari's village credit systems and their specifically female orientation? In the next section, I briefly survey the ethnographic literature on women and credit in other fishing societies to see what light they shed on such questions.

Women and credit in fishing villages: a comparative ethnographic assessment

The data on credit giving and receiving among women in coastal Kanyakumari contrasts in a number of ways with the kind of picture sketched in other ethnographic accounts of fishing communities, and of the role of women in credit. Thus Norr (1972), in her ethnography of a fishing village near Madras, mentions women handling sums of money, but claims that: 'Women deal only with petty sums of money—larger amounts for sudden expenses or investments are *men's* affairs. If quarrels occur in this realm they are long lasting and serious. They are avoided by only loaning to *men* already close—kin, close friends, employees—since sanctions for repayments are only informal' [emphasis added] (Chapter 2, p.116).

In Norr's account, women's financial affairs are subsidiary to men's. The data from Kanyakumari contrast with this conclusion in virtually every one of these respects. Firstly, consumption loans are not necessarily small sums of money. Indeed, some of the largest loans raised in the village are for the purpose of dowry. The smallest sums involved in loan raising are rarely less than Re500, itself no mean amount. Secondly, the division between productive and consumption loans does not fall along sexual lines. Finally, if the seriousness of fights is an index of the relative weight attached to men's and women's affairs, this hardly provides ground for inferring the primacy of men's realm. One of the two fights which have ended in murder in KaDalkarai Uuru involved inter-household tension between women over the payment of loans (see Case A, p.155), and resulted in the permanent expulsion of one of the households involved.

A recent article by Abraham (1985) based on fieldwork in a fishing village in Kerala comes closer to one part of the kind of assessment I have argued for in this chapter: that is, of the credit system as a popular and flexible alternative to the power of middlemen, as a strategy of self-reliance when faced with the vagaries of a fishing economy. However, Abraham, like Norr, finds the system to be confined to subsistence needs, with amounts rarely exceeding Re500. In her experience, loans up to Re100 are exempt of interest, which operates to keep the scale of loans smaller than in KaDalkarai Uuru. Investment-related loans in this Kerala village are given by an entirely different category of households—that is, those with substantial surplus cash, charging interest at normal rates.

An even more striking contrast with Kanyakumari fishing villages is that there is simply no mention in Abraham's account of the role of women in the subsistence credit system she describes. While it is possible that there is an entirely different sexual division of labour in Kerala fishing villages, one suspects that it is the account which is flawed by the dominant tendency in social theory to 'de-gender' one's data, particularly in economic analyses of production and finance.

This suspicion is strengthened by the association between women and financial management which consistently emerges from accounts of fishing communities elsewhere in Asia. Rosemary Firth, in a piece of work which quite explicitly recommends and embodies notions of a sexual division of labour within anthropological fieldwork (1943), makes several references to the role of Malay fisherwomen as bankers:

All money earned by the fisherman is given to the woman both to spend and to save. The peasants say that this is natural, 'for who should guard the money while we are away all day, if not the woman?' A friend of ours once remarked, when his wife was very ill, that it was difficult because he had to keep an eye on the cash, which he could not do all the time when he was out and about working. The same man told us that he did not know exactly how much money his wife had in the house. If he wanted sums for the purchase of boats or nets, he would ask his wife, and she would tell him if she thought they could afford it or not (p.17).

The strength of this tradition that the woman is the banker is shown in many ways. One man told us that he would be willing to give more money to an old relative of his, but as he was no connection of his wife's she did not like to give much. Although wages to our Kelantan servant and his wife were always handed by me to him, when he wanted to borrow some money for a ceremonial occasion, he came to me with the request 'Che Mbong [his wife] would like four dollars in advance.' I met one woman who complained bitterly of the way her husband treated her; the climax of it all was that he never gave her any money, but insisted on buying the rice and so on himself. This she regarded as quite outrageous, and it was certainly unusual (p.18).

Firth adds a few more anecdotes of this kind, but makes no analysis of the mechanisms of credit. However, these details are included in Alexander's ethnography on a Sri Lankan fishing village (1982):

Despite their small role in the main productive activities, it is women who manage the household's resources. In all but the richest households, wives receive their husbands' earnings intact and plan consumption until further income is received. Apart from patron and client or advances from middlemen to fishermen, credit is also arranged by the women. All the village moneylenders (eight) are women, as are the revolving credit associations (*sittuwa*) organisers (four), and men can only participate in these through their wives. Women make the financial arrangements for ceremonies, especially weddings or funerals, and the decisions to invest in land or fishing gear, although the actual purchases are arranged by men (1982:41)

In two of the three categories of loans described by Alexander, women play a key role either as borrowers or lenders, and even in the third category, women organise the social occasions for which loans are sought. As in KaDalkarai Uuru jewellery is the preferred form of security and gives women a certain edge in being able to conduct credit transactions.

In sum, then, most accounts confirm the special role of women in the credit economy of fishing villages, but significant variations occur in the size of the loans for which women are responsible, the purposes for which these loans are taken and the degree of reliance on professional money-lenders, whether male or female.

By all accounts, KaDalkarai Uuru still emerges as unusual in that women are able to utilise their own, non-professional social networks in order to generate loans which range from small to large according to Alexander's schema. It would seem particularly important to acknowledge this evidence, given the tendency to assume the periph-erality of women to financial management, and the operation of the cash economy in general. In India at least, women's exchanges have been ethnographically conceptualised mainly in terms of ritual exchange. As Sharma puts it in a recent article on dowry:

> It is largely women, and especially senior women, who control the flow and pace of gift-giving both within the household and with other households ... the proper regulation of gift-making at all ritual occasions (life-cycle rites, seasonal festivals, etc.) is an important function of the women of the household, and where these gifts consist of goods (sweets, clothing, household items) as opposed to cash, it is the senior woman of the household who has the prime responsibility for seeing that the obligations are met and proper relationships maintained (1984:65).

Such gift-giving has been shown to be an essential element in maintaining social continuity, mending broken relations and expressing the niceties of the social distribution of prestige. However, the kind of power women exercise through these activities is typically confined within a narrowly defined sphere of domesticity: its importance must never be overtly recognised, and it must always subordinate itself to male policies and initiatives. Naveed-i-Rahat (1981) describes women's participation in reciprocal gift relations in the Punjab as oriented primarily to the maintenance and strengthening of the social base on which the success of male enterprises implicitly rests.

In such accounts, women emerge very much as the covert manipulators of men, who can only act vicariously through men, even while they work hard at producing the goods and services that cement men's social relationships. Women's exchanges in the ritual sphere are here the precondition to the economic and political activities which are strictly a male domain.

Mukkuvar women's financial transactions provide a pointed exception to the generalised picture of 'women in south Asia' one may otherwise be tempted to extract from such accounts. Once again, the view from the coastal margins of a land-based economy proves significantly different from, even the inverse, of received orthodoxy on models of gender.

In Mukkuvar villages women utilise social and ritual bonds, established through marriage, work, neighbourhood and fictive kin relationships, to undertake financial transactions which owe little to male intervention, which blur any clear distinction between domestic and extra-domestic worlds, and which are recognised as vital to the daily and seasonal survival of households. In utilising social and ritual relationships in this perhaps unorthodox fashion, not only are women performing functions usually considered outside their domain, but they are also involved in other institutional subversions.

Within institutions such as dowry and marriage exchanges, women show considerable inventiveness at giving the economic and social capital at their disposal a whole new orientation. Dowry, which is examined in detail in Chapter 8, has as a whole operated to obscure the fact of women's dispossession from the main productive resources in the fishing economy. Nevertheless we find women skilfully utilising the one component of dowry over which they can exercise control—their jewellery—to make it serve as the basis for an elaborate redistribution of the available income. Formally gifted for the personal use of the bride, it has been adapted by Mukkuvar women to answer their special needs in a fishing economy, to serve as the guarantor of inter-household financial agreements. Similarly, the practice of exogamy, atypical as it is in the Mukkuvar context, still becomes, in women's hands, a way of extending the scope of their social networks and financial 'catchment' area. Their role as intermediaries between different families and villages allows them to act as intermediaries in the sphere of finance and credit.

In Mukkuvar society, it is the social and economic activity which helps explain the common apprehensions of femininity—expressed most directly in the religious and ritual spheres—as powerful and possibly dangerous to patriarchal control. Equally, such practices reinforce the special affinity women feel for those religious deities that are specifically responsible for the local environment and the female world of social relations. In the following chapter I examine another of the areas of practice which underpins female solidarity in Mukkuvar society—kinship and household formation.

7 Kinship and cultural power: the politics of caste and gender in kinship, marriage and household formation

The gift in general is an extremely meritorious action: one acquires merit by the gift of goods to the Brahmans, meaning that one thereby exchanges raw materials of no value for spiritual goods. Now the 'gift of a maiden' is a special form of gift, and it is meritorious on condition that no payment is received for the girl; here the girl is, on the whole, assimilated to a material good, and the giving of her is in fact accompanied by material gifts and by as lavish receptions as possible. In the hypergamous pattern, the superior status of the bridegroom's family makes it more demanding about the prestations it receives with the girl, as if it would only accept marriage into an inferior family on condition of receiving hard cash; but this precisely squares with the pattern of the gift: one gives a daughter and goods to a superior in exchange, not in this case for spiritual merit, but for something similar, namely the prestige or consideration which results from intermarriage with him (Dumont, 1980:117).

The relations of domination and subordination between the sexes in India, and overarching this, the relations of power between castes of superior and inferior status, impinge on and shape the practices of kinship, marriage and marriage payments. In the West, marriage and family have increasingly become shrouded in an ideology of individualism, privatisation and even a seeming opposition to the outside world. In India, in contrast, it requires no strenuous leap of theoretical or political imagination to find, in the principle of hierarchy which codifies the wider society, the conceptual model and mechanism that turns kinship into an extension of the politics of caste.

These connections need not be made afresh: they have been explicitly elaborated for us over the centuries by the efforts of Hindu lawgivers, who have attempted not only to codify, regulate and render homogeneous the tenets of Brahmanic ideology, but have applied and extended them to all cultural forms and practices, including those concerning the household and the family.

In the area of marriage, the principle of hierarchy translates itself into a clear distinction between wife-givers and wife-takers. Marriages which take the form of the gift of a virgin daughter are exalted, while more equal and egalitarian conceptions of marriage are denigrated. Manu the lawgiver sternly denounces any attempt by the father of the bride to share the burden of marriage expenses: 'No father who knows [the law] must take even the smallest gratuity for his daughter; for a man, who, through avarice, takes a gratuity, is a seller of his offspring' (*Manu* III, 51, cited Tambiah 1973:68).

The weight of authority and tradition vested in Sanskrit textual codification has meant that South Asian kinship and marriage systems tend to be evaluated largely in terms of the Brahmanic ideals. Yet in the south of India, non-Brahman kinship still remains vital and enshrines a coherent alternative set of principles and values which place considerations of ritual purity and hierarchy secondary to the consolidation of economic power, and emphasise the continuance of strong bonds between brother and sister even after marriage.

The Mukkuvars share certain important features of this southern pattern of marriage and kinship, placing their already pronounced cultural distance from Sanskritic Hinduism on an even firmer footing. At the same time the anomalous status of the Mukkuvars in caste society is confirmed all over again in the realm of kinship: aspects of marriage recruitment and household formation 'fit' neither of the polarities of Brahman or non-Brahman kinship, and instead suggest important modifications to the classic ethnographic model of Tamil social structure.

In order to enable the reader to appreciate the various contrasts presented by Mukkuvar kinship, I will briefly describe the opposing principles of Sanskritic and non-Sanskritic (Tamil) kinship, particularly focusing on their contrasting implications for the status of women.

The Brahmanical view of marriage

The textual tradition referred to as Brahmanic is in fact not a homogeneous one—it can be referred to in the singular only for convenience's sake. Texts such as the Arthasastras and the Manusmritis, written and compiled over a period between 400BC and AD400, are marked by internal inconsistencies which reflect the historical process of accumulation and accretion by which they were compiled (Mukherjee 1978:97*ff.*). Nevertheless, the texts also employed linguistic and textual devices, explored by Guha (1983:38–39), to manufacture an appearance of internal rigour and to 'systematise codes of authority'.

These codes of authority, which arranged social relations into hierarchical dyads (father/son, husband/wife, king/subject, god/devotee) posited certain ideals of the family and of marriage. The ideal family is a 'patrilineal joint family consisting of a three to four generation agnatic descent group of males, their wives and unmarried daughters' (Grey 1982:213). Authority is organised in such a family according to a hierarchy of age and gender, with men ranking over women, and older men over younger men. Women derive authority, in this model, through their relationships with men—as their wives, and secondarily as their mothers. The solidarity of this joint family is brought about by the ideological fusion of what are in fact distinctive and separable sets of practices: economic functions, ritual functions and the tasks of domestic reproduction are all brought under a hierarchically imposed unity of interests. Thus, conflicts of economic interest are hypothetically dissolved by enjoining all earning members to pool their contributions, leaving the redistribution of resources to the senior male head of the family. Similarly, all tasks associated with domestic reproduction are meant to be shared—in this case by the women.

The two fundamental principles of the joint family, that is, shared property and a shared domestic hearth, are not only ideologically defined to fuse functions and interests which could be otherwise separated, but are also defined in a way that enshrines a sexual division of labour.

In the area of marriage, the ideology of hierarchy and the ideology of the gift have fused in the manner indicated by Dumont in the opening quotation of this chapter: the giving of a woman, assimilated to the status of other movable 'goods', becomes the most prestigious way in which human beings can seek to establish a relationship with the sacred or with their earthly superiors. As a mobile counter in an exchange whereby her father gains status and her husband's family gains a woman and accompanying wealth, the woman's inheritance can necessarily only consist of a portion of other goods which, like herself, are movable. The implications of this for the woman's property right are examined in the next chapter. But the principle of woman-as-gift brings with it important structural consequences. The merit of giving away the daughter can best be consolidated by giving the daughter to someone superior in rank, purity and merit—that is, the principle of hypergamy becomes the basis for seeking marriage alliances. The logic of the system also drives the wife-givers to seek prestigious connections from greater and greater distances, since repeated marriage would only fix and solidify status inequalities between wife-takers and wife-givers (Tambiah 1973:93). The practice of virilocality is a further extension of the logic of giving the woman away as gift—the daughter is given by the father to the groom, not only to reside with him, but to be absorbed into his family. In extreme cases this may be expressed in terms of the wife coming to share the natural substances of the husband, becoming a natural extension of her husband and ceasing definitively to be a member of her father's clan (Barnett 1976).[1]

The connections between a particular ideology and features such as dowry, patrilocality and hypergamy are not of a causal kind. Obviously the latter can and do exist in many societies without the precise ideological gloss found in India. Rather, it is a matter of Sanskritic ideology finding fuller expression in certain social arrangements rather than others.

As against the south Indian patterns of marriage and kinship, which we shall look at next, the north of India has tended to more closely approximate the Sanskritic ideals of virilocal and patrilocal residence, village exogamy and hypergamy. Its effect on women's lives has been, quite simply, to split them in two: the relatively free, asexual daughter in one's *peke* (the village of birth and childhood) versus the fertile, sexual wife who is hedged about with rules of concealment, constraint and hierarchy in the *saure* (village one is married into, where one's parents-in-law live). The distinction comes up repeatedly in ethnographies sensitive to women's experiences:

> For a young wife, the change from her natal to conjugal home is drastic. Whereas in the former she is a divine human worthy of worship, enjoying comfortable relations with her brothers and sisters, in her conjugal home she is a stranger with strictly hierarchical relations with husband and affines. She is also the focus of the contradiction in the household structure—a contradiction with the potential to disrupt most relations within the *pariwar* [household] (Grey 1982:221–222; cf. also Sharma 1980:41).

The Tamil (Dravidian) system of kinship

Mukkuvar kinship reveals itself to be part of a wider configuration of South Indian kinship, which must be characterised as specific to the non-Brahman castes of the south. At its core, the distinctiveness of non-Brahman kinship is a simple one: the non-Brahman south expresses, through its marriage rules and kinship terminology, a positive preference for cross cousin marriages, i.e. where Ego is male, marriage with the mother's brother's daughter or father's sister's daughter, and in certain areas, with the elder sister's daughter. All relatives in one's own (Ego's) generation and at least the first ascending and descending generation are divided into two categories, 'cross' and 'parallel'. Marriages are permitted with immediate genealogical cross-cousins and with more remote relatives falling into the same category. Beck has pointed out (1972:217–218) that there are no terms in the language, at least in Tamil, to designate cross and parallel categories—they are simply reflected in the classification of relatives under a single four-fold scheme, which in turn governs marriage behaviour and, by extension, general behaviour.[2]

The marriage preferences are not necessarily of a statistically dominant character among the castes of southern India. Beck's tabulation of various ethnographic accounts of different regions of Tamil Nadu indicates that the percentage of cross marriages varies between 5–15 per cent (1972:253). However, Dumont has argued, along structuralist lines, that the rules are dominant in the sense that they serve as normative models which structure behaviour, kinship terminology and overall kinship ideology, in much the same way that hypergamy serves as a conscious model in the north of India, even among castes that do not actually practise it (1966).

Dumont, as usual, has managed to express the distinctiveness of the southern pattern in a controversial and theoretically striking formulation. He has argued in *Affinity As a Value* (1983) that in the south, relations of affinity are actually inherited from one generation to another without being transformed into relations of consanguinity. The Tamil terms for individuals related in the cross category cannot, he argues, be rendered as, for example, mother's brother's sons or father's sister's sons: the terms for these individuals (*macaan, ataan*), from a woman's point of view, 'are words which describe people already defined as affines, i.e., charged with sexual significance and license.'[3] The difficulty of understanding this inheritance of affinity has been responsible, according to Dumont, for many anthropological misreadings of Dravidian kinship.

The second feature singled out by Dumont is that the marriage system sets up a pattern of localised alliances. Unlike north India, where marriage with close cognates and into the lineages/clans of one's mother, father's mother, mother's mother, etc. is disallowed, the system in the south has 'overtones of restricted exchange' (Tambiah 1973:93). For Dumont, the southern system of kinship is not profoundly shaped by the concern for hierarchy as is northern kinship. He is therefore moved to describe southern kinship as a sphere of relative egalitarianism in a world of hierarchy.

Dumont's argument is amply borne out by the work of other ethnographers of south Indian kinship. Beck's study of the 'Konku' region of Tamil Nadu (1972) demonstrates a striking concern for equality between wife-givers and wife-takers in the marriage rules and rituals among non-Brahman agricultural castes. An expressed preference for matrilateral cross-cousin marriage with the mother's brother's daughter or her category equivalent ensures that sisters and brothers remain of sufficiently equal status to allow their offspring to wed. There are no separate terms to distinguish wife-takers from wife-givers, while the matter of post-marital residence is determined by considerations of economic and political power rather than ritual rules. Uxorilocality may be adopted if it suits these purposes and marriages tend to be arranged within a narrow local territory of a five mile radius (cf. Harris 1982:139–144).

These features are important to bear in mind when we look at the characteristics of Mukkuvar kinship, since it situates Mukkuvars as part of this wider non-Brahman cultural configuration and reinforces their structural distance from Brahman culture. Brahman kinship (in the south), embodies concerns quite foreign to the Mukkuvars. For example, Brahman concern with the preservation of hierarchy and ritual purity rules out uxorilocality, since it undermines the respect that ought to be given by the bride and her family to the groom (Beck 1972:233). Their kin terminology distinguishes wife-givers and wife-takers to enable the latter to be given more respect. The marriage ceremony has no ritual bonding between brother and sister, and marriage payments take the form of dowry. The search for ritually pure partners spreads Brahman marriage alliances over a broader territory of up to 25–30 kilometres.

Not all anthropologists are happy with Dumont's way of contrasting northern and southern kinship systems and attempts have been made to dissolve the differences into an overall unity of a pan-Indian nature.[4] Certainly, it would be true to say that Brahman models of kinship are valorised in the south as they are in the north. However, Brahman kinship in the south is a compromised structure, attempting to strike a bargain between two coherent but opposed principles. Thus, Brahmans too have adopted the southern practice of cross-cousin marriage, but they attempt to distinguish themselves by preferring patrilateral cross-cousin marriage to the father's sister's daughter (FZD). In this way, instead of repeating an existing connection between clans and lineages, as occurs in marriages with the mother's brother's daughter (MBD), the Brahmans prefer to marry a woman in the same direction, transferring her from one descent group to a second in generation after generation (cf. Gough 1956:844).

As we have seen for the north, the seemingly technical details of kinship have vast implications for the status of women. The southern emphasis on close brother-sister bonding, enshrined in cross-cousin marriage, allows the woman continued access and even responsibility towards the family of origin. We have seen earlier that south Indian women do not escape the symbolic traps and double-binds by which male-dominated culture encompasses female sexuality. Nevertheless, as the crucial link in a male kin-nucleus of father, brother, husband and son, the woman is the guarantor of kinship relations. According to Beck (1974), the importance of the woman's fertility and ritual power is such that she forms the very basis of the kinship system, and consciously ensures its proper functioning. In a system where affines are inherited, and the distinction between affines and natal kin is blurred, the transition from one to another is hardly a jarring break in the woman's life. Her fertility and the well-being of her offspring continue to be of vital concern to her natal family even after marriage, for they provide future marriage partners (Wadley 1980: 164–165).

Kinship among the Mukkuvars

Mukkuvar kinship conforms with the main feature of the south Indian pattern of kinship: the emphasis on cross-cousin marriage—*sonda kalyanam* as the Mukkuvars describe it—marriage with one's own relatives. We may see this reflected in the kinship terminology. Parallel cousins are assimilated to the status of siblings, with whom marriage would be incestuous. Thus parallel male cousins are called *anna* or *thambi* (elder or younger brother), and parallel female cousins are called *akka* or *thangachi* (elder or younger sister). A further distinction is made between these parallel cousins and one's own siblings: the latter are described as '*kuuDai poranda thangachi/akka/* etc.', 'sibling who has been born *with* oneself'. The most salient contrast in the kinship system is the opposition between parallel cousins and cross-cousins. Terms such as *ataan* and *macaan* used to describe male cross-cousins are laden with the significance of viewing them as potential bridegrooms. Mukkuvars also call the male cross-cousin the *more mapillai* for the girl, that is, the bridegroom by customary law. Furthermore, after marriage, the husband and wife continue to use the same terminology to describe each other's relatives as they used before marriage—a practice which only makes sense if we assume that the affines are also related in a consanguineal fashion.

The kinship vocabulary also allows for the relative equality of wife-givers and wife-takers, as against the distinctions embedded in hypergamous systems. For example, the bride and groom both refer to their in-laws as *maama* and *maamii*. These are not purely affinal terms either: they refer simultaneously to consanguineal categories, since the *maama* is also a mother's brother and his categorical equivalent, the *maamii* a mother's brother's wife. Other such transpositions are apparent in the brief list of kin terms given in Table 7.1.

In terms of a broad Brahman versus non-Brahman division in the area of kinship and marriage, Mukkuvars fall squarely within the non-Brahman model. Not only does their kinship terminology allow for little distinction between wife-givers and wife-takers, but their patterns of post-marital residence emphasise economic rather than ritualistic concerns, allowing greater room for individual circumstances to modify prescribed forms.[5] On the whole, a greater proportion of marriages result in virilocal residence, but opportunities also exist for uxorilocal and neolocal residence (see Table 7.2).

The issue of post-marital residence is evaluated on the basis of practical considerations: the economic opportunities presented by the fishing seasons and the types of fishing employed in a given area; the

Table 7.1   Mukkuvar kinship terminology, showing equivalences between consanguineal and affinal classifications

		The same terms are used for the following categories
Man's terms for wife's kin		
Wife's father and mother	*maamaa/maamii*	mother's brother, mother's brother's wife
Wife's elder sister	*anni/mahini*	younger brother's wife
Wife's younger sister	*kolundi*	younger brother's wife
Wife's younger brother	*machaan*	younger sister's husband
Wife's elder brother	*machaan*	elder sister's husband
Woman's terms for husband's kin		
Husband's father and mother	*maamaa/maamii*	
Husband's elder sister	*anni/mahini*	elder brother's wife
Husband's younger sister	*anni/mahini*	younger brother's wife
Husband's younger brother	*kolundan*	younger sister's husband
Husband's elder brother	*machaan/ataan*	elder sister's husband

Source: Fieldwork data from KaDalkarai Uuru.

amount of kin cooperation available to men (e.g. in the provision of fishing gear) and to women (e.g. financial cooperation in their credit transactions). Such considerations may lead not only to uxorilocality, but to a pattern of shifting residence, followed by about five per cent of households in KaDalkarai Uuru. Consider the following cases:

Case A
In household A, the wife had initially moved to her husband's home for two years. The marriage had been conducted against the wishes of the groom's family, and as a result, the bride had to contend with a hostile environment. The couple returned to KaDalkarai Uuru at her wishes. The husband quotes a Tamil proverb to explain this move: '*Thai ki pin thaarum*', or 'behind the mother, go the family'. The husband continues to return to his village for two to three months of the year to dive for oysters, but they reside in KaDalkarai Uuru.

Case B
After a period of six years of seasonally shifting migration between the wife's and the husband's village the couple has settled in favour of residence in the wife's village. The move is attributed to recurring illness on the part of the husband, and the offer of financial aid from the wife's mother.

Case C
In this household, the wife is an educated woman, and works as the nursery schoolteacher at KaDalkarai Uuru. The permanency of her job, and the income she can earn, has caused the couple to move from Kadiapatnam, a village five kilometres away.

The contrast between non-Brahman and Brahman kinship carries us a certain distance in our attempt to place the Mukkuvars in a wider context. However, ethnographic models which divide the Tamil

Table 7.2   Type of residence taken up by those marrying out of KaDalkarai Uuru during the years 1972–82

Year	Virilocal number	Residence percentage	Uxorilocal number	Residence percentage	Neolocal number	Residence percentage
1972	4/8	50	—	—	—	—
1973	6/14	43	—	—	1/14	7
1974	4/9	44	—	11	1/9	12
1975	3/9	33	—	—	3/9	33
1976	2/17	11	5/17	30	4/17	24
1977	6/14	42	2/14	14	2/14	14
1978	5/13	39	1/13	8	3/13	23
1979	4/9	45	2/9	22	—	—
1980	3/10	30	1/10	10	3/10	30
1981	3/13	23	—	—	3/13	23
1982	5/8	62	—	—	—	—

Note: The above figures do not add up to a hundred per cent, since they do not include the group of people who marry *within* the village and continue to reside within it (see Table 7.5).

Source: Personal census conducted, following up information contained in the marriage registry.

social structure into two neat, opposed categories of Brahman versus non-Brahman, or left-hand versus right-hand castes (Beck 1972) do not successfully explain all features of Mukkuvar kinship. Mukkuvar marriage alliances reflect neither concern with preserving ritual purity—they are too low-ranking for that—nor concern with consolidating economic power, since they are too poor for that as well. They do not even fit the pattern of marriage alliances of low-ranking service castes, whose populations are localised and scattered, forcing them to marry over a wide area (Beck 1972:232). Instead, Mukkuvar marriages show a concern with preserving the highly particular and 'closed' cultural universe of fishing communities, which their pattern of settlement in a dense, continuous belt helps them to sustain. These settlements also strictly define the boundaries of marriage networks. Not only is caste endogamy closely observed, but marriages are rarely conducted with Mukkuvars who have given up fishing and settled further into the interior, if only to work as fish-traders. The concern for caste endogamy, a characteristic feature of Hindu marriage rules, remains undimmed by conversion to Catholicism.

Church parish records of marriages bear out this Mukkuvar preference for conducting marriages close at hand. In the ten years 1972–1982, between 90–100 per cent of marriages were conducted within Kanyakumari District (see Table 7.3). A majority of these marriages united families in coastal villages (see Table 7.4). The preference for local marriages was carried one step further: a high proportion of marriages (30 to 50 per cent over those ten years in KaDalkarai Uuru) were conducted within the village itself (see Table 7.5).

Data for earlier years are sketchy and incomplete since KaDalkarai Uuru did not have its own independent church records until 1972.

Table 7.3   Proportion of marriage partners found within Kanyakumari District for the years 1972–82

Year	Numbers	Percentage
1972	11/11	100
1973	14/15	93
1974	9/10	90
1975	9/9	100
1976	20/20	100
1977	19/19	100
1978	13/13	100
1979	11/13	85
1980	—	—
1981	12/13	92
1982	8/8	100

Source: Church marriage registry at KaDalkarai Uuru.

Until then KaDalkarai Uuru, along with numerous other coastal and inland villages, registered its marriages, births and deaths with the Church of Colachel. However, where KaDalkarai Uuru is mentioned in these earlier records (1870–1970) at the Colachel Church registry, the pattern seems to hold. Throughout this period, there are only two years (1920, 1930) when women from KaDalkarai Uuru married into non-coastal villages in the interior. Similarly, the records indicate that the proportion of intra-village marriages averaged around 40–50 per cent in this period.

For most people, marriage within the village also involves residence within the village; all the couples who married within the village in the ten years between 1972–82 remained residents of the village.

I will come back to the significance of these patterns of marriage alliance from the perspective of Mukkuvar women a little later. But first, I wish to develop more fully the striking divergence of Mukkuvars from other castes in Tamil society, whether high or low ranking, whether of left-hand or right-hand division, in the context of household formation.

Household formation

Throughout India the family has been seen to be divided, according to function, into two spheres: a male-dominated sphere concerned with property and property management, and a female-dominated sphere concerned with the domestic hearth (Beck 1978, Grey 1982). While the symbolic importance of the female-centred hearth is readily granted, when it comes to explaining conflict, fission and the restructuring of the family anthropologists have tended to minimise the importance of the peasant view on the matter. Where peasants

Table 7.4   Proportion of marriage alliances with partners from non-coastal villages, for the years 1972–82

Year	Numbers	Percentage
1972	—	—
1973	2/14	14
1974	—	—
1975	—	—
1976	1/17	6
1977	—	—
1978	2/13	15
1979	1/9	11
1980	1/10	10
1981	—	—
1982	1/8	13

Source: Church marriage registry at KaDalkarai Uuru.

Table 7.5   Proportion of marriage partners found within the village of KaDalkarai 1972–82

Year	Numbers	Percentage
1972	4/8	50
1973	7/14	50
1974	3/9	33
1975	3/9	33
1976	6/17	35
1977	4/14	29
1978	4/13	30
1979	3/9	33
1980	3/10	30
1981	7/13	54
1982	3/8	38

Source: Marriage registry at KaDalkarai Uuru.

point to the tensions between women as primary in splitting up a joint family into nuclear components, anthropologists (Grey 1982, Mandelbaum 1972, Ishwaran 1968) have preferred to view this explanation as a smoke-screen to hide the 'real' tensions between men over conflicting interests in property.

The entire debate needs re-casting if we are to see it from the perspective of the Mukkuvars, where women control not only the hearth but also several important areas within the so-called male sphere of property. Women are important in the day-to-day financial management of the home as well, and are identified with the household in ways that are of far more than symbolic significance. Indeed, women have in some cases succeeded in giving their names to their clans, over at least a couple of generations. These kin-based groupings in the village (described to me by villagers with the English word 'set'), are often identified by idiosyncratic names rather than the formal name of the senior male head. The names are not enduring;

they may hinge around an individual worthy of note, such as a man noted for his fishing skills, as with names such as *kalla chaalai* (cunning sardine), and *marathu kaaran* (a hook-and-line fisherman of particular repute). Others referred to a well-known deformity, such as the *nondiyaar* (the lame one). A third type of name refers to a distinctive group occupation which sets members apart from other villagers (such as the *madi ketti* clan who tie nets together, or the Anthony clan, who work as barbers). However, women of unusual capability often give their names to their clan. The house I lived in was identified as the Colombo *kaari veeDu*, or the 'house of the Colombo woman', referring to the fact that the grandmother had been married into a Colombo family early in her life. My research assistant typically introduced herself to villagers in the neighbouring village of Colachel as belonging to the house of Claramma, her grandmother. Other women's names (such as Pichai, Konathan, Poocha, Pillai) were among the twenty-three named clan groupings given to me.

Given this unusual situation, where nearly all the key functions of the household are associated with women rather than men, women's ability to cooperate within the household has far greater repercussions on the form taken by the household than have relations between men. The likelihood of clashes occurring is also greater between women than between men. Conflict over the management of financial and domestic resources is seen by villagers to be almost inevitable. Men's property—at least, in its material and tangible forms such as nets, boats, and fishing gear—is not a major source of tension between male kinsmen, nor do these items affect the structure of the household as such.[6] By contrast, women's property, mainly jewellery given as part of their dowry, is important to the entire household to which the bride belongs, and the distribution of its value to other members of her natal as well as her conjugal household may be a source of considerable tension. As described in the previous chapter, jewellery forms the basis for raising credit for daily consumption needs. It may also be called upon to finance other marriages. These may include the marriages of the bride's husband's unmarried sisters, but her natal family may also feel entitled to call upon her to assist in financing her own sisters' marriages. This in itself may cause tensions between the bride and the parents-in-law. In recent times, women's dowry is also increasingly called upon to finance men's purchase of capital equipment. These different uses have varying degrees of cultural legitimacy, as I will show in the next chapter, but are also factors which strain cooperation between senior and junior women co-residing in a joint family.

Brahmanic ideology seemingly resolves this conflict of interests between women by imposing a hierarchy of seniority and representing the joint family as an indissolubly fused entity. Traces of such an ideology are certainly present among the Mukkuvars. Older women informants in particular recalled that in their youth they had been expected to subordinate themselves to their mothers-in-law. 'In that age, all things were shared, and had to be shared,' recalled a sixty-year-old woman. Even now, only a minority of women openly show their anger if they feel their dowry has been squandered by their in-laws. In two of the three cases I came across or heard about, the women went back to their own parents, in one case living there for three years before returning. In the third case, the rift became serious enough to initiate a move to set up separate households, with in-laws and the young couple living apart. In Mukkuvar society, as elsewhere in India, the ability of the woman to follow through her opposition to her in-laws depends a great deal on the support the husband is prepared to give his wife, and such support may not always be forthcoming, as the details noted on one of the above three cases illustrates:

> The husband of Virgin has been taking her jewellery and passing it on to his parents to finance a costly court litigation that they are involved in with their neighbours. The husband's assurances that he was placing the jewellery in a bank were finally discovered to be a lie by Virgin, and she went back to live with her parents. Relations between Virgin and her husband were already soured by the fact that the husband had loved another woman before his marriage, and this woman has now come back to live in the village. Virgin's departure for her parents angered the husband so much that he threw all her belongings, including her best wedding saris, into the ocean. Virgin has now returned, and is living with her husband and in-laws, but enjoying a markedly diminished status within the family.

However, the hierarchy within the joint family is not seen by Mukkuvars as something to be preserved at all costs—the ideology of a fused unity is countermanded by a recognition of separate interests. Villagers were fond of saying '*taayum pillaiyum vaayum vayarum veerai*' ('the mother and child have separate mouths and stomachs'). Even in the most intimate of relationships, between mother and child, there is a separation of functions and interests.

This recognition is built structurally into household arrangements. Fifty-seven per cent of all the households in KaDalkarai Uuru were nuclear. In this the Mukkuvars are no different to other low-caste groupings. Those at the bottom of the hierarchy tend to live in small households, in nuclear families (Cohn 1955, Searle-Chatterjee 1981, Gough 1956, Beck 1972, Kolenda 1967).

In addition to this preference for nuclear families, Mukkuvars structure even their apparently 'joint' families on a radically disaggregated model of living. Households which appear to be joint kin groups turn out to be discrete nuclear entities sharing only residence under one roof. All other facets of joint living—the sharing of resources, cooking and property—are missing. The incomes and cooking arrangements of each nuclear family are kept discrete and separate. Similar arrangements hold even in cases of uxorilocal residence, with the married daughter cooking and managing finances separately from her mother. The conflict that is feared is therefore not merely between women in the husband's household—it is seen as possible even between mother and daughter. One of the key bases for the 'naturalisation' of familial functions—the fusion of a biological relationship with social activities such as the cooking and sharing of food and residence—is here radically disrupted. Daughters and daughters-in-law maintain their own discrete areas of autonomy, separate from mothers and mothers-in-law, sharing only the area of residence and cooperating on a selective basis. Such an arrangement undermines the relations of authority not only between men and women, but also between senior and junior women—a power relationship which may be even more critical to women's status at an immediate daily level of existence. Further, if conflicts do emerge despite these arrangements, junior women are in a stronger position to bring pressure to bear on their husbands to move out and form a separate establishment.

Separation into separate nuclear establishments occurs in the vast majority of the cases. There were only three instances in the entire village where hearths were shared outside the boundaries of a nuclear unit: married brothers living with parents; married sisters, living next door to each other but sharing cooking arrangements; and a married couple sharing the hearth with the husband's parents, but keeping incomes separate. Evidently, the nuclear unit structures even the joint household. It seems more than possible that the sharing of residence has more to do with the scarcity of alternative accommodation than with any emulation of a patrilineal ideal.

Such a hypothesis is strengthened by the wide variety of types of households found in KaDalkarai Uuru, arrangements which challenge the assumption of male-centredness. Scholarly typologies of familial forms, such as found in Kolenda (1967), stand in need of considerable re-definition before they can be used to classify Mukkuvar households. Kolenda's schema[7] assumes that relatives living in a conjugal unit are necessarily related only to the husband—but in KaDalkarai Uuru, these households, defined as 'supplemented conjugal households', most often contain relatives of the wife—either her parent(s) or sibling(s). Again, for Kolenda, there is a sharp distinction between a 'lineal joint family' and a 'supplemented nuclear family' because it is assumed that authority will shift from a senior married couple to their son with the death of one of the parents. For Mukkuvars on the other hand, very little changes in the event of such a death, since there is no clear-cut hierarchy, and the various functions of a joint household are radically disaggregated in any case.

The typology used to examine household types in KaDalkarai

Uuru is therefore a modified one and needs to be interpreted with the above important caveats in mind.

Some of the unique features of the data presented in Table 7.6— such as the high percentage of conjugal households (57 per cent), and the co-existence of uxorilocal with virilocal residence—have received some comment already. The fuller ramifications of uxorilocality come through in the table, and deserve further comment. Firstly, among lineal joint families the number of uxorilocal and virilocal families is equal—that is, a married daughter is equally as likely as a married son to live with the parents. Twenty-three households fall into each category. Secondly, in cases where married siblings share residence, one is just as likely to find married sisters living together as married brothers or married brothers and sisters. There are two households falling into each of these categories in KaDalkarai Uuru.

These uxorilocal patterns of residence, combined with the prevalence of intra-village marriages, indicate the extent to which women can hope to retain close ties with their natal kin after marriage. In 46 per cent of households classified as 'supplemented conjugal', parents were being supported and looked after by their daughter and her husband. In four households, the married woman and her husband had undertaken responsibility for the woman's younger brother since the death of the woman's parents; and this included sharing their income and their cooking arrangements. The very fact that a married woman could undertake such responsibilities and be in a position to help her natal family must once again be related to the relative status equality of wife-givers and wife-takers in the cross-cousin marriage system, but it is further accentuated by the bias towards marrying within a small geographical area, and the permissibility of uxorilocality.

We do not get a full idea of the extent of kinship-based cooperation and mutual support if we concentrate exclusively on those sharing the one roof, minimising the amount of cooperation in matters of finances and food arrangements. While Mukkuvars prefer clear-cut differentiation of incomes and hearths, once granted this autonomy they establish relations of cooperation between households. The ideal is separate residences closely clustered in proximity to others of the same kin group. Fifty-three per cent of households are interrelated by kin ties. There are discernible patterns of kin clustering in the residential pattern of the village. Here again, bi-local patterns of residence make it possible for married women to remain near their natal kin, either parents or siblings. The most common kin relationship on which the residential clustering is based is that of married siblings living near one another. Here again, sibling bonds are not only the brother–sister bond emphasised by other ethnographers such as Beck. They also include bonds between sister and sister, and between brother and brother.

Sibling clusters are the dominant pattern, other patterns merely

Table 7.6   Types of households in KaDalkarai Uuru

Types of household	Numbers (out of 288)	Percentage
Conjugal	163	57
Sub-conjugal	16	6
Supplemented conjugal	28	10
Supplemented sub-conjugal	9	3
Lineal joint:		
Uxorilocal	23	8
Virilocal	23	8
Supplemented lineal joint	3	1
Collateral joint:		
Fraternal	2	0.6
Sororal	2	0.6
Cognatic	2	0.6
Supplemented collateral joint:		
Fraternal	1	0.3
Sororal	-	-
Cognatic	3	1
Supplemented lineal collateral joint	1	0.3
Single person household	4	1
Other	2	1

Source: Village census, conducted during fieldwork, 1983

extensions of this core. Table 7.7 sets out the variations: siblings plus married children, siblings with parents living close by and finally, married siblings plus married children or affinal kin.

In the course of describing the north Indian untouchable *mohulla* (residential neighbourhood) of Varanasi sweepers, Searle-Chatterjee (1981:51) points out that contrary to the stereotypic model of Indian social structure, the kin links in the *mohulla* are primarily of a uterine and affinal nature, not of an agnatic kind. This is true of KaDalkarai Uuru as well. Not only are the residential links uterine, but whereas the *mohulla* emphasises uterine and affinal relations, in KaDalkarai Uuru consanguineal and uterine links are crucial. Kin support is sought, by men and women alike, from siblings of both sexes, as well as parents.

By separating themselves into nuclear units, but living close together, Mukkuvars attempt to maintain their independence and minimise possibilities of conflict (particularly between women) while at the same time gaining the advantages of cooperation and solidarity.

Implications for Mukkuvar women

The patterns of marriage, household formation and residence all help explain the social forces which sustain women in fulfilling their challenging role within the sexual division of labour—namely, in keeping

Table 7.7   Patterns of kin-based residential clustering in KaDalkarai Uuru

(h'h. = household)

A   3 Groups based on sororal clustering

B   3 Groups based on fraternal clustering

C   7 Groups based on cognatic clustering

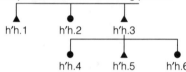

Extensions of these three patterns:

D   11 Groups based on the following pattern:

E   6 Groups based on the following pattern:

F   5 Groups based on the following pattern:

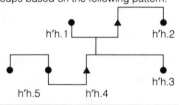

Source: Census, conducted during fieldwork, 1983

the domestic unit afloat, and in sustaining and reproducing it on a daily basis despite the uncertainties and fluctuations of the male-dominated economy of fishing. Let us glance at the data presented so far from the point of view of women. Marriage does not represent a radical change in women's lives, either in terms of the distances they have to travel, or in terms of their social roles. They marry others of the same fishing caste, and over half may expect to remain within the same village. Few women who marry out of the village go further than another coastal village within Kanyakumari District.

Thanks to the southern kinship system, with its emphasis on cross-cousin marriages, women and their natal families enjoy relative status equality with their husbands and the husbands' families. The dominance of the alliance model of marriage, rather than hypergamy, is partly reflected in the kinship terminology employed by husbands and wives towards affines. The continuity of the terminology also reflects the absence of a sharp break in women's lives at the time of marriage.

Within the village, women may live in the same house as their married brothers or sisters, or at least in separate but nearby houses. They may also live with their own parents, or in many cases look after them in their old age with their husband's support. Many are able to extend similar support to young unmarried brothers after their parents' death, and may be expected as a matter of course to extend financial help in getting their younger sisters married. The bonds with one's natal family therefore remain strong and viable well after marriage.

Those women who live with their husband's family avoid the close supervision and authority relations of a patrilineal joint family by maintaining separate cooking arrangements and separate financial management of their husband's income. If conflict between the bride and the mother-in-law escalates despite these arrangements, the former can legitimately move out and establish a separate residence without offending cultural norms—provided, of course, that scarce accommodation is available. Having moved out, the likelihood is that the nuclear family will establish its residence close to another married brother or sister in a kin-cluster which can be called upon for the kind of support that provides the basis for the female-run credit economy. The brother-sister bond is not merely about sisters seeking protection in case of maltreatment in the affinal home, as is the case in northern India, but about sisters being in a position to offer financial and material aid to brothers in times of need, by such means as pawning their jewellery to raise money for an overseas trip or offering their homes in case of a housing crisis. It should be stressed that married women also keep in close touch with their sisters and offer them similar forms of assistance.

The capacity of women to offer help to their natal families is in direct proportion to their control over household finances and the lack of status distinctions between their natal and conjugal families. Women call these families by different names: the former is their *sonda veeDu* (one's own home) and the latter their *poonda veeDu* (the home one enters), but these two terms are not laden with the heavy emotional connotations of the north Indian *peke* and *saure*, where the former represents, in retrospect, a lost era of childhood freedom. The implications of this contrast with the north carry over to the evaluation of daughters in the two cultures. Early in my stay I came across statements puzzling to anyone familiar with the status of women in Indian families: remarks that parents, or at least women, tried to 'keep their daughters close at hand' when they arranged their marriages. In the course of my investigations on health and healing practices, I came across a woman who had borne three sons, and was worrying over the survival chances of her ailing one-and-a-half year old daughter. She had already lost two daughters. She explained her larger concern: 'A daughter looks after you—at least when you are thirsty she will be there to give you water. A son marries and moves away—and especially once he partitions off his household, he won't even peep in to see how a mother is faring.' It seems that here it is sons and not daughters who are viewed as 'birds of the courtyard', destined to move away with marriage and therefore unreliable (Wadley 1980:165).

Household formation and proletarianisation

It is commonplace to point out that surveys and household classifica-tions necessarily freeze the fluctuating composition of the households, which is in some ways the very essence of south Asian households. Fluctuations may be related to the normal cyclical changes in the formation and fission of households, with marriage and the birth of children, and their eventual partition to form independent units. Numerous temporary changes also occur as a result of extended visits by kin, such as the visit of a daughter to her natal home on the occasion of her first pregnancy (Desai 1964, Dube 1955, Madan 1965).

Further changes may occur as a result of economic and material scarcities, exacerbated by the large-scale changes in the mode of production (Chapter 5). 'Joint families' may very well be a spurious category of analysis, given that families in many cases live under one roof simply because there is nowhere else for them to live. The sharing of accommodation as a form of mutual aid occurs regularly on an emergency basis. Poorer dwellings built of palm leaf and thatch are located on the beachfront and are periodically subject to mon-soonal flooding. The threat of fire is also ever-present: three houses of a superior (brick) variety were gutted by fire during my residence. I found households extending help to kin-related families whose houses had been damaged. In the first case, a married brother and family moved in with a married sister; in the second, a married daughter and family moved into her parents' household; in the third instance, a married woman and family moved into her married brother's household. (Again, note the importance of the women's parents and siblings). However, such mutual aid also extends beyond the circle of kin. A married woman of fifty, who worked as a fish vendor, stayed with her woman friend (*kumbadri*) who was also a vendor. The first was widowed and unwanted at home; her brother, with whom she had begun to live after the death of their mother, had found his own family too large to accommodate his sister easily. In another case, two families were living together temporarily as a result of work-based ties between the men, with one working as coolie for another.

Other forms of household fluctuations occur as a result of the built-in seasonal scarcity in fishing economies. I have already mentioned the incidence of men and families moving seasonally from husband's village to the wife's in order to take advantage of fishing opportunities in both places. In one household, a man had worked out reciprocal rights with the village of his *urimai penn*, the girl whom he was entitled to marry, his MBD—even though she was not actually his wife.

However, far more substantial changes are being wrought in household composition by the changing patterns of capitalist utilisation of male and female labour. Labour migration involves prolonged absences from the household. With 56 per cent of households experiencing the absence of male workers for periods of three to six months of the year, such alterations can no longer be seen as aberrant, but must be included in an understanding of the household.

Here traditionally evolved definitions of household types such as those of Kolenda appear inadequate. In well over half of the households in fishing villages, men ostensibly classified as members of the household are non-resident for a good part of the year. Yet they are part of the household insofar as they send money home and return for kin and religious occasions. If we take economic cooperation to be the key criterion for defining a household, as Sharma does in a similar situation in Punjab and Himachal Pradesh (1980), then we must conclude, as she does, that the boundaries of the household extend well beyond the boundaries of the village. Orthodox definitions concentrating on co-residence would find this a problem. We have already seen that sharing a residence is not necessarily a guide to the sharing of incomes, financial responsibilities and cooking arrangements in Mukkuvar villages. We now confront the opposite, but related paradox, where residence and economic cooperation do not go together. In fact, such cooperation increasingly requires rural men to move further afield in search of employment.

It has been suggested that the occupational diversification of household members, across rural and urban sectors, has actually favoured the persistence of the joint family (Rao 1968). But in KaDalkarai

Uuru there is no joint family in the traditional sense. During ordinary seasonal migration undertaken by the men in neighbouring districts or in Kerala, the women simply continue to reside in 'sub-conjugal units'. However, during the more prolonged absences of men who seek work overseas and are away for several years, the community feels it necessary to provide some symbolic protection for the women left behind, and here it is possible to find the creation of joint households. But in this case again, the Mukkuvar community allows for forms other than the patrilineal joint household—a married woman in such a situation may live either with her parents or her in-laws. Of the two cases in KaDalkarai Uuru, one woman lived with her parents and her children while her husband worked in the ship-yards of Vishakapatnam on the east coast; the other, recently married, lived with her in-laws and six brothers-in-law while her husband tried his luck at Bahrein. Under these new and unprecedented circumstances, women who would normally have looked forward to setting up their own independent units are now faced with the prospect of living with parents or in-laws for indefinite periods of time.

My concern with examining the impact of historical forces, particularly class formation, on the seemingly natural sphere of 'the family' is continued in the next chapter, where I examine the changing nature and significance of marriage payments.

8 Capitalism and marriage payments: the transformation of dowry from *sirdanam* (women's wealth) to male capital accumulation

Feminist campaigns in north Indian cities have, over the last few years, highlighted the occurrence of violence against women within the family, and simultaneously politicised the whole question of the way that marriages and marriage payments have become increasingly commercial transactions. While the political activism of the last decade has generated an intuitive understanding that we are confronting not only a quantitative increase, but a qualitative shift in the very meaning of dowry, we still have at our disposal remarkably few theoretical tools in order to examine the domestic domain historically, and establish connections between household, economy and political processes.

It is not as though anthropology has been indifferent to the question of linking marriage payments with broader economic and cultural processes. Indeed, one of the major preoccupations of Indian anthropology has been to describe the cultural ramifications of economic upward mobility in a caste-stratified order. In this process, described variously as Brahmanisation (van der Veen 1971) or Sanskritisation (Srinivas 1966), the shift from one mode of marriage payments, bride-price, to another, dowry, is an important way of consolidating the rise of a low-caste group in the ritual hierarchy. The model condenses within its argument two sorts of theories linking marriage payments with the wider social order: a cultural theory and an economic theory.

The cultural theory, implicit in the model of Sanskritisation, refers to the cultural hegemony of the Brahmanic view of marriage discussed in the previous chapter. The Sanskritisation model does not articulate any explicit theory of hegemony, or how it is achieved: it is merely taken for granted as something which has been established for all time, so that the only form of social change possible is upward mobility, which is culturally translated into the aspiration of lower castes to become as similar to upper castes as possible.

The economic theory which informs the Sanskritisation model is a version of Comaroff's argument (1980) linking marriage payments with the nature of women's work. In this view, where women's work takes the form of productive labour, marriage represents a loss of women's labour to her family, who must therefore be compensated with bride-price. Where women are unproductive, dependent members, dowry compensates the groom's family for having to incur the expenses of maintaining an extra dependent. Outside India, in the hands of writers such as Goody (1976) and Boserup (1970), the argument takes on a more global and complex form. Drawing on the traditions of nineteenth century theory and its interest in linking property institutions, marriage and women's status (Hirschon 1984:1), these writers link marriage payments and female property with the nature of the dominant mode of production, the form of agriculture and the degree of class stratification. Boserup (1970) associates shifting hoe cultivation with the centrality of female labour, relative freedom of movement, some economic independence, polygamy and bridewealth. Plough cultivation, she argues, marginalises women's role in production, and generates female dependency along with its associate, dowry. Goody elaborates on the theme of the consequences of plough cultivation and its concomitant, fixed-field agriculture: it generates enough surplus to support a noncultivating class in which women are valued more for their reproductive capacities than for their productive ones. Hence we have class endogamy and various institutions limiting women's social and sexual freedom (1976:20).

The coexistence of dowry and bride-price in the one society, as in India, is explained by recourse to the argument that there are two different norms for female labour which polarise at the two ends of the caste/class spectrum. At the upper end, where dowry marriages predominate, women are unproductive; at the lower end, where bride-price is paid, women perform productive labour. The shift from bride-price to dowry should theoretically then be accompanied by a shift in the nature of female labour from productive to unproductive labour—and indeed, such a change has been ethnographically recorded for India (Epstein 1973).

Most of the underlying assumptions in both the cultural and economic components of the Sanskritisation model seem unsatisfactory from the point of view of the Mukkuvars. Their caste status alone is a matter of some ambiguity (Chapter 1). Although officially designated a low caste, Mukkuvars perceive themselves as outsiders in relation to the agricultural castes rather than as their lowly dependants.

Secondly, the preoccupation of the Sanskritisation model with upward mobility in an otherwise static social order seems singularly inappropriate to describe the kinds of transformations (outlined in Chapter 5) which are changing the very economic framework within which the community performs its labour. The assumption of a purely caste-based system becomes inadequate to deal with wage labour and a world market, the realities with which Mukkuvars are currently having to deal. Such change cannot be captured in simple terms of either upward or downward mobility—a different paradigm is needed.

Similar confusions arise when we try and assess the Mukkuvars' status in terms of property ownership. The material means of production are slight and destructible, while the most important means of production are cultural and intangible (Chapter 3). I have argued that the intangible nature of property renders it more susceptible to cultural rules and prohibitions governing its acquisition—thus consolidating a fundamental separation between women and the ocean's economic resources (Chapter 3). Nevertheless, the very incorporeal and mobile nature of property also lends itself to flexibility in other areas of social arrangements, in ways beneficial to women. We have just seen that the patterns of marriage and residence among Mukkuvars embody a strong preference for intra-village alliance and a bilateral pattern of residence (both uxorilocal and virilocal). In a land-based society, such a system would not normally coexist with male inheritance of land, at least not without substantial modifications to the latter. According to Tambiah, it is the question of residence which is crucial in determining whether or not women inherit land. Whatever the mode of reckoning descent may be, women inherit land only if residence is both matrilocal and uxorilocal. Under all other arrangements, women inherit only 'movables'.

However, the entire distinction between movables and immovables becomes irrelevant once land drops out of the picture. Although we can look at the Mukkuvar situation in a positive light and conclude that women are able to enjoy the advantages of a more flexible marriage and residential pattern, it also means that such social arrangements can coexist with a basic economic dispossession embedded in the sexual division of labour.

With such complications already in place, no easy connections can be made between the community's status and the nature of women's work within it. Thanks to cultural norms and an ideology of sexual propriety (which is supposed to have no place among the egalitarian lower castes of India), Mukkuvar women do not hold the central place in the fishing economy enjoyed by men. This dependency has been further deepened by the displacement of men's work, as they work in areas further and further away from their native villages. Yet does this mean that we can go ahead and declare women in this community to be unproductive, dependent and an economic burden to their natal and conjugal families? This would be far too simplistic, for women continue to perform a variety of tasks. Some of these we have already examined as part of their function in running a credit-based economy, and others are examined in more detail in the next and last chapter. Whether we pronounce their work productive or unproductive depends on what criteria we use. In any case, the variety of types of female work coexisting within the one community covers virtually every type of distinction one might wish to draw. If the relevant distinction is between publicly visible versus private 'invisible' forms of work, then both forms coexist within the community. Ideologies of sexual modesty structure women's work (see the next chapter), but not with such uniform severity as to enforce total public invisibility. Rather, the visibility of the female labour force is structured by age and marital status. Older women who have established themselves as mothers and mothers-in-law perform public forms of work such as marketing fish. But among younger women too, the ideology of seclusion merely restricts the scope of various forms of work which they can perform. Women take in tailoring, sell vegetables, spices and cooked food items, trade in rice, weave fishing nets at piece-rate wages. If the relevant distinction is between waged and non-waged forms of work, then here too, women perform both types of work. With forms of female labour so varied within the one community, the relevance of the form of marriage payments to the nature of women's work seems tenuous.[1]

If we were to accept the Sanskritisation model, then Mukkuvars—with their officially low status, their women performing important economic tasks, and a kinship system emphasising relative equality between wife-givers and wife-takers—should be paying bride-price. Instead, I found the community was giving extremely large dowries, in which I include not only payments and gifts given at the time of marriage, but the pattern of gift-giving between affines which continues particularly over into the first years of marriage and more generally, throughout the lifetime of the bride.[2]

If we take the obligations to host major feasts at the time of the wedding, the bride's family hosts two major feasts as against the one feast required of the groom's family. The bride's family hosts one on the day of the marriage when the main ceremonial feasting takes place, as well as a feast for the groom's party on the day the bride leaves home. The groom is obliged to present his siblings, their partners and children, his own parents, their siblings and his grandparents with new clothes. Seven days after the marriage (during which the couple stay at the bride's home), the groom's party arrives to fetch the bride and groom from the bride's home; the party must bring gifts of raw and cooked foods (*shomadu*), and the entry of the bride into the groom's house must be celebrated with a feast which the bride's relatives attend. However, any gifts the bride's kin may receive during the feast held in their honour must be returned in increased value. Moreover, the dowry paid by the bride's family always includes a component of cash payment to cover marriage-related expenses incurred by the groom's family. The apparently reciprocal nature of some of these transactions turns out, on closer examination, to be unilateral.

An average dowry at the time of fieldwork (1982–83) added up in cash terms to anywhere between 10 000–30 000 rupees. This total sum of what the Mukkuvars called *sirdanam* (in Sanskrit, *stridhanam*) would be composed of three component parts. First, a cash payment which is an outright payment to the groom's kin. Informants describe it as designed to cover any marriage expenses incurred by the groom's family. Second, another cash payment, towards the future of the newly married couple. Ideally, it should be spent on items that will benefit them both. A typical use of such money would be the purchase of items of fishing capital, either nets or boats. Third, jewellery made specifically for the bride. This will always include a gold *tali*, the ornament of central symbolic significance in denoting the woman's married status, which is tied around the neck of the bride by the groom at the time of marriage. If possible, the jewellery will also include a full 'set': gold bangles, earrings, and at least one other gold chain for the neck.

In addition, cooking vessels and pots are presented, not directly to the bride, but to the groom's 'party' which comes to take her to the husband's home. If separate cooking arrangements are instituted in the new home, the bride will use her own vessels. If we judge the relative cash value of each of these three items of marriage payments between 1981–83, jewellery ranks by far as the weightiest component, seldom below sixty per cent of the total cash value, and occasionally as much as eighty per cent. Cash payments range from twenty to forty per cent of the total cash value of dowry, and of this, the section specifically designated for the couple comprises only two to three per cent.

Another hidden dimension to these payments is the customary payment of the *moy*. This consists of cash payments made by wedding guests which are publicly announced at the time of the evening function. The burden on the girl's family is thus reduced by the villagers themselves, in a practice reminiscent of that found in other low castes described by Beck (1972).

Following the payments through to the early years of marriage, the expenses of the first childbirth must be borne by the bride's parents. The bride's mother is central in this function and if she is not alive, her place must be taken by the mother's sister. The first child is an occasion for a further bonding between mother (or mother-substitute) and daughter, thus reinforcing a matrifocal principle. The expenses met by the mother of the bride include the costs of a midwife or hospitalisation. The daughter must be fed special meals and medicines for forty-one days. The mother's brother pays for a silver hip girdle for the new-born child. The bride's parents also present the child with a chain and a ring, and pay the costs of a christening ceremony. Subsequent births, if they occur while the bride is still resident with the husband's parents, are financed by the latter, but these include only the costs of medical expenses and do not involve presentation of jewellery.

Having established the details of the current practice of dowry, I then spent a long and unproductive hunt trying to trace whether there had been a historical shift in the community from bride-price to dowry, egged on by the discovery of a small detail regarding the Mukkuvars of Cochin (Iyer 1909). Iyer writes of this, a Hindu community: 'The bride's price is ten rupees and a half, and at the time of departure, the bridegroom places a rupee on the lighted lamp, in the shed and takes leave of his father-in-law with the present of a rupee' (Iyer 1908:268).

However, in interviews with women, some of whom were married in the 1940s, I was unable to locate any evidence of this practice. The earliest marriage I was able to record among current residents in the village was of a woman married in 1925, and this marriage already had a dowry form. Ultimately, the search for a perhaps mythical bride-price past, a search inspired by the reigning theory of marriage payments among the lower castes, nearly obscured for me the historical changes that have occurred within the dowry form.[3] Yet these changes are, on examination, virtually as important and significant for women as any shift from bride-price to dowry.

The central distinction to be made here is between the jewellery and the cash components of the dowry. The cash component, which I have just described as an outright payment to the family of the groom or to the groom himself, is not only the component of dowry which has grown and continues to grow, but is also quite a new component of dowry altogether. The earliest two marriages for which I have data include no cash payments whatsoever, and the quantities of jewellery presented were modest by today's standards. One marriage, conducted in 1925, endowed the bride with jewellery worth '10 *powan*' of gold, or 100 grams (approximately) of gold. Using the gold prices current at the time of fieldwork, where 1 *powan* of gold was worth Re1500, the bride received Re14 300 worth of jewellery. The next marriage, which occurred in 1933, had no cash payments, and jewellery worth Re5720—reflecting the poverty of the girl's family, which was unable to provide anything but a token dowry. Selik's small-scale study of the nearby coastal village of Muttom (1980) also records that before 1930, dowry took the form of gold ornaments for the bride, and included no cash payments.

The striking spiral in the rates expected of wife-givers can be traced in the space of a generation, between mother/daughter, mother-in-law/daughter-in-law, as illustrated in Table 8.1, which presents the information in the form of abbreviated case examples.

Case C in Table 8.1 is particularly significant in illustrating one of the principal factors behind the sudden escalation in dowry. Sibling B is a woman who was married in 1982 to a groom owning a third of a

Table 8.1   Case examples illustrating the spiral in the cash component of dowry in the space of a generation

Case A: Mother-in-law, married in 1953
Dowry: Re18 000 worth of jewellery
Re10 125 in cash
Total: Re28 125

Daughter-in-law, married in 1981
Dowry: Re15 000 worth of jewellery
Re 30 000 in cash
Total: Re45 000

Case B: Mother-in-law, married in 1943
Dowry: Re7500 in jewellery
Re5192 in cash
Total: Re12 692

Daughter-in-law, married in 1981
Dowry: Re15 000 in jewellery
Re6500 in cash
Total: Re21 500

Case C: Sibling A (brother), married in 1965
Dowry: Re15 300 in jewellery
Re300 in cash
Total: Re15 300

Sibling B (sister), married in 1982
Dowry: Re40 000 in jewellery
Re10 000 in cash
Total: Re50 000

Sibling C (brother), married in 1983
Dowry: Re15 000 in jewellery
Re10 000 in cash
Total: Re25 000

Note: To allow comparison of dowries across generations, the following procedure has been adopted. All jewellery is converted to the cash value of gold in the year that fieldwork was conducted (1983). The cash component has been calculated as a percentage of the original dowry and then giving it a cash value in 1983's money terms
Source: Data gathered in fieldwork, KaDalkarai Uuru, 1983

share in a mechanised boat, which he operates with two other men off the coast of Colachel. There were other factors which made him an eligible groom, such as the fact that he did not drink too much alcohol, but it was the share in the mechanised boat that escalated his dowry value. As against this, Sibling C is a man who married in 1983, but was only able to 'command' Re25 000. He is a skilled artisanal fisherman, and valuable according to traditional criteria because of his ability to work with a variety of different types of equipment. Given the seasonality of fishing, too narrow a specialisation means economic hardship for the family, so this man would have normally been considered a good groom—yet he can only fetch half the price of his brother-in-law.

As this case shows, grooms who have a share in mechanised boats can command dowries far in excess of anything even a skilled fisherman working with artisanal craft and gear can hope to command. A fisherman working as a coolie on mechanised trawlers could command up to Re40 000, while someone who actually owns a share can ask for up to Re70 000. Such fishermen, owning shares, usually do not exist in KaDalkarai Uuru—we are talking here about grooms in Colachel. A man working with artisanal equipment, no matter how skilled, could not command more than Re30 000.

As Sharma points out (1984), the principle in determining the value of dowry, particularly the cash component, is not based on a predetermined share of the family fortune to be handed over to a woman, but on the basis of the economic promise of the groom. The principle itself is not an entirely new one in the Mukkuvar community. Well before the advent of mechanised fishing, grooms were being evaluated in terms of their reliability—whether known to squander money on alcohol, whether able to work on different types of equipment. Certain highly specialised forms of fishing skills, such as hook-and-line fishing, have also been traditionally prestigious and accordingly attracted higher dowries. A hook-and-line fisherman or *tuuNDilkaaran* is noted for his knowledge of the ocean and his ability to catch single specimens of the larger species; and since he works alone, he does not have to share his earnings with crew members. The prestige of such men has dimmed in recent years, since they are in direct competition with the fishing zones and specimens of mechanised trawlers and the particular species of fish sought by them. However, in villages further away from the disruptions of the trawlers in Colachel, hook-and-line men are still able to draw higher dowries than in KaDalkarai Uuru. Such a marriage was being negotiated during my stay between a girl from KaDalkarai Uuru and a groom in Enayam, fifteen kilometres away; the groom's family were demanding a total of Re40 000 in dowry. As one woman slyly put it: 'A good hook-and-line fisherman can catch women as easily as his fish! Having learned deception with his fish, he then comes and deceives us!' So while the principle itself is not a new one, the balance is shifting in favour of grooms with new sorts of economic skills or opportunities, and their price—the 'groom-price'—is vastly escalated in the process.

Similar continuities and discontinuities are evident if we look at the way in which dowries are not only inflated in order to match the prestige and increased earning capacity of men, but are also used to finance such ventures. The principle that women's dowries may be used to finance the purchase of new capital stock for men in the household is well-established in the community. As an extension of this principle, however, women are now being asked to finance much more ambitious ventures: the purchase of shares in mechanised boats and associated gear, and in a smaller minority of cases, the financing of overseas immigration to the Middle East for men who fail to make a living as fishermen. In one case, half the wife's jewellery and all the cash payments went into financing her husband's overseas trip, while in another case, a woman got into trouble with her husband's family for secretly selling nearly all her jewellery to finance her brother's trip to Bahrein.

Not only does the scale of investment involved in the new technology entail an enormous leap in costs (compare the costs of trawlers and gear, even second-hand equipment, with the cost of artisanal equipment: Chapter 1), but the new ventures are far more risky and likely to be unsuccessful than the traditional forms of capital investment. In KaDalkarai Uuru, only three of the eleven households which originally invested in mechanised trawlers continue to maintain their share. Most of these households have not only suffered a loss of their original investments but have entered into deeper levels of indebtedness, which in turn are financed by whatever is left of women's jewellery. Even where such investment is successful, the implications of this success are ambiguous for women. The cash remittances that men send back to the women in the villages as part-owners or coolies in mechanised fishing, or as workers in the Middle East, are in no way equivalent to their traditional financial control over earnings generated at the village itself.

Women are on the one hand bearing the brunt of the costs associated with the formation of a male labour force for mechanised fishing, and on the other hand reaping far fewer benefits than they did from the old forms of male work. While the principles on which dowry is evaluated and utilised remain roughly consistent with the pre-mechanisation period, the new relations of production have expanded the market for male labour and the scale of investments involved, thus changing the very meaning of marriage payments within the fishing community.

The utilisation of dowry in the Mukkuvar community

What does dowry mean to women in the community? Has it ever operated as *sirdanam* or women's wealth? If it has, can that description still apply to it?

Anthropologists mainly concerned with linking payments to the theme of social stratification have focused on the shift from bridewealth to dowry. Yet Brahmanic ideology claims a good deal more for the significance of dowry: it professes to endow women with wealth which is equivalent to male inheritance, and which is controlled by the bride to the extent of being passed on intact to her daughters.[4] Most ethnography is either silent on this issue, content instead to quantify the flow of gifts between affines and the kinship obligations embedded in them (Lewis 1958, Mayer 1960, Srinivas

1952), or else accepts on faith the notion of dowry as compensatory or complementary to male patrimony. I refer in particular to Tambiah (1973) and Goody (1976), both of whom reproduce uncritically the purely jural or juridical ideology represented in the classic texts of the Smritis. Goody, in his argument on property and female status referred to earlier, takes a strangely contradictory position. On the one hand he links dowry with the increased sequestration of women, and yet on the other he sees dowry as an enhancement of women's legal rights, as an instance of 'diverging devolution' where women have inheritance rights in the parental estate. For Goody, the 'even-handed approach' implicit in dowry makes it imperative for the society to control the marriages of women in the propertied classes. Yet he does not question how the reality of sequestration and seclusion would affect women's ability to own this property in any but the most formal sense of the word (see also Sharma's criticisms of Goody: 1980, 1984). Tambiah lists the kinds of items in which 'a woman exercised dominion independently of her husband', namely: 'clothes and jewellery received by the bride from her parents before marriage, betrothal presents from the bridegroom, presents received by her at marriage from her parents and kin, and gifts received after marriage from her husband' (1973:86). Yet these gifts are treated as an equivalent complement to the man's inheritance of land. It seems timely to point out that the difference between the two types of property is not simply a technical difference between movable and immovable forms of property, as it is neutrally represented in anthropological literature: it is the distinction between a woman's right to maintenance conditional on the basis of a socially approved marriage, and a man's unconditional right to inherit the means of production. The differing forms of inheritance dictate an entirely different relationship to marriage for men and women. For a man, marriage means the acquisition of a wife, access to her unpaid labour and to her fertility and sexuality. However, it is not essential to his survival. For a woman, marriage in accordance with parental wishes becomes the only way to lay claim to the dowry, and even then it is not a productive fund that she can live off for the rest of her life.

Among Mukkuvars, the distinction between male and female inheritance does not take the same form as in land-based society, but the inequalities run along parallel lines. Men inherit the means by which to exploit the chief productive resource of the community—the rights to the sea—and the cultural and physical means of production required to extract a living out of that resource. Whatever cash payments they are given at the time of marriage are also converted into productive assets such as nets, gear and craft.

Can dowry be considered an equivalent form of female property? According to the Dharmasastras, dowry may be enjoyed by husband and wife together, but is not supposed to merge with the property of the husband. The husband cannot, for example, transfer the dowry to finance his sister's marriage. Here again, anthropologists assume that social and moral pressures protect the woman from having her dowry misappropriated by her husband and his family. According to Srinivas '. . . only during a real crisis may a husband utilise her money or pawn her jewellery. But he is obliged to return it as soon as conditions return to normal. In a great part of rural society, women stick up for their rights against their men, and public opinion supports them in this' (1978:12). For Tambiah, and more recently, Randeria and Viseria (1984), such misappropriations are aberrant because they occur in a covert manner: 'Such pilferage of the wife/daughter-in-law's dowry or *stridhan* is considered shameful and would not be publicly acknowledged. In this sense dowry does not form part of a rotating capital fund in India' (Randeria and Viseria 1984:277).

However, if such 'misappropriations' occur on a sufficiently wide-spread basis, and further, if there are no inbuilt structural sanctions against such practices, then at the very least we are faced with a dissonance between the ethico-juridical ideology and the actual rights enjoyed by women in the area of property. At the outset, the fact that dowries are calculated on the basis of the economic potential of the groom rather than on the basis of the daughter's share of the parent's property raises substantial doubts about the equivalence of male and female property. The role dowry plays as a 'marriage ticket' belies its function as female inheritance.

On the basis of my dissatisfactions with the prevailing anthropological treatment of dowry in India, I gathered survey data from 86 households in KaDalkarai Uuru, asking questions as to who benefited from the dowry and what its uses were. The questions pertain to those components of the dowry conventionally regarded as belonging to the bride. That is, the jewellery, and those cash payments earmarked as belonging to the couple. It excludes those cash payments that are presented to finance the marriage and the expenses of the groom's family. The results of this line of questioning are summarised in Tables 8.2 and 8.3.

The empirical data make it obvious that the bride does not have exclusive control over dowry and continual inroads are made into women's property by the rest of the household. With or without the woman's consent, in-laws and husbands in the Mukkuvar community benefit substantially from the incoming dowry. Such usage is far too systematic and widespread for us to treat it as aberrant.

However, if the Hindu ethico-juridical conception of dowry is inadequate, neither is it at all clear what kind of alternative concepts of property one ought to bring to bear in an enquiry of this kind. Concepts of inalienable rights implicitly rest on the construction of the person as an individual, as well as on assumptions regarding property as a private possession. The assumptions are not universally generalisable. Instead, they form part of a very specific economic history associated with the development of capitalism (Hirschon 1984,

Table 8.2   The utilisation of dowry by members of the Mukkuvar household

Nature of utilisation	Numbers (out of 86)	Percentage
1 Appropriation by bride's in-laws	23	26
2 Appropriation by the husband for capital investment	26	30
3 Appropriation by the husband for non-productive uses	2	1
4 Appropriation by the bride's natal kin (mainly for marriages of younger sisters)	14	16
5 Usage of dowry as a 'survival fund' by entire household	52	60
6 Appropriation by in-laws for purposes in which the bride obtains no economic return (mainly to finance marriages in the husband's family)	14	16

Note: Each household generally appears under more than one heading. The *percentages* are therefore a rough, rather than an exact guide, since the total is more than 100 per cent. The actual *numbers* (out of 86) are more reliable.
Source: Survey of 86 households in KaDalkarai Uuru on the theme of marriage payments; fieldwork, 1983

Table 8.3   Relative numerical proportions of different forms of dowry-appropriation

People appropriating the dowry jewellery (involving appropriation of 50% or more of jewellery)			Appropriation of entire dowry jewellery	
	Incidence	Percentage	Incidence	Percentage
Bride's in-laws	5/86	6	3/86	3
Bride's own kin	5/86	6	1	1
Bride's husband	13/86	15	9	10
Household as a whole (for daily subsistence needs)	37/86	43	25	29

Note: Some idea of the relative proportion of dowry used in the above ways is given in this table, which shows the number of cases in each category where 50 per cent or more of the dowry was used up. A third column gives the number of instances where the *entire* dowry was used by a given party other than the bride, the ostensible owner of the jewellery.
Source: Fieldwork, 1983

Macpherson 1973). Such preconceptions are particularly ill-suited to the economic and cultural realities of life in a poor south Indian fishing community. Certain types of corporate familial usages of dowry are either regarded as necessary by women or are even positively encouraged by them. Any investment that increases the men's economic assets in fishing equipment has an implicit benefit for the rest of the family, including the women. In exceptional cases, this share may even be explicitly acknowledged in the form of cash,[5] but women see themselves as having a stake in increasing the productive assets of the household regardless of any immediate and tangible returns. One woman's comments brought out well the mixture of approval and reluctance with which a bride may countenance the sale or pawning of her jewellery: 'A thousand rupees worth of jewellery was taken from me by my mother-in-law to buy a net. Since my husband is her only son, any money spent in this way could only benefit me and my children. However, the decision was taken entirely by my widowed mother-in-law. A mother-in-law can be ignored or disobeyed in some families, but not mine.'[6]

Fifty-six per cent of the households interviewed gave evidence of either the in-laws or the husband utilising part of the woman's jewellery to raise funds for the purchase of new capital equipment (adding categories 1 and 4 in Table 8.2). Husbands in particular reported substantial usage of the wife's dowry—26 of the 86 interviewed households reported some utilisation. In nine of the households, all of the woman's dowry had been used up in this fashion, and in thirteen of them, more than 50 per cent had been used in capital equipment purchase. However, one cannot view this as the dowry being taken away from the passive bride—the women are often themselves the active agents in pawning their own jewellery and raising credit for such purposes. Although not reported in Tables 8.2 and 8.3, the men who benefit from women's dowry also include members of the bride's natal kin. It is also not uncommon for women to pawn their jewellery to help their brothers.

By far the greatest bulk of dowries are used up over a period of time to cope with the sheer inadequacy of income from fishing. Sixty per cent of households report having sold some portion of dowry jewellery to buy food, medicines and clothes, and pay for building repairs to houses damaged by monsoons and surf. If this jewellery is not directly sold, it is pawned in order to raise credit, but it eventually passes out of the owner's hands due to inability to repay the loan. Forty-three per cent of households had used up half or more of the dowry in this fashion, while 29 per cent of households had used up all of the dowry simply for daily survival. It is very common to see a woman wearing a simple black thread around her neck, to symbolically denote her marital status: she has sold the gold *tali* that she was married in.

Conclusion

Dowry represents above all a survival fund for the household, rather than a productive resource that women use in investments. We have seen in the chapter on credit that women use jewellery, which comes mainly from their dowries, to raise credit. Most of the decisions as to when to pawn a particular piece of jewellery and which piece to part with are made by the woman whose dowry it is. However, this kind of 'control' is as meaningless as the notorious 'freedom' of the wage-earning proletariat to sell its labour power in the market place. Women may express a strong stake in the continuation of dowry as a system, but this has a great deal to do with reasons of poverty and economic uncertainty. The economic circumstances make a mockery both of the traditional Hindu notion of jewellery, pots and pans as things to be preserved, kept intact in order to be handed down from mother to daughter as a female line of inheritance, and of the bourgeois concept of women's property as an item for private enjoyment or security.

Not all familial forms of dowry utilisation are approved of by women. Women make distinctions between uses which are forced on them by economic circumstances and uses they see as unproductive, a drain on their meagre resources. The latter cause resentment, tensions and fights. In a few cases, the women bitterly resent having to finance their husband's drinking habits with their dowry jewellery. A far more common source of tension is the use of dowry to finance other marriages. A peculiarity of the Mukkuvar community, which is linked to the pattern of kinship, marriage and residence, is that both affinal and natal kin feel equally entitled to make financial claims on the bride after her marriage. Most of these claims are made to raise dowry for the marriage of the bride's younger sisters or her sisters-in-law. Both types of demands cause tension and resentment on the part of the bride.

In the fourteen households which used dowry for marriages in the husband's family, there was tension, but little evidence of the moral pressure or threat of dishonour which ethnographies have described to be the protection of the bride in such situations. The only escape route for the bride is to await the partition of the household, at which point she may be able to move out and form her own household—but by then a substantial part of the dowry may be whittled away. While pressures from affines have been recorded by the few anthropologists interested in such matters (e.g. Jacobson 1976:162), financial assistance to natal kin would be quite rare in north India, since it goes against the principle of hierarchy between wife-givers and wife-takers. Among the Mukkuvars, however, the demands of natal kin are just as high as the demands of the husband's family (see Table 8.2). Sixteen per cent of the households report instances of each kind. The only difference is that the parents of the girl represent the use of her jewellery as a loan rather than as a form of appropriation, but the difference amounts to little—the loans are rarely repaid. In practice, then, parents use a daughter's dowry as something which gains her an entry-point into marriage. Once the crisis is over, and the daughter safely married, her dowry is utilised to perform the same function for another daughter. Dowry therefore operates as a rotating marriage fund, as well as a survival fund.

Anthropologists such as Sharma (1984) and Strathern (1984) have raised important questions about feminism in a non-Western context, particularly in relation to women and property. Sharma points out that management of property in India is subordinated to the corporate ideology of the family, which is of larger concern than the rights of any individual within it. Among Mukkuvars the notion of the family as a corporate, property-managing entity is blunted by the minimal presence of property in the conventional sense, and by the dispersal of the various functions of the joint family into smaller nuclear components. Nevertheless, women take very seriously their responsibility to ensure the survival of the domestic unit, and subordinate all the economic resources at their disposal to that end.

Feminist intuitions about the radical shifts in the meaning of dowry are quite accurate in important respects. Among Mukkuvars the emphasis is shifting away from the jewellery component of dowry towards cash. Both are used for the family's economic survival, but the former is under female control, and the latter under male control. Further, the items under female control are distributed more directly and evenly over the family members, whereas the cash—which as we have seen is used to finance male ventures in gear, shares in trawlers and overseas trips—benefits the family only indirectly in the form of remittances. These historical shifts in the domestic arena, an area all too often conceived of as outside history, have disturbing implications for women. At the same time, we have seen the problems that arise when we impose an alien, bourgeois framework of property onto women's dowry. Such a framework fails to explain, among other things, why even impoverished women may be compliant and active perpetuators of the system of dowry payment.

9 The sexual codification of women's work: domesticity and female proletarianisation in the Mukkuvar community

In this final chapter I wish to consolidate several of the themes which have already dominated my treatment of the position of women in the fishing community. The consideration of women's work in the fishing community is very well suited to my purposes of consolidation and synthesis: women's paid and unpaid labour raises questions concerning the relation between culture and economy, and more specifically, between the construction of female sexuality and the historical patterning of female proletarianisation. Whether we consider the work Mukkuvar women perform without any monetary remuneration, in their capacity as the wives, mothers and daughters of men, or the work women perform as wage workers, their labour raises fundamental questions about the categories of political economy. In particular, we are led to question the way that political economy conceives of the transition from pre-capitalist to capitalist modes of production as an economic process. Its categories of analysis are unable to recognise or theoretically assimilate the process of sexual differentiation which is always at the heart of the old as well as the newly emergent relations of production.

I have classified my presentation of women's work according to one of the distinctions central to economic theory: the presence or absence of a wage or cash payment in exchange for command over labour. My discussion of unpaid work is more condensed than the treatment of paid work, since it draws on material previously introduced in the book. Here the same material is used to raise broader questions on the nature of domesticity as it is redefined by new relations of production. My discussion of paid work requires introducing some new material on the various forms of petty trade and piece-work performed by Mukkuvar women. I have deliberately left this material till the last chapter to demonstrate the fundamental continuity between women's unpaid and paid labour, neither of which can be satisfactorily understood without referring back to the overarching cultural construction of sexual difference. Although I utilise the paid/unpaid distinction for purposes of presentation, my ultimate purpose is to undermine the conventional bases of the distinction.

Women, domesticity and domestication: the public/private distinction in social theory

Mukkuvar women find the central focus of their identity and their social roles in the work they perform as wives, mothers and daughters. This includes a variety of different types of tasks, ranging from tasks which would be readily classified and recognised by Western political economy as labour, such as drying and salting fish in peak fishing seasons, to tasks which would not find such ready acknowledgement. Into the latter category, however, fall the bulk of women's activities, which go towards maintaining the daily reproduction of the fishing households. Those include travelling to markets to buy vegetables, purchasing firewood from agricultural households in the hinterland, searching for water with which to cook, clean and also to drink, and caring for the sick and the young. Women's responsibility for such activities readily finds a cultural framework in the special kind of popular religion practised by the Mukkuvars, primarily concerned as it is with this everyday, social world. Women exercise special responsibilities in the religious sphere more or less as an extension of their domestic tasks.

In addition, in their capacity as domestic caretakers, women in the fishing community have tasks which set them apart from their female counterparts in agricultural peasant households. We have seen how, in order to counter-balance the precarious and fluctuating nature of the fishing economy and the cash generated by men's work, women engage in a wide variety of attempts to raise credit to keep households functioning on a day-to-day basis. In this enormous task the women are aided by their ability to mobilise different kinds of social relations: networks of kinship, neighbourhood, friendship and work. We have seen how peculiarities of kinship, household formation and neighbourhood settlement strengthen women's social base, enabling them to establish a striking continuity in their relationships with parents and siblings even after their own marriages. The typical pattern of settlement in Mukkuvar villages is conducive not only to a density in female social relations, but also to a degree of female autonomy inconceivable to a junior female in a conventional hierarchical joint family. If the peculiarities of the fishing economy place a considerable social burden on Mukkuvar women, the idiosyncrasies of kinship and residential patterns give women some means with which to meet the challenge. Both kinship and the sexual division of labour give women considerable presence in the daily life of the community and in other land-based activity.

The underside of this female centrality in land-based social relations is women's marginality to all sea-based activities. The two aspects of female identity are inseparably linked according to the codes of popular culture and religion. These codes construct women as powerfully sexual and as potentially dangerous to men and (male) social order. In the name of this threat women are both excluded from spaces (such as the sea and the sea-front which men have claimed as their own) and legitimately assigned to the space of the home and domesticity.

Mukkuvars conform to a pattern common among fishing communities the world over in excluding women from fishing. This exclusion, where noticed by outside observers, has often been described and theorised in purely economic terms, as in the following Marxist account of fisherwomen in Ghana:

> Usually the women take a proportion of the income for themselves, but this relies upon the ability of the men to secure the catch. It is not founded upon the independence of the women, but upon the way in which the spheres of reproduction and production interact ...
> ... It is rare for a woman from the fishing community to be wealthy, either in terms of the community or beyond it. Women are subordinate and their role in distribution, rather than production itself, reinforces their subordination (Westwood 1984:149).

This female 'subordination', as analysed by Westood, is the result of the way the spheres of distribution and reproduction are secondary to and dependent on male-dominated production. The problem is thus clothed in an economic terminology which masks many troubling questions behind a seemingly neutral and technical tone. Categories such as production, reproduction and distribution have been here applied without any adjustment or re-definition in the context of a non-European culture which is not even operating entirely within capitalist relations of production.

Among the Mukkuvars, at least, women's separation from the material means of production must be viewed quite differently. It is not merely that this dispossession is brought about by cultural means. Rather, resources such as access to space and the skills obtained in those spaces are simultaneously economic and cultural in their character. Dispossession is not a simple negative exercise of power. It is at the same time positive, in that it confers on women other forms of empowerment in the sphere of the domestic through which they construct a very positive identity and social role for themselves.

Symbolic anthropology has been more keenly aware of this ambiguity and paradox in the cultural models of femininity in Tamil society. The central observation of the ethnographic studies of the 1970s (Baker-Reynolds 1978, Beck 1974, Egnor 1978, Wadley 1980) takes the following form: women, so essential for the spiritual and material well-being of the Tamil male, are also entirely dependent for their own status on marriage and motherhood, which in Tamil culture entail submission to the guardianship and control of men. This sweeping conclusion is based on a fairly narrow examination of women's roles, which are confined by and large to what this brand of anthropology has designated as the sphere of 'culture': that is, kinship and symbolic practices (ritual, texts, language). Once again, economic categories escape any serious scrutiny, since the analysis is not extended to women's labour, either paid or unpaid.

Feminist theory in the 1970s, whether Marxist or cultural-symbolist in orientation, seems to have concurred on at least one point: both strands equate domestic*ity* with domestic*ation* in the sense of female subordination. Anthropologists such as Rosaldo have argued that there is 'a universal opposition between domestic versus public roles which is necessarily a-symmetrical: women, confined to the domestic sphere, do not have access to the sorts of authority, prestige and cultural value that are the prerogatives of men' (1974:8). The 'universal framework for conceptualising the activities of the sexes' proposed by Rosaldo defines the 'domestic' as those 'minimal institutions and modes of activity that are organised immediately around one or more mothers and their children' (p.23), while the 'public' is defined as those 'activities, institutions, and forms of association that link, rank, organise or subsume particular mother-child groups' (p.23). In this formulation, the domestic is, by definition an extremely narrow and minimal social institution, since everything outside the mother-child dyad(s) is public. Moreover, the claim is that this way of drawing the dividing line is universal, and further, that women's association with the domestic is the basis of women's subordination to men.

I do not propose to overturn this kind of argument with an inversion that is equally universalistic and a-historical. Rather, I wish to delimit my argument regarding the domestic sphere in the Mukkuvar community in terms of both the community's historical location and its location in the social structure of caste society. We are dealing here with a *community* in the full sense of the word: work and social life among the Mukkuvars are not experienced as distinct parts of life, as they are in industrial society. Although radically affected by transformations in the fishing economy, this transformation does not take the form of a unilinear historical trajectory envisaged by the term 'transition to capitalism'. In such a community, domesticity is organised very differently from the domesticity of the Western housewife whose work is carried on in isolation from any socially recognised or valued forms of labour. The point is often made that the bifurcation between the private, domestic sphere and the public, socially-organised world became particularly acute with the development of capitalism in the West (Mitchell 1971, Barrett and MacIntosh 1982). The force of this observation is particularly noticeable in this fishing caste, where the distinction between the domestic and the public is extremely blurred. A similar point may be made with regard to the contrast between the Mukkuvars and the more culturally proximate domesticity of the upper caste Tamil Brahman wife. The kind of confined picture of domesticity one gets from Rosaldo's definition may be relevant to the latter, but fits ill with the kinds of tasks performed by Mukkuvar women in the name of their domestic responsibilities.

I base my argument not purely on the symbolic meaning attached to the concept of domesticity among the Mukkuvars but on the actual types of work performed by Mukkuvar women. Some, such as the salting and drying of fish, are more analogous to what would be called 'processing work' in an industrialised economy. Nevertheless, the work is performed by Mukkuvar women as unpaid labour, and very much as part of their familial role, as the wives and mothers of fishermen.

Other tasks, such as the raising of credit and the frequent loan-giving and receiving among women, also sit uneasily with Western categories of economic analysis. These tasks have no equivalent in the Western household, which is both more atomised and less liable to continuous fluctuations in income. Such credit activity probably has a closer affinity with the makeshift ways in which households survive in the informal sector of any Third World city, or among the casually-employed sub-proletariat all over the world. However, the 'work' that goes into ensuring survival in such precarious conditions has never been given much theoretical attention, precisely because it defies neat classification into either domestic or public spheres, and can be neither designated as unproductive or productive. Yet the work of raising credit is an indispensable component of the subsistence economy of Mukkuvar villages, an instance of the way in which the domestic and the wider economies flow into one another. The economy of each individual domestic unit relies crucially on the wider social relations of kinship and neighbourhood, which link each household not only to the rest of the village, but to the entire coastal *tinai*. Women inhabit and dominate not only the individual domestic unit, but also the extended counterpart of the domestic domain.

If women's credit-related activities are a more striking instance of the unusually wide parameters of domesticity among the Mukkuvars, the way in which women perform the types of work more conventionally described as housework also points to the social basis of such work. As with low-caste settlements of agricultural untouchables, no individual Mukkuvar house is spatially isolated from its environment. Here are no shady groves of fruit trees such as one finds in the wealthier agricultural households—the settlements are densely packed, huddled together in their poverty but also in their interdependence. The social relations of women's domestic work reflects this physical density in settlement patterns. A large amount of informal mutual aid occurs in domestic labour, most typically when younger women from other households are called in by older women unable any longer to perform such physically arduous tasks as pounding rice into flour, or carrying water from the taps. Given an unusually high incidence of widows living alone, and the even more widespread occurrence of older women living in nuclear units with no younger women in the family to call upon, such mutual aid is critically necessary.

Even where women are essentially performing tasks for their own domestic unit, the work does not necessarily take place within the physical boundaries of the home, or on an individual basis. The sandy lands and alleyways in front of and between households become transformed into a makeshift work-area for groups of four or five women who come together informally to perform tasks such as pounding rice flour or grain, or weaving nets. In the cool of the morning or in the late evening, women perform their individual chores side-by-side, allowing the conversation and conviviality of the group to alleviate the tedium of the tasks. Certain of these tasks, such as net-weaving (now paid on a piece-rate basis and therefore considered later in this chapter under the heading of 'paid work'), have historically been considered as work women perform as an extension of their domestic tasks. They are still performed principally by the young, unmarried daughters of fishing households. Nor is there any differentiation between the way the girls collectively perform their (paid) weaving and the way their mothers collectively pound their grain and rice.

Symbolic rules and cultural practice

The wide-ranging social relations that enter into women's performance of domestic tasks in turn have important repercussions for their ability to contest implicitly the more restrictive versions of domesticity that are undoubtedly present in Tamil culture. Indeed, we have seen that Mukkuvar rituals and symbolic practices themselves abound with images of confinement, binding, and cooling female sexuality and anger within the bounds of marriage, and of restrictive codes of speech, clothing and bodily movement. It is not that the symbolic analysis of ritual is wrong in any simple sense—the problem is rather that if we restrict our analysis to exegesis of symbolic practice alone, then in the very process of codifying meaning we render it in the form of 'cultural rules', and convey an overly rigid account of people's lives. Bourdieu (1977) has argued against this tendency in social theory which he diagnoses as the problem of 'objectivism', a practice whose tendency is 'to reify abstractions, by the fallacy of treating the objects constructed by science, whether "culture", "structures", or "modes of production", as realities endowed with a social efficacy, capable of acting as agents responsible for historical actions or as a power capable of constraining practices' (Bourdieu 1977:27).

Bourdieu's polemic against 'objectivism' is also the basis for his sustained argument in favour of a theory of 'practice'. If, following Bourdieu, we direct our attention to the actual practices of women's labour in the domestic sphere, we find that the purely symbolic definitions of women's space, deliberately narrow and confining in their scope and intention, are in fact significantly widened. Far from remaining confined to the four walls of the home—the only space where the threat of female sexuality is, in theory, firmly contained—women in practice extend the practical meaning of domestic space to include not only parts of the village, but also other coastal villages, and potentially the agrarian hinterland itself. In each case this extension is implicitly justified by reference to the domestic duties performed. In the course of processing their food grains or weaving their nets, women claim the spaces immediately around their homes as spaces for domestic work. In their efforts to raise credit, and to consolidate social relations and kinship networks, women circulate within the village but also travel by bus from one coastal village to another. Their religio-medical responsibilities take them even further afield from the home—in the course of their trips to healers and Christian shrines, they travel all over the district and even into adjacent districts of Tamil Nadu such as Tirunelveli, and to the neighbouring state of Kerala. Domestic space therefore extends imperceptibly into sacred space, a terrain which is in principle without any strict physical boundaries.

However, while this means that symbolic meanings are constantly being contested and subtly redefined in practice, it does not mean that social and economic practice somehow takes place outside symbolic meaning. The expansion of women's space which occurs in the course of practice is understood and legitimised in Mukkuvar culture only through its implicit reference to women's cultural responsibilities as wives, mothers and daughters. Women's ability to travel with impunity and even authority within the coastal belt and to the markets and shrines of the agricultural hinterland stems from a collective understanding that they are carrying out the tasks and duties proper to them as *women*: that is, in the name of domestic responsibilities associated with a cultural model of femininity. It is only thus that the threat which their very presence outside the home poses to male dominance in public space becomes somewhat neutralised. The significance of this symbolic process of legitimation becomes more sharply apparent when we consider, in the next section, the plight of women who invade men's space, not as domestic caretakers but as economic competitors.

The cover of domestic responsibility does not extend far enough to allow all women to travel or move about freely with equal impunity. The threat posed by female sexuality, as it is constructed by patriarchal culture, is not evenly distributed among all categories of women. We have seen this reflected in Mukkuvar ritual: the threat is perceived most clearly in the young girl whose sexuality has 'flowered' with the onset of menstruation, but who has yet to experience the social constraints of marriage and motherhood. The threat is weakest among those women who have not only been 'bound' by marriage and maternity, but whose age is such as to culturally 'de-sex' their bodies. The extent to which women's practice is able to extend the spaces available to them is severely constrained by this differentiated view of female sexuality. It is particularly striking during periods of intense demands on female labour. During the anchovy season, the fish seem to occupy every inch of space in the village. They are laid out to dry on the beaches, along sandy alley-ways, even inside the huts and houses of the fisherpeople. Men need women to cooperate almost continuously through the day and into the night. It is the women's job to spread the catch, and in so doing to carve out a little piece of the beach for themselves. Each woman must keep a vigilant eye not only on the weather and predators, but on her competitors, each guarding her little piles of drying fish. However, even with such urgency in the task at hand, the demand for all available female labour is overridden by the culturally dangerous possibilities unleashed by allowing all women access to the public spaces on the sea-front. What actually happens in practice is that only the married women work on the beaches; no self-respecting household would allow their young daughters to help out on the sea-front.

Similarly, the trips older women may undertake unaccompanied cannot be undertaken by younger, unmarried women, even for the most respectable of domestic reasons. Younger women do travel to shrines and to other coastal villages, but they must be accompanied by a *toNai*, a female companion, preferably older and socially qualified to chaperone them. Occasionally a whole group of younger girls may be permitted to travel together, but only for a limited time. Younger girls can still extend their domestic space, but they need more props to do so than older women. For younger women, the segregated all-female group provides a kind of additional symbolic screen which is culturally required before they can travel safely through spaces which have been implicitly colonised by men.[1]

This complex interaction between cultural meaning, symbolic constructions of femininity and the social practices of women's labour can be observed once again in the various forms of work performed by women. By situating this examination immediately after the discussion of women's domestic labour, I hope to show that the two types of work, paid and unpaid, are not as radically distinct in the way they are structured as may initially be assumed.

Women's paid work

If, on the one hand, domestic labour in Mukkuvar communities is more empowering to women than has been argued in economic and anthropological theory, the reverse is true in the case of women's paid work, which has been less empowering than conventional economic models assume. Western political economy draws an enormous distinction between unpaid and paid work. The former, particularly when it takes the form of housework, has been undervalued not only by economic models, but by the very logic of an economy oriented towards wage labour in its mode of operation. In Western economies, wage-work or paid work is socially recognised, valued as 'productive', viewed as the definitive feature of 'modernisation'.

The Marxist variant of political economy not only sustains this distinction between unpaid and wage labour, but adds to it various political prescriptions which have had vast implications for the proposed model of women's liberation. In the Marxist paradigm, housework is productive only of use-values, and is not socially recognised because it is not productive of exchange values (Seccombe 1973, Gardiner *et al.* 1980). The social gulf between housework and paid work is enormous, each occurring within an entirely different set of social relations. Housework occurs in isolated domestic units, is produced and consumed within the family. It is virtually a historical anachronism within capitalist society. Wage work, on the other hand, is at the very heart of capitalism. For the first time in human history, capitalism makes apparent the social character of human labour; associated with this, it amasses people into large-scale productive units, characterised by a complex division of labour. We are by now familiar with the prescription for the solution of the troublesome 'woman question' which flowed out of this kind of analysis: remove women from the isolation of privatised labour into the public world of wage labour, where they can be organised as workers rather than as women. The question of sexual difference is thus safely dissolved into the question of class conflict.

Western feminists have criticised this Marxist legacy from a number of vantage points. The housework debate of the 1970s made it clear that the persistence of unpaid domestic work in advanced capitalism is no historical accident. The critique that flows out of a consideration of the Mukkuvar community is necessarily somewhat different. We have seen that 'housework' among the Mukkuvars is not the privatised, socially unrecognised category of work it is in the West. I now wish to extend the critique further by arguing that in fact wage work or paid work in such a community may well occur under far more confining and socially unvalidated conditions than domestic work. Instead of being separated by a revolutionary break in the organisation of the relations of production, both domestic and paid work are in a social continuum, often located in the same physical and social space. If there is a distinction, in terms of women's paid work being articulated with the wider market economy in a way their domestic work is not, the distinction is almost a theoretical one: it does not alter women's daily lives in any significant way. Both types of work keep women within the village, often in the immediate vicinity of the home if not inside the home itself. In both cases the restrictions of sexual discipline operate with particular force on younger unmarried women. The relations of production in both cases are subordinate to the sexual, cultural discourse on female sexuality. Indeed, the only real difference is that the cultural legitimacy given by that discourse to women's domestic work, which allows them to extend their territory or space, is missing in the case of women's paid work, so that in a sense their world shrinks instead of expanding as predicted by the different variants of Western modernisation theory, both non-Marxist and Marxist.

In what follows I will be concentrating on the forms of wage work and paid work undertaken by the minimally educated, untrained female labour force typical of this impoverished low-caste community. This may seem outwardly to be an economically defined category of female workers, characterised by lack of economic skills and marketable qualifications. But even this category is internally riven by social and cultural distinctions, distinctions which refer at an empirical level to the age and marital status of the woman worker, and derive their cultural force by implicit reference to the polysemic religious model of femininity. I have referred to the way in which these very distinctions structure women's unpaid domestic tasks. The same logic now surfaces to segment women's paid work. One cannot treat the paid work options available to uneducated women under one heading. Instead, I have been forced by the logic of my material to deal separately with the paid work typical of the young unmarried women, the young married women and the older women (who may be married or unmarried/widowed). I will go on to consider the difference made by education and training to the scope of paid work opportunities available to women, particularly younger women. These educated young women are definitely in a minority in the female population, but they nevertheless must be considered carefully, for they are a culturally and politically significant minority. Consideration of their status in the community in turn poses fresh questions about the cultural pre-conditions of women's paid work.

Paid work for young, unmarried girls: piece-work and 'soap and powder' money

The sexual disciplining of the female body operates with greatest rigour, and even a degree of ferocity, on one whose body is perceived as sexual but as yet uncontained: that is, the young, unmarried female. Her access to space is defined in the narrowest of terms: the only 'safe', culturally legitimate area she is allowed to occupy is within the four walls of the home. Even the most acute demand for female labour, as in the peak fishing seasons, does not override this cultural preoccupation with containing the double-edged threat of female sexuality, simultaneously a threat to men, and in danger from men and supernatural powers.

Young girls, like their mothers, can negotiate the strict application of these cultural rules and expand the space available to them. However, the scope of paid employment undertaken by most younger unmarried women reflects only the harshness of the restrictions imposed on them. For most unmarried girls, safe employment is employment that does not involve setting foot outside the front door of the home. Given the limitations of the skills actually available to young girls, this comes down to the one paid economic activity characteristically associated with them in coastal villages of Kanyakumari District: the weaving of fishing nets. The sight of girls weaving fishing nets is a regional peculiarity of Kanyakumari. Other fishing communities, further north into Kerala or on the east coast of Tamil Nadu, do not define net-weaving as women's work.

In Kanyakumari District, net-weaving is doubly acceptable as a means for young girls to earn some cash. Firstly, it may be performed at home, but it also flows directly out of a sexual division of labour which historically pre-dates the advent of a market in fishing nets, from a period in which women wove nets as an extension of their unpaid domestic duties. According to Belgian Catholic missionaries who have established one of the few social work organisations with any significant interest in the coastal belt, the transition of net-weaving from unpaid to paid work was the result, not of a relentless economic expansion in market relations, but of a political struggle waged by the mission and the girls. The isolation of the girls at home meant that both a wage and a market for net-weaving had to be created by conscious and organised social intervention. The struggle to establish wages and a market for the girls' products necessarily coincided with the attempt by the missionaries to set up a collective space outside the home as the site in which production would take place. In the late 1960s the Belgian Catholic Mission, which had already established branches of the Kottar Social Service Society (KSSS), decided to expand its services and establish net-weaving centres for coastal women and girls. Altogether, thirteen such centres were established, drawing in about 1300 girls by the mid-seventies. The woman most intimately associated with the organisation of the scheme, Sister Lieve, reflected in the course of an interview on the success of the operation:

> The centres were a tremendous success. We were receiving any number of orders, particularly in the southern villages near the Cape, who receive orders from the east-coast villages. This gave them a strong bargaining

base to combat opposition from local men to the higher wages they were demanding. Such opposition was more of a problem for the women from the northern villages, but even here the women stood firm and refused to release the nets unless wages were paid. So wages came in as a mode of payment and grew steadily until the introduction of the net-making machines (personal communication).

In villages which were not lucky enough to be the site of one of these centres, such as KaDalkarai Uuru itself, girls continued to weave for a very limited market, barely larger than the village in which they lived. This is still the case in KaDalkarai Uuru today. Although the principle of payment has been established, the market is only slightly bigger than the old familial unit for which they previously wove their nets, and they are paid on a piece-rate basis. The number of pieces, known as the *kaNi*, in a net determines the amount paid to the girls. Each piece of net involves a greater or lesser number of pieces, and a different type of weave, but payment is ultimately decided by the weight of the net. A small-meshed gill-net weighing seven kilograms would bring the weaver an income of Re70, but this represents the labour of nearly two months.

The low payment for net-weaving strengthens its characterisation as the work most appropriate to young unmarried girls. Older married women with children say they no longer have the time to devote to the continuous work required to fetch a sum as meagre as Re35 a month. Younger girls, unhampered by the domestic responsibility of child-care, and socially prevented from participating in public tasks such as processing and drying fish, are seen to have the 'leisure' to perform the work. The efforts of the girls to relieve the boredom, isolation and repetitiveness of the job brings them together in small groups of three to five. As they weave, talk and sometimes sing Church songs in the front porch of their homes or in the sandy lanes outside the home by lamplight in the evening, one is tempted to forget the complex restrictions which have narrowed their options to this one poorly-paid activity.

The romantic gloss which colours perceptions of this activity is a temptation not only for outside observers but for the community itself. It is a temptation fostered by the preoccupations of the young girls, which revolve around nylon saris and the desire to afford soap and powder, both of which are luxuries in this poor community. The money from net-weaving is perceived not only by the girls, but by the fishing households and social work organisations such as the KSSS, as 'powder money'. The girls' income is seen as important to the extent that their families are spared the additional burden of having to cater to their frivolous hankerings. In the process, the important contribution made by the girls to the fishing economy, whose very nets they weave, is obscured.

Although the centrality of the labour performed by the girls has received recognition only by a few isolated organisers, their activity has acquired an enormous symbolic significance to the fishing community, largely the result of a community mobilisation against the introduction of mechanisation into net production. In 1978, five net-weaving machines were purchased by the Tamil Nadu government and introduced into the state. One of these was bought by a Muslim trader and installed in Manavala Kuruchi, a coastal village in Kanyakumari District. According to the women, men in the fishing community failed to take into account or give due importance to the displacement of female labour, and gave preference to the speed and cheapness of the machine-made products. The orders placed with the girls slumped dramatically. This was particularly obvious in the more centralised locations of production, the net-weaving centres set up by the KSSS. The social workers employed by the KSSS cooperated with various 'voluntary action' groups in the district[2] to lead coastal women and girls into agitation against the machines, which lasted a year. The agitation has succeeded only partially in its aims: the state government has placed a ban on any further licensing of machines within the state, but as participants in the protest are quick to point out, the orders for nets continue to flow away from the coastal villages to neighbouring states where the machines are still in operation. Only three of the net-weaving centres originally set up by the KSSS continue to function today.

In the grip of the current mood of economic and political defeat, the demands of the Mukkuvar women are minimal: they ask only that net-weaving continue to be made available to them as a source of income, however meagre that income may be. However, the success of these net-weaving centres, both in the early attempt to centralise the organisation of weaving and in the political struggle that followed the introduction of machines, indicates that the task of widening the economic horizons available to young unmarried women has to somehow address the mixture of sexual, cultural and economic factors which limits their work participation. Without being fully aware of what they were doing, the organisers of the net-weaving centres provided the girls with a space away from home where they not only wove nets, but came into contact with girls from different coastal villages and with the nuns and social workers who ran the centres. At one of the few centres that still survives, located at the tip of the cape itself, one can get a sense of the way in which such weaving collectives, particularly when guided by politicised female clergy, easily transform themselves into consciousness-raising groups. In such groups, the relaxation of the young girls' usual sexual and social disciplining is as important as the activity of weaving itself. The resultant explosion of female energy is remarkable. At the session I went to the girls maintained a lively and critical discussion of social mores and government policies, directing as many questions at me regarding gender roles in Australian society as I was able to ask them. Under the leadership of the nuns and social workers, who rapidly become idolised, the coastal girls attend political rallies and demonstrations with the same enthusiasm and high spirits with which they go and see a film in town. As an older woman said of the net-weaving protests: 'For nearly four months, we women and girls had fun though we fasted.'

It follows closely from my argument that the convergence of female politicisation and female pleasure is not an accidental feature confined to this particular experience: it reflects the unity of the politics of the body with the politics of the workplace.

The young, married women: home-based petty trade and piece-work

The rituals of marriage in Tamil Nadu culminate in the tying of the *tali* around the bride's neck, by which, the bridegroom symbolically lays claim to future control over the otherwise dangerous power of female sexuality.

Yet if we look at the work options available to the younger groups of married women, it is apparent that the dangers of female sexuality are not quite extinguished to male satisfaction by the social controls of marriage. As long as women are young, it seems, their bodies are always threatening to overflow the boundaries of male control. Precautions still need to be taken—married women, too, are preferably kept within the home.

The paid work options of married women are therefore not much wider in range than those of unmarried girls. In practice they no longer have available to them the option of weaving nets, since the demands of child-care and domestic duties fragment their time much more and prevent them from earning as much as the girls from net-weaving. The characteristic work performed by these women is petty trade. The trade is distinctive not only in terms of the small scale of the enterprise but in terms of its typical physical location, which is closely bound up with the location of the domestic dwelling. Trade is pursued either from the front porch of the home, in street stalls set up on the ground in front of the home, or in small shops which are extensions of the home. Not only is the space an extension of a woman's domestic space, but the articles sold are extensions of the items she produces as part of her unpaid domestic labour. Items of food constitute the bulk of women's trade. Some women sell vegetables, rice and spices bought wholesale at the rural markets, but others sell food items that they have actually cooked themselves. The latter include local snacks such as boiled and seasoned tapioca and popcorn. Those women who have become established as petty traders in bulk items such as rice may also use their customer networks to lend money and make a little extra profit from the interest.

The physical limitations on the space which may be occupied by young married women have drastic consequences. Despite the fact that over half of the women engaged in such trade are widowed and have no other means of economic support, the scale of the petty trade and its rate of turnover is too small to be profitable. Requirements of seclusion prevent them from making their own purchases at wholesale markets. They must therefore rely on the cooperation of men or older women who can spare some time. Further, since they are buying wholesale from outside their own community, the terms of credit are set more severely against women retailers. Unlike fish traders who buy on credit and then pay the men back after sales are completed, the vegetable traders buy with cash, but are forced to sell on credit to villagers who are always short of cash in between the sales of fish. The market supplied by these women is also not large enough to be economically viable. Home-based sales effectively restrict the market to the village of residence. Informal norms restrict the market even further—a petty trader will typically service, not the entire village, but her particular section of the village.[3] Within this limited market, the trader must compete with the cheaper prices and the much fresher produce which rural wholesale markets can offer. With no means of storage at her disposal, the trader has no way to keep her food items fresh and saleable under the hot coastal sun. Many women have either given up their trade, or are hovering on the brink of closing their businesses.

The income that women draw from these kinds of home-based wage work is summarised in Table 9.1, along with the proportion of households engaged in each type of work. A subsidiary category of employment for the unqualified village women (also included in Table 9.1). concerns the few jobs made available by the Church, as cooks and *ayah*s or nannies in the village primary school. Such jobs are included in the category of home-based paid work in Table 9.1 because they fit the criteria of respectability: they do not take women outside the village. The jobs are poorly paid, but expose the women to the envy of other villagers who suspect them of corruption and pilfering supplies for their own use.

As with men's earnings, the female earnings from petty trade fluctuate considerably from one month to the next. In fact, the seasonal cycles of male and female earnings are interlinked: apart from the seasonal nature of the vegetable produce marketed by the women, profit in women's petty trade also depends on the amount of money circulating within the limited market of the village itself. This amount in turn depends on the cycle of the fishing seasons. However, though male and female earnings both vary considerably, the discrepancy between the two is striking: most women earn little more than one-third of the amount men earn, if we take Re300 to be a rough averaging out of male income for the bulk of the fishermen (55 per cent of households) who either own no equipment or a minimal amount of equipment. Women's income lags even further behind the income of those men who own enough equipment to be classified as

Table 9.1   Home-based paid forms of work performed by women in fishing families, KaDalkarai Uuru

Types of activity	Number of families (N = 286)*	Percentage	Income (rupees per month per household)
Tailoring	8	2	60–200
Sale of vegetables and spices	6	2	25–120
Sale of cooked food	7	2	30– 90
Sale of rice and cooked food	8	2	75–100
Net-making and thread-making	34	11	20– 40
Money-lending	8	2	35–100
Cook and *ayah* for primary school	6	2	60
	—	—	
	77	23	

Note: 1. *N = 286, i.e. the number of nuclear families engaged in fishing in KaDalkarai Uuru.

2. Figures in Table 8.1 add up to a percentage when taken in conjunction with the rest of the families in Table 9.2 (women in 'public' paid jobs and women not earning any cash).

Source: Household survey; fieldwork 1982–83

Table 9.2   'Public' forms of paid work performed by women in fishing families, KaDalkarai Uuru

Types of activity	Number of families (N = 286)	Percentage	Income (rupees per month per household)
Uneducated women:			
Fish trading	51	18	50– 75
Educated women:			
Social work	11	3	200–500
Teaching			400
Typing/clerical work	—	—	150
Total number of families in which women contribute income from 'public' forms of work	62	21	

	Number	Percentage	
Total number of families in which women contribute income (Tables 9.1 and 9.2)	139	44	
Other (i.e. households where women are not engaged in paid work)	147	56	
	—	—	
	286	100	

Source: Household survey; fieldwork 1982–83

'masters' or employers of coolies, or if compared to that other category of men who work as labourers on mechanised craft (where the average income is twice that earned on the *kaTTumaram*).

When it comes to paid work, therefore, there is not much to choose between the options available to unmarried women and married women: the youth of the women concerned overrides their marital status. Not only do both groups of women have to perform their paid tasks within or around the home, but certain types of paid work are also common to both groups. Although unmarried girls tend to rely on net-weaving, and married women on petty trade, the two groups have in common the work of tailoring. Women and girls are supplied with sewing machines by local tailoring shops to sew and tailor at home. Items of clothing such as women's blouses, petticoats and men's shirts are manufactured in fishing households. Other women manage to hire the machines at their own expense and set themselves up as semi-independent producers, paying the cost of hire out of the orders they supply. Such forms of tailoring, which bring in a sum anywhere between Re60–200 a month, account for two per cent of the households in which women earn cash.

Feminist criticism within India during the 1970s raised, among other issues, the question of the significant underestimation of female unemployment in economic statistics. The criticism has had some impact. The National Sample Survey (NSS) is, along with the census, one of the two main official sources of information on rural women's work participation in India. For the first time, the 1981 questionnaire (the 32nd round) has added some questions on the type of location in which women would like to see work made available. The response to this set of questions reveals that 23 per cent of women categorised as engaged in domestic work, and hence usually discounted from the official labour force, reported a willingness to accept paid work if it were made available in the home.

At least one feminist commentator, Agarwal (1985), has interpreted the women's response as a function of the other unpaid domestic tasks they already perform—that is, as a by-product of the sexual division of labour. Such an interpretation implicitly attributes to the women's responses a purely practical, utilitarian logic: the women prefer to earn cash at home because it fits in with their other tasks. However, such a practical logic is complicated by and even subordinate to the highly charged cultural overtones of the question which was put to the women in the National Sample Survey. The question of where women earn money, whether it is located in a respectable domestic space, or in a public space dominated by men, is a heavily loaded one, and we cannot analyse women's preferences in a voluntarist fashion without also taking into account the costs they incur by venturing into alien territory. These costs are made only too obvious when we consider the next category of women workers, the fish-traders.

The older women: kuttai kaari[4] *or the 'basket' fish-trader*

The peculiar status of the female fish-traders of Kanyakumari District can perhaps be best highlighted by reviewing the assumptions about women traders with which I came to the field. I came with the expectation of documenting the lives of bold and assertive women. I planned to qualify the popular mythology of the aggressive fish-wife, and to affirm their unconventional model of femininity. My expectations had been fed by reading ethnographies of women traders in other parts of the world, and in other parts of India. It seemed that whereas there is no necessary relation between female participation in subsistence production and extra-domestic power (Sanday 1974), female participation in the wider world of trade and exchange has provided the basis for women exercising positions of community leadership and being active in political mobilisations (Chaki Sircar 1984, Ifeka 1975).

There is some force to the picture one gets from reading ethnographies of women traders in Nigeria and north-east India as mediators of a wide-ranging set of social relations. Among Mukkuvars, those who work as fish-traders have the opportunity to forge strong work-based associations with other traders. Women may begin their working lives trading on an individual basis, but once they have shown themselves to be competent and enterprising market-women, they are eligible to become recruited into work-teams of four to five women who operate as a *kuuTam* or group. The *kuuTam* involves a flexible arrangement between the women concerned, designed to deal with the seasonality of trade. Women come together as a *kuuTam* in peak seasons, after having worked as individuals in the slack season. If the catch is particularly large, more than one *kuuTam* may merge. Within these larger groups, the tasks of buying the fish at the sea-front, drying it if necessary, and marketing the catch, are shared by about eight women.

The work relations between fish-trading women can also give rise to strong cooperative relations of mutual aid in other areas of life. I have earlier mentioned the case of a fifty-year-old woman trader who was widowed and virtually homeless. She had lived with her mother and brother until the time her mother died. Her brother eventually felt that his family had grown too large to be able to accommodate his widowed sister. At the time of fieldwork, she was living for an indefinite period with a workmate, another trader of about the same age.

It would also be true to say that women who work as fish-traders enjoy a unique access to other castes and communities in the agrarian hinterland, an access equalled only by the women healers in the district. In their daily movement to and from the market place, the women develop social relations with other caste groups such as the Nadars. The network may be mobilised by traders in the same way that other non-trading women utilise their kinship networks: to raise small amounts of credit. Traders themselves see these alternative sources of credit outside the village as leading to less acrimony and tensions than credit from neighbours or members of the Mukkuvar community. Those trader women who have developed relations of direct barter with Nadar households exchange fish for rice and firewood, and may develop long-term personal contact with the women of these agricultural households.

Relationships of this kind present a direct contrast to the normally hierarchical model of interaction found in agricultural caste society. Although fishing communities as a whole present a challenge to the hierarchy of caste-based interaction, it is the women fish-traders who exemplify this most clearly in their trade with agricultural society. The men's world of fishing is oriented away from the hinterland and out to sea. The market women, through their work, not only enjoy the leverage that comes from the cash they earn, but perhaps as importantly, they daily move right outside the domestic space of the home, as well as the extended versions of domestic space in the village and in the rest of the coastal *tinai*. Unlike women doing every other type of work, they widen their area of operation, not in the name of domestic responsibilities, but as traders. I will come back to the significance of this feature of their work, and deal with it in some detail.

Certainly, the widening of horizons has its advantages for these women. The proverbial independence and individualism of the female fish-traders is a by-word in the Mukkuvar villages themselves. I came across a couple of examples of this myself. An ex-trader, now aged seventy, is still so fiercely independent that she prefers to support herself from the meagre earnings she makes by selling root vegetables than allow herself to be economically dependent on her three sons. Another trader, whom I shall call Claramma, began an affair with a married man when she was at a young age. She has remained unmarried, and in the intervening years has borne the man three children. The social pressures on her have been immense. The Church refused her children baptism due to their illegitimacy, her brother fought her lover, and at a later stage the lover was sent to prison on a murder charge. A great part of Claramma's ability to withstand and survive all of these tribulations comes (according to her own account and the account of other villagers) not only from her ability to support herself and her children, but from her daily escape route out of the village and its various modes of surveillance and censure. Indeed, with the long hours of work involved in buying at the beach, walking distances of 5–10 kilometres, selling at the markets and then back again, the traders are a fugitive presence within the village. My efforts to talk to Claramma about her unusual life were long thwarted by the sheer impossibility of finding her in the village except late at night.

The physical appearance of the trader women itself separates them from other groups of women. Their faces are weathered from working outdoors, and they have a brisk loping gait which comes from walking long distances, carrying up to twenty kilograms in their characteristic woven baskets or *kuTTai* (from which they derive their occupational name, *kuTTai kaari*).[5] Their manner is usually business-like, and a little preoccupied, unless one is a customer of course—but when they decide to relax, they are bold and audacious in their humour, delighting in sexual puns and innuendo. They care little about their appearance or the clothes they wear. A traditional cotton *cheelai* worn in the traditional simple style, without any elaborate pleats and allowing for maximum freedom of movement, their hair in a careless knot, underline their partial escape from the normally bounded and contained forms of bodily discipline demanded of women in the fishing community.

However, their very escape is a problematic one, precisely because it sets them apart from other women in the community, and ultimately undermines the advantages I have outlined so far, which come with the wider social and territorial networks enjoyed by the women traders.

The first criterion which sets them apart from other women, and which emphasises the minority character of fish traders, is their age. The second characteristic of the trader women is their marital status. With the exception of Claramma, none of the vendors is unmarried, but a quarter of them are widowed. However, age is the prime consideration: widows, despite their obvious economic hardship, have to be at least thirty years of age before they go out to work as fish-traders. Widows below thirty are engaged in the types of home-based employment described in the previous section. A little less than half the women who now work as fish-traders in KaDalkarai Uuru are aged fifty and over. None is below thirty, although a few women such as Claramma did report circumstances (such as an alcoholic father), which forced them to start learning marketing skills with their mother at a much younger age.

As a result of these social prerequisites, the actual number of women fish-traders in the village is limited. Only 18 per cent of the women in KaDalkarai Uuru work as fish-traders. This is to be compared with the total figure of households where women are engaged in some form of paid work, which comes to 44 per cent of all households in the village (see Table 9.2). The small size of the occupational category of trader-women only expresses in numerical terms the socially and sexually anomalous character of their work. Let us consider briefly the way the work of the fish-trader requires systematic transgression of the sexual codification of space and the segregation of genders.

Women traders wait on the sea-front for auctions. They wait along-side men who come not only from their own village but from other castes and communities, such as the Nadars and the Muslims. During auctions, women must bid in the midst of physical jostling, excitement and aggression. Purchase is followed by a walk through the country roads, and the shortcuts to the markets take women through the paddy fields, through which they return late in the evening as well. The atmosphere at the markets is not as aggressively and exclusively male as the bazaars of north India, but women who are selling fish must adopt tough and vocal strategies to compete effectively.

The threat represented by the transgressions is a double one. Not only are women present on spaces which have been defined as male, but they are not there under cover of some feminine role or domestic obligation. Thus the cultural purdah which metaphorically shields women and renders them culturally invisible or protected when they travel to religious shrines, healers or on social errands, or even to the market-place itself (as consumers and purchasers of items for domestic consumption), is conspicuously not available for women who work as fish-traders. Traders cannot exploit any cultural ambiguities about their role to legitimise their activities: when they appear on the beaches and market-places, they are there, at least in theory, to perform a role identical to other traders who are male.

Such a transgression is simply not permitted to occur in situations where the woman's sexual presence is her key defining characteristic. As a result, no young woman works as a fish-trader. When she is over the age of thirty, and certainly over the age of fifty, the sexuality of a woman no longer poses such a threat because it is regarded as diminished, if not extinguished. Her presence on male-dominated space can then be tolerated with more equanimity, but the tolerance is still grudging and accords her an anomalous status. Women traders occupy a culturally intermediate position where they are accorded neither the same status as male traders nor the same sexual and social status as younger women who remain within a domestic space.

In the world of male traders and commerce, women traders may be seen as old and de-sexualised, but they are still women and must obey some rules of modesty and propriety, rules which are among the most compelling forces ensuring that they occupy the least powerful rung of the trading hierarchy in the fish trade. Unlike the cycle-traders, women do not possess any means of transport. With the aid of cycles, they could compete with men in servicing a wider market, covering over forty kilometres in radius, instead of the ten kilometres they can currently manage on foot. The cycles also carry larger loads of fish, fifty to sixty kilograms as against the twenty kilograms that women carry on their heads. Women refrain from purchasing cycles not simply from lack of capital, since women traders are prepared to hire taxis and 'Dimbos' or small trucks when the volume of trade permits. What restrains them is the certainty of public ridicule and harassment were they to cycle along rural roads, whereas taxis offer a 'closed' way of travelling in public.

It would be easy to conceive of the women's problems as purely economic, relating to their lack of access to credit and to sources of capital. Yet the general lack of capital to invest in items such as means of transportation is itself linked to restrictions which prevent women from being able to stay overnight away from the village. Male traders will stay in cheap hotels, but women, even if over forty years of age, cannot take such risks with their reputations. Similar problems restrain women from making contact with sources of credit located outside their own village, if these are controlled by men. The women's only source of advantage is the personal links they keep up with the fishermen of their own village. Thanks to these they are able to purchase the fish on trust, and pay the men back when they return from the market. This privilege, which is not extended to traders outside the community, is of little weight when compared with the scale of operations mounted by male traders, even when these are located residentially inside Mukkuvar villages. In KaDalkarai Uuru, the best-established of these male traders hires agents to send fish to markets outside the district: to the adjacent district of Tirunelveli, to Madras, and interstate to Kerala. Like all traders, he needs working capital and ready sources of credit to tide him over the long interval—which could be a month—between purchase and sale. To meet these needs the trader has developed close contacts with wealthy boat-owners in nearby Colachel. By no means the wealthiest in the fish trading business, this man averages a profit of Re300–500 a month. This may be compared with the uncertain Re50–75 net profit averaged by women traders.

In the world of men, women traders are therefore treated as women, albeit women of a strange and anomalous variety. The lingering stamp of femininity functions to disqualify even older women from competing on the same footing as male traders. Increasingly, these disqualifications serve to intensify the poverty and inability of women to survive as traders in the face of the new mercantile capital in the sea-food business. The produce, even in the small fishing villages of Kanyakumari, is marketed through a chain of middlemen who eventually link up with larger sea-food companies interested in supplying an export market. The traditional practice of women fish-traders has been to buy on credit and pay back the auctioneer after sales are complete. Middlemen who are affiliated to companies can offer fishermen ready cash well before the catch is actually in, and at far higher prices than the women could afford. Profitable species of fish are now siphoned off from the local market to service the national and international markets.

Simultaneously, the ecological impact of mechanised fishing has affected the variety and scale of fishing available on the western coast of southern India (see Chapter 5). This affects all categories of traders supplying local markets within the district, but is particularly disastrous for the small-scale operators, like the women, who are surviving on a marginal profit. An increased variety of provisioners of mercantile capital are therefore fighting over a dwindling catch. According to villagers in KaDalkarai Uuru, the number of traders who are wealthy enough to employ small trucks has doubled in the last five years. They recall that five years ago, there were fifty to sixty cycle-traders, as well as four traders who hired the occasional taxis and two who owned trucks. Today there are still only about sixty cycle-traders, but ten traders who hire taxis, and seven who own trucks. The tendency favours those who already command some capital.

The sexual codification of femininity and the ensuing disciplining of the female body thus reinforce the low economic status of women traders. In turn, their economic powerlessness feeds back into their low cultural status within the community. Having given up the security of the sexual status of the young confined woman, the female traders have not gained much in return. If in the world of traders they are still derogated and limited by their female status, in the world of the Mukkuvar community and to caste society at large they are neither men nor women. While respected within the community for their independence and self-reliance, they are also the target of easy ridicule. Young children run behind them on the roads, mimicking their unfeminine gait as they move at a brisk pace, hips swaying fast and elbows thrust for balance under their heavy head-loads. But most damning of all, they are rejected by their own daughters, who dream of clothes and marriage and safe, feminine occupations. The unremitting toil of the fish-traders and their loss of feminine status disqualify them as role-models for younger women. Unlike the socially validated existence of women traders in other areas such as Nigeria, Manipur or Java (Alexander 1987), the female fish-traders of Kanyakumari remain locked into a liminal space where they transgress the sexual norms of femininity without being able to redefine these norms.[6] The price they pay for their inability to do so is at once economic and cultural.

Education and women's paid work: the case of qualified, unmarried girls

I have left the case of educated, trained or qualified women until the end of this discussion of paid work for the simple reason that they are unrepresentative of the female community as a whole. Firstly, Mukkuvars as a group have a lower rate of literacy than the rest of the district: 34.3 per cent as against the 48.6 per cent calculated for Kanyakumari District as a whole (Selik 1980). In the village of KaDalkarai Uuru, only 77 individuals, male and female, have studied up to the Senior School Leaving Certificate (SSLC) and beyond. Within this overall low rate of literacy and education, however, the discrepancy between male and female education is not as heavily weighted in favour of men as it is in the rest of India.[7] If we break the group of literate villagers into male and female components, forty-one of the seventy-seven are men, and thirty-six are women.

This near parity in male and female education is largely the result of the very high rate of withdrawal of boys from schools. Most fishing households still regard fishing as the most reliable and readily available form of male employment, and to train the boys in their trade, begin their apprenticeship by the age of seven or eight. The education of boys is therefore passed over in favour of their traditional training out at sea.

As we can see from the figures for KaDalkarai Uuru, only a minority of girls remains in school right through till the SSLC. They are withdrawn, to be absorbed into household tasks, by parents who find even the cost of buying notebooks and pencils for the children too onerous. However, there is more of an economic incentive to let girls complete their education and acquire some kind of certification and training. Households are keenly aware of the paltry sums uneducated women and girls can hope to earn. An educated and qualified daughter represents a welcome widening in the economic strategies available to a poor household. A girl may not receive a great deal of help in getting through school, but once she does, the family will support her, at least in principle, in trying for further training and qualification.

The attitude of the daughters in turn encourages the parents to regard their education as an asset. Educated daughters, particularly while still unmarried, take very seriously their role as financial contributors to the family. In doing so they continue the female tradition in the Mukkuvar community. As with mothers, the daughters are at the heart of the strategies of survival and reproduction pursued by households. Like their mothers, they are busy raising money for dowries, looking after younger children, cooking meals. If in addition they are educated and employed, they dutifully contribute money to the household pool, and help younger children with their schoolwork.

Although the number of educated girls is small, they are a significant minority and raise some interesting questions for my general argument about the kinds of cultural forces which shape women's access to wage work, and the conditions under which they may extend their areas of activity. Here we have a group of women who are young and unmarried and should therefore be subject to the greatest degree of restriction in their movement. Further, like the women traders, when these girls move in search of training and employment they do not have the symbolic screen of domesticity to cloak their movement. Yet, unlike the women fish-traders, the young educated girls do not occupy a disadvantaged status bereft of cultural validation. Instead, they are well regarded by the community, by the Church and by educated outsiders. Although young and unmarried, many are travelling distances further away from home than their mothers ever did, either in the course of domestic duties, or in their capacity as fish-traders. Many of those who train as teachers travel interstate to Bangalore in the state of Karnataka, to a Catholic teacher's training institute. Employment in turn takes the girls to other districts within Tamil Nadu.

How, then, is it possible for these girls to travel such distances, work in new areas of employment and still remain legitimised in their activity? No doubt a great deal of respectability and legitimacy is conferred on them by the very process of certification and the social power of the institutions which train and employ them. Teaching and social work are recognised by the wider society as prestigious occupations in a way that trading in fish is not. They do not carry the stain of a low-caste occupation. These occupations are also formally recognised, in contrast to other forms of female employment such as piece-work performed at home.

But there is another, more subtle, process at work. Girls are only allowed to take jobs which can be legitimised—that is, jobs in which the requirements of modesty and chaperonage can be maintained and verified. Girls may travel and stay away from home in order to send home the cash which is desperately needed—but they cannot simply move about in search of work, and arrive in a strange town on the off-chance that there may be work available. Mukkuvar men can go to the port town of Neendakara in Kerala or to the Middle East with no job and no accommodation. With girls, every detail of work and accommodation must be arranged before they leave home, and places where they live and work must be sexually segregated and supervised.

Ordinarily, such requirements would place an insurmountable obstacle in the way of most fishing households. Not only do they lack the requisite finances, but their ability to provide girls with pre-existing social contacts is hampered by the insularity and self-contained economic and marital networks of coastal people. The Mukkuvar villages have the Catholic Church to step into this gap, to act as financier, institutional guarantor of respectability and chaperonage, and provider of employment. Its activities in this regard are only a further extension of the tendency of the Church to regard the coastal belt as its own private constituency. Girls train as teachers in all-girl boarding colleges run by the Church. Afterwards, the lucky ones may find employment in a Catholic school, boarding in a convent, supervised by nuns. Others find work in mission-based social service organisations such as the KSSS, running health programmes for mothers and children within the district.

Such social mediation with the outside world offered by the Church provides girls with a respectable way out of the village, but even here there are costs. While the girls spoke with enthusiasm of the pleasures of student life at teacher's training college, employment in a strange district in the closed atmosphere of a convent struck them as quite another matter. I receive frequent letters from one of my research assistants, describing the loneliness and the petty tyranny of the convent sisters in foiling her attempts to study for a higher degree by correspondence. For such girls, the village offers a more relaxed and convivial existence. Other girls who receive this form of Church patronage suffer the ridicule and suspicion of gossip, for the Church itself is locally represented by a male: often a young and attractive parish priest. In cases such as that of my first research assistant, who was already inclined to regard herself as a cut above other uneducated villagers, such gossip can further alienate the educated girl from her community.

On the whole, however, once the Mukkuvar villagers are satisfied of suitable chaperonage and supervision, there is no limit to the actual physical distance they are prepared to send their unmarried daughters in search of employment. With chaperonage and patronage, even Australia is not out of bounds; I was repeatedly approached by parents to find jobs for their daughters. Nor do the Mukkuvars necessarily entertain pre-conceived ideas of what sorts of jobs the girls should occupy, and they have little trouble contemplating the idea of women in positions of authority.

Ultimately, it is the wider society which imposes its more impoverished vision of female roles onto the girls. The narrowing of girls' training to teaching, social work and clerical/typing skills reflects an ideology of women as nurturant and subservient to men which is more indicative of women's status in the modern, industrial economy than of women in the Mukkuvar community. By contrast, Mukkuvar boys who have moved out of fishing and obtained jobs in the industrial sector work as engineers, teachers at the Polytechnic Institute in Nagercoil (rather than in primary and secondary schools as do women), in factories, small repair workshops, and in one rather unusual case, in the police force. Not only is there a greater variety in these male jobs, but they are also more readily employable skills. Of the forty-one qualified and educated men in the village only two are unemployed, and one of them voluntarily so. On the other hand, a quarter of the thirty-six educated girls are unemployed and actively seeking work, some with a growing sense of desperation.

The tragedy of the educated, trained girls is unemployment, and in many more cases, underemployment. Trained teachers find they can at best obtain occasional work as casual relief workers. Girls who study shorthand and typing find limited scope for employment in an already over-saturated labour market. In the absence of employment, the gap between the forms of paid work performed by educated girls and uneducated girls narrows and becomes blurred. Even qualified girls take in tailoring, weave nets for piece-rate wages, in fact do anything to bring in some money. Their problem is not the cultural marginality which haunts the status of the fish-traders. The prestige of their education, the fact that the jobs they aspire to represent a form of upward mobility for the community, and do not contravene the norms of respectability for women, all combine to give these young women tremendous cultural confidence. The older fish-traders also have a kind of boldness and independence of their own—but their insecure status enables them only just to maintain that independence. They cannot win the respect of the community, or even of their own daughters. The educated girls, on the other hand, have such a secure status that they are able to take part in the politics of village reform, which is bound up with the social work jobs a number of them take on, and even to a certain extent to participate in the politics of protest. They are often in key positions of responsibility in the voluntary unpaid youth groups, village health and education programmes run by the more politicised sections of the Catholic clergy.

I came to know this group of young women particularly well. Like other outsiders seeking to work within the community, I turned to the educated girls as social go-betweens and as research assistants in conducting surveys and interviews. But many came to mean much more to me than that, as I relied on them heavily for daily companionship and friendship in the village.

To give an idea of the impressive range of responsibilities handled by many of these young women, I have reproduced below the bio-data of my second research assistant. It gives some idea of the way girls perform tasks that, strictly speaking, fall outside their area of qualifications. It is as though their status as women who are both of the coastal village, and educated, equips them in the eyes of the Church and of villagers to run a whole range of organisational services.

Bio-data of V. Serapheenal, age 24

Educational qualification:	Colachel High School
Professional qualification:	Typewriting, lower grade English and Tamil proficiency Teachers certificate, specialising in teaching mathematics, SJES Training Institute, Bangalore, Karnatala
Work experience: 1978–1980	• Volunteer social worker in Kottar Social Service Society (KSSS) • Part-time coordinator in Social Education Development, conducting village adult education classes, health and legal counselling
1982–1983	• Casual teaching as replacement teacher in Kadiapattnam and KaDalkrai Uuru in local village schools • Assistant president and accountant in KaDalkarai Credit Society

	• Accountant and animator in KaDalkarai Fish Vendors Association
1983	• Casual work as Research Assistant to PhD scholar from The Australian National University, Canberra, Australia
Other experience: 1978–1982	• Conducting religious associations in the village • Catechism teacher • Animator in Little Way Association • Catechism teacher • Secretary to Little Way Association at Colachel Vicarage • Assistant president in Little Way Association at Kottar Diocese level • President in Catechism Teachers' Association in KaDalkarai Uuru village

The sexual construction of economic and political experience

I have argued that in the Mukkuvar community the domestic sphere is more empowering of women than is the kind of paid work available to most uneducated girls and women, a conclusion in direct contrast to what we have come to expect on the basis of modernisation theory. The missing element in the Western economic diagnosis is culture. It is the cultural construction of sexual difference that provides the fundamental key to the allocation of economic roles. Women's sexuality is culturally defined as requiring restriction and control. This on the one hand restricts women's relationship to the labour market, and on the other hand, confines them to the domestic spheres. In Mukkuvar society, however, the domestic sphere is remarkably fluid and extended in its boundaries—women enjoy considerable freedom of movement in practice, so long as they stick to a domestic definition of their role. The case of the fish-traders illustrates the dangers to women who give up the respectability of domesticity to compete in the market-place with men. They end up as neither respectable women nor successful traders. The case of the educated girls shows that certification and training can partially re-define women's relationship to wage labour, allowing an easing of the isolation and restrictions imposed on uneducated young girls. But here, too, the requirement of chaperonage and segregation combines with the prevailing narrow definition of 'women's jobs' in the modern industrial economy to allow girls a very limited escape from the village, one which takes them only as far as Catholic-run convents and social work institutions inside and outside the district.

In none of these different versions of women's work are we allowed to forget even for a moment that we are not dealing simply with a group of workers, but with *women* workers. Women's work is not subject to a simple form of determination, rather, it is overdetermined, a term used by Freud to describe the representation of dream thoughts in certain images which are favoured, since they allow a condensation of a number of thoughts or else displacement of the energy from sexual impulses to apparently trivial images (1915). That is, the final product, the manifest dream, has a misleading coherence and unity: each image stands for many, deriving its psychic energy from thoughts which are hidden from us in the process. Women's work is roughly analogous: it seems an economic function, the result of a division of labour which may even appear as natural and biological in its origin. But the division of labour is created by a process which is hidden to the observer, a process which is both cultural and historical. As in the case of dreams, the hidden content of this seemingly neutral category of work is overwhelmingly sexual.

I have no real scope to develop here the political implications of my argument, at variance with all prescriptions which would obliterate the question of sexual difference in favour of some larger unity. Political experiences within the coastal women's community over the last ten years are immensely suggestive in this regard. Those groups of women who are culturally validated in their work have been far more receptive to organisational initiatives from politicised clergy and social workers than those the culture confines, restricts or else ignores altogether. As mothers, wives and caretakers of the local environment, village women have participated in a number of campaigns. They have fought the mining companies which are eroding their *tinai*, blindly oblivious to the people who live in it. Organised into 'mothers' groups, they have marched and petitioned municipal authorities to provide water, sanitation and electricity. As preparers of food and domestic budgets, they have participated in district-wide agitations against price rises in basic food items such as rice. The educated girls have also proved a readily mobilisable group. Many are already involved in literacy and health programmes and readily extend this work to organising village women into marches and rallies. The combination of education, cultural self-confidence and unemployment can be explosive. During the period of my stay in the village, the Tamil Nadu government announced its decision to de-recognise teaching diplomas received outside the state. This affected many Mukkuvar girls. Rallies were held in Nagercoil to protest the decision, and my assistant travelled three hours daily by bus for a week in order to take part, and participated in the culminating hunger strike held on the last day.

By contrast, the women and girls who work at home performing piece-work and petty trade have had little access to organisations and political action. Equally conspicuous in their absence from any organised action are the fish-traders, even though the village credit society has been trying to enlist their support for some time now. These divisions in political involvement may change in time—the activism of one group of women has repercussions on all others in this tight-knit community. But the salient point here is that it is not the experience of paid work which acts in itself as a force capable of generating political mobilisation; nor is domesticity the equivalent of female domestication in this community. Rather, the relation between work and women's ability to mobilise in political ways is mediated by the cultural organisation of sexual difference.

Conclusion

In undertaking the detailed work of an ethnographic analysis, I have sought to address central issues in Indian sociology and culture, as well as more general issues of social theory. In analysing the Mukkuvar past and present, change and continuity, the lives of men and of women, I have sought to show a gulf between two major bodies of social theory, the inadequacies of each, and the possibility of going beyond them, in a way that can begin to span the gulf.

The first body of social theory is the Marxist tradition. Despite all attempts at reassigning a greater role to the 'superstructure' in Marxist theory (such as the Althusserian attempt to delay economic determination 'till the last instance'), the crushing weight of 'economism', and even more fundamentally, of an attempt to separate out culture from material practice, allows the residual power of old Western dualisms to continue to haunt the philosophical premises of Marxist theory and political practice.

The inadequacies of such an approach are particularly striking if we consider the ways in which the subjects of the book—women in a low caste community—have been considered previously. For many Marxist writers on caste (Mencher 1974, Meillassoux 1973, Gough 1971) it is precisely what is distinctive about caste—namely, the organisation of power around a moral hierarchy of purity and pollution—that is seen as epiphenomenal, reducible to the exercise of economic power in the appropriation and exploitation of labour. A similar logic is played out in explanations of women's subordination: women become subsumed under a broader social category, that of the class to which they belong.

The anthropological concept of culture, as 'meaningful orders of persons and things' (Sahlins 1976:x) has the potential, according to Sahlins, to 'leave behind just such antique dualisms as mind and matter, idealism and materialism' (p.ix). Yet the analysis of social

230

systems and historical processes in terms of culture and symbolic structures is not necessarily more productive of insight than a materialist approach. History and process may disappear from sight under the weight of static, quasi-eternal, intellectually elaborated structures of explication which bear the all-too-visible mark of the privileged standpoint of the Western scholar. Economistic studies of caste have their 'culturalist' counterparts: the work of Dumont, for all its suggestive insights, stresses the moral and ideational elements in the organisation of social structure virtually at the expense of materialist concerns, for example, with labour and livelihood. A more striking example is the understanding of caste, kinship and gender in India, fostered from the 1970s by the Chicago brand of cultural anthropology. These categories have been interpreted in terms of culturally-defined transactions in food, bodily fluids and blood (Marriott and Inden 1977; Inden and Nicholas 1977). Daniel (1984) in exploring how Tamils construct their view of the 'person', has carried further the notion of 'ranked substances' as the basis for negotiating everyday life in a Tamil village. Studies of Tamil women by Egnor (1978), Wadley (1980), and Reynolds (1978), again exhibit the strengths and weaknesses of what I am calling a purely culturalist account, conveying a vivid sense of symbolic constructions of meaning, located in the context of kinship and ritual, but ignoring or minimising historical processes, relations of power, and what in the Marxist account would be called 'relations of production'.

In the book I have explored areas of Mukkuvar life which are quite intractable if viewed in terms of these European polarities of thought. Mukkuvar interaction with the physical environment cannot be explained wholly in terms of economic relations. Geographical data and the question of people's location in the physical landscape have long been culturally overlain by the ancient Tamil conceptualisation of geo-cultural zones or *tinais*. The geographical zones are inscribed with cultural meanings reflecting a sense of hierarchical ordering which plays just as important a part in Mukkuvar self-definition as do habitation or occupation. The system of ranking social groups according to criteria of purity and pollution is a later historical accretion, adding another layer of cultural determination to the issue of people's relationship with their physical environment. The agrarian orientation of the ancient Tamil world-view, combined with caste society's labelling of fisher-castes as polluted and inferior, has intimately shaped the historical evolution of the Mukkuvar's definition of their work, their community and of caste itself.

At the same time these cultural determinations have been radically shaped by the specificities of fishing as a sub-economy and labour process, which is not directly dependent on the dominant land-holding groups in Tamil society. The fact that the relations of the Mukkuvars with caste society are based on trade and monetary exchange, rather than direct servitude, has had enormous implications in

tempering the lowly status ascribed to them. It means that Mukkuvars, particularly the men who are directly engaged in fishing, are
able to construct an alternative self-image based on their relation to
the sea rather than to the land. But here again, their relation to the
sea is not a material relation as such: it is dominated by a religious
conceptualisation of the sea and of nature in general. Such concep-
tualisations are remote from the mind-body dualism of Western
philosophy. Mukkuvar religion is this-worldly, without being merely
pragmatic; it focuses on the physical environment without ceasing to
be mystical and transcendental. An investigation of the religious
framework has proved essential to my argument; without this
investigation it would prove impossible to evaluate Mukkuvar ideas of
the female body, which serves as a particularly apt locus for the
condensation and materialisation of religious values. By privileging the
female body, the Mukkuvars lay the basis for a very specific cultural
model of gender relations, one in which female identity is at once
valorised and feared. This model of the feminine body is in marked
contrast to what some feminists (Lloyd 1984, Pateman and Gross
1986) have argued to be the case for European religion and philosophy, in which the female body occupies a merely negative space.

In my presentation of these cultural constructions (of caste, the
landscape, the female body, the labour process), I have tried to avoid
discussing them as static, unified, internally consistent cultural products. Rather, I have argued for culture as a field of conflict, internally
split by relations of power and contestation between dominant and
subordinated groups. The Mukkuvars contest the upper caste Hindu
view of them by emphasising the independence of their existence out
at sea, the internal homogeneity and tight-knit nature of their community, their Catholicism and, above all, the positive valence of their
sense of difference from agrarian society. The contestation is often a
latent one, full of implicit possibilities which only partially come to
the foreground in specific historical settings.

I have argued that the religious consciousness of the Mukkuvars
mirrors tensions, not only between Mukkuvars and Hindus, but
also between popular Catholicism and the Church itself. Interpretations of popular village Catholicism overstep the boundaries set by
institutionally-based doctrines, borrowing from certain strands of
Hinduism and subverting them in turn. This tension in religious
consciousness once again finds its most fully elaborated version in the
split constitution of the feminine. The ultimate hegemony of the
Church finds expression in the dominance of the Virgin Mary or
Maataa as the highest, most positively valorised form of femininity.
But the power of the Church's religious definitions is modified by the
particular interpretation of the Maataa offered by popular Christianity. First, she is more important to the belief system than the figure of
Christ. Further, the Maataa has acquired certain features which
closely resemble the Hindu village goddess, particularly in her

capacity to heal through possession of human bodies. The Church's representations of the Maataa are further challenged by the subterranean presence of Hindu spirits and the malevolent Eseki who brings disease and misfortune.

Through its definition of Eseki and the spirits as Hindu and alien the Mukkuvars' construction of femininity becomes centrally implicated in the politics of caste. The battles which rage between the female spirits Virgin and Eseki, within the bodies of the sick, the afflicted and the possessed, are not only condensed, metonymic representations of conflicting models of femininity, but also condensations of the oppositional relations between Mukkuvars and the rest of caste society. Insofar as these battles can be represented by specifically religious modes of consciousness, as battles between Christian and Hindu spirits, Mukkuvars are incorporated into a wider community of Tamil Christians, who also perceive themselves as a minority in Hindu society. I have argued that while this Christian community is not entirely under the control of the Church, its consciousness of itself as a minority makes it easily mobilisable, under Church leadership, against its Hindu peasant counterpart.

The different modalities of caste, religious and gender consciousness therefore coalesce around the conflicting interpretations of 'good' femininity versus 'evil' femininity which prevail within this popular Christianity.

As the objects of these complex and contradictory attributes, Mukkuvar women enter into relationships with their physical environment, the economic resources available to the community and with the labour process, not simply as versions of the 'economic man' posited by materialism, but as bearers of a (contradictory) gender-specific subjectivity. The battle between the Maataa and Eseki can be seen as a metaphor, as well as a very real site for the cultural tensions which feed into all the activities and relationships into which women enter. Their means of access to the resources of nature is not the same as that of the men in their community: they cannot go out to the sea and fish, and indeed, they cannot even occupy the spaces contiguous to the sea, for fear of upsetting the balance between men and their environment. The Virgin who guards the men out at sea cannot tolerate the presence of the latent Eseki-like sexuality of real women.

In the Mukkuvar rituals of cooling, binding and confinement, as well as in the pervasive practice of the containment of women within spaces defined as 'domestic', female sexuality is attributed with power, only to be then subjected to constraints intended to control it. This subterranean view of women, distinct and even opposed to the official Church's representations of femininity, is fed by the unusually wide area of responsibilities shouldered by women in household management, credit-generation and kinship maintenance. The domesticity of Mukkuvar women comes very close to the forbidden Eseki-model of female power. Nowhere, however, is this powerful female officially worshipped. She is recognised, only to be feared and bound. Official veneration is reserved for the meek, serene and domesticated Maataa, who has none of the elusive and unpredictable changeability of the goddess worshipped by Hindu villagers. The reigning representation of femininity is therefore one of a fixed and immutable essence, the feminine represented as pure maternal nurturance. Even though women's domestic practice may come closer to the Eseki-model of femininity, they can seek legitimacy for their practice only in terms of a fictive, Virgin-like domesticity. Eseki can be claimed by women only in states of altered consciousness, where their possession by Eseki is treated as illness, to be cured by the Church, or by other ordinary women healing in the name of the Maataa.

As long as women view maternal nurturance (of children and men) as their prime area of self-definition and keep their Eseki-like dimensions under restraint, they are accepted. Indeed, they may even succeed, as I have suggested, in covertly enlarging the actual physical spaces allotted to them. But if women step outside the charmed circle or the Lakshman Rekha (to use an image from Hindu mythology), of domesticity, legitimised by the Maataa model, they run a profound risk. The fish-traders in the Mukkuvar community are a living example of what awaits the women who compete directly with men for trade and cultural space. Like Eseki herself, they are culturally disowned and their femininity subject to hostile rejection. Their success or failure as traders cannot be judged or even adequately described in purely economic terms.

The view I have argued for, placing culture and sexuality at the centre of capitalist transformation and the new division of labour between men and women, renders problematic one of the key distinctions between pre-capitalist and capitalist society as we have inherited this distinction from Marx. In Marx's formulation, the distinction revolved around this very question of determination. In his characterisation of 'Forms which precede capitalist production' in the *Grundrisse* ([1857–58], 1973:471–479), he describes pastoral society as one where 'the communality of blood, language, customs' is the 'first presupposition ... for the appropriation of the objective conditions of their life, and of their life's reproducing and objectifying activity ...' (1973:472). Similarly, in Asiatic landforms, the relation of the individual to the conditions of labour is mediated by 'the total community' (1973:473). In sharp contrast, the situation under capitalism ruptures the mediating role of culture and the community, between the individual and the conditions of labour: the economy comes into its own as the ultimate determinant of all human activity, once 'production appears as the aim of all mankind and wealth ... the aim of production' (1973:487,488). There are a number of problematic features in Marx's formulation, not least of all his association of pre-capitalist culture with the sphere of nature, a stage where man is no more than a 'species-being' (1973:496). The inadequacies of such a position from the perspective of contemporary anthropology have been clearly articulated by Sahlins (1976:49).

The thrust of my critique of Marx's position lies elsewhere: it is aimed at the model of determination he posits. I have shown that culture does not cease to play a crucially formative and shaping role with the advent of capitalism. Despite the loss of control over the organisation of production and domestic life in the community, culture is mediating the very process of capitalist transformation among the Mukkuvars. There is by now a vast literature demonstrating that capitalist forms of production, new technology and market relations of exchange do not simply displace pre-existing social formations. Instead, as writers such as Frank (1978), Laclau (1977), Wallerstein (1974), and Wolf (1982) try to show, capitalism typically enters into complicit relations with pre-capitalist relations of labour utilisation and exploitation, propping them up and even accentuating them in the process. The debate has largely been confined to a strictly economic and political terrain. Ironically, the closest one gets to an appreciation of cultural factors is in the 'modernisation' theory of the 1960s, where 'culture' was singled out as one of the key obstacles to progress in the Third World (Foster 1967, Huntington 1968). Modernisation theory is now largely discredited for its intellectually and politically unacceptable premises, entailing an uncritical universalisation of the European model of modernisation. However, the alternative model which has replaced modernisation theory is a mechanistic one. Systemic forces such as modes of production operate without any reference to the cultural construction of meaning, let alone the capacity of social subjects to negotiate and reconstruct the social meanings of their world (Banaji 1977, Hindess and Hirst 1977, and even Wolf 1982).

In the book I have tried to show the importance of cultural constructions of sexuality, particularly female sexuality, in rendering capitalism itself a gender-specific historical process. I have also presented this culture as a relatively fluid system of meanings, such that even those who are most constrained by the system can also selectively modify and re-interpret its hegemonic interpretations. These re-interpretations range from the unconscious, 'hysterical' resistance of ill and possessed women who rupture the smooth reproduction of daily life, to the older women who travel far and wide in the name of their religious and familial obligations and extend the spaces of domesticity well beyond the confinement of the domestic dwelling; and finally to the select group of educated young girls who have succeeded in manipulating the cultural capital available to them to pursue upward mobility without sacrificing their acceptability within the community.

Is this, then, an interpretation which leans towards the 'culturalist'

side of the old culture/materialism dichotomy? I have tried throughout the book to anchor my account of culture firmly in a recognition
of the independent transformative power of capitalism. I have traced
the effects of capitalism not only on work and the labour process, but
on important aspects of daily life which are of equal importance to
women. For example, marriage payments play a fundamentally
different role in today's fishing economy. Women's dowry, once the
basis of their control over a subsistence-credit economy, now functions increasingly as a source of capital, to be invested in male
ventures either into wage labour or into small-scale capitalist entrep-
reneurship in ownership of trawlers, paddy land and coir factories.
Similarly, in household formation, the pattern favouring female solidarity and management of household finances is slowly altering.
Men's incorporation into wage labour is taking them further away
from the village, whereas women's wage labour ties them more firmly
to the four walls of the home than was the case even with domestic
work. Given such divergent modes of work, the patterns of living and
residence are drastically affected. Households become environments
of women, children and the very old for several months of the year.
Where separation from the male wage-earner lasts even longer, as
where men have gone to the Middle East, the woman may find
herself pressured to live with in-laws or parents, thus conforming to
the pattern of the joint family, close to the Brahmanic patrilineal
ideal, rather than to the pattern of matrifocal, nuclear families typical
of the Mukkuvar settlements.

However, rather than collapse culture into social relations of
power, I have found it important to keep distinct, at least analytically,
the three conceptual fields of discourse, social relations and practice.
Culturally constituted subjects are not formed by any one of these in
isolation, nor do the three fields reinforce a common tendency.
Indeed, it is precisely the dissonances that emerge within each field,
and between them, which allow us to avoid the determinism of a
widely prevalent extreme sociologism which reduces the problem of
the construction of the subject to an effect of social relations of
power. The dissonance or lack of a neat fit between discourse, practices and social relations allows room in which to posit a degree of
agency for the subject. Thus, women successfully evade the full force
of the Catholic discourse on the domesticated and maternal 'feminine', and carve out for themselves a much wider sphere of legitimate
action in their *practice*. Such practice in turn becomes possible only
because the discursive field is itself internally riven. The hegemony of
the Church's discourse is in perpetual tension with popular Catholicism, thanks to the ambiguous figure of Eseki who occupies a position
in Mukkuvar consciousness analogous to the figure of the repressed:
disowned, but always reappearing. The counter-hegemonic discursive
field occupied by the figure of Eseki is in turn reinforced by social

relations which assign to women a position of authority in kin and economic matters.

There is nothing immutable about this balance of forces between the different fields. New kinds of social relations, involving male migration and a tendency to female dependency, erode key aspects of women's ability to negotiate the more restrictive interpretations of femininity. Representations of women such as one finds in the journal of the young, ambitious migrant fisherman John—in which women, while remaining maternal, are relied on to supply romantic intimacies missing in life away from home—may already register a discursive shift, one which women may be in a weaker position to negotiate in practice.

The book has explored the lives of Mukkuvar women as social subjects who are situated at the nodal point of heterogeneous and distinct relations of power. The women have to be considered as members of an occupationally polluted community, which is also a religious minority community, as much as in terms of the relations of power based on gender and class. Attention to the multiple determinations of women's lives may take us a little further in challenging European representations of Indian women, which often emerge untransformed in ethnography. The 'Tamil woman', rich in spiritual strength but oppressed materially, as she emerges from the cultural anthropology of the 1970s, is not so different from the woman who inhabited the discourse constructed in the nineteenth century in the dialogue between colonisers and male elites. The polarisation between the confined, spiritual upper caste woman and the lower caste woman who is free from the burdens of caste purity and sexual disciplines (read: free of culture itself), but exploited simply as a member of her class, partakes of a complex history. It has been my aim to show that in giving an adequate and meaningful account of the lives of Mukkuvar women, one is necessarily engaged in the wider project of transgressing and subverting such artificial polarities.

Notes

Chapter 1

[1] The incorporation of the district into Tamil Nadu was also orchestrated by the upwardly mobile Nadar community in what is now Kanyakumari District. The Nadar community is even more of a social force in the adjacent district of Tirunelveli, and the Nadars of Kanyakumari felt more confident of a future that kept their caste intact, operating within the political party in which Nadars had already made a mark—the Congress in Tamil Nadu. To the Mukkuvars, who have never had a representative either in the State Parliament, or in the State Legislative Assembly of Tamil Nadu, the linguistic re-division has brought little benefit.

[2] Alexander notes this reputation to be shared by fishing communities all over the world (1982). See also p.33 of this chapter.

[3] The traditional caste name of ShaaNaar carries with it connotations of the lowly occupation of toddy tapping. It is an association the upwardly mobile community would like to shed, and they prefer to be called the Nadars (see Hardgrave 1969).

[4] Recent anthropological work amply bears out both these themes, namely, the contextually shifting definitions of space, and the centrality of 'place' to definitions of community and personhood. Beck's usage of the term 'Natu' in her work on the 'Konku Natu' (1972:19) marks an important point in the increasing foregrounding of indigenous categories of space in scholarly work on Tamil Nadu. Daniel (1984) has since developed the theme further. He points out that Tamil speakers are not lacking in spatial terms whose meaning is relatively context-free, universal and fixed. The terms *tecam* and *kiramam* are of this kind. However, he argues that these terms, which are of Sanskrit origin, are not as culturally significant as the indigenous terms *ur* and *natu*, which derive their meaning from the contextually shifting spatial orientation of the person (1984:68–79).

[5] See Hardy (1983:124).

[6] Alexander's book (1982) is one of the few attempts to explore this question.

[7] I will initially restrict my examination to those means of production which have a physical, material form—namely, the various styles of craft and the

238

types of nets and gear which are associated with the kinds of fishing practised in the district. Later, the concept of property is submitted to a critical examination from the point of view of its applicability to fishing communities, where various non-material skills and privileges play a crucial role (see Chapters 3 and 9).

8 Details regarding the construction of the *kaTTumaram*, and the types of fishing, are elaborated in J. Kurien and R. Willman (1982). Sketches of the different types of fishing are also taken from here.

Chapter 2

1 I have no precise figures on the social background of Tamil priests, since I did not realise the importance of such data in the course of fieldwork.

2 See McGilvray for a similar argument regarding the Mukkuvars of Sri Lanka (1983). Fuller (1975) has argued that Christians in Kerala do not subscribe to pollution ideology—but his own evidence indicates that these attitudes are in great measure determined by the place of the different Christian castes in the local power structure. To put it very crudely, Syrian Christians, who are landlords and merchants, have every incentive to support the caste hierarchy, whereas the 'New Christians', converted in the nineteenth century, are landless labourers and would prefer to ignore pollution norms. See also Stirrat's work on caste in a Sri Lankan fishing community (1983).

Chapter 3

1 Hirschon (1984:1) has pointed out that these ideas were not unique to Engels—they were part of the nineteenth-century's interest in the relationship between property, marriage and women's position.

2 The details of the medical model need not be entered into for my purposes, which are that of documenting its influence on popular religion. The diffusion of Ayurveda into popular categories of thought, ritual, daily practices of diet, bathing and healing, is beginning to receive documentation (Beck 1969, Babb 1975, Obeyesekere 1975, McGilvray 1982). According to McGilvray: 'Some of the results [of this research] have been quite promising, demonstrating that ideas of ritual temperature, configurations of colour, states of pollution and possession and the attributes of male versus female sexuality are often linked by an implicit ritual logic which has wide distribution in South Asia (1982:25).'

3 It would be easy to draw this conclusion from the kinds of statements that ethnographers such as McGilvray make:

> Professional Ayurvedic physicians are capable of extremely subtle and complex combinations of humoral influences, but for most ordinary people in Batticaloa, there is paramount concern for environments, substances and foods conveying the three following qualities: cutu (heating), kulir (cooling) and kiranti (eruptive) . . . As one might expect, the ideal of bodily health is an equilibrium of all these qualities (1982).

4 Nichter (1987) has singled out the hot vs. cold opposition to be: 'a dominant binary opposition and symbol in the Sinhalese conceptual universe at large and in Sri Lankan semantic illness networks where it has polysemous reference and inference'.

5 In a comparative vein, see Herrin (1982) on the importance of icons to women in early Christianity.

6 Ethnographies of Hindu fishing communities recorded at the turn of the century reveal details of cults of the goddess. E. Thurston (1909), citing an even earlier account by Buchanan (1807), describes the Mukkuvars of Malabar worshipping BhadraKali with sacrifices of fowl and fruit. A.K. Iyer, also describing the Mukkuvars of Malabar (1909), describes the worship of Visnu and Siva as equally reverent—but includes the Tamil gods Subramania and Sastha to be especially favoured. The guardian deity, however, is female: Kodungallur Bhagavathi, and he adds that they are 'Sakthi worshippers'. The Rev. Whitehead (1921) presents a nice instance of a Mukkuvar 'take-over' of a Sanskritic goddess: punning on the name 'Meenakshi' (eyes shaped like the fish), the fishing community of Cuddaloor, on the east coast of Tamil Nadu, converted the wife of Siva, worshipped at the great temple of Madurai, to the 'fish goddess' who is depicted seated on the *ullan* (ocean fish) with her male consort. An account which bases itself on the ancient Tamil Cankam literature of the 4th–6th centuries AD refers to the religion of the *neytal tinai* or coastal area as involving the prominence of female worshippers. At the annual festival in honour of Kaman, the god of love, whose emblem was the shark, men and women danced. Married women prayed for the protection of their husbands, and unmarried girls sought his assistance for a suitable groom. The chief god, Kadalon, represented by the backbone of a great shark, protected the men at sea—but was worshipped by women on full moon nights when the men were at sea. They adorned the spine with little lamps filled with fish oil and with offerings of dried fish implored protection for the men of the clan (C. Amirtha Raj 1980).

7 The communal riots of 1982 actualised much of this potential. Reports of this period stress the influence of pulpit rhetoric and harangues from the priests (see Iyengar 1985:2153). Such a form of reporting underestimates the double-edged nature of religious consciousness even at times when there is no overt conflict. A similar examination should, of course be made, of Hindu popular consciousness.

8 This is particularly a problem when historically reconstructing the transition from the pre-Sanskritic to the Sanskritic. Wulff, discussing the problem for Bengal, finds that 'historical evidence is far too fragmentary to allow us to link prevailing conceptions of divinity among a certain group or in a given period with the actual social circumstances of women. Furthermore, the evidence we have from the ancient and medieval periods is limited by and large, to the elite strata of the population' (1985:220). The establishment of a Brahmanic paradigm in religion itself may be sub-divided into several historical periods as far as women's social status was concerned. The early Vedic period (c.1200–600 BC) allowed women the status of *ardhangini* or partner to her husband in religious rites, a status which presupposed female education. The decline in female religious status was a gradual affair until finally the Dharmasastras in the early centuries BC declared women to be the equivalent of men of the lowest caste (Findly 1985).

9 See Robinson (1985) for a similar reinterpretation of traditions in Bengali female devotionalism.

10 The prestige of the Cape Comorin as a focus for pan-Indian religious sentiment has increased enormously with the establishment of an off-shore memorial to Vivekananda, a nineteenth century Hindu revivalist, located close to the temple of the goddess. The flurry of construction work which

has accompanied the development of the Cape as a pilgrim and tourist resort has been a source of ongoing conflict between the fisherpeople and the Hindu religious organisations.

11 This information is based on personal communication with the priest.

12 Since writing this, an article by S. Bayly (1986) has come to hand. Based on her work on coastal communities on the eastern coast of Tamil Nadu, the Muslim Labbais and the Christian Paravas, she advances an argument which strikingly parallels mine. She argues for the centrality of the worship of Hindu 'folk' goddesses, which 'has long served as a bridge linking members of the three religious groups within local systems of shared belief and practice' (1986:59). Furthermore, she recognises that this is no simple syncretism: 'Ultimately ... the Tamil goddess tradition operated in two seemingly contradictory ways ... the same Tamil amman tradition which simultaneously bridged the gulf between these separate communal affiliations ... also allowed both Christians and Muslims to express their attachment to their own religious community ... This is as much a confrontation with alien religious traditions, as it is an expression of shared values and shared ideology' (1986:64, 65).

Chapter 4

1 Beck illustrates this theme with an ancient poem celebrating the auspiciousness of young girls:

> The kannimar [virgin daughters] are playing in the prosperous village of Taiyanur/ ... The five hundred men of Taiyanur live like Kuberan with plenty of wealth/ ... In order that they may live, our kannimar are playing like this ... (1972:8).

2 Home remedies using simple ingredients considered cooling are used in accordance with specific properties attributed to each. Thus spices such as dill and garlic, roots, oils and liquids such as coconut milk play an important part in the remedies women make at home. Beck (1969) has used the attributes of heating and cooling to classify foods, liquids and colours in a single grid.

She raises several difficulties in constructing general rules of classification, since they make no reference to characteristics of colour, taste, texture, caloric content, or the temperature at which the substance is prepared or eaten (1969:561). Nevertheless, she suggests certain possible guidelines in the classification of foods, for example. Citrus fruits, all products of the cow, most oils and spices are cooling. Many grains and all strong liquors are heating, while meats, pulses and fruits divide equally between the two categories (1969:561).

Daniel (1984:184) has added further qualifications with respect to Beck's classification. He makes the point that foods are strung along a hot-cold gradient, not neatly divided into one category or the other. Furthermore, the classification is variable according to region, caste, context and may even vary from one individual to another.

3 Such an association is reminiscent of similar links made between women and the Devil in medieval Europe, exemplified in the witch hunt (Larner 1984) and in Islam (Sabbah 1984:112*ff*.).

4 See Shorter (1982:293) for a similar practice in medieval Europe, said to 'help ward off all that brings evil and harm'.

5 Gilbert points to the etymological roots of 'hysteria' in the Greek *hyster* or

womb (1986:xiii). 'The guilt of reproduction is fixed on the ill female organs', as Clement puts it (1986:6).

6 Cf. Gross on Kristeva: 'The semiotic is thus both the precondition and the excessive overflow of the symbolic. It is necessary for symbolic functioning, but because it cannot be spoken as such, it also continues to exert a possible resistance to and subversion of symbolic norms ... Like the dream or symptom, a repressed eruption in the discourse of consciousness, the semiotic threatens at certain privileged moments, to transgress its subordinated, unacknowledged position, breaching the limits of textual intelligibility and destabilising symbolic efficacy' (1986:129–130).

7 In setting my argument out in this form, my views have been sharpened and clarified by Partha Chatterjee's recent work on nationalism in India (1986). Chatterjee is concerned with a very similar question: what are the tensions, contradictions and suppressions which mark nationalist thought as the discourse of a subordinate class, in his case, the indigenous bourgeoise of colonial India.

Chapter 5

1 The story of these departures is complicated by the fact that the men are not setting out for similar destinations or even identical forms of work— two groups are destined to work on mechanised fishing vessels, in different parts of the southern coastline, but a third group takes with it artisanal fishing gear and *kaTTumaram* to work in other parts of Kerala. I will concentrate on those working in mechanised fishing in this section.

2 This figure is based on the village census I conducted during fieldwork.

3 Variously known as *jobber*, *sardar*, *jamadar* and *mistri* in the north of India, and *kangani* in the south, these middlemen have provided labour for the cotton and jute textile mills, the coal mining industry, and continue to operate in industries requiring casual labour on a seasonal basis, such as the construction and building industry.

4 On these aspects of the labour broker in Indian industry, see Morris 1965, Kooiman 1977, Murphy 1976, Simmons 1976.

5 Neendakara is located ten kilometres north of the town of Quilon, in the southern part of Kerala. It was the site for the location of a project to modernise fishing in the early fifties, under the aegis of a Norwegian Aid Programme.

6 Puthenthurai is a fishing village in Kanyakumari District: the boat-owner's wife is therefore a fellow Mukkuvar.

7 The institution of the *chit fund* is explored in Chapter 5.

8 The rough weather is between June–August, but December–April, the winter season, is also a difficult period. The peak seasons fall between April–May, and then again between the end of August and November.

9 The famous 'irregularity' of 'pre-industrial man' celebrated by both Thompson (1967) and Sahlins (1974) is a privilege of gender: the 'idle' periods were enjoyed by men alone for the most part, and at the expense of the women. Cf. for example, Lee, Richard B. *!Kung (San): Men, Women and Work in a Foraging Society*, London, Cambridge University Press, 1980, which argues that female gathering is 67 per cent more efficient than male hunting in a given ecological context; and Zihlmann, A.L. 'Women as shapers of human adaptation' in Dahlberg, 1980, who indicates that the necessary floor of subsistence among modern, non-arctic hunter-gatherers is maintained by gathering and not by hunting.

[10] The English word was used by the man.
[11] In 1982, the problem was exacerbated by the ethnic tensions between the Tamils and Sinhalese in Sri Lanka. Men justly feared that the punishments dealt out by Sinhala-manned patrol boats would be far more severe than before, and as a result there were far fewer men bound for Rameswaram that year. Presumably the trend has only intensified since completing fieldwork.
[12] The concessions included: (i) making available 'soft loans' schemes covering up to 95 per cent of the cost of imported and indigenously built trawlers; (ii) treating fishing vessels as ships and allowing special tax-holiday benefits applicable to newly established undertakings; (iii) waiving all import duty on goods imported for use as containers for packing marine products; (iv) waiving excise duty for diesel oil used in fishing boats (see *The Hindu*, 13 September 1982).

Chapter 7

[1] See also Dumont (1983:157) for comments in which he describes this idea as 'of Brahmanical parentage', and contrary to low-caste practices in South India.
[2] Beck suggests that the terms *pangaali* and *macaan* or *cammanti* (her spellings) are the closest Tamil equivalents for parallel and cross cousins. (See also Harris 1982, p.139 on this point.)
[3] The actual quote is from Beck (1972:220).
[4] The 'Chicago school' of cultural anthropology has had its exponents in the area of south Indian kinship, and in Indian kinship generally. Along with Fruzzetti and Ostor whose work has been generalised from Bengali material (1982), Barnett (1976a and 1976b) has applied a concept they argue to be pan-Indian, that of 'blood-purity', to the south Indian context. Starting from the premise that kinship must be studied in terms of cultural constructions of the self, this group argues that 'blood purity' provides the basis of caste codes of conduct, of which marriage is a nucleus. The methodological individualism and essentialism of this approach has been ably highlighted by Dumont's own critique (1983:153–159). The second approach, put forward by A.D. Carter, argues that cross-cousin marriage is a mere 'surface effect', with the underlying structure being a pan-Indian 'segmentary' concept of caste and kinship (1974). For a critique of Dumont's 'structuralist analogy from phonetics to semantics' in the area of Tamil kinship, see also Scheffler (1977).
[5] In this, Mukkuvars are similar to other low castes. See Gough (1956), Beck (1972) and Harper (1969) on this point.
[6] Individual thefts of gear and boats are of some importance in generating fights and violence between men, but fall outside the kind of intra-household structural conflict of interests being discussed here.
[7] Kolenda has suggested the following definitions of 'family types' to classify various regions of India (Kolenda 1967:149–150):

Single person household;
Sub-nuclear family: a fragment of a former nuclear conjugal household (e.g., a widow with unmarried children, or unmarried, divorced or widowed siblings living together);
Nuclear family: a couple and their unmarried children;
Supplemented nuclear family: nuclear family plus other unmarried or widowed relatives;

Lineal joint family: parents and unmarried children, plus one married child and family;
Supplemented collateral joint family: collateral joint family plus some other unmarried, widowed and divorced relatives;
Lineal collateral joint family: collateral joint family plus two or more married sons with their wives and married or unmarried children;
Supplemented lineal collateral joint family: a lineal collateral joint family plus some relatives who are not a member of any of the nuclear families involved;
Other: as defined by the researcher.

Chapter 8

[1] It is time we questioned the equation between dowry and female seclusion on the one hand, and between bride-price and female autonomy on the other. Bride-price itself is associated with a variety of cultural systems. Many of the practices associated with a bride-price system in other cultures are equally restrictive of women's ability to freely conduct marriage transactions: levirate is one such practice, where the widow is 'taken over' as part of her deceased husband's property by male kinsmen. Another is marriage by abduction (Hirschon 1984:13–14).

[2] The 1982 Report of the Joint Committee of Upper and Lower Houses of Parliament notes:

> These subsequent expenses are often regarded as making up for the deficiencies in the initial giving of dowry and cause hardship to the girl's parents. In the first few years of marriage, in most cases, the girl's treatment in her husband's home is linked to these gifts . . . Thus 'dowry' is not one isolated payment initially at the time of marriage, but a series of gifts given over a period of time before and after the marriage.

Citation of the Report may be found in *Economic and Political Weekly*, vol.xix, no.37.

[3] A minority of ethnographers now dispute whether marriage payments among lower castes can be accurately described as bride-price in any case. Dumont (1980:379, fn.54c) describes the notion of marriage-as-purchase to be a fiction concocted by Brahmans and echoed by modern-day anthropologists to describe situations where bilateral prestations, rather than unilateral ones, are to be found. Randeria and Viseria (1984) have also argued that we take a closer look at the *totality* of gift exchanges. In Gujarat, they find that bride-price payments are, at the most, episodic reversals of the usual pattern of gift-flow. 'In both ideology and practice, it is the bride-giver who is the gift-giver among the lower castes as well.' (p.650).

[4] *Yautaka* or property given at nuptials is described in the following terms: 'Let the daughters share the nuptial gift of their mother' (Vasishta xvii, 24) and 'Property given to the mother on her marriage (*yautaka*) is inherited by her [unmarried] daughters' (Manu ix, 131). Quoted by Tambiah (1973:89).

[5] In one case, the woman was given a share of Re300 in the two nets that were bought with the sale of her jewellery. In another case, the woman was given a share of the sale value of her in-laws' house to be inherited post-mortem. Her jewellery had been sold, fetching a price of Re4500, in order to buy equipment which was subsequently lost at sea.

[6] It is possible that female attitudes towards this kind of usage are conditioned by the Tamil traditional law, or *Tesawalamai*. According to its code, *chidenam* or dowry formally belongs to the wife, but if dowry is used

to acquire other forms of property during the marriage, it is converted into the *Thediattetam*. As such it not only belongs to both spouses, but the husband can sell or otherwise dispose of it without the wife's consent, while the wife can only do so by agreement of the husband. Details of this system are taken from Skonsberg (1982:83). Villagers in KaDalkarai Uuru rarely referred to such legal codes in explanation of their practices and attitudes, however.

Chapter 9

[1] The point I am making may be usefully compared to Farida Shaheed's (1990) revealing comments on the use women make of the veil or *burquah* in extending the space available to them in the much harsher environment of fundamentalist Islamic Pakistan. She argues that the veil, seemingly the harshest version of the generalised purdah complex, in fact allows women 'safe conduct' through public space, where they can see without being seen by men. By contrast, an interpretation of purdah as meaning strict domestic confinement, also found in Pakistan, has far more isolating consequences for women.

[2] These groups may be roughly characterised as development agencies, of diverse philosophies and sources of funding, but all of whom share an autonomy from government bureaucracy and political parties. The KSSS is itself, therefore, a group of this kind.

[3] Similar norms divide male activities based in the village into geographically based zones: for example, the auctioneers each have their particular part of the beach front. However, these divisions have a less devastating effect on the income of the men.

[4] The *kuTTai* is the woven basket carried on their heads by female fish-traders. The different grades of traders are distinguished by descriptive terms referring implicitly to the size of their enterprise. Thus we have the 'cycle-traders' and the larger merchants who use a *maaTu vanDi* or bullock cart, or else hire trucks.

[5] There is also a smaller basket used to carry weights up to ten kilograms, called a *kaDavam*.

[6] See also the work of Lessinger (1984) on women traders in the city of Madras, and Sharma (1980) for other examinations of the sexual restrictions on women traders in India.

[7] The 1981 census of India estimates that the percentage of male literacy on an all-India basis is 38 per cent, as compared to 18–20 per cent of women who are literate.

References

Abraham, A. (1985) 'Subsistence credit: Survival strategies among traditional fishermen' *Economic and Political Weekly* xx(6):247–252

Adamson, W.A. (1980) *Hegemony and Revolution: A study of Antonio Gramsci's Political and Cultural Theory* Berkeley: University of California Press

Agarwal, B. (1985) 'Work participation of rural women in the Third World: Some conceptual problems' *Economic and Political Weekly* xx(51, 52): A-155–A-164

Alexander J. (1987) *Trader, Traders and Trading in Rural Java* Oxford: Oxford University Press

Alexander, P. (1982) *Sri Lankan Fishermen: Rural Capitalism and Peasant Society* ANU Monographs on South Asia, no.7, Canberra: The Australian National University

Amirtha Raj, C. (1980) 'Theologising by the Diocese of Kottar in the District of Kanyakumari', MA thesis, Paris: Institute Catholique de Paris

Ardener, E. (1975a) 'Belief and the problem of women' in S. Ardener (ed.) *Perceiving Women* London: Malaby, pp.1–18

—— (1975b) 'The problem revisited' in S. Ardener (ed.) *Perceiving Women* London: Malaby, pp.19–28

Babb, L.A. (1975) *The Divine Hierarchy: Popular Hinduism in Central India* New York: Colombia University Press

Babcock, B. (ed.) (1978) *The Reversible World: Symbolic Inversions in Art and Society* London: Cornell University Press

Baker-Reynolds, H. (1978) 'To keep the *tali* strong: Women's rituals in Tamil Nadu', PhD thesis, Madison: University of Wisconsin-Madison

Banaji (1977) 'Modes of production in a materialist conception of history' *Capital and Class* 3:1–44

Barnett, S. (1976a) 'Coconuts and gold: Relational identity in a south Indian caste' *Contributions to Indian Sociology* (n.s.) 10(1):133–156

—— (1976b) *See* Fruzetti, Ostor and Barnett

Barrett, M. and McIntosh, M. (1982) *The Anti-Social Family* London: Verso Editions/NLB

Barrington, Moore, Jr. (1966) *Social Origins of Dictatorship and Democracy:*

Lord and Peasant in the Making of the Modern World Harmondsworth: Penguin
Bayly, S. (1981) 'A Christian caste in Hindu society' *Modern Asian Studies* 15(2):203–234
—— (1986) 'Islam in southern India: "Purist" or "syncretic"?' in C.A. Bayly and D.H.A. Kolff (eds) *Two Colonial Empires* Dordrecht: Martin Nijhoff Publishers, pp.35–73
—— (1989) *Saints, Goddesses and Kings: Muslims and Christians in South Indian Society, 1700–1900* Cambridge: Cambridge University Press
Beck, B. (1969) 'Colour and heat in south Indian rituals', *Man* 4(4):553–572
—— (1972) *Peasant Society in Konku: A Study of Right and Left Sub-castes in South India* Vancouver: University of British Columbia Press
—— (1974) 'The kin nucleus in Tamil folklore' in T. Trautmann (ed.) *Kinship and History in South Asia* Michigan Papers on South and Southeast Asia, no.7, Ann Arbor: University of Michigan, pp.1–28
—— (1981) 'The goddess and the demon: A local south Indian festival and its wider context' in M. Biardeau (ed.) *Autour de la Déesse Hindoue* Etidues reunies Par, Paris: Edition de l'Ecole des Hautes Etudes en Sciences Sociales, pp.83–136
Beidelman, T. (1959) *A Comparative Analysis of the Jajmani System* Monographs of the Association for Asian Studies VIII, Locust Valley, New York
Berger, J. and Mohr, J. (1975) *A Seventh Man: The Story of a Migrant Worker in Europe* Harmondsworth: Penguin
Berreman, G.D. and Dumont, L. (1962) 'Caste, racism and stratification' *Contributions to Indian Sociology* vi:122–124
Boserup, E. (1970) *Women's Role in Economic Development* London: Allen and Unwin
Bourdieu, P. (1977) *Outline of a Theory of Practice* Cambridge: Cambridge University Press
Brown, P., Macintyre, M., Morpeth, R. and Prendergast, S. (1981) 'A daughter: A thing to be given away' in The Cambridge Women Studies Group (eds) *Women in Society* London: Virago, pp.127–145
Brubaker, R. (1978) 'The ambivalent mistress: A study of south Indian village goddesses and their religious meaning,' PhD thesis, Chicago: University of Chicago
—— (1979) 'Barbers, washermen and other priests: Servants of the south Indian village and its goddess' *History of Religions* xix(2):128–152
Carter, A.T. (1974) 'A comparative analysis of systems of kinship and marriage in south Asia' *Proceedings of the Royal Anthropological Institute (for 1973)*:29–54
Chaki Sircar, M. (1984) *Feminism in a Traditional Society: Women of the Manipur Valley* Delhi: Shakthi Books
Chatterjee, P. (1986) *Nationalist Thought and the Colonial World—a Derivative Discourse* London: Zed Press Ltd for The United Nations University
Clement, C. (1986) 'The guilty one' in H. Cixous and C. Clement *The Newly Born Woman* Minneapolis: University of Minnesota Press, pp.1–59
Clifford, J. (1986) 'Introduction: Partial truths' in J. Clifford and G.E. Marcus (eds) *Writing Culture: The Poetics and Politics of Ethnography* Berkeley and Los Angeles: University of California Press, pp.1–26

Clothey, F.W. (1978) *The Many Faces of Murukan: The History and Meaning of a South Indian God* The Hague: Mouton

Coburn, T.B. (1984) *Devi Mahatmya: The Crystallisation of the Goddess Tradition* Delhi: Motilal Banarsidas

Cohn, B. (1955) 'The changing status of a depressed caste' in M. Marriott (ed.) *Village India* Chicago and London: University of Chicago Press, pp.53–77

Comaroff, J.L. (ed.) (1980) *The Meaning of Marriage Payments* London: Academic Press

Connor, L. (1982) 'In darkness and in light: A study of peasant intellectuals in Bali', PhD thesis, Sydney: University of Sydney

Constantinides, P. (1978) 'Women's spirit possession and urban adaptation' in J. Bujra and P. Caplan (eds) *Women United, Women Divided* London: Tavistock, pp.185–205

Crapanzano, V. (1986) 'Hermes' dilemma: The masking of subversion in ethnographic description' in J. Clifford and G.E. Marcus (eds) *Writing Culture: The Poetics and Politics of Ethnography* Berkeley and Los Angeles: University of California Press, pp.51–76

Cronin, V. (1966) [1959] *A Pearl to India* Norwich: R. Hart Davis, republished by Libra Books, London

Curley, R.T. (1973) *Elders, Shades and Women: Ceremonial Change in Lango, Uganda* Berkeley and Los Angeles: University of California Press

Daniel, V. (1984) *Fluid Signs: Being a Person the Tamil Way* Berkeley and Los Angeles: University of California Press

Darnton, R. (1985) *The Great Cat Massacre* New York: Vintage Books

Das Gupta, A. (1967) *Malabar in Asian Trade, 1740–1800* Cambridge: Cambridge University Press

David, K. (1977) 'Hierarchy and equivalence in Jaffna, North Ceylon: Normative codes as mediator' in K. David (ed.) *The New Wind: Changing Identities in South Asia* The Hague: Mouton

Davis, N.Z. (1978) 'Women on top: Symbolic sexual inversion and political disorder in early modern Europe' in B. Babcock (ed.) *The Reversible World: Symbolic Inversions in Art and Society* London: Cornell University Press, pp.147–189

Desai, I.P. (1964) *Some Aspects of Family in Mahwa* New York: Asia Publishing House

Dirks, N.B. (1987) *The Hollow Crown: Ethnohistory of an Indian Kingdom* Cambridge: Cambridge University Press

Dube, S.C. (1955) *Indian Village* New York: Cornell University Press

Dumont, L. (1966) 'Marriage in India: The present state of the question. North India in relation to South India' *Contributions to Indian Sociology* 9:90–114

—— (1980) *Homo Hierarchicus: The Caste System and Its Implications* [Revised ed.] Chicago: University of Chicago Press

—— (1983) *Affinity as a Value: Marriage Alliance in South India, with Comparative Essays on Australia* Chicago: University of Chicago Press

Egnor, M. (1978) 'The sacred spell and other conceptions of life in Tamil culture', PhD thesis, University of Chicago

Elmore, W.T. (1925) *Dravidian Gods in Modern Hinduism: A Study of Local and Village Deities of Southern India* Christian Literature Society for India, Madras [reprint ed. from the University Studies of the University of Nebraska, vol.15, 1915]

Engels, F. (1972) [1884] *The Origin of the Family, Private Property and the State* New York: Pathfinder Press

Epstein, T.S. (1973) *South India, Yesterday, Today and Tomorrow* London: Macmillan

FAO-SIDA Bay of Bengal Programme for the Development of Small Scale Fisheries (1983) *Marine Small Scale Fisheries of Tamil Nadu: A General Description* Information Document (published) FAO, Madras

Ferro Luzzi, G. (1974) 'Women's pollution periods in Tamil Nadu' *Anthropos* 69:113–161

Findly, E.B. (1985) 'Gargi at the king's court: Women and philosophical innovation in ancient India' in Y.Y. Haddad and E.B. Findly (eds) *Women, Religion, and Social Change* New York: State University of New York Press

Firth, Raymond (1966) *Malay Fishermen: Their Peasant Economy* London: Routledge and Kegan Paul

Firth, Rosemary (1943) *Housekeeping Among Malay Peasants* published for the London School of Economics and Political Science by Percy Lund, Humphries and Co. Ltd., London

Food and Agriculture Organisation (FAO) (1978) 'Assessment of problems and needs in marine small scale fisheries, Orissa' RAS/74/131, Working Paper no.10, FAO Rome

Forrester, D. (1979) *Caste and Christianity: Attitudes and Policies on Caste of Anglo-Saxon Protestant Missions in India* London: Curzon Press

Foster, G. (1967) *Tzintzuntzan* Boston: Little Brown

Foucault, M. (1976) *The Archaeology of Knowledge* New York: Harper and Row

Frank, G. (1978) *World Accumulation, 1492–1789* New York: Monthly Review Press

Freed, R. and Freed, S. (1964) 'Spirit possession as illness in a north Indian village' *Ethnology* 3(2):152–168

Freud, S. (1973) [1915–16] 'Dreams' *Introductory Lectures on Psychoanalysis* vol.1, Transl. by J. Strachey, J. Strachey and A. Richards (eds) Harmondsworth: Penguin

Friedmann, H. (1979) 'Peasants and simple commodity reproducers: Analytical distinctions', Centre of International Area Studies, Peasants Seminar, University of London, London

Fruzetti, L. and Ostor, A. (1982) *Concepts of Person: Kinship, Caste and Marriage in India* Cambridge, Mass: Harvard University Press

Fruzetti, L., Ostor, A. and Barnett, S. (1976) 'The cultural construction of the person in Bengal and Tamil Nadu' *Contributions to Indian Sociology* 10(1):157–182

Fuller, C.J. (1975) 'Kerala Christians and the caste system' *Man* 11:53–70

Gardiner, J., S. Himmelweit and Mackintosh, M. (1980) 'Women's domestic labour' in E. Malos (ed.) *The Politics of Housework* London: Allison and Busby

Gilbert, S.M. 'Introduction: A Tarantella of Theory' in H. Cixous and C. Clement *The Newly Born Woman* Minneapolis: University of Minnesota Press, pp.ix–xviii

Gluckman, M. (1963) *Order and Rebellion in Tribal Africa: Collected Essays* London: Cohen

Goody, J. (1976) *Production and Reproduction—A Comparative Study of the Domestic Domain* Cambridge: Cambridge University Press

Gore, M.S. (1970) *Immigrants and Neighborhoods: Two Aspects of Life in a Metropolitan City* Bombay: Tata Institute of Social Sciences

Gough, K. (1956) 'Brahmin kinship in a Tamil village' *American Anthropologist* 58(5):826–853

—— (1971) 'Caste in a Tanjore village' in E.R. Leach (ed.) *Aspects of Caste in South India, Ceylon and NW Pakistan* London: Cambridge University Press, pp.11–60

—— (1973) 'Harijans in Thanjavur' in K. Gough and H.P. Sharma (eds) *Imperialism and Revolution in South Asia* New York: Monthly Review Press, pp.222–245

Gramsci, A. (1971) *Selections from the Prison Notebooks* edited and translated by Q. Hoare and G.N. Smith, London: Lawrence and Wishart

Grey, J. (1982) 'Chetri women in domestic groups and rituals' in M. Allen and S. Mukherjee (eds) *Women in India and Nepal* ANU Monographs on South Asia, no. 8, Canberra: The Australian National University, pp.211–241

Gross, E. (1986) 'Philosophy, subjectivity and the body: Kristeva and Irigaray' in C. Pateman and E. Gross (eds) *Feminist Challenges: Social and Political Theory* Sydney: Allen and Unwin, pp.125–143

Guha, R. (1983) *Elementary Aspects of Peasant Insurgency in Colonial India* New Delhi: Oxford University Press

—— (1985) 'The career of an anti-god in heaven and on earth' in A. Mitra (ed.) *The Truth Unites: Essays in Tribute to Samar Sen* Calcutta: Subarna Rekha, pp.1–25

Gulati, L. (1983) 'Women and technological change—a case study of three fishing villages', Working Paper no.143, Centre for Development Studies, Trivandrum

Hall, S. (1981) 'Notes on deconstruction of "the popular"' in R. Samuel (ed.) *People's History and Socialist Theory* London: Routledge and Kegan Paul, pp.227–240

Hardgrave, R.L. (1969) *The Nadars of Tamil Nadu: The Political Culture of a Community in Change* Berkeley: University of California Press

Hardy, F. (1983) *Viraha Bhakti: The Early History of Krisna Devotion in South India* Delhi: Oxford University Press

Harper, E.B. 'Fear and the Status of Women' in *South Western Journal of Anthropology*, Vol.25, No.1, Spring 1969, pp.81–95

Harris, J. (1982) *Capitalism and Peasant Farming: Agrarian Structure and Ideology in Northern Tamil Nadu* Delhi: Oxford University Press

Hart, G. (1974) 'Some aspects of kinship in ancient Tamil literature' in T. Trautmann (ed.) *Kinship and History in South India*, Michigan Papers on South and Southeast Asia, no.7, Ann Arbor: University of Michigan, pp.41–63

—— (1975) 'Ancient Tamil literature: Its scholarly past and future' in B. Stein (ed.) *Essays on South India* University Press of Hawaii

Herrin, J. (1982) 'Women and the faith in icons in early Christianity' in R. Samuel and G. Stedman Jones (eds) *Culture, Ideology and Politics* London: Routledge and Kegan Paul, pp.56–83

Hill, P. (1982) *Dry Grain Farming Families: Hausaland (Nigeria) and Karnataka (India) Compared* Cambridge: Cambridge University Press

Hiltebeitel, A. (1981) 'Draupadi's hair' in M. Biardeau (ed.) *Autour de la*

Déesse Hindoue Etidues Reunies Par, Paris: Editions de l'Ecole des Hautes Etudes en Sciences Sociales, pp.179–214

—— (1988) *The Cult of Draupadi—Mythologies: From Gingee to Kuruk-shetra* Chicago: University of Chicago Press

Hindess, B. and P. Hirst (1977) *Mode of Production and Social Formation* London: Macmillan

Hirschon, R. (ed.) (1984) *Women and Property, Women as Property* London: Croom Helm

Holmström, M. (1984) *Industry and Inequality: The Social Anthropology of Indian Labour* Cambridge: Cambridge University Press

Huntington, S.P. (1968) *Political Order in Changing Societies* New Haven: Yale University Press

Ifeka, C. (1975) 'Female militancy and colonial revolt—the women's war of 1929, East Nigeria' in S. Ardener (ed.) *Perceiving Women* London: Malaby, pp.127–157

Inden, R.B. and Nicholas, R. (1977) *Kinship in Bengali Culture* Chicago: University of Chicago Press

Irigaray, L. (1985) *Speculum of the Other Woman* New York: Cornell University Press

Ishwaran, K.S. (1968) *A South Indian Village* London: Routledge and Kegan Paul

Iyengar, V.L. (1985) 'Fisherpeople of Kerala: a plea for rational growth' *Economic and Political Weekly* xx(49):2149–2154

Iyer, A.K. (1981) [1909] *The Tribes and Castes of Cochin* vol.1 New Delhi: Cosmo Publications

Jacobson, D. (1976) 'Women and jewellery in rural India' in G.R. Gupta (ed.) *Family and Social Change in Modern India* Main Currents in Indian Sociology, III, New Delhi: Vikas Publishing House, pp.135–183

—— (1982) 'Purdah and the Hindu family in central India' in H. Papanek and G. Minault (eds) *Separate Worlds: Studies of Purdah in South Asia* New Delhi: Chanakya, pp.81–109

Jain, D. (1980) 'Street vendors of Ahmedabad' in D. Jain (ed.) *Women's Quest for Power* Delhi: Vikas Publishing House, pp.19–76

Jameson, F. (1981) *The Political Unconscious: Narrative as a Socially Symbolic Act* London: Methuen and Co.

Jeffrey, P. (1979) *Frogs in a Well: Indian Women in Purdah* London: Zed Press

Joshi, H. and Joshi, V. (1976) *Surplus Labour and the City: A Study of Bombay* Delhi: Oxford University Press

Kakar, S. (1981) *The Inner World: A Psychoanalytic Study of Childhood and Society in India* Delhi: Oxford University Press

—— (1982) *Shamans, Mystics and Doctors* Delhi: Oxford University Press

Khare, R.S. (1984) *The Untouchable as Himself: Ideology, Identity and Pragmatism Among the Lucknow Chamars* Cambridge: Cambridge University Press

Klausen, A.M. (1968) *Kerala Fishermen and the Indo-Norwegian Project* London: Allen and Unwin

Kolenda, P. (1964) 'Religious anxiety and Hindu fate' in S. Harper (ed.) *Religion in South Asia* Seattle: Washington University Press, pp.71–81

—— (1967) 'Regional differences in family structure' in R.I. Crane (ed.) *Regions and Regionalism in South Asian Studies: An Exploratory*

Study Durham: Duke University Programme, Monograph no.5, pp. 147–226

Kooiman, D. (1977) 'Jobbers and the emergence of trade unions in Bombay city' *International Review of Social History* xxxi:566–572

Kosambi, D.D. (1956) *Introduction to the Study of Indian History* Bombay: Popular Book Depot

Kovakanandy, R. (1984) 'Purse Seine Fishing in Kerala: Its economics and politics' *Economic and Political Weekly* Vol.xix, No.13, March 31, pp.566–572

Krygier, J. (1982) 'Caste and female pollution' in M. Allen and S. Mukherjee (eds) *Women in India and Nepal* ANU Monographs on South Asia, no.8, Canberra: The Australian National University, pp.76–104

Kurien, J. (1985) 'Technical assistance projects and socio-economic change: Norwegian intervention in Kerala's fisheries development' *Economic and Political Weekly* xx(25,26):A-70–A-87

Kurien, J. and Mathew, S. (1982) *Technological Change in Fishing: Its Impact on Fishermen* Centre for Development Studies, Trivandrum: Unpublished paper prepared for Indian Council of Social Science Research

Kurien, J. and Willmann, R. (1982) *Economics of Artisanal and Mechanised Fisheries in Kerala: A Study of Costs and Earnings of Fishing Units* Working Paper no.34, Food and Agricultural Organisation of the US and United Nations Development Programme, Madras

Laclau, E. (1977) *Politics and Ideology in Marxist Theory* London: New Left Books

Larner, C. (1984) *Witchcraft and Religion: The Politics of Popular Belief* Oxford: Basil Blackwell

Lee, R.B. (1980) *!Kung(San): Men, Women and Work in a Foraging Society* London: Cambridge University Press

Lessinger, J. (1985) 'Caught between work and modesty: the dilemma of women traders in Madras' *Manushi* 28:7–12

Lévi-Strauss, C. (1969) [1949] *The Elementary Structures of Kinship* Revised edn transl. by J. Bell and J. von Sturmer, edited by R. Needham, Boston: Beacon Press

Lewis, I. (1971) *Ecstatic Religion: An Anthropological Study of Spirit Possession and Shamanism* Harmondsworth: Penguin

Lewis, O. (1958) *Village Life in Northern India: Studies in a Delhi Village* New York: Random House

Lloyd, G. (1984) *The Man of Reason: 'Male' and 'Female' in Western Philosophy* London: Methuen

Lowie, R.H. (1929) *Primitive Society*, London: Routledge and Kegan Paul

MacCormack, C.P. (1980) 'Nature, culture and gender: a critique' in C.P. MacCormack and M. Strathern (eds) *Nature, Culture and Gender* Cambridge: Cambridge University Press, pp.1–24

Macpherson, C.B. (1973) 'A political theory of property' in C.B. Macpherson (ed.) *Democratic Theory: Essays in Retrieval* Oxford: Oxford University Press

Madan, T.N. (1965) *Family and Kinship* Bombay: Asia Publishing House

Mandelbaum, D. (1964) 'Introduction: Process and structure in South Asian religion' in E.B. Harper (ed.) *Religion in South Asia* Seattle: Washington University Press, pp.5–20

—— (1966) 'Transcendental and pragmatic aspects of religion' *American Anthropologist* 68:1174–1191

Mani, L. (1987) 'The construction of women as tradition in early nineteenth-century Bengal' *Cultural Critique* 7:119–156

Marriott, M. and Inden, R.B. (1977) 'Towards an ethnosociology of south Asian caste systems' in K. David (ed.) *The New Wind: Changing Identities in South Asia* The Hague: Mouton

Marx, K. (1973) [1857–58] *Grundrisse* Harmondsworth: Penguin

Mayer, A. (1960) *Caste and Kinship in Central India: A Village and its Region* London: Routledge and Kegan Paul

Mazumdar, V. (1979) *Traditional Women and Their Integration into Modern Development: An Inquiry into Two Models in India* Delhi: Indian Council of Social Science Research

McGilvray, D.B. (1982) 'Sexual power and fertility in Sri Lanka: Batticaloan Tamils and Moors' in C.P. MacCormack (ed.) *Ethnography of Fertility and Birth* London: Academic Press, pp.25–73

—— (1983) 'Mukkuvar *vannimai*: Tamil caste and matriclan ideology in Batticaloan, Sri Lanka' in D.B. McGilvray (ed.) *Caste, Ideology and Interaction* Cambridge: Oxford University Press, pp.34–97

Meillasoux, C. (1973) 'Are there castes in India?' in *Economy and Society* Vol.2, pp.89–111

Mencher, J. (1974) 'The caste system upside down: or the not so mysterious east' *Current Anthropology* 15(4):469–494

Menefee Singh, A. (1984) 'Rural to urban migration of women in India: patterns and implications' in Fawcett, T., Khoo, S. and Smith, P.C. (eds) *Women in the Cities of Asia: Migration and Urban Adaptation* Colorado: Westview Press, pp.87–107

Mersch, W. (1977) 'Factory labour during the early years of industrialisation—a comment' *Indian Economic and Social History Review* xiv(3): 385–389

Mines, M. (1984) *The Warrior Merchants: Textiles, Trade and Territory in South India* Cambridge: Cambridge University Press

Mitchell, J. (1971) *Woman's Estate* Harmondsworth: Penguin

Moffatt, M. (1979) *An Untouchable Community in South India: Structure and Consensus* Princeton: Princeton University Press

Molyneux, M. (1981) 'Women in socialist societies: problems of theory and practice' in K. Young, C. Wolkowitz and R. McCullagh (eds) *Of Marriage and Market* London: CSE Books, pp.167–202

Moreno, Manuel (1985) 'God's forceful call: possession as a divine strategy' in Waghorne, J.P. and Cutler, N. (eds) *Gods of Flesh, Gods of Stone: The Embodiment of Divinity in India* Chambersburg: Anima, pp.103–120

Morris, M.D. (1965) *The Emergence of an Industrial Labour Force in India: A study of the Bombay Cotton Mills, 1854–1947* Bombay: Oxford University Press

Mukherjee, P. (1978) *Hindu Women: Normative Models* New Delhi: Orient Longman

Murphy, E.D. (1981) *Unions in Conflict: A Comparative Study of Four South Indian Textile Centres, 1918–1939*, ANU Monographs on South Asia, no.5, Canberra: The Australian National University

Nair, K., P. Sivanandan and V.C.V. Ratnam (1984) 'Education, employment and land-holding patterns in a Tamil village' *Economic and Political Weekly* xix(24,25):948–956

National Sample Survey Organisation (1981) *Sarvakshena* vol.5 (1 and 2), New Delhi: Government of India

Naveed-i-Rahat (1981) 'The role of women in a Punjab village' in Epstein, T.S. and Watts, R.A. (eds) *The Endless Day: Some Case Material on Asian Rural Women* Oxford: Pergamon Press, pp.47–81

Nichter, M. (1987) 'Cultural dimensions of hot, cold and sema in Sri Lankan health culture' *Social Science and Medicine* 25(4)

Norr, K. (1972) 'A south Indian fishing village in comparative perspective' PhD thesis, Michigan: University of Michigan

Obeyesekere, G. (1975) 'Impact of Ayurvedic ideas on culture and the individual in Ceylon' in C. Leslie (ed.) *Comparative Studies in Asian Medical Systems* Berkeley: University of California Press, pp.201–226

—— (1981) *Medusa's Hair: An Essay on Personal Symbols and Religious Experience* Chicago: University of Chicago Press

Oddie, G.A. (ed.) (1977) *Religion in South Asia: Religious Conversion and Revival Movements in South Asia in Medieval and Modern Times* New Delhi: Manohar

O'Flaherty, W. (1975) *Hindu Myths* Harmondsworth: Penguin

—— (1980) *Women, Androgynes and Other Mythical Beasts* Chicago: University of Chicago Press

Omvedt, G. (1978) 'Migration in colonial India: the articulation of feudalism and capitalism by the colonial state' *Journal of Peasant Studies* 7(2):185–212

Ortner, S. (1974) 'Is female to male as nature is to culture?' in M.Z. Rosaldo and L. Lamphere (eds) *Woman, Culture and Society* Stanford: Stanford University Press, pp.67–88

Pateman, C. and E. Gross (eds) (1986) *Feminist Challenges: Social and Political Theory* Sydney: Allen and Unwin

Pillai, S. (1962) *Chemmeen* New York: Harper and Brothers

Platteau, J. (1982) *The Drive Towards Mechanisation of Small-Scale Fisheries in Kerala: A Microstudy of the Transformation Process of Traditional Village Societies* Unpublished paper, Vienna Colloqium on Contemporary India, Nath Pai Memorial Session, Vienna

Pratt, M.L. (1986) 'Fieldwork in common places' in J. Clifford and G.E. Marcus (eds) *Writing Culture: The poetics and politics of ethnography* Berkeley: University of California Press, pp.27–50

Premi, M.K. (1980) 'Aspects of female migration in India' *Economic and Political Weekly* xv(15):714–720

Ram, K. (1981) 'The Indian working class: critical issues in the study of class formation in the Third World' MA thesis, Sydney: Macquarie University

Ramachandran, P. (1981) 'The history of Nancinad, 1600–1858' PhD thesis, Trivandrum: University of Kerala

Ramanujan, A.K. (1967) *The Interior Landscape: Love Poems from a Classical Tamil Anthology* Bloomington: Indiana University Press

Randeria, S. and L. Viseria (1984) 'Sociology of brideprice and dowry' *Economic and Political Weekly* xix(15):275–279

Rao, M.S.A. (1968) 'Occupational mobility and joint household organisation' *Contributions to Indian Sociology* (n.s.) ii:98–111

Ratte, L. (1985) 'Goddesses, mothers and heroines: Hindu women and the feminine in the early nationalist movement' in Y.Y. Haddad and E.B. Findly (eds) *Women, Religion and Social Change* Albany: State University of New York Press, pp.321–350

Report of the Conservation Committee (1981) Report of the Committee to study the need for conservation of fishery resources during certain seasons of the year and allied matters, State Government of Kerala, Trivandrum

Report of Joint Committee of Upper and Lower Houses of Parliament (1982) Extracts in 'Dowry Amendment Bill. Another toothless legislation' *Economic and Political Weekly* xix(37):1609–1610

Robinson, S. (1985) 'Hindu paradigms of women: image and values' in Y.Y. Haddad and E.B. Findly (eds) *Women, Religion and Social Change* Albany: State University of New York Press, pp.181–215

Roche, P. (1984) *The Fishermen of the Coromandel: The Social Study of the Paravas of the Coromandel* New Delhi: Manohar

Rosaldo, M. (1974) 'Woman, culture and society: a theoretical overview' in M. Rosaldo and L. Lamphere (eds) *Woman, Culture and Society* Stanford: Stanford University Press

Rosaldo, R. (1986) 'From the door of his tent: the fieldworker and the inquisitor' in J. Clifford and G.E. Marcus (eds) *Writing Culture: The Poetics and Politics of Ethnography* Berkeley: University of California Press, pp.77–97

Sabbah, F. (1984) *Woman in the Muslim Unconscious* New York: Pergamon Press

Sahlins, M. (1974) 'The original affluent society' in *Stone Age Economics* London: Tavistock Publications, pp.1–40

—— (1976) *Culture and Practical Reason* Chicago: University of Chicago Press

Sanday, P. (1974) 'Female status in the public domain' in M. Rosaldo and L. Lamphere (eds) *Woman, Culture and Society* Stanford: Stanford University Press, pp.189–206

Scheffler, H.W. (1977) 'Kinship and alliance in south India and Australia' *American Anthropologist* 79:869–882

Scott, J.C. (1979) *The Moral Economy of the Peasant: Rebellion and Subsistence in Southeast Asia* New Haven: Yale University Press

Searle-Chatterjee, M. (1981) *Reversible Sex Roles: The Special Case of the Benares Sweepers* Oxford: Pergamon Press

Seccombe, W. (1974) 'The housewife and her labour under capitalism' *New Left Review* no.83, pp.3–24

Selik, A. (1980) *The Fishing Castes of Muttom, South India* Unpublished monograph, financed by Education and Welfare Departments, Washington DC and University of Houston

Selvarathnam, J. (1985) 'Where sunlight is scarce: changes in cropping patterns in Kanyakumari' *Economic and Political Weekly* 45,46,47:1961–1964

Shah, K.T. (1948) *National Planning Committee, Animal Husbandry, Dairying, Fisheries, and Horticulture* Bombay: Vora and Company

Shaheed, F. (1989) 'Purdah and Poverty in Pakistan' in H. Afshar and B. Agarwal (eds) *Women, Poverty and Ideology in Asia* London: Macmillan, pp.17–42

Shanin, T. (ed.) (1971) *Peasants and Peasant Societies* Harmondsworth: Penguin

Sharma, U. (1978) 'Segregation and its consequences in India' in P. Caplan and J.M. Bujra (eds) *Women United, Women Divided* London: Tavistock, pp.259–282

—— (1980) *Women, Work and Property in Northwest India* London: Tavistock

—— (1984) 'Dowry in north India: its consequences for women' in R. Hirschon (ed.) *Women and Property, Women as Property* London: Croom Helm, pp.62–73

Shorter, E. (1982) *A History of Women's Bodies* Harmondsworth: Penguin

Shulman, D. (1976) 'The murderous bride: Tamil versions of the myth of Devi and the Buffalo Demon' *History of Religions* xvi(2):120–146

Simmons, C.P. (1976) 'Recruiting and organising an industrial work force in colonial India: the case of the coal mining industry, 1880–1939' *Indian Economic and Social History Review* xiii(4):455–482

Sivakumar, S.S., D. Kumar, and B. VasantKumar (1979) 'From Toori to thirtyfooter: a preliminary study of the political economy of fishing in Tamil Nadu' *Bulletin Seminar Series* 19(12):15–36

Skjonsberg, E. (1982) *A Special Caste? Tamil Women of Sri Lanka* London: Zed Press

Sophie, Sister (1980) A study of the fishermen community of Colachel, Unpublished report, Madras: Stella Maris College

Srinivas, M.N. (1966) *Social Change in Modern India* Berkeley: University of California Press

—— (1978) *The Changing Position of Indian Women* The Huxley Memorial Lecture, Bombay: Oxford University Press

Standing, H. and V. Bandopadhyay (1985) 'Women's employment and the household: some findings from Calcutta' *Economic and Political Weekly* xx(17):WS-23-WS-38

Stein B. (1980) *Peasant State and Society in Medieval South India* New Delhi: Oxford University Press

Stirrat, R.L. (1981) 'The shrine of St Sebastian at Mirisgama: an aspect of the cult of the saints in Catholic Sri Lanka' *Man* (n.s.) 16(2):183–200

—— (1983) 'Caste conundrums: views of caste in a Sinhalese Catholic fishing village' in D.B. McGilvray (ed.) *Caste, Ideology and Interaction* Cambridge: Oxford University Press, pp.8–33

Strathern, M. (1984) 'Subject or object? Women and the circulation of valuables in Highland New Guinea' in R. Hirschon (ed.) *Women and Property, Women as Property* London: Croom Helm, pp.158–175

Tambiah, J. (1973) 'Dowry, bridewealth and women's property rights' in J. Goody and S.J. Tambiah (eds) *Bridewealth and Dowry* Cambridge: Cambridge University Press, pp.59–169

Taussig, M. (1980a) 'Folk healing and the structure of conquest in southwest Colombia' *Journal of Latin American Lore* 6(2):217–218

—— (1980b) *The Devil and Commodity Fetishism in South America* Chapel Hill: University of North Carolina Press

—— (1987) *Shamanism, Colonialism and the Wild Man* Chicago: University of Chicago Press

Thompson, E.P. (1967) 'Time, work discipline and industrial capitalism' *Past and Present* 38:56–97

Thorner, D. (1957) 'Casual employment of a factory labour force in the case of India, 1850–1939' *Economic and Political Weekly* January

—— (1964) *Agricultural Cooperatives in India* Bombay: Asia Publishing House

Thurston, E. (1909) *Castes and Tribes of Southern India* vol.5, Madras: Government Press

Turner, B. (1984) 'Towards an economic model of virtuoso religion' in

E. Gellner (ed.) *Islamic Dilemmas, Reformers, Nationalists and Industrialisation* New York: Mouton, pp.49–72

Vattamattam, J. (1978) 'Factors that determine the income of fishermen: a case study of Poonthura village in Trivandrum District', MPhil thesis, Trivandrum: Jawaharlal Nehru University and Centre for Development Studies.

Veen, Klaas W. van der (1971) *I Give Thee My Daughter: A Study of Marriage and Hierarchy Among the Anavil Brahmans of South Gujarat* Assen: Van Gorcum

Vijayan, A.J. (1980) *Migrant Fishermen in Paradeep, Orissa* Report sponsored by Fisheries Research Cell of the Program for Community Organisation, Trivandrum

Wadley, S. (1977) 'Women in the Hindu tradition' *Signs* 3(1):113–135

Wadley, S. (ed.) (1980) *The Powers of Tamil Women* Syracuse: Syracuse University Press

Wallerstein, E. (1974) *The Modern World System: Capitalist Agriculture and the Origins of the European World System* New York: Academic Press

Warner, M. (1976) *Alone of All Her Sex: The Myth and Cult of the Virgin Mary* London: Picador

Westwood, S. (1984) ' "Fear woman": property and modes of production in urban Ghana' in R. Hirschon (ed.) *Woman and Property, Women as Property* London: Croom Helm, pp.140–157

White, H. (1978) *Tropics of Discourse: Essays in Cultural Criticism* Baltimore: The John Hopkins University Press

Whitehead, Rev. Henry (1921) *The Village Gods of South India* Calcutta: Oxford University Press

Williams, R. (1976) *Culture and Society 1780–1950* Harmondsworth: Penguin

Wolf, E.R. (1966) *Peasants* Englewood Cliffs: Prentice Hall

—— (1982) *Europe and the People Without History* Berkeley: University of California Press

Wulff, D.M. (1985) 'Images and roles of women in Bengali Vaisnava *padāvalī kīrtan*' in Y.Y. Haddad and E.B. Findly (eds) *Women, Religion and Social Change* Albany: State University of New York Press, pp.217–246

Yalman, N. (1963) 'On the purity of women in the castes of Ceylon and Malabar' *Journal of the Royal Anthropological Institute* 93:25–58

Zachariah, K.C. (1968) *Migration in Greater Bombay* Bombay: Asia Publishing House

Zihlman, A.L. (1980) 'Women as shapers of human adaptation' in F. Dahlberg (ed.) *Woman the Gatherer* New Haven: Yale University Press, pp.75–121

Zvelebil, K. (1973) *The Smile of Murugan: On Tamil Literature of South India* Leiden: E.J. Brill

Select glossary

All words are Tamil unless otherwise specified, e.g. Skt for Sanskrit

aaTam dance
aavi ghosts
akam poetic category of Cankam literature (*cf*. Cankam), dealing with themes of the 'interior': inner emotions, and love
ammai noyvu, vysoori the disease of the goddess, small-pox
ananku concept of ancient Tamil origin, denoting power of a particularly erratic and malevolent kind
arudal to give comfort in times of mental/physical stress
asan practitioner of specialised branch of Siddha Vaidya medicine

beta money for meals cooked on board a mechanised trawler
bhakti (Skt) emotional devotionalism: one of the means to *moksa* (salvation)

Cankam literature term given to Tamil literature of first to sixth centuries AD
chaalaa valai sardine net
chaDangu auspicious ceremony
chelai sari, worn by mature women
chilla maram tree (*Albyzzia stipulata*) used for making the *kaTTumaram*

dharma (Skt) code of ethical normative conduct appropriate to one's subject-position in the social hierarchy, in one's life-cycle and in terms of one's gender and marital status
dhoti (Skt) male attire for lower half of body
eetanam fishing gear, nets and boats

Eseki (*Isaakai*) colloquial pronunciation of the Hindu village goddess worshipped in Kanyakumari District

iDangkai 'left hand', opposed to *valangkai*, symbolic designation of artisans, itinerant merchants and lesser agriculturalist castes *ishTamaana toDarpu* lit. 'free willing relationship' to other castes, based on market exchange: characterised as a feature of 'left hand' castes in Tamil society

jaati (Skt) genus, species, kind, type: used widely in conversation with a variety of like meanings, among them 'caste' and 'sub-caste'
jaati taaivar (Skt, Tamil) caste headman
jabam prayers
jaba maalai rosary beads
jajmani (Skt) lit. pertaining to the *jajman*, 'lord/master': a colonial construct interpreting the Indian social structure as bound by patron/client relations of hierarchical reciprocity between *jajman* and *praja* (subjects, the people)

kaaka kuTumpam lit. 'crowfamily': a unified clan
kacha valai anchovy net
kaDavaa perch fish
kanakapillai catechist, office created by Francis Xavier in 1542
kaNaku shollaravaa those who heal on the basis of possession
karamaDi beach-seine net
karma (Skt) Hindu doctrine of deeds bearing fruit, carried over from re-birth to re-birth, and exercising a determining influence on the destiny of all living things
karyasthani ecclesiastical functionaries of the Catholic Church
katavul early Tamil term for God
kaTTumaram lit. 'tied wood', catamaran: colloquially referred to as *maram*
kavati pots of water carried in ritual of self-mortification
kolle noyvu cholera
korati gypsy
kshatriya (Skt) one of the four varnas or traditional social orders, that of warriors: warrior caste
kudipu meen type of fish, big-jawed jumper
kumbadri (from Portuguese *compadre*) friend
kumkum (Skt) vermilion coloured mark on forehead, indicating auspiciousness
kuTTai kaari women fish-traders, distinguished by their woven baskets or *kuTTai*
kuTTi raja (Tamil and Skt) lit. 'petty king': ironic title given to the Catholic Church by villagers
kutukai tax traditionally levied by the King of Travancore, but used in coastal areas to mean the tax levied by the Catholic Church on the fishing catch
kuTumpam family
kuuTam lit. crowd or group: work team of female fish-traders

makkaL the 'people': hence KaDalkarai *makkaL* or people of the sea-shore, linking up with the notion of sea-shore as a specific cultural as well as geographical zone (*cf. tinai*)
mantravaaDi exorcist, using *mantras* or *aksharam* (sacred syllables)
melingi church bellringer
modom overseer of ecclesiastical duties
moy cash payments by wedding guests
muzhi divine gaze, trance state

naadigal three humors or elements in Siddha Vaidya, the south Indian variant of Ayurveda

naaTu vaidiyar specialists in indigenous systems of medicine, the Ayurveda and the Siddha Vaidya

NaDar dominant agricultural caste in Kanyakumari District

naital sea-shore tract

orupaDi jewellery

paavaaDai chokkai skirt worn by pre-pubescent girl

paavaaDai meelaaku skirt and cloth covering upper part of female body, after puberty

paavam sin, wretchedness, pitiability: often used by Mukkuvar villagers with reference to the self or one's own collectivity, hence '*paavangaL uDiya uuru*' or 'village of the wretched'

paDukkai offerings to shrines

peey spirits

peey aaTam dance of those possessed by demonic spirits

pishaashu demon

podu nanmai First Communion

poraamai envy, the infinite capacity of human beings to desire, in excess of what can be possessed or enjoyed

pradhani (Skt) headman

puram poetic category of Cankam literature (*cf.* Cankam), dealing with 'external' themes of war, politics and trade

purdah (Arabic) form of female seclusion

purohit (Skt) ritual officiant, priest

raal valai prawn net

sakti (Skt) form of bio-religious power often conceived of as intrinsically feminine in character

sammanasu conscience

shuuTu 'heat', one of the three humors, associated with the goddess' extreme emotions

shuuTu vyaadigal diseases caused by excess of heat

sirdanam (Mukkuvar Tamil) and *stridhanam* (Skt) lit. 'woman's wealth: dowry

sumangali an auspicious, married woman

tahaDu metal cylinder inscribed with *mantra*, worn on waist to ward off evil

talai toTTamma godmother

tali gold necklace tied around bride's neck by groom, henceforth denoting her marital status

taluka (Arabic, *taluqa*) an administrative sub-unit within a district

tapascharya (Skt) rigorous practices of asceticism and meditation, designed to accumulate one's *sakti*

taTTumaDi boat seines

thozil work, labour, with connotations of a 'calling' in the Christian sense: hence *kaDal thozil*, labour pertaining to the sea; *maram thozil*, labour pertaining to the *kaTTumaram*

tinai physical landscapes or zones, used as poetic metaphors in Tamil bardic and literary traditions between first and sixth centuries AD

tiiTu pollution

toNai companion

tuuNDil veelai profession of hook-and-line fishing

ubadesiar sacristan

ul naaDu lit. 'country of the interior': term used for agricultural hinterland by people of the coast

uuchaali local Mukkuvar term for the 'strongmen' of the coastal villagers, often used to enforce the authority of powerful elites

uuru one's place of origin, which may, depending on context, refer to one's village, town or region

uuru kuuTam village meeting

uuru nilam communal land, technically owned by the Church, but regarded by Mukkuvar villagers as common property

vaalai mackerel

vaatiyaar lit. 'teacher': used for Hindu and Christian teachers, in either religious or secular context

valangkai 'right hand', symbolic designation of agriculturalist and interdependent service castes

vaLLam plank canoe

veepa ellai leaf of sacred margasa tree

vetalai betel leaf

viibudi sacred ash

viiTukku duuram lit. 'far from house', period of menstrual seclusion or separation

viraKaarar lit. 'men of heroism': key element in the construction of corporate identity among warrior and chiefly groups of Tamil Nadu, elements of which are to be found among men in fishing castes

yoga (Skt) forms of bodily manipulation and meditative practice used as one of the disciplines leading to spiritual power

Index

Alexander, Jenniffer, 222
Alexander, Paul, 7–8, 161
ananku: etymology, 69–70; contrast with karma, 62; and women's bodies, 69–70; and goddess worship, 70–3; and Christianity, 62–4

Battle of Colachel, 27–8
Beck, Brenda, 23, 67, 70, 71, 74, 86, 87, 167–70, 172, 173, 189
binary oppositions: as a consequence of domination, 64–6; and Catholicism, 61–6; and Hinduism, 66–8; and European polarities of thought, 53, 59, 230–1, 237; blurring of oppositions in Mukkuvar culture, 53–7, 59–60, 82–3, 231–7
body, the: and popular religion, 53–9; equilibrium of hot and cold elements, 54–5, 85–7; ambiguity of bodily signifiers, 56, 58, 74–5, 102, 104; symbolic inversion, 100, 101; pollution, 79–82; symbolism, 56, 57, 88, 89; *see also* illness; female body; envy; healing; healers; popular religion
Boserup, Esther, 46, 186
Bourdieu, Pierre, 48, 205, 206
Brahman kinship, 165–7; ideology, 164, 165; in southern India, 169; and marriage payments, 185, 193,

194, 195; *see also* Tamil kinship; Mukkuvar kinship
Brubaker, Richard L., 71, 72, 73

capitalism: in fishing versus agriculture, 9, 10; and world market, 113, 114, 130, 131, 132, 133, 134, 136, 137; labour recruitment, 116, 242n; and gender specificity, 48, 50, 113–34, 137–143, 200–5, 208–29, 233, 234, 235, 236; *see also* male migration; female migration; dowry; household; the state; the domestic
cash, *see* credit; male migration
caste: and Indology, 8, 9, 185; and *'jajmani* relations', 8, 9; 'Left Hand' and 'Right Hand' castes, 21–5, 27, 28, 109, 171, 172, 231, 232; 'Backward Caste', 41; and landscape, 1, 2, 3, 4, 5, 6, 7; untouchability, 6, 45, 76, 77, 109, 110; pollution, 76, 77, 79, 80, 81, 82, 109, 111, 112; and Marxism, 9, 230
Catholic Church: and conversion, 30, 31, 32; and education, 33, 222, 223; and caste, 32, 33; recruitment into priesthood, 33, 34; taxation, 34; hegemony, 35–44; female employment, 224, 225, 226; voluntary associations,

12–14; labour relations, 14–16;
distribution, 16–18; types of fish
caught, 11, 12; ritual construction
of, 50–1, 60–1; and time, 120–4;
as part of wider social caste bloc,
21–5

gender as ideology, *see* femininity;
masculinity
gender as practice(s), 205–7, 236–7;
women's religious practices, 61,
94; *see also* healing; widening of
domestic sphere in women's
practice, 145–53, 162–3, 174–7,
203–5, 217–18, 223–7, 228
gender as social relations: of
kinship, 167–73; of household
formation, 173–9, 179–82; of
marriage payments and
inheritance, 187–90; of
capitalism, *see* capitalism
Gluckmann, Max, 74, 104
goddess, the: in local form, 62–3,
71–3; in Kanyakumari, 73–4;
Sanskritic, 67; as non-unitary,
66–75 *passim*; in illness and
possession, 58, 69, 71–3; and
social inversion, 72–3, 99–103;
see also the body; *ananku*;
Virgin–Maataa
Goody, Jack, 46, 186, 194
Guha, Ranajit, 102, 110, 165

Hall, Stuart, 112
Hardy, Friedrich, 68–9, 72, 104
Harris, John, 155
healers: Christian, 55, 56, 57, 58, 59,
61, 94–8, 102–3, 104, 109; *korati*
(gypsy) and night-singers, 23;
mantravaaDi (exorcists), 23, 55,
56, 57; *naaTu vaidiyar* (herbalists)
23; Siddha Vaidya, 54, 55, 56; *see
also* spirit possession; Virgin–
Maataa; saints; sorcery; healing;
goddess, the; popular religion
healing: femininity and, 57–61, 81,
98–9, 103–5, 107; and Tamil
codifications of the body, 53–9,
69–73; and religious tensions,
61–6, 78–9, 93–103; *see also*
healers; spirit possession; popular
religion; female body, the

hegemony: and the Catholic
Church, 35–43, 61–6, 78–9; and
Hinduism, 66–75; Brahmanic and
non-Brahmanic cultural models,
23–5, 27–8; Brahman and non-
Brahman kinship, 164–184;
marriage payments, 185–88,
193–5; and women's work, *see*
women's work; *see also* caste,
'Left-Hand' and 'Right-hand';
counter-discourses
Hill, Polly, 153
household: formation, 173–9,
182–4; fissure, 15, 176–81;
cooperation, 14, 178–82; women
and, 174–5; typologies, 177–9,
183; joint and nuclear, 166,
175–7; sibling bonds, 177–9, 181,
197; and dowry, *see* dowry

identity, 29–30; and territory (*tinai*),
1–7; occupational, 10–28 *passim*;
religious, 29–44; sexual, 25–28;
see also femininity; masculinity
illness, 53–7, 58–9, 64, 70, 85–7,
89–92, 98–105, 105–9; *see also*
envy; healing; healers;
spirit possession; sorcery
inequality, 9, 23–5, 45–6;
ownership, 12–13; mobility, 14;
male work relationships, 16–18;
mercantile groups, 18–21, 24;
religious, *see* Catholic church;
sexual, 45–53, 200–29, 137–144;
ritual, 79–80; regional, 131–33;
see also poverty; capitalism;
gender
Iyer, Anantha Krishna, 1, 6, 190

Kakar, Sudhir, 67, 103
Khare, R.S., 110
Kolenda, Pauline, 109–110, 176,
177, 183
Kottar Social Service Society
(KSSS), 210–13

Lowie, Robert, 47
Lewis, Ioan, 64

male migration, 113–140;
fishermen's journalistic
description, 117–120; numerical